THE BOOK OF INDIAN ESSAYS

by the same author

POETRY

Nine Enclosures
Distance in Statute Miles
Middle Earth
The Transfiguring Places
Collected Poems: 1969–2014
Collected Poems
Selected Poems and Translations

PROSE

Partial Recall: Essays on Literature and Literary History
Translating the Indian Past

TRANSLATIONS

The Absent Traveller: Prakrit Love Poetry
Songs of Kabir
Blue is Like Blue: Stories by Vinod Kumar Shukla
(with Sara Rai)

EDITED BOOKS

Twenty Indian Poems
The Oxford India Anthology of Twelve Modern Indian Poets
Periplus: Poetry in Translation (with Daniel Weissbort)
An Illustrated History of Indian Literature in English
A Concise History of Indian Literature in English
The Last Bungalow: Writings on Allahabad
Collected Poems in English by Arun Kolatkar

THE BOOK OF

INDIAN ESSAYS

Two Hundred Years of English Prose

Arvind Krishna Mehrotra

editor

black kite
AN IMPRINT OF PERMANENT BLACK

ASHOKA UNIVERSITY

The Book of Indian Essays, first published in hardback 2020
by Black Kite (an imprint of Permanent Black)

in association with

ashoka
UNIVERSITY

and

Hachette India
(an Hachette UK company)

All editorial management by Black Kite

ISBN 13: 978-93-89253-63-4

10 9 8 7 6 5 4 3

Black Kite/Permanent Black
D28 Oxford Apartments, 11 IP Extension,
Delhi 10092

Printed in India by Manipal Technologies Limited, Manipal

in memory of

RAM ADVANI

Bookseller

(1920–2016)

"The only book I hung on to was George and Weedon Grossmith's *Diary of a Nobody*, which I'd got for acting the part of a tipsy imposter in a one-act play called *Borrowed Plumes*. I had chosen this book myself, at Ram Advani's Bookshop on the Simla Mall."

– Ruskin Bond, *Scenes from a Writer's Life*

Contents

Acknowledgements xi

INTRODUCTION
When the Gas Cylinder Comes 1

HENRY LOUIS VIVIAN DEROZIO (1809–1831)
Chit-chat – Scandal – Tea-parties 20

ANON. HINDU YOUTH (*FLORUIT 1830*)
The Colonisation of India 24

BANKIM CHANDRA CHATTOPADHYAY (1838–1894)
The Confessions of a Young Bengal 39

SHOSHEE CHUNDER DUTT (1848–1909)
The Street-Music of Calcutta 43

RABINDRANATH TAGORE (1861–1941)
The Nation 55

JAWAHARLAL NEHRU (1889–1964)
The Tribal Folk 62

HASAN SHAHID SUHRAWARDY (1890–1965)
Tagore at Oxford 70

SÁLIM ALI (1896–1987)
The Indian House-Crow 82

NIRAD C. CHAUDHURI (1897–1999)
Apologia Pro Scripta Sua 88

SUDHINDRANATH DATTA (1901–1960)
Calcutta 95

VERRIER ELWIN (1902–1964)
Do We Really Want to Keep Them in a Zoo? 113

R.K. NARAYAN (1906–2001)
Elephant in the Pit 129

BUDDHADEVA BOSE (1908–1974)
To Remember Is to Live Again 132

G.V. DESANI (1909–2000)
The Benares that Was 142

AUBREY MENEN (1912–1989)
My Grandmother and the Dirty English 152

M. KRISHNAN (1912–1996)
The Jellicut 163

AMRITA SHER-GIL (1913–1941)
Modern Indian Art: Imitating the Forms of the Past 167

SANTHA RAMA RAU (1923–2009)
With Shivan and Kitty in New Delhi 173

NISSIM EZEKIEL (1924–2004)
Naipaul's India and Mine 185

FRANCIS NEWTON SOUZA (1924–2002)
Nirvana of a Maggot 206

QURRATULAIN HYDER (1927–2007)
My Aunt Gracie 216

ASHOK MITRA (1928–2018)
An Ordinary Man 229

DHARMA KUMAR (1928–2001)
108 Varieties 235

SHEILA DHAR (1929–2001)
Baua 242

VICTOR ANANT (1929–1999)
The Three Faces of an Indian 260

ARUN KOLATKAR (1931–2004)
House with Nine Rooms 278

MADHUR JAFFREY (1933–)
The Dining Room – Winter Evenings – Dining at the Long Tables 289

RUSKIN BOND (1934–)
The Last Time I Saw Delhi 297

ANITA DESAI (1937–)
A Secret Connivance 302

DOM MORAES (1938–2004)
On God 310

ADIL JUSSAWALLA (1940–)
When Earth Rose Up to Get Me 317

CHITRITA BANERJI (1947–)
Patoler Ma 322

IRWIN ALLAN SEALY (1951–)
The Anglo-Indians 328

MEENA ALEXANDER (1951–2018)
In Whitman's Country 334

GAUTAM BHATIA (1952–)
Art as Politics 344

SHAMA FUTEHALLY (1952–2004)
March 354

AMITAV GHOSH (1956–)
The Imam and the Indian 356

SARA RAI (1956–)
On Not Writing 370

MUKUL KESAVAN (1957–)
The Ugliness of the Indian Male 385

RAMACHANDRA GUHA (1958–)
The Coconuts of Bengal: Brown Men, White Affinities 389

SUNIL KHILNANI (1960–)
Gandhi's Styled Life 397

SHOHINI GHOSH (1961–)
Sky Above and Grass Below 405

SANJAY SUBRAHMANYAM (1961–)
Another Booker Flop 412

AMIT CHAUDHURI (1962–)
Money Matters 426

PANKAJ MISHRA (1969–)
Mashobra 431

Acknowledgements

THE WORLDCAT TOOK .07 seconds to tell me that the library nearest Dehra Dun to have a copy of Shama Futehally's *The Right Words: Selected Essays* was Zentralbibliothek Zurich, 3700 miles distant. Not every book that I wanted to consult was, like Futehally's, in print, affordable, and orderable online; nor did I know beforehand of every essay that I have included. Many essays were pointed out to me, and many others had to be sent for – from distant libraries. I am grateful to Rukun Advani, Zaheer Baber, Amit Chaudhuri, Rosinka Chaudhuri, Sukanta Chaudhuri, Ramachandra Guha, Kaiser Haq, Adil Jussawalla, Graziano Krätli, Sanjay Krishnan, and Anuradha Roy for making this anthology possible.

Sources and Copyright

The editor and publishers have made every effort to trace and contact copyright holders of the material under copyright reproduced in this book. Any omissions in this respect that are brought to the notice of the publishers will be rectified in this book's first future reprint.

Sources and dates of first publication have been provided where these could be ascertained. In most cases, the source cited is the one from which the essay was drawn.

Henry Louis Vivian Derozio, "Chit-chat – Scandal – Tea-parties", out of copyright essay, in Rosinka Chaudhuri, ed., *Derozio, Poet of India: The Definitive Edition* (Delhi: Oxford University Press, 2008).

Anonymous, "The Colonisation of India", out of copyright essay, in *Asiatic Journal*, New Series, vol. III (Sept.–Dec. 1830), pp. 79–86.

Bankim Chandra Chattopadhyay, "The Confessions of a Young Bengal", out of copyright essay, in Amiya P. Sen, ed., *Bankim's Hinduism* (Ranikhet: Permanent Black, 2011).

Shoshee Chunder Dutt, "Street-Music of Calcutta", out of copyright essay, in Alex Tickell, ed., *Selections from 'Bengaliana'* (Nottingham: Trent Editions, 2005).

Rabindranath Tagore, "The Nation", out of copyright essay, in Rabindranath Tagore, *Creative Unity* (London: Macmillan, 1922).

Jawaharlal Nehru, "The Tribal Folk", in *The Adivasis* (New Delhi: Publications Division, 1955).

Hasan Shahid Suhrawardy, "Tagore at Oxford", in the *Calcutta Municipal Gazette*, 1941.

Sálim Ali, "The Indian House-Crow", in Tara Gandhi, ed., *A Bird's Eye View*, vol. 2 (Ranikhet: Permanent Black, 2007). First published in Sálim Ali and Humayun Abdulali, "The Birds of Bombay and Salsette", *Journal of the Bombay Natural History Society*, vol. 39 (1936), pp. 91–3.

Nirad C. Chaudhuri, "Apologia Pro Scripta Sua", in Nirad C. Chaudhuri, *Why I Mourn for England* (Calcutta: Mitra & Ghosh Publishers Pvt. Ltd, 1998). First published in *Granta: Special Indian Number* (May 1997).

Sudhindranath Datta, "Calcutta", out of copyright essay, in Sudhindranath Datta, *The World of Twilight* (Bombay: Oxford University Press, 1970).

Verrier Elwin, "Do We Really Want Them in a Zoo?", in *The Adivasis* (New Delhi: Publications Division, 1955).

R.K. Narayan, "Elephant in the Pit", in *A Writer's Nightmare* (New Delhi: Penguin, 1988), © legal heirs of R.K. Narayan, reprinted by their permission.

Buddhadeva Bose, "To Remember Is to Live Again", in Rosinka Chaudhuri, ed., *An Acre of Green Grass: English Writings of Buddhadeva Bose* (New Delhi: Oxford University Press, 2018), reprinted by permission of Damayanti Bose.

G.V. Desani, "The Benares that Was", https: www.desani.org/other writings, © Unicef.

Aubrey Menen, "My Grandmother and the Dirty English", in Aubrey Menen, *Dead Man in the Silver Market* (London: Chatto and Windus, 1953).

M. Krishnan, "The Jellicut", in Ramachandra Guha, ed., *M. Krishnan: Nature's Spokesman* (Delhi: Oxford University Press, 2000), reprinted by permission of M. Harikrishnan.

Amrita Sher-Gil, "Modern Indian Art: Imitating the Forms of the Past", in *Amrita Sher-Gil: A Self-portrait in Letters & Writings*, introduced, annotated, and edited by Vivan Sundaram, vol. 1 (New Delhi: Tulika Books, 2010), reprinted by permission of Vivan Sundaram. First published in *The Hindu* on 1 November 1936, it was reprinted twice: in *The Khalsa Review*, 16 November 1936; and then as two essays, titled "Evolution of My Art" and "Appreciation of Art", in *The Usha* (Lahore), vol. III, no. II (August 1942).

Santha Rama Rau, "With Shivan and Kitty in New Delhi", in Santha Rama Rau, *Home to India* (New York: Harper & Brothers, 1945).

Nissim Ezekiel, "Naipaul's India and Mine", in *Journal of South Asian Literature*, vol. 11, no. 3/4 (1976). First published in *Imprint* (1965).

Francis Newton Souza, "Nirvana of a Maggot", in *Words and Lines* (New Delhi: Nitin Bhayana Publishing, 2000). First published in *Words and Lines* (London: Villiers, 1959).

Qurratulain Hyder, "My Aunt Gracie", in *The Sound of Falling Leaves* (New Delhi: Sahitya Akademi, 1994), reprinted by permission of the Sahitya Akademi.

Ashok Mitra, "An Ordinary Man", in *Calcutta Diary* (New Delhi: Authors Upfront, 2014). First published in *Calcutta Diary* (Calcutta: Rupa & Co., 1977), reprinted by permission of Paranjoy Guha-Thakurta.

Dharma Kumar, "108 Varieties", in *Seminar*, no. 321 (May 1986), copyright Seminar Publications, reprinted by permission of *Seminar*.

Sheila Dhar, "Baua", in Sheila Dhar, *Raga'n Josh: Stories from a Musical Life* (Ranikhet: Permanent Black, 2005), reprinted by permission of the publisher.

Victor Anant, "The Three Faces of an Indian", in Timothy O'Keefe, ed., *Alienation* (London: MacGibbon & Kee, 1960).

Arun Kolatkar, "House with Nine Rooms", hitherto unpublished, read at the Festival of India, Stockholm, in 1987, sourced from the Kolatkar Papers, essay title provided by Arvind Krishna Mehrotra.

Madhur Jaffrey, "The Dining Room – Winter Evenings – Dining at the Long Tables", in Madhur Jaffrey, *Climbing the Mango Trees* (London: Ebury Press, 2005), reprinted by permission of the author.

Ruskin Bond, "The Last Time I Saw Delhi", in Ruskin Bond, *Our Trees Still Grow in Dehra* (New Delhi: Penguin, 1991), reprinted by permission of the author.

Anita Desai, "A Secret Connivance", *The Times Literary Supplement* (14 September 1990).

Dom Moraes, "On God", in Dom Moraes, *From East and West: A Collection of Essays* (New Delhi: Vikas, 1971), reprinted by permission of Sarayu Ahuja.

Adil Jussawalla, "When Earth Rose Up to Get Me", in Adil Jussawalla, *Maps for the Mortal Moon* (New Delhi: Aleph, 2014), reprinted by permission of the author.

Chitrita Banerji, "Patóler Ma", in Chitrita Banerji, *The Hour of the Goddess* (Kolkata: Seagull, 2001), reprinted by permission of the author.

Irwin Allan Sealy, "The Anglo-Indians", in *The Anglo-Indians* (New Delhi: Photoink, 2007), reprinted by permission of the author.

Meena Alexander, "In Whitman's Country", in *Virginia Quarterly Review*, vol. 81, no. 2 (2005), reprinted by permission of David Lelyveld.

Gautam Bhatia, "Art as Politics", in Gautam Bhatia, *Stories of Storeys* (New Delhi: Yoda Press-Sage, 2018), reprinted by permission of the author.

Shama Futehally, "March", in Shama Futehally, *The Right Words* (New Delhi: Penguin, 2006), reprinted by permission of Zai Whitaker.

Amitav Ghosh, "The Imam and the Indian", in Amitav Ghosh, *The Imam and the Indian: Prose Pieces* (New Delhi: Ravi Dayal, 2002), reprinted by permission of the author and Mala Dayal.

Sara Rai, "On Not Writing", in *Caravan Magazine* (January 2019), reprinted (retitled) by permission of the author.

Mukul Kesavan, "The Ugliness of the Indian Male", in Mukul Kesavan, *The Ugliness of the Indian Male and Other Propositions* (Ranikhet: Permanent Black, 2008), reprinted by permission of the publisher and the author.

Ramachandra Guha, "The Coconuts of Bengal: Brown Men,

White Affinities", in Ramachandra Guha, *The Last Liberal and Other Essays* (Ranikhet: Permanent Black, 2004), reprinted by permission of the publisher and the author.

Sunil Khilnani, "Gandhi's Styled Life", transcription of a BBC Radio 3 broadcast (2010), reprinted by permission of the author.

Sanjay Subrahmanyam, "Another Booker Flop", in *London Review of Books* (6 November 2008), reprinted by permission of the author.

Amit Chaudhuri, "Money Matters" in Amit Chaudhuri, *Telling Tales* (London: Union Books, 2013), reprinted by permission of the author.

Pankaj Mishra, "Mashobra", by permission of the author.

ARVIND KRISHNA MEHROTRA

When the Gas Cylinder Comes

INTRODUCTION

"WHERE ARE THE OLD Magazines and Registers," wrote Henry Louis Vivian Derozio in 1826 in *India Gazette*, "the Helter-Skelters, the Higgledy-Piggledies, and others, which have appeared 'like angel-visits, few and far between'? – We ask, 'Where are they;' and an Echo answers 'Where!' – But the very appearance of these is a positive indication that talents are not wanting to tend and nurse the literary flower."[1] Attracted by the bright light of literature, as short-lived as bugs, and not so infrequent as angel-visits, *Kaleidoscope, Mookerjee's Magazine, Tornado, Wastepaper, Prisoner, Dialogue, Miscellany, Fulcrum, Dionysus, damn you, Vrishchik, Bombay Duck, Indian Literary Review, Fakir, Nether*, and *Kavi* are the names of some of the "little magazines" that nursed the literary flower in India over the last two hundred years. Among the very early ones is *Helter-Skelter*. In it, in 1824, the fifteen-year-old Henry Derozio published an essay, "On Drunkenness". It appeared under a pseudonym, Leporello, derived by Derozio from Mozart's 1787 opera *Don Giovanni*, which is based on the legend of the great libertine and seducer Don Juan. Leporello is Don Giovanni's servant, who helps him out of not a few tight

[1] Rosinka Chaudhuri, ed., *Derozio, Poet of India: The Definitive Edition* (New Delhi: Oxford University Press, 2008), p. 82.

situations, sometimes by impersonating his master. Derozio's choice of pseudonym may hint at his sympathy for those who overstep the boundaries of social acceptability, as Derozio himself was to do later in his short life.

"On Drunkenness" has epigraphs from Byron – "Man, being reasonable, must get drunk;/ The best of life is but intoxication"; and from Beaumont and Fletcher – "Would I were drunk, dead drunk". In the essay, completely sober himself, Derozio says his "classical learning is prodigious", and, either by direct quotation or allusion, shows his acquaintance with "Quintillian, Pope, de Staël, Samuel Johnson, Godwin, Addison and Steele, Fielding, Ovid, Horace, Scott, Lesage, the Old Testament (2 Samuel and Esther), Homer, Cervantes, Campbell, Plato, Xenophon, Dryden, Tacitus, Blackstone, Shakespeare, Moore, and Newton."[2] And of course with Montaigne, whose "On Drunkenness" he would have read. The malarial air of "Little London", as Calcutta was called, was thick with literature. Derozio could scarcely have foreseen that only seven years later, because he encouraged his students to read widely, freely exchange ideas, and question religious orthodoxies, including dietary taboos, the native managers of Hindu College would compel him to leave the institution. As one contemporary observer remarked in the *Oriental Magazine*, the "progress" the students were making was "by actually cutting their way through ham and beef and wading to liberalism through tumblers of beer."[3]

[2] Daniel E. White, *From Little London to Little Bengal: Religion, Print, and Modernity in Early British India, 1793–1835* (Baltimore: Johns Hopkins University Press, 2013), p. 121.

[3] See Rudrangshu Mukherjee, "The Derozio Affair: An Annal of Early Modern Calcutta", *Economic and Political Weekly*, LII, 36 (9 September 2017), pp. 54–60 (57).

Derozio onwards, Indian writers, and not only those who write in English, have been literary cosmopolitans. In 1876 Toru Dutt published *A Sheaf Gleaned in French Fields*, her translation of some 200 French poems that included, along with those by Hugo, Lamartine, and Nerval, two of Baudelaire's – "The Broken Bell" and "Man and the Sea" – their first appearance in an English anthology. A hundred years later, asked by the Marathi "little magazine" *Rucha* about his influences, Arun Kolatkar, a little impatiently, rattled off a list of some eighty names, from Whitman to Laurel and Hardy and from Catullus to Howling Wolf.

If English was used to write *belles-lettres* such as "On Drunkenness" and "Chit-chat – Scandal – Tea-parties" (the latter is reproduced in this anthology), it was used also by Derozio and his students – the Young Bengal of literary and social history – to write vigorous petitions, put out reformist pamphlets, draw attention to the poor quality of education in Calcutta, and debate the virtues of colonisation.

"Stare; pry; listen; eavesdrop. Die knowing something. You are not here long", the twentieth-century photographer Walker Evans wrote. In "Drawn to that Moment", John Berger says: "Because the faculty of sight is continuous,

> one tends to forget that the visual is always the result of an unrepeatable, momentary encounter. Appearances, at any given moment, are a construction emerging from the debris of everything that has previously appeared. It is something like this that I understand in those words of Cézanne which so often come back to me: "One minute in the life of the world is going by. Paint it as it is."

Seeing that same "minute in the life of the world going by", the poet William Carlos Williams writes in his *Autobiography*: "It is an identifiable thing, and its characteristic, its chief characteristic is that it is sure, all of a piece and, as I have said, instant and perfect: it comes, it is there, and it vanishes."

All three writers are struck by the evanescence of life when discussing photography, painting, and poetry. But what they say describes another art form too – the literary essay. Brevity and evanescence seem to lie at the heart of this genre, making only a few of its manifestations memorable.

Take the cry of a hawker. It fades even as you hear it, but you have the assurance that you'll hear it again, at roughly the same hour tomorrow. It's a little like knowing that when you wake up after a night's sleep there'll be a sun in the sky. Not all street cries are so fortunate. Their numbers keep dwindling and a few are always on the brink of extinction. "Almost the first cry every morning," Shoshee Chunder Dutt writes in "Street-Music of Calcutta",

> is of the *Kooar-ghotee-tollah.* Be the day ever so cold or so rainy there is the man ready to extricate from the bottom of the well whatever you may have dropt in it, though the cry speaks of brass *lotahs* only. He must dive at least five or six times a day to earn a decent pittance, for two or three pice is all he gets each time.

But times change, people do not need to go to wells for their supply of water, there are no more brass *lotahs* – or ear-rings, nose-rings, or finger-rings – to retrieve. The diver stops coming, and the cry dies with him. It is as though you were looking at a sepia-toned photograph, and in a way you are.

"Street-Music of Calcutta" is from Dutt's *Bengaliana: A Dish of Rice and Curry, and Other Indigestible Ingredients* (1878). By then, between 1868 and 1875, the eight-volume *People of*

India had come out, with 468 "Photographic Illustrations" and "Descriptive Letterpress". The man whose cry was "*Kooar-ghotee-tollah*" could have been one of the illustrations. This was the great age of collecting, documenting, categorising, and listing everything, from people and their physical measurements to the languages they spoke and the trades they plied. The first Census of India was undertaken in 1872, and in the following decade G.A. Grierson made his proposal for a Linguistic Survey of India. In 1879 we get S.W. Fallon's *A New Hindustani–English Dictionary, with illustrations from Hindustani literature and folk-lore*. The illustrations come from songs, proverbs, poems, and street cries: "*Makkhan hai malāī se mīṭhā!*" (Butter ho! sweeter than cream!). Henry Mayhew's *London Labour and the London Poor*, described as a "Cyclopaedia" of street life, had appeared in four volumes in 1861–2. A dying street cry, if you follow it to the end of the lane, will soon open out to reveal a small library, and millions of words.

Tables, chairs, shelves, racks, in the old days typewriters and now computers in government offices, are marked with an inventory number. Written in black or white enamel paint with a thick brush, the number is almost the first thing you notice, even before you see the man sitting behind the desk. Sometimes the items are typed up into a list, which is then displayed on a wall, where you see it pasted or hanging from a lightly cobwebbed string. Gautam Bhatia ("Art as Politics") has kept an eye open for such lists: "One desk D/2/Vig Bhav/Rm 7/Chair, Nos. 3, Paper Weight – two nos. Portrait of Gandhi – one." The enumeration, which is to use Williams' phrase "instant and perfect", stands for an entire government room with its three chairs and two paperweights, in Vigyan Bhavan, Delhi; it stands, too, for the Government of India.

When she looks out of the window of her Delhi house, Shama Futehally sees the trees in "March" and thinks not of a particular season but the cycle of seasons, not of that particular March but of those to come. Closing her ears to the scream of "Today" coming out of television screens, she notices the purple jacaranda in full bloom and acknowledges the "unnamed horticultural official, on whom be peace", the unremembered soul who thought not of today but of "tomorrow" when he planted it.

Qurratulain Hyder's "Aunt Gracie" appears in a book of her Urdu stories published by the Sahitya Akademi, *The Sound of Falling Leaves* (1994). The book is a translation, her own, of *Pathjhar ki Awaaz*, which won the 1968 Sahitya Akademi Award for Urdu. In her preface to the English translation she says that the "collection includes four autobiographical pieces", one of the four being "Aunt Gracie". She does not specify the language she wrote the four pieces in, but since "Aunt Gracie" does not appear in *Pathjhar ki Awaaz*, the book that won the award, I felt it safe to assume she wrote it in English for *The Sound of Falling Leaves*, making it eligible for inclusion here.

Just as Indian authors flit between languages – Qurratulain Hyder between English and Urdu, Sara Rai between English and Hindi/Hindustani, Buddhadeva Bose and Nirad Chaudhuri between English and Bengali – the essay flits between genres. It can come disguised as a story, as with Ruskin Bond; or appear as an obituary, as with Ashok Mitra; or take the form of a weekly shopping list, as with Shoshee Chunder Dutt; or be a book review, as in Nissim Ezekiel's "Naipaul's India and Mine" and Sanjay Subrahmanyam's "Another Booker Flop"; or have been written as a newspaper column, where the tight limit imposed on word length can be an advantage – the writer's equivalent of keeping a penknife handy. Many things can be done with a 1000- to 1500-word column, as they can with a penknife. Amit Chaudhuri's "Money Matters" answers a question that has often been on our tongues but is never asked: Why do Indians spend a good part of their thinking lives worrying about small change? And Mukul Kesavan wields it to carve up what stares us in the face: ourselves. In "The Ugliness of the Indian Male" he says that "The oddest aspect of the Indian man is the things he's willing to wear", before turning his penknife into a rapier by pointing out what gives the North Indian male his dash: "the thick bands of rotting pink threads" he wears around his wrist. (It is a fair guess that the proposed Rama temple in Ayodhya will be an extension of this aesthetic, the "rotting threads" transmuted into sky-kissing domes of gold.)

Unlike a novel, an essay can be discovered at random and quickly read. "Some of my best reading," Adil Jussawalla says, "has been casual, literally picked off the streets." The other day the novelist Allan Sealy found an essay in a newspaper spread on the bottom of a trunk that had accompanied him to boarding school. Emptied of dark memories and lined with a pretty face from the Sunday supplement, the trunk now held spare copies of his novels. Spring-cleaning thirty years after that Sunday, he discovered – behind the model in the cigarette ad – a piece by Dom Moraes he had missed. He devoured it on the spot and laid the essay back on its bed, pretty face up. The essay, like a penknife, can be put to many uses; like a newspaper aeroplane, it can fly and crash and fly again; as a literary genre, it is unfussy. An essay gathers no dust.

There's only one way in which a literature recognises itself: by constantly returning to the mirror of history, by making connections between authors, revisiting those that might have been overlooked, seeing resemblances, divergences, offshoots. It is in the mirror, if you hold it close enough, that authors who had appeared dead have a chance of coming back to life. Your dead author could still be breathing.

There are in fact two mirrors. One will reflect the world's writers, who are but a conglomeration of well-known faces that you identify or group by nationality: Irish, British, Australian, Chinese, South African; the other mirror reflects a specific locale – in this case India – and in it you are one of the faces you see, if only from the corner of your eye. It is the looking glass to which you keep returning.

It is the same with books. When this book of Indian essays in English confronts the wider mirror of books, it sees the *Oxford Book of English Essays* (1991), the annual volumes of *Best American Essays*, John D'Agata's *The Making of the American Essay* (2016) – in which one of the essays is T.S. Eliot's poem "The Dry Salvages" – and dozens of other such. It then looks in the second mirror, the smaller one, and there finds a blank: two hundred years, and an empty mirror to stare at. Ours is a literature that refuses to look at itself. This is in contrast to the modern Indian author, especially the one that writes in English, who, in part because of the prevailing culture of book promotion, does little else except preen and hustle, hustle and preen. And who constantly asks, with a worried look, "Mirror, mirror, on the wall, who is the fairest of us all."

To the emptiness of the mirror, one exception: *Statements*, edited by Eunice de Souza and Adil Jussawalla.[4] *Statements* and the present anthology are aimed at different markets. The earlier volume is a slim textbook for colleges and universities, some of

[4] Hyderabad: Orient Longman, 1976.

its essays (by D.D. Kosambi, Romila Thapar) meant to educate and shape young minds. The present anthology is for the general reader. However, it is not as though the general reader's mind cannot be shaped. Three of the ten essayists in *Statements* also figure here, and one essay, F.N. Souza's, is common to both.

~

While Indians may not have produced writers who are known primarily for their essays, as for example Lamb and Hazlitt in Britain, the nineteenth century is in particular not short of journals that carried them on a regular basis. The *Bengal Spectator* and the *Calcutta Review*, both of which started in the 1840s, are just two. While the objective of the short-lived *Bengal Spectator* was "to lay before the Government the wants and grievances of the native community, and pray for those advantages to which they may be deemed entitled", the subject of colonisation itself and the damage it had done to the colonised had been raised and debated in Calcutta's English and Bengali press much earlier. Colonisation would have allowed Europeans to settle in India, purchase land, and effectively become "Jummeendars and Talookdars", but also, since they would then be coming in greater numbers, to take over Indian jobs. As one commentator opposed to colonisation graphically described it, native tailors who had led decent enough lives before the arrival of Gibson and Co. were driven into poverty; those who lived by the needle, he said, through want of food became thin as needles. Goldsmiths, carpenters, *mistrees*, and even boatmen had fared no better.

The debate on colonisation could seldom have been joined more passionately or with greater historical awareness than it was in the pages of the *India Gazette* of 12 February 1830, when it carried an anonymous essay by a Hindu youth, "On the Colonisation of India". Reprinted the same year in the *Asiatic Journal*, it remained undiscovered until recently, when it was revealed and discussed.[5] Read "before a Hindu literary society, composed chiefly of native gentlemen", the essay put colonialism in perspective, while also asking whether we have any evidence of colonisation benefiting the colonised, though the colonising power will always say there is. "Large cabbages and fine blue indigo would be produced no doubt, but who would care if the produce of rice was bettered or not . . ." At the end of the essay we find the author looking in the mirror of literature, where he sees the figure of Washington Irving, from whose satirical *A History of New York* (1809) he quotes at length. In the second mirror he would have seen his teacher, Derozio. The society at which the paper was read was probably the Academic Association run by Derozio and David Hare in the years 1828–31.

The author of "On the Colonisation of India" may be anonymous, but the manner in which he argues his case against colonisation – giving examples from ancient Greece, the Roman colonies, and the colonies of the Phonecians, before coming to the settlement of the British in Ireland, North America, and New South Wales, and of the Spanish in Mexico and Peru, and rounding off his argument with a reference to a contemporary author, the American Washington Irving – reminds you of his later avatar, Pankaj Mishra, whose essay recollecting his days in Mashobra is utterly unlike the political essays he is well known for.

[5] Rosinka Chaudhuri, "'On the Colonisation of India (1829)': Public Meetings, Debates and Later Disputes", *The Indian Economic and Social History Review*, 55, 4 (2018), pp. 463–89.

If the nineteenth-century essay is neglected by those who are supposed to manage literary affairs, so is the twentieth. One only has to shake out the files of the *Modern Review* or the *Illustrated Weekly of India* to find Jadunath Sarkar and Fredoon Kabraji, flattened in their pages like dead moths, fluttering out.

A not-so-dead moth fluttering out is V.S. Naipaul, who contributed to the *Weekly* an occasional Newsletter: all of these newsletters are still uncollected. The one of 14 April 1963, called "A Return to England", began: "I have been living in England for nearly fifteen years, but have never ceased to think of myself as more than a visitor. The attitudes of non-residence have hardened into a habit of feeling which now extends, alarmingly, to all countries." The feeling never left him, hence *The Enigma of Arrival*, whose narrator describes himself as "a man from another hemisphere".

For reasons of space rather than for parochial reasons, it was decided to restrict this anthology as far as possible to "Indian" writers. Literary geography, unfortunately, had to be mapped on to the political one, but only loosely. So while Naipaul, Salman Rushdie, Ved Mehta, Vikram Chandra, Vijay Seshadri, Jhumpa Lahiri and so many others were stopped at the border, Santha Rama Rau and Victor Anant were allowed in. Anuradha Roy was stopped for entirely different reasons; she is the book's publisher. These exclusions created space for fine pieces by people such as Amrita Sher-Gil and Gautam Bhatia, who are not really seen as essayists but who would otherwise have had to be excluded.

On the whole, though, in this anthology the twentieth century is better shown than the nineteenth. The latter period – represented here by Derozio, the anonymous author of "On the Colonisation of India", Bankim Chandra Chattopadhyay, and Shoshee Chunder Dutt – could more truly be said to show gaps in the representation. The same is true of women writers:

their presence here is inadequate. This is not for reasons of space but because the country's early women writers in English were relatively few in number, and because the few that existed at all – such as Cornelia Sorabji (1866–1954) and Iqbalunnisa Hussain (1897–1954) – devoted their energies generally to issues of social reform and particularly to improving the lives of women. The one exception was Toru Dutt (1856–1877). But she died young, her energies went into poetry, and her engaging prose is mainly to be found in letters to her friend Mary Martin in England or in her notes to *A Sheaf Gleaned in French Fields*. "An Eurasian Poet", first published in the *Bengal Magazine* in 1874 and not reprinted in its entirety since, is a short piece of delightful, even mischievous literary criticism – "'Ah – it's the hackneyed subject of Derozio with the innumerable Christian names again' – exclaims the reader glancing at my title" it begins. As Dutt had foreseen, readers for the next hundred and forty years did believe that the piece was on Derozio. It is not.[6]

Voices such as Sorabji's and Hussain's can be found in an anthology edited by Eunice de Souza and Lindsay Pereira, *Women's Voices: Selections from Nineteenth and Early-Twentieth Century Indian Writing in English* (2002). And, as de Souza puts it in the book's introduction, "For the most part these were writers writing for a cause. There is little of the 'art for art's sake' present in their writing." Buddhadeva Bose, writing on the Bengali essay, says he goes to the essay for "the highest level of prose", and makes a distinction similar to the one made by de Souza: "I wish to confine my attention to those whom I would call 'pure' writers as opposed to 'applied' writers; in other words, to

[6] See my "Toru Dutt and 'An Eurasian Poet'", in Arvind Krishna Mehrotra, *Translating the Indian Past and Other Literary Histories* (Ranikhet: Permanent Black, 2019), pp. 19–38.

those who write not primarily to impart instruction or convey information, but as practitioners of an art whose validity, apart from the value of the content, they recognise."[7]

It is not till we come to Attia Hosain (1913–1998) that we have women who might have written the kind of essay in English that I have searched for when compiling this anthology: the essay that has something of Berger's "unrepeatable, momentary encounter"; one whose theme may range from "what the author notices from his window, to what he sees in his waste-paper basket, to a world cataclysm" (R.K. Narayan);[8] one that captures "the movement of the wing . . . not the bird".[9] The words are Anita Desai's, borrowing a line from one of Nissim Ezekiel's poems, "Poet, Lover, Birdwatcher". Even with Hosain, however, only one of her essays, "Deep Roots", is in print and it is about the difficulties of writing on a feudal culture that was steeped in Persian and Urdu and yet had to be re-imagined in English, the only language in which she could write her fiction. (The rest of Hosain's non-fiction prose is still in the form of clippings and typescripts and kept in an archive in London which I could not access.) As it happens, this is also partly the world of Sara Rai, though here the situation is almost reversed. Coming, on her mother's side, from a feudal Shia Muslim background similar to Hosain's, Sara Rai's Hindi is laced with Urdu words, but her reading is mainly in English, the language in which she has

[7] I am grateful to Rosinka Chaudhuri for drawing my attention to this quotation from *An Acre of Green Grass and Other English Writings of Buddhadeva Bose*, ed. Rosinka Chaudhuri (New Delhi: Oxford University Press, 2018), p. 63.

[8] R.K. Narayan, *A Writer's Nightmare: Selected Essays 1958–1988* (New Delhi: Penguin Books, 1988), p. 8.

[9] Anita Desai, "The Timid Movement of a Wing", *Indian Literary Review* (August 1978), pp. 11–13.

the first stirrings of what she writes. But then it gets more complex. While she is a bilingual writer, there is always more than one language pressing down on the one that she's doing her writing in. Out of this linguistic confusion, or linguistic richness, comes the title of her essay, "On Not Writing".

The essays by women in the anthology may be comparatively few, but, not unexpectedly, a passage in one essay illuminates a passage in another. Sheila Dhar's mother, "Baua", silently bore her husband's emotional neglect throughout her married life, a lapse that her husband extended to their children. A month before she died, Sheila Dhar asked Baua a question that had long troubled her: Why had she not walked out of the marriage? After three days of rumination, Baua came up with her answer: "The truth is that I loved him." Could part of Baua's truth have lain elsewhere? "Beaten, bullied and tormented, not infrequently to the point of death," Anita Desai writes in "A Secret Connivance", "a woman will state in her dying words that her man is not guilty . . . she is so indoctrinated with the ideals of honour and status and respectability that nothing will make her go against them. If she did, she would be questioning her own being – if she is not there to uphold the honour of her husband, her family, her society, then what is she *for*?" This is what Dhar too had suspected before she got her answer.

Madhur Jaffrey, describing how the large joint family in which she grew up spent a winter evening at home in Delhi, throws on her cousin Sheila Dhar's essay a different light. It is personal, familial. Sheila Dhar's Baua is Madhur Jaffrey's Taiji, her father's elder brother's wife. This is how Madhur Jaffrey ends her essay:

> If Taiji was trying to compensate her children with choice foods for their emotional deprivations, this could be written off as one of the smaller ripples created by Shibbudada's behaviour towards his family. As we all got older, the ripples would reach further and

further and enmesh Shibbudada's family and ours in the worst tangle of human relationships.

Jaffrey's essay is a chapter from her book, *Climbing the Mango Trees* (2005), as is Santha Rama Rau's from *Home to India* (1954). These are the only two chapters from books. Within the two memoirs they also stand as independent self-contained pieces, which is why they are included here. None of the essays in here is an extract.

There are essays that unexpectedly dovetail. R.K. Narayan's essay is about the death of an elephant, whereas all that the men around the animal wanted was to trap it. M. Krishnan's is about a bull, "light and quick-muscled", killing a man, whereas all the bull wanted was to get the man out of its way.

From essays that dovetail to essays that form a daisy chain: what if one were to read this anthology as a book of interlinked stories, as a single piece of non-fictional fiction; or as something else again, as an exercise in social history?

Coming up the Hoogly is the East Indiaman *Vansittart*, commanded by Captain William Henry Clarence Dalrymple. It had sailed from the East India docks at Blackwall, London, and had taken six months to make the voyage round the Cape of Good Hope. Among those eagerly awaiting its arrival is an East Indian by the name of Henry Derozio. Calcutta's been having the "rainy" and there's a great dearth of news; the docking of the boat changes all that. With it come people, merchandise, gossip; the chit-chat revives. A young student wonders if all this is for the good. What if the "Europeans" start arriving in even greater numbers, what if they buy up all the land, turn small farmers into farm labourers? A little later, Calcutta street cries are meticulously noted down; also noted, in the same decade, are the changes everywhere to be seen. With the boats (many of them made in Calcutta from Burma teak) come new styles of furniture, dress, locomotion, and a new cuisine. Hinduism, deservedly, gets kicked out of the door, but what's to take its place? Worries set in. What if taking its place is the Cult of the Nation? We see a crowd of people, all wearing the same mask. Those not wearing the mask panic; those wearing it strut around with pride; there's hatred in the air. The moral sense is blurred. Meanwhile, someone has other worries on her mind: how to paint a chair or a pair of boots. When the nation is born, its first prime minister wishes he were a nomad and could walk away from it all. A contemporary of his spends his time observing the habits of crows. In Lutyens' New Delhi, the men eat Quaker Oats, the women "call off the menus for the day", the servants have apprentices. If you do not live in a Lutyens house in New Delhi, you build a lookalike in Old Delhi. The people who live in them are identified by their house numbers: "They're from Number 7." Joint families break up. Private libraries are sold by the kilo as wastepaper. The English we speak changes, as does the cityscape. People once again become reflective. They think about the languages they write in, the books they read, the food they eat. They retreat from the world, while still observing it closely. Someone even remembers the East Indian Derozio.

Poetry should be at least as well written as prose, Ford Madox Ford once said. By prose he meant the prose of Stendhal and Flaubert. It is hoped that the well-written sentences of this anthology will give its readers pleasure and make their lives, as they have mine, a little more endurable. "What helps me can perhaps help somebody else," wrote Montaigne in "On

Practice", though he said it as the author of the *Essays* and not as the editor of an anthology containing them.

Truth, Anita Desai says in "A Secret Connivance", is "often ordinary, commonplace, colourless and dull." Which is why we avoid it in our writing, though it is also what makes the writing convincing and sets it alight. It is this very truth, "colourless and dull", that Shama Futehally was looking for in her older contemporaries when she started out as a writer but never found. Here she is remembering Behram Contractor, who wrote columns for several Bombay papers under the pseudonym Busybee:

> For me personally, however, the most important thing which that column did was to make me realize – long before a Rushdie or a Ghosh had appeared on the scene – that there could be such a thing as real Indian English writing. Because in the early seventies, if you aspired to write in English, you were aspiring to an activity which did not exist. Writers in English were either expatriates (mental or physical) like V.S. Naipaul or Dom Moraes – or they were self-consciously native like Kamala Markandeya. Writers who looked neither upwards nor downwards, who looked unpretendingly back at us and spoke our own idiom – and, yes, who were always out when the gas cylinder came – these did not exist. I still remember my youthful despair about not being able to write, not for lack of will but because there was no world for the writing to inhabit.
>
> – "Busybee's Stray Thoughts"

This is a passage that only a woman of the middle classes living in India, and gifted with an exquisite writerly instinct, could have put down. Who else will wait as anxiously for the arrival of the van carrying cooking-gas cylinders, or follow the rattling sound that the cylinders make as the van approaches the house before coming to a stop? Not Markandeya in London; not Moraes. And who else will ask, despairingly, "Where is that world my writing can inhabit?" Ironically, someone who was troubled by the same question was V.S. Naipaul. "Very little of what I read was of help," he wrote, referring to his reading Dickens as a schoolboy in Trinidad. "The vision was alien, it diminished my own and did not give me courage to do a simple thing like mentioning the name of a Port of Spain street."[10]

Political essays, however truthful, well written, and convincing, such as Arundhati Roy's, have not been included here. Political writing is urgent, but it is soon replaced by something as urgent the next day, often the next hour, even the next minute if we follow it on Twitter. As we in India pass through a dark phase in our history, similar to Europe of the 1930s, we need it more than ever before; but so do we, as urgently, the essays in this anthology.

"The light at the end of the tunnel," wrote Robert Lowell, "is just the light of an oncoming train." Our particular oncoming train is called Shri Ramayana Express and it carries pilgrims on an IRCTC religious circuit tour. The sleeper class package costs Rs 16,065.00 per person and during Navratra "food served to the travellers will be cooked without onion and garlic. Fasting food will also be available for the tourists, including Sabudana Khichdi, fruits, curd and potato chaat."[11] As a character in Aleksandar Tišma's novel *The Use of Man*, set in Novi Sad in the closing years of World War II, says: "Mysticism now rules the world, the cult of blood and violence, darkness, the longing for the past, nationalism." In brief, the world of "potato chaat" – and spare a thought for the Portuguese, who, some

[10] Quoted by Adil Jussawalla in *Maps for a Mortal Moon: Essays and Entertainments* (Delhi: Aleph, 2014), p. 19.

[11] https://www.zeebiz.com/india/news-special-train-shri-ramayana-express-fare-booking-routes-and-everything-you-need-to-know-120307

500 years ago, introduced what they thought was a harmless tuber to this country.

Where we are now, others have been before and left a record in fiction, poetry, diary, and newspaper column. In 1921, in a column for a Berlin paper, Joseph Roth wrote: "It's only the minutiae of life that are important . . . I no longer have any use for the sweeping gestures of heroes on the global stage. I'm going for a walk."[12] In 1933, the year Hitler came to power, Roth left Germany and moved to Paris, which is where he heard of the Nazi book-burnings. That same year he wrote in an essay, "The Auto-da-Fé of the Mind": "Now, as the smoke of our burned books rises into the sky, we German writers of Jewish descent must acknowledge above all that we have been defeated. Let us, who are fighting on the front line, under the banner of the European mind, let us fulfil the noblest duty of the defeated warrior: Let us concede our defeat."[13]

The two exceptions to not including political essays are Tagore's "The Nation" and Gautam Bhatia's "Art as Politics". Both are far from straightforwardly political: Tagore's by its defence of "self-expression" over "showy" patriotism and the "crowd mind", and Bhatia's because the essay is not so much about politics as about the statues and monuments our political leaders, when in power, lavish on themselves or erect to those they wish to invoke, emulate, or be blessed by. But whereas monuments, whether to gods, men, or women, will be swallowed up by rising sea levels or be destroyed by earthquakes or be pulled down by an irate public that has had enough, the lowly sentence, though defeated, could still be around, ready to crawl out of the slime and reclaim the pedestal.

[12] Joseph Roth, *What I Saw: Reports from Berlin 1920–1933*, translated by Michael Hofmann (New York: W.W. Norton, 2003), pp. 24–5.

[13] Ibid., p. 207.

HENRY LOUIS VIVIAN DEROZIO

Chit-chat – Scandal – Tea-parties

During the rainy, which is invariably the most unfashionable season in Calcutta, there prevails a great dearth of news, unless it should so happen that the arrival of a ship or two from England, brings matter of much political importance, or intelligence which is interesting, if it can only make the multitude gape with wonder, and exclaim "strange, strange, passing strange". But cases like those of Thurtell, Fontleroy, and the more unfortunate Elephant that was put lately to death for having manifested symptoms of rebellion, are of very rare occurrence; and when these are wanting, *Chit-Chat* flags, and becomes "weary, stale, flat, and unprofitable", in spite of the benevolent efforts of newspaper Editors who occasionally *make* murders and suicides, with the hope of keeping public attention alive. Now, with deference to the opinion of all those who differ from me, I certainly think that it was charitable, most charitable on the part of the wag who, some time ago, reported the arrival of a ship named the *Frederick the 1st* – it excited interest; everyone spoke of it, the newspaper Editors wrote about it; some wished to know what was the authority for such a rumour, others credited without inquiring about it, it was the aqua vitae of conversation – it was, in a word, the Chit-chat of the day. But, when these little ingenious manoeuvres are not played or rather palmed upon the public, there is an awful paucity of conversational topics; indeed it causes some people more distress than the present want of Bullion in England has created among the Mercantile Community. All that can be said by good folks in "these weak piping times of peace" may be summed up in a few words.

The *weather*, however, I must admit, is an exhaustless subject; you may first remark that it is very sultry or very pleasant, *as the case may be*; then, add that the state of the weather for the last few days, has been fitful, or settled, *as the case may have been*; then, that it will probably continue fitful, or settled, as the face of the heavens appears to you at the time you are speaking; after all this, it will be necessary to inform the person you are in conversation with, although he may be only your nextdoor neighbour, that it blew very freshly from the East on Tuesday night, and the consequence was, that you slept more soundly then than you had done for a fortnight past.

The Thermometer is the next subject; though from its connexion with the one I have already mentioned, it may be called the memorandum Book of the Seasons. On it, you may make voluminous remarks; say that the Thermometer was up to 98° in the shade on Monday last about noon; then immediately complain of having panted, and of having been nearly suffocated, &c., &c., although perhaps if the truth were told, you saw not a Thermometer for a week, and on the very day and hour which you have mentioned, probably you were driving your Buggy all over Calcutta, from Auction to Auction, Shop to Shop, here, there, and everywhere. Indeed, the weather and its concomitants, or, as the lawyers would say, "all appurtenances thereto belonging", are subjects which may be spoken of *ad infinitum*.

But even the weather is not sufficient to afford good conversation for an hour; at least not *agreeable* Confab. What then is to be done? How is the time to be whiled away? I know of no other thing which so effectually kills the moments as they pass, and makes the sand in the old man's glass appear like diamond sparks, as when two good people of lively imagination sit and talk *scandal*, without intending any mischief to any individual. Now, I think that it is not so easy to talk scandal *cleverly*, as some people suppose it is. It requires management, and is just as much an art as anything which has that name. (Memo: to write a folio volume on this prolific subject, pointing out its agreeable varieties, with complete instructions for the uninitiated.) Add to all this, that the poetical faculty, i.e. imagination, is very requisite to *create* such intelligence, or rumour, or whatever you choose to call it, as "It is said that Mrs. &c. &c." And to give these "*says*" an historical effect, it is always necessary to conclude, and frequently to intersperse your narrative with "I heard it on very good, and indisputable authority." Be it remembered, that this is brought in to strengthen your veracity, in the same manner that an author who deals in the marvellous, refers you in a note to some antiquated writer whose works are only to be seen in the Public Libraries at Oxford, in the Museum, or in the collections of private individuals. Thus, the correctness of what you assert will be rarely impeached, but should you be so unfortunate as to be detected, you have that ever ready "I heard it" as an excellent hole to creep out of. The best and *fittest* time to exert your imaginative *bump*, and to ascertain or exhibit your true powers in the pleasant art of scandal is at those charming coteries called

Tea Parties – Oh! The very name of tea bring to the mind a thousand associations fraught with everything delightful and entertaining. What the ruby liquid is to the poet, *that* the inspiring green Hyson is to – what shall I say? – the conversationist. I know not how it is, that one insensibly begins to be agreeable at tea; particularly when two or three "lovely ones" are telling the twenty-fourth edition of a tale which they "heard on very good authority". It is impossible even for a dull Hypochondriac to be silent when a "budding Miss" talks of Mr–'s attentions to Mrs–; and then sweetly condemns her coquettish cousin Ella for having so many young men constantly at her heels, &c., &c. – I say it is impossible for any man to be silent after such pretty things have been said.

So sweet a language from so fair a mouth –
Ah! To what effort could it not persuade?

It is all delightful, pleasant and "very refreshing", as Mr Jeffry says in the *Edinburgh Review*. In short, Chit-chat is necessary for the well being of society, Scandal for the life of Chit-chat, and Tea Parties for the preservation of all these.

– *Calcutta, July 20, 1826*

"ANON. HINDU YOUTH"

The Colonisation of India

FROM THE *INDIA GAZETTE* OF 12 FEBRUARY 1830

THE SUBJECT WHICH I am desirous of introducing to the society, is of very great importance to the natives of this country, particularly as it may involve them in a change not easily or perhaps never after to be repealed. To judge of the consequences that would ensue from such a measure, requires more judgment and far greater literary talents than I can boast of. Perfectly sensible therefore of my incapacity in pronouncing proper and just opinions on subjects of this nature, I do not refrain from making these observations, for fear that it should be said of my countrymen, that they did not utter even one single word of remonstrance when their fate hung suspended as by a cobweb over their heads. For this reason I beg to bring forward the subject to the notice of the worthy president and members of the society, hoping that their clear judgments will be able to bring into proper shape that which I merely introduce before them; and soliciting at the same time their kind indulgence, I beg to commence on the subject without farther preface.

The term "colony" has been defined to be "a body of people drawn from the mother country, to inhabit some distant place, and remaining even there either under the government of the mother country, or under a government of their own." The colonies of the ancients were mostly of the latter sort.

From time immemorial, Greece had been so colonised by the people of Asia Minor, who were obliged on account of a very rapid increase of their numbers, and their incapacity to supply themselves with the proper necessaries of life in their own country, to seek other lands for their maintenance and support. They therefore went over to Greece, that being the nearest country to themselves, where they established several colonies, amongst which were all the most celebrated states of Greece. But about the year 1044 BC some of these Grecians migrated back into their former country (Asia Minor), and established themselves by expelling the original inhabitants; and although these settlers certainly spoke the same language, and although their manners and customs were of course the same as the inhabitants of Greece Proper, yet they did not remain either under their management or under their jurisdiction. The Greeks established colonies in several other countries also, in most of which the settlers established governments of their own, and in all of them the original inhabitants were expelled.

The Romans made colonies in almost all those places they conquered, both in order to make some recompense to their worn-out soldiers and countrymen, as also to keep the vanquished in perfect awe, by a display in their country of their superior skill and power. The Roman colonies were in fact a sort of military stations, where their veteran soldiers received a certain portion of land for their past services, and spent the remainder of their lives in executing such orders of justice or tyranny as they might receive from Rome. Almost in all parts of the then known world, Roman colonies had been so established. For among the Roman colonies may be named several of the most considerable cities in England, France, Spain, and even in Asia and Africa. Those towns in England, the names of which end in Caster or "Chester", are all Roman colonies. The city of Cologne on the Rhine is a Roman colony; its ancient name "Colonia", means a "colony". The Romans considered that they had a right to take possession of any portion of land they pleased. In the earlier part of the republic, whenever they thought their territories were not large enough, they took by force of arms a certain portion of the lands in Italy, and expelled the inhabitants thereof. Whenever a foreign country was conquered, the inhabitants, after being led under the yoke, were either carried as prisoners to Rome, or left in their country to serve almost as slaves to the Roman settlers, neither possessing the rights of Roman citizens nor those of their own country.

Of three different sorts of colonies, I have already mentioned two, namely, colonies for sending away from the mother country an unusual increase of population, &c. and those established for keeping any vanquished nation in obedience. The third sort are colonies of trade. Of this, among the ancients the Phoenicians established the greatest number. These people, for the purpose of extending their already overflowing commerce, established their countrymen in many foreign countries, in order that by this means their transactions in trade might be facilitated. This, of course, of all sorts of colonies is the least exceptionable, as commerce is generally conducive to the improvement of a country, and this sort of colonies would perhaps be a great blessing to the land in which they are established. This would certainly have been the case with the Phoenician colonies, but they also drove away the original inhabitants into the further part of the country, and established their own people. Among the Phoenician colonies may be mentioned Carthage, the rival of Rome. Such were the colonies among the ancients.

Among the modern colonies may be mentioned the settlement of the British in Ireland in the year 1612, and in North

America in the reigns of Elizabeth and James, and that in New South Wales in the year 1786; as also the settlement of the Spanish in Mexico and Peru, &c. &c. It was in the reign of James I that the British first settled in Ulster. That province fell to the crown by attainders. On account of the Irish then being considered rebels, no price was given to them for their lands. Conspiracies were formed and barbarously executed, but this only served to dispossess them of those lands and properties which they still held. Their inhumanity in destroying the settlers is treated at great length by historians, and this at once points out how they hated and detested them. And it is possible that they so much disliked those that acted as friends towards them.

About the year 1497 AD in the reign of Henry the First of England, the British, in order, if possible, to equal the Portuguese and Spaniards in their discoveries, fitted out a fleet, under the command of a Venetian named Cabot. This man discovered the greatest part of the northern regions of America, to which he gave the general name of Newfoundland; no attempts were then made to colonise the country. In the reign of Elizabeth, Sir Walter Raleigh, with some British adventurers, first settled in these parts. Mighty disputes ensued between the red and white men, the red man neither seeking nor desiring for any good or evil which the white man might do him; whilst the white on his part, was so very desirous of imparting these things to them, that he was obliged often to have recourse to harsh means. An eminent modern author observes, that "no sooner did the benevolent inhabitants of Europe behold their sad condition, than they immediately go to work to ameliorate and improve it. They introduced among them rum, gin, brandy, and the other comforts of life; and it is astonishing to read how soon the poor savages learnt to estimate these blessings. They likewise made known to them a thousand remedies by which the most inveterate diseases are alleviated and healed; and that they may comprehend the benefit and enjoy the comforts of these medicines, they previously introduced among them the diseases they were calculated to cure." On account of the settlers coming and possessing themselves of the finest lands, the enraged sachems, or Indian chieftains, began to harass them by frequent petty attacks. The Indian, with all his rudeness, barbarity, long bows and arrows, soon felt the powers and strength of gunpowder. A great many of the settlers, however, fell by the hands of the natives, others died by several diseases incident to the change of climate, so that the adventure was by no means very prosperous. It is related, that of 9000 Europeans only 1800 remained alive at the end of twenty years. But even all this did not make the white desist from his undertaking. In the reign of James I some people migrated to America, on account of their differing in some points from the established forms of worship. Charles II granted charters to several persons to colonise America; amongst these was William Penn, a Quaker, who settled in Pennsylvania. Amongst other things mentioned in the history of this settlement, it is expressly stated that the settlers of this colony paid money to the Indians for the lands they took possession of, and did take nothing by force. This was certainly considered something new, as the best way of taking possession of the lands was by force. In this manner several colonies were established, and at present the settlers have formed a republican government of their own, and the aborigines are driven into the interior parts of the country, where they even to this day adhere to their ancient rites and manners, and, however rude they may be, are by no means desirous of being slaves to the white men.

New Holland was discovered by the Dutch and English about the year 1618, and was colonised by the English about the year 1779. A certain number of convicts was subsequently sent from

Britain to this new colony, to serve the colonists there. The first settlers on their arrival presented the natives of this country with beads, glass, and other trifles, which however, they afterwards threw away, refusing to give anything in return for such useless baubles. The convicts made a great deal of disturbance on their first landing; by degrees, however, and after a good deal of trouble, the people were somewhat tamed; but even to the present period we are informed a man dare hardly sleep without a pair of pistols at his bed-side. The country, however, being not much peopled, the necessity of expelling the aborigines was not very much resorted to. Such of these as remained, however, retreated to the wilds and forests of the country, abandoning those places, which (to their idea at least) they had cultivated, to the settlers.

The colonies of the Spaniards, however, afford a far greater example of oppression and cruelty. When the West-Indies were discovered and taken possession of by the Spaniards, the Pope issued an order, that should the natives of the newly discovered colonies yield to the settlers a certain portion of land, and should they all embrace Christianity, all would be well; otherwise the settlers were authorised to pursue them with fire and sword, and even to extinguish, if possible a race, as his holiness was pleased to observe, totally barbarous and unchristian.

Such were the orders of his holiness, and these orders were given to such people as would in every way "better the instruction". A Spaniard, on his return from an embassy (or rather espial) to the court of Peru, informed his brother settlers of the immense wealth of the Peruvians. Their general, in order to possess it, formed a plan as bold as it was treacherous. The Emperor of Peru, being invited by the Spanish general to visit him, next day proceeded in great pomp and splendour to the Spanish camp. The first man that he met there was a Spanish monk, who immediately after his arrival began a long harangue, in which, among other things, he observed that the Pope had made a grant to the Spaniards of the whole of America, and that he should, after having embraced Christianity, yield to the king of Spain as his lawful sovereign. On hearing this, the monarch was perfectly astonished, and said that he wondered how a foreign priest dared to dispose of his hereditary lands; and that he would not "leave the immortal Sun to worship the God of the Spaniards who was but a mortal." Saying this, he threw away the breviary which the monk had put into his hands. The Spaniards immediately rushed from their lurking places, and after some skirmishing, took the king prisoner. "Four thousand Peruvians were killed, but not a single Spaniard fell." An immense ransom, consisting of as many gold plates as would almost fill up a room 16 feet square, was received by the Spaniards, on their promising to set the king at liberty. But even after this they were as treacherous as ever. After a mock trial, in which the king, among other things, was accused of having many wives, he was ordered for execution: he however became baptised in the hope that he should be freed, but even after this he was most shamefully strangled at a stake.

The history of the world affords not another parallel to the inhumanity of the Spaniards towards the natives of the Indies. The historian appears to be perfectly shocked at the audacious barbarity, and bigoted, but unprincipled zeal, with which they treated these Indians. It would draw down disgrace on the most brutal tribes of savages; how much then must it do so on a nation that pretended to be one of the most civilised of its time? But it must also at the same time be confessed, however, that the Supreme Spanish government was not wholly in fault; for, correctly speaking, it was principally the work of Pizarro, one of the chief Spanish adventurers, a vain and selfish man, in whose hands the government had put the reins, perhaps not knowing him to be so perfectly void of humanity and feeling to his fellow-creatures as he was found to be.

After having thus far given a short detail of the historical facts connected with the subject, I shall next proceed to state what change would be produced by means of colonisation in this country in particular. In not even one of the historical facts above quoted, can be found an example in which the condition of the aboriginal inhabitants of a country has ever been bettered by colonisation. Nay, so far from it, that it can safely be asserted, that in every part of the world, since colonies were first established to the present day, the original inhabitants of a country have always suffered from the experiment.

In India, if there were a large portion of extra and uncultivated land, the sufferings of the natives would of a certainty be less; but such is not the case: for by the collectors' accounts in the Mofussil, it will be observed that this country has not more waste lands than the most civilised countries in the earth; much less is it like America in its former state, or New Holland in its present one. But even if there were immense waste lands, and if good and honest English farmers, leaving their delightful homes, and the farms which they and their fathers have enjoyed, should condescend to visit a foreign clime, is it certain that they would cultivate such things as would be beneficial to the natives of the country? Large cabbages and fine blue indigo would be produced no doubt, but who would care if the produce of rice was bettered or not, provided there could be found meat sufficient to afford them ample food? Men of respectability and capital, nay even simple craftsmen, who have barely some common means of subsistence, would not leave their homes for the purely philanthropic object of ameliorating the condition of the inhabitants thereof, whose manners and customs widely differ from their own, and the climate of whose country is by no means adapted to their constitutions. None but needy and adventuring desperadoes, who have neither families nor homes, would come to settle here in the expectation of expelling the timid natives, as their fathers had done to the natives of America.

Such being the case, therefore, little can colonisation benefit the inhabitants of this country. It may, however, be affirmed by those gentlemen who are desirous of colonisation, that by the superior skill of the Europeans in machinery, the preparation of thread, cloth, and other articles, and even sugar and such things, would be facilitated – to which it may be answered, that it is a question whether the preparation of articles by these means would be for the benefit or evil of a country; for my own part, I am of opinion, from the several examples already seen in Manchester, Glasgow, and other manufacturing towns, that the use of machinery is always for evil.

The idea of the Zemindars of receiving high prices for their land, is equally delusive. It has been already shown that none but needy adventurers would come out to settle in this country, and they will not be able to make actual payment for lands, which they will by some means or other get possession of. In Ireland, as I have before observed, no price was paid for the lands taken possession of by the settlers on account of the Irish being rebels. In America, although a remuneration was pretended to have been given, yet very few Indians received any adequate recompense for their property. As for the Spaniards, they had the Pope's order to take possession of any portion of land in America they pleased. Besides, the settlement of Lord Cornwallis will be at an end as soon as the country is colonised, so that the government revenue may also be increased. Further, that it would be impossible for the Zemindars to get any redress for the encroachment of the European settlers, who may purchase neighbouring zemindaries. As for the Ryots, it is perfectly out of the question for them to go to law with their European masters, illustrations of whose oppression, at least to those who have observed the operations of several indigo planters, are superfluous.

The daily labourer would also suffer; for besides the fall of wages, which would be the case by means of an increase of population, he may perhaps be totally unable to obtain any livelihood at all; for even at present the natives complain, and do so with some justice, that they can obtain no respectable situations, all which are conferred on Europeans; how much more reason then would they have to do so, when the office of even menial servants would be filled by Europeans. I regret that circumstances oblige me to quote a passage from one of Bishop Heber's letters to the Dean of St Asaph. The Right Rev. Prelate observes, that "many of the adventurers who come hither from Europe, are the greatest profligates the sun ever saw; men whom nothing but despotism can manage, and who would insult, beat, and plunder the natives without shame or pity"; and ask a native ryot, and his answer will not in any point deviate from the above observation.

The religion of the Hindoos would also suffer; but on this point I shall refrain from making any remarks, believing it to be a rule of the Society not to make any discussions concerning religion. It has been asserted by some Europeans that English labourers could do work a great deal more than the natives of this country. But it is prejudice alone that makes them say so. The European also is a human being as well as the native; and I, for my own part, sincerely believe that the native can work as much as any European workman could do. Nay, I may even add, that in a climate like this the native could work more than the European.

Everyone therefore would suffer, whether they be zemindars, ryots, persons living by handicraft or by agriculture. In fact, India requires no importation of articles from other countries to promote the welfare and happiness of its inhabitants. The natives of this country would not by any means whatever suffer should the manufacturing of indigo or the importation of all sorts of wines, &c. be prevented. The success of the settlers themselves also, however sanguine they might be at first, is doubtful and precarious; for although some money might have been made in indigo, &c. in this country by the Europeans that have already come here, yet, generally speaking, adventures have been attended with considerable loss.

The transportation of convicts into colonies points out the light in which they are regarded by the mother country. In short we need not wish for colonisation any more than, as Mr Irving observes in one of his works, the inhabitants of Europe would desire their country to be colonised by the men in the moon.* Our author, who is a citizen of the United States of North America, adds, "Neither would the prodigy of sailing in the air and cruising among the stars, be a whit more astonishing and incomprehensible to us, than was the European mystery of navigating floating castles through the world of waters to the simple savages. We have already discovered the art of coasting along the shores of our planet by means of balloons, as the savages had of venturing along their sea-coasts in canoes, &c."

"To return, then, to my supposition," says the author, "let us suppose that the aerial visitants I have mentioned, possessed of vastly superior knowledge to ourselves; that is to say, possessed of superior knowledge in the art of extermination, riding on hypogriffs, defended with impenetrable armour, armed with

*The reference is to Washington Irving, *A History of New York* (1809).

concentrated sun-beams, and provided with vast engines to hurl enormous moonstones. All this is very possible, it is only our self-sufficiency that makes us think otherwise; and I warrant the poor savages, before they had any knowledge of the white men, armed in all the terrors of glittering steel and tremendous gun-powder, were as perfectly convinced that they themselves were the wisest, the most virtuous, powerful, and perfect of created beings, as are to the present moment the lordly inhabitants of old England, the volatile populace of France, or even the self-satisfied citizens of this most enlightened republic.

"Let us suppose, moreover, the aerial voyagers finding this planet nothing but a howling wilderness, inhabited by us poor savages and wild beasts, shall take formal possession of it in the name of his most gracious and philosophic excellency the Man in the Moon. Finding however, that their numbers are incompetent to hold it in complete subjection on account of the ferocious barbarity of its inhabitants, they shall take our worthy president, the King of England, the Emperor of Hayti, the great King of Bantam, and returning to their native planet, shall carry them to court, as were the Indian chiefs led about as spectacles in the courts of Europe. Then making such obeisance as the etiquette of the court requires, they shall address the puissant man in the moon in, as near as I can conjecture, the following terms:

'Most serene and mighty potentate, whose dominions extend as far as I can reach, who rideth on the great bear, useth the sun as a looking glass, and maintaineth unrivalled controul over tides, madmen, and seacrabs; we thy liege subjects have just returned from a voyage of discovery, in the course of which we have landed and taken possession of that obscure little dirty planet which thou beholdest rolling at a distance. The four uncouth monsters which we have brought into thy august presence, were once very important chiefs among their fellow savages, who are a race of beings destitute of the common attributes of humanity, and differing in everything from the inhabitants of the moon, as they carry their heads upon their shoulders, instead of under their arms, have two eyes instead of one, are utterly destitute of tails, and are of a variety of unseemly complexions, particularly of a horrible whiteness instead of a pea-green.

'We have moreover found these miserable savages sunk into a state of the utmost ignorance and depravity; every man shamelessly living with his own wife and rearing his own children, instead of indulging in that community of wives enjoined by the law of nature, as expounded by the philosophers of the moon. In a word they have scarcely a gleam of true philosophy among them, but are in fact utter heretics, ignoramuses, and barbarians. Taking compassion therefore on the sad condition of these sublunary wretches, we have endeavoured while we remained on their planet, to introduce among them the lights of reason and the comforts of the moon. We have treated them to mouthfuls of moonshine and draughts of nitrous oxide, which they swallowed with incredible voracity, particularly the females. We have insisted upon their renouncing the contemptible shackles of religion and common sense, and adoring the profound, omnipotent, and all-perfect energy, and the ecstatic, immutable, immovable perfection. But such was the unparalleled obstinacy of these wretched savages, that they persisted in cleaving to their wives and adhering to their religion, and absolutely set at nought the sublime doctrines of the moon. Nay among other abominable heresies they even went so far as blasphemously to declare, that this ineffable planet was made of nothing more nor less than green cheese!'

"At these words the great Man in the Moon being a profound philosopher, shall fall into a terrible passion, and possessing equal authority over things that do not belong to him, as did whilome his holiness the Pope, shall forthwith issue a formidable Bull, specifying 'that whereas a certain crew of Lunatics having lately discovered and taken possession of a newly discovered planet called the Earth, and that whereas it is inhabited by none but a race of two-legged animals that carry their heads on their shoulders instead of under their arms; cannot talk the lunatic language; have two eyes instead of one; are destitute of tails; and are of a horrible whiteness instead of a pea-green; therefore, and for a variety of other excellent reasons, they are considered incapable of possessing any property in the planet they infest, and the right and title to it are confirmed to its original discoverers. And furthermore the colonists, who are now about to depart to the aforesaid planet, are authorised and commanded to use every means to convert these infidel savages from the darkness of Christianity, and make them thorough and absolute Lunatics.'

"In consequence of this absolute Bull, our philosophic benefactors go to work with hearty zeal, they seize upon our fertile territories, scourge us from our rightful possessions, relieve us from our wives, and when we are unreasonable enough to complain, they will turn upon us and say: 'Miserable barbarians! Ungrateful wretches! Have we not come thousands of miles to improve your worthless planet? Have we not fed you with moonshine; have we not intoxicated you with nitrous oxide; does not our moon give you light every night, and have you the baseness to murmur when we claim a pitiful return for all these benefits?' But finding we not only persist in absolute contempt of their reasoning and disbelief in their philosophy, but even go so far as daringly to defend our property, their patience shall be exhausted and they shall resort to their superior powers of argument, hunt us with hypogriffs, transfix us with concentrated sun-beams, demolish our cities with moonstones; until having by main force converted us to the true faith, they shall graciously permit us to exist in the torrid deserts of Arabia or the frozen regions of Lapland, there to enjoy the blessings of civilisation, and the charms of lunar philosophy, in much the same manner as the reformed and enlightened savages of this country (America) are kindly suffered to inhabit the inhospitable forests of the North, or the impenetrable wilderness of South America."

Even such would be the fruits of colonisation here. A greater evil than colonisation can in fact never happen, so very much is it to the disadvantage of the natives; and I therefore most sincerely hope, that it will please our gracious sovereign to renew the charter of the East-India Company on its expiration, and thereby obtain the blessings of his loyal and loving subjects in the East.

BANKIM CHANDRA CHATTOPADHYAY

The Confessions of a Young Bengal

THAT IN THE OUTWARD circumstances of social and personal life English-educated Bengalis are rapidly getting anglicised, few English-educated Bengalis will deny. The stamp of the Anglo-Saxon foreigner is upon our houses, our furniture, our carriages, our food, our drink, our dress, our very familiar letters and conversation. He who reads may read it on every inch of our outward life. We build and fit up our houses according to English ideas of architectural beauty, ventilation, and general comfort. Our ancestors, in building houses of any pretension or grandeur, invariably postponed all considerations of the ease and comfort of the human inmates to a pious regard for the benefiting accommodation of the various celestials during their thirteen appointed visits in the course of twelve months. The *Poojah Dalan*, the apartment dedicated to the idols, was invariably the portion of the house upon which the lion's share of the whole estimated cost was spent, which was most adorned with the architectural decorations of the time, which, in its dimensions, surpassed every other apartment – which, in short, determined by its style and magnificence the owner's position in society. In the houses built by the English-educated Bengalis the *Poojah Dalan* is only conspicuous by its absence, so much so that it would not, perhaps, be altogether superfluous to refer to a piece of philological evidence to prove that it was not always so: in many rural villages of Bengal, *Dalan*, is to this day, synonymous with a brick-built house. Chairs, tables, *punkhas* seldom meant to be pulled, American clocks, glassware of variegated hues, pictures for which the *Illustrated London News* is liberally laid under contribution [*sic*],[1] kerosene lamps, bookshelves filled with Reynolds' *Mysteries*, Tom Paine's *Age of Reason* and the *Complete Poetical Works* of Lord Byron, English musical-boxes, compose the fashionable furniture of the sitting-rooms of Young Bengal . . .

We have no objection, on principle, to dine on roast beef or veal cutlets, nor any, either, on principle or in practice, to *drink*, in the idiomatic English sense, and after English fashion. Our conversation is nine parts broken English and one part pure Bengali. We have exchanged the cumbrous forms of Bengali epistolary correspondence for those of Cook's Universal Letter-writer and the tight-fitting jackets and loose-fitting *chapkans* of our grandfathers for shirts *d'anglaise* and *chapkans* that are every day steadily approaching towards the shape and size of English coats, to say nothing of our English shoes, the eyesore of official Anglo-Indians.

English education, administered with the most rigid economy and the example of Englishmen, wrapped up with the threefold covering of national, political, and religious exclusiveness, has in a single generation sufficed to work these changes in the external features of Bengali society. Paradoxical as it may seem, the second is by much the most powerful agency of the two, though, without *some* share of the first it cannot have free scope for its operation. A six months' visit to England, accomplished with the lightest possible equipment of English, does far more

[1] The meaning of "liberally laid under contribution" is not clear; it was presumably clear to Bankim's readers – unless the phrase contains a printer's mistake that escaped the author's notice. – Ed.

to anglicise one's tastes, manners, and fashion than a lifelong devotion to English literature at home. Cases of conflict between the action of English education and that of English example are not rare, in which the result has proved to demonstrate the superior energy of the latter.

The very idea that external life is a worthy subject of the attention of a rational being, except in its connection with religion, is, amongst ourselves, unmistakably of English origin. In spite of their emphatic inculcation of the duty of self-preservation, the prevailing tendency of our *Shastras* was towards severe asceticism, founded upon a profound feeling of the transitoriness and unreality of this world . . . English civilisation has pulled down the three hundred and thirty million deities of Hinduism, and set up, in the total space once occupied by them, its own tutelary deities, Comfort and his brother, Respectability . . .

We have cast away caste. We have outlived the absurdity of a social classification based upon the accident of birth. But we are not such ultra radicals as to adopt for our watchword the impracticable formula of "Equality and Fraternity". Thank God, we are not so far as Frenchified as that. We have received a High English education. Our culture is thoroughly English and we mean to reconstruct society according to English notions . . .

Our Deism, our Theism, our Brahmoism, progressive or ultra-progressive, our Compteism, apparently an indigenous religious development, the morality of which was recently discussed under that strange designation, with equal ability and learning in more than one issue of a Calcutta newspaper – what are all these *isms* at bottom but merely so many different embodiments of a strong desire to exempt ourselves from the obligations of Hinduism. No enlightened human being can endure semi-barbarous restrictions concerning drink; no enlightened human being can afford to forgo the commonest comforts of life for finding means for the extravagantly expansive superstitions of benighted parents; no enlightened human being can find it in his heart to respect a man whose only claim to respect is founded on an old-fashioned ascetic purity of life, and an intimate acquaintance with a literature, false history, false geography, and false physics; no enlightened human being can bring himself to believe in the moral excellence of perpetual widowhood; and so on, to the end of the chapter of grievances, the necessary minor premises being assumed, sound logic compels us to cry with one voice, "Hinduism must be destroyed."

Agreed. But the spiritual nature of man abhors a vacuum. Between our various *isms*, the Hindu code of personal and social ethics has been well nigh wholly repealed, and its precepts are universally seen and felt to be more honoured in the breach than in the observance. Where is our new code of morality? Where is the new public opinion to enforce its rules? Where is the man amongst us who in personal purity, in meekness, in self-forgetfulness, in genuine non-political patriotic feeling, in tenderness for the least sentient thing, in lifelong and systematic devotion to knowledge and virtue for its own sake, can stand a moment's comparison with the better order of minds nurtured in the cradle of Hinduism? Let the tree be judged by its fruit.

SHOSHEE CHUNDER DUTT

The Street-Music of Calcutta

I DEVOTED A WHOLE DAY to listen to the street-music of Calcutta, and report the result for the information of my readers. The cries to which I refer are to be heard daily in the native part of the town. Those peculiar to the European portion of it are of course very different.

I. Kooar-Ghotee-Tollah!

Almost the first cry every morning is that of the *Kooar-ghotee-tollah*. Be the day ever so cold or so rainy there is the man ready to extricate from the bottom of the well whatever you may have dropt in it, though the cry speaks of brass *lotahs* only. The Moorish lady cried her heart out for the earrings she had dropt in the well, which she could not recover. There must have been no *kooar-ghotee-tollah* in Spain in her day, for ear-rings, or nose-rings, or finger-rings, are all picked out of wells in Calcutta with the greatest facility. Look at the man as he stands before you – an elderly, stout fellow, with elephantiasis on one leg – and you would hardly think him capable of the feat by which he earns his daily bread. He must dive at least five or six times a day to earn a decent pittance, for two or three pice is all he gets each time; and the frail steps on the well-side by which he gets down are not contemptible dangers to brave for the price paid to him. Talk of old Bazaine's escape from Fort St Marguerite! It surely was not half so perilous as these incessant descents into wells kept as dirty as can be imagined and in indifferent repair; and yet who has ever heard of a *ghotee-tollah* having died in the execution of his duty?

But have not water-pipes superseded the use of wells in every family-residence in Calcutta, asks the English reader, entirely innocent of native ways and doings. No, Aryan brother, they have not. The supply of Municipal water is little to be depended upon, and fails frequently at very inconvenient hours; and our Hindu ladies are so aquatic in their habits, and delight so much in water, that an unfailing supply of it from 4 a.m. to 10 p.m. is an absolute necessity of their lives. Almost every act of housewifery requires the washing of hands or clothes, and many make entire ablutions of the body imperative; and since the filtered water of the Municipality is not to be had at all hours, there is no alternative for the mass but the well and the *ghotee*. They speak again, of the compulsory setting-up of meters in private houses to regulate the supply of water according to the rate paid for it. The idea is not particularly liberal; to our thinking the supply of water, like that of air and light, should be unchecked. But, as our sapient commissioners seem to think otherwise, "don't fill up your wells yet" is our warning and advice to all whom it may concern.

II. The Song of the Makhum Chora

This is a song of the boyhood of Krishna, when that mischievous urchin used to go about from dairy to dairy stealing butter. The itinerant singer goes, Homer-like, from house to house, singing the delinquencies of the little god, that the morning might be commenced auspiciously by all, with the achievements of the deity fresh in their recollections. It is rather odd giving lessons in thieving to business-people at this early hour, as the instruction is not unapt to stick in the minds of those who buy and sell, and to influence their actions throughout the day. Songs about Ramchandra are also sung. For these regular reminders the singers claim a small *buxis* (varying from four pice to two annas) at the end of each month. The songs are good to hear, and some of the singers have very musical voices; and so, for one reason or another, the imposition is tolerated by all families.

III. Jye Radhay! Bhikayapye Baba?

The begging appeals in Calcutta are intolerable nuisances that recur from daybreak to dusk; and there is no means of putting them down, as the police will *never* interfere. I don't object to an old woman, or a blind or lame man, appealing to one for charity; but for two real objects of sympathy that accost you, there are four or six stalwart claimants whose only plea for appeal is that they are Vysnubs, which they think gives them a right to *demand* alms. They actually give you *gallee* if you send them away empty-handed. "What, such a Burra Baboo, with such a house to live in, and not give alms! Remember there is another place to go to; for he that turns away the beggar from his door gets no admittance in Vycant." Cheek of this sort is constantly given; and as you can't condescend to resent it, you are obliged to submit to it with the best grace you can. Often, very often, a sturdy beggar will refuse to leave your door without a reasonable dole. If you ask the *paharawalla* to eject him, the man of authority laughs at your face; if you tell your own people to push out the applicant, there is an action for assault, sometimes resulting in a fine: at all events, I remember having once read of such a case, in which the learned magistrate held that force should not have been used for expulsion, without laying down however how the expulsion was otherwise to be effected when the party to be dealt with is strong-limbed, obstinate, and clamorous.

Of course, as I have said, there are many real objects of charity, who, in a city where there is absolutely no provision for them, well deserve the attention of the humane. But, when your temper is once upset by stubbornness, it rarely happens that you are able to do your duty to the rest. "Don't admit any of them" is the snappish order the master gives to his door-keeper; and so many a poor woman loses the pice or grain that she would otherwise have received.

IV. Sissee, Bottole Bikree!

This is an expressive cry, a proof of the march of civilisation as represented by the brandy-bottle. From house to house the *Bikreewalla* collects all the empty bottles, in broad daylight, as a matter of course, and without any attempt whatever at concealment. The cry is constantly raised that Young Bengal is afraid to avow his liberalism; but surely the avowal, as regards the consumption of spirituous liquors, is distinct enough. *Sissees* (medicine phials) are, of course, also asked for; but you see every *Bikreewalla* passing by loaded with champagne, beer, and brandy bottles, with their labels on. It is an every-day and every-hour matter now, and the number of *Bikreewallas* is so large that one is staggered in attempting to compute the amount of consumption it represents. If you detect me in giving out bottles from my house, I have my answer ready: "Some rose-water bottles only, which I do not know what to do with. But pray, don't smell them; bad gases may have generated in them, and you may fare the worse for doing so."

V. Poorana Kagoch!

What a stentorian voice that bearded Mahomedan has who every morning cries out at your door for old newspapers! Do the worthy gents of the fourth estate know what their bad grammar and worse taste actually sell for second-hand in the Calcutta *bazaars*? Fourteen pice the quire; not a cowrie more! I haggled very hard once for 4 annas; but the devout Mahomedan swore by Allah Bismallah that he barely gets that rate from the shop-keepers, and could not therefore give me more than the fixed 3½ annas a quire. Twenty-four sheets of an *Indian Thunderer* for fourteen pice only! With this data given, will any B.A. or M.A. work out for us how much each furious leader is appraised at? I am not a dab at figures, but my calculations give just 9½ cowries for the biggest thunder – English or Patriotic. Some of these thunder-makers have sought sedulously for immortality by having blind-lanes named after them. The immortality of the whole genus will be found in the shops of the *Panchunwallahs*, if they will only seek for it there.

Akin to the above cry are the cries of

VI. Poorana Loha Bikree!
VII. Poorana Chatta Bikree!
VIII. Poorana Nakra Kani Bikree!

There is no such thing as destruction in the world, says the philosopher. What we consider as such is only change. Your old iron, your old *chatta* or parasol, all your tattered rags, are marketable articles: there is no destruction for them, but a salutary change. The broken padlock will do service again in another shape; the *chatta* will receive a new era of existence after it is mended and a new cloth put on to it; the rags will be converted into paper – probably to print some big daily, to be sold again at 3½ annas a quire! *O tempora! O mores!*

IX. Dhong! Dhong! Dhong!

There goes the Kansari's music! A cooly carries with him all the articles he has for sale. The gong and the bell are for *poojahs*, if you are particularly fond of them; the *thalla*, or dining plate, for your first-born, if he has commenced to eat rice; the *lotah*, the *pilsooj*, the *garoo*, anything you stand in need of, sir! But I don't want anything; still the infernal *dhong! dhong!* continues. It is enough to awaken the dead in their graves!

The Kansari is a man well-to-do in life. He has a shop in the nearest bazaar, and both in going to it and in coming back from it he makes it a point to carry a cooly's load with him, if only to try the temper of the people whose houses he passes by. Braziers from other places, especially from Jagganath, also frequent the streets, crying, *Thakoorbateer bassan go! Thakoorbateer bassan!* But this you don't hear every day, probably because the sellers are few in number, and perambulate different parts of the town by turns.

X. Katao Sell-Chaktee, Janta!

This is a horrible voice between a bawl and a screech. I wonder how much the man makes a day by this cry. Who on earth requires grinding-stones to be recut and repaired? And yet here is a man who makes his living by cutting them anew.

XI. Bhalo, Bhalo, Naya, Naya, Sap; Sapay Bandoray Tamashar Khayle

Here is poetry for you, reader; the serpent-charmer's poetry, as he goes about with his baskets full of serpents, a baboon following at his heels that will play many tricks with the serpents, if you will pay a trifle for the *tamasha*. It is, of course, well known that the serpents are fangless; but what if one of the reptiles escapes while being played with and burrows in your house? Won't it get new fangs in time? Why then is the play permitted in a densely crowded city? I never could look at serpents without dread. Our native dress at home gives us no protection against them if they are unwarily crossed and I would unhesitatingly vote for the expulsion of all such players from the town. I know that there are many who take a delight in looking at the reptiles – particularly children. The impression left on these little fellows is various. One child, after such a sight in the day, woke up at night in convulsions, with the cry of "Sap, Sap", and with froth foaming in his mouth. But this was an exceptional case. Generally, they are well pleased with the play so long as it lasts, and forget all about it afterwards; what especially delights them being the music of the charmer, which certainly does charm all simple-hearted listeners – including the serpents, of course. These charmers, they say, can charm out serpents from their holes and capture them. I saw one attempt myself, but that was a failure. The serpent did come out to listen to the music, but snapped at the charmer every time that he approached it; and, as it was a rather large-sized cobra, the man did not much like the idea of cultivating any intimate acquaintance with it. But there is no doubt that they do capture many serpents in this way, for many good people have seen them do so.

XII. Chye Moong-ke-Dal?

A very good edible is *Moong-ke-dal*, the Arabica Revelenta of the doctors, which has been known in this country from time anterior to the flood as a very wholesome food for the convalescent. The man who sells the *dal* is an up-country man, and the grains are very clean and have been well picked. The Bengali does not know, or does not care, to clean his grains in the way these up-country people do it. The fact is he is more partial to his fish and *torkaree* than to his *dal*, though the *dal* is both more wholesome and more strengthening. Altogether, in the matter of food, the natives of Bengal are very much less particular than up-country Hindus. The former will take anything they can get that caste rules allow, and then hurry on to money-making; while the latter, though not less fond of money-making, will still find full time for cleaning and cooking their dinner well.

XIII. Hansayr Deem Chye; Hansayr Deem, Go? Hansayr Deem!

How loud the man bawls! His custom perhaps is not as profitable as it used to be of old. Young Bengal is more fond of *Moorgeer Deem* (fowls' eggs) than of *Hansayr Deem* (ducks' eggs); but of course the former cannot be hawked about openly except in Mahomedan quarters. The *Hansayr Deem* is a loathsome food. Of fowls' eggs I have no personal experience, but they are said to be better. Both are taken by some people raw!!! And I have heard that doctors advise their being so taken. The idea makes the blood run cold.

XIV. Belatee Amra Chye; Chye Pat-Badam!
XV. Aloo Chye; Piaz Chye?

The first may pass without comment; but *Aloo* (potatoes) and *Piaz* (onions) selling together in the streets of an orthodox town! Oh Menu and Vyasa! What are we coming to? There was a time when people lost caste for eating onions; while now potatoes and onions are carried round in the same basket from door to door, and even widows and Brahmans buy the potatoes quite heedless of their unorthodox contamination.

XVI. Chye Malsee Dohi; Malsee Dohi Chye, Go!

The cry is drawn out in lengthened sweetness, and reaches a great distance; and very great is the demand for the *Dohi.* All people who can afford to pay for it buy it eagerly, for it very much facilitates the taking of rice – particularly when the days are hot. It is also very wholesome, notwithstanding some medical opinions expressed of late to the contrary. In bowel complaints it acts as a charm. The other variety of it, called *Malye Dohi*, is less digestible, and is only liked because it is more acid. They both sell in the streets with the greatest promptitude.

XVII. Took-Tap, Took-Toom

Play-things to sell! What a crowd of ragged children follow in the wake of the seller; all anxious to buy; but having no pice to pay! And what a variety or nicknacks the man has got; birds made of coloured rags and decked with tinsel, paper *palkees, gharries*, umbrellas, trees, flowers, whistles, bells, cards, balloons, looking-glasses; everything, in fact, that is likely to catch a child's fancy. With villainous pertinacity these are displayed ostentatiously at every door. In vain do poor mothers tell the man to pass on, not having the pice to pay for what their children clamorously ask for. The man knows that the pice will be forthcoming, and generally succeeds in getting it out.

XVIII. Chooree Libee, Go!

What a sweet melodious voice that girl has who goes from house to house selling *choorees*, or bracelets made of sealing-wax or glass! But all the poetry evoked by her voice vanishes the moment you get a full view of her face. The phiz of Medusa could scarcely have had a more petrifying effect. You close your eyes involuntarily, while the ear continues to drink the melody that floats by. *Chooree libee, go!* Yes, my love, I will buy up all your *choorees* if you will go on hawking them in your own pretty way;

but don't break the spell by turning your face towards me, or you will convert me into stone. Throw a veil over your features, and you will enhance the value of your wares.

XIX. Ghotee Batee Sarabay! Ghora, Pilsooj Sartay Achya! Bhangabasun Sartay Achay!

No, man, no! I have no broken utensils to repair; pass on, please; your pertinacity is most annoying. Who can possibly require a tinker at his door every day of the year?

XX. Ripoor Kormo!
XXI. Salie Jootea; Joota Broosh!
XXII. Do Golie Soota Ek Pysa!
XXIII. Dhama Bandabay, Go!
XXIV. Baxo Sartay Achay?

These shrieks and screeches are very trying indeed. There is no poetry in the voices. They are all matter-of-fact calls, for things or services which you cannot possibly stand in need of more than, say, once, twice, or four times a year; and yet you have to bear with the calls every blessed day of your existence, and fortunate is he who does not receive each more than once in twenty-four hours.

XXV. Jaruck Laboo, Belmoroba, Huzmee Golee, Ambachar, Topacool, Kasundi!

A good long yarn this, and rather melodiously bawled out, hawking for sale *chutnies* and acids which are dear to every epicure and gourmand.

XXVI. Monda, Metoy!
XXVII. Rootee, Biskoot, Nankhataye!
XXVIII. Golapee Aooree Chye?
XXIX. Chye Nakole Dana?

We pass over all these cries as calling for no particular remark. Immediately after them follows the cry of

XXX. Chanachoor Gurma-Gurrum

Your *syce* is a great scoundrel and steals gram; the horse is getting thinner; you are afraid of being some day hauled up before the Magistrate by the Cruelty-Prevention-Society, which is so vigilant. But where the deuce does the gram go to? Ask this man and you will know. All the stolen gram is converted into *Chanachoor*, which, made hot with chillies, is much valued by drunkards both of high and low degree. *Brandy-pawny* and *Chanachoor Gurma-Gurrum* comprise a feast for the gods, leaving aside the exquisites of the Calcutta University. What Young Bengal is there who has been able to resist the temptation of sharing them with his *syce* or his *sirdar-bearer*, if not in worse company?

XXXI. Chye Buroph?

And there is the *Burophwalla* coming in good time to cool down both the liquid-fire and chillied-gram! Does anyone wish to have revelations of pandemonium or the purgatory without the intervention of the Planchette? Let him accompany a *Burophwalla* for the nonce, and he will see both places with his open eyes and learn all that he may require to know. Oh, what secrets these *Burophwallas* could divulge if they had a mind to!

Night now closes up the city of palaces, brothels, and iniquities for a brief while; and no calls but those of the *Paharawalla* and the jackal will be heard for the next few hours. I may therefore close for the present with –

XXXII. Yapeed Mooshkillashan Karayga

Which is announced by a broad flaring light in the hands of a bearded *fakir*, who goes about from door to door, asking for that dole in the name of a Mahomedan saint which no Hindu housewife dares to refuse. All *Mooshkill*, or difficulties, will be made *ashan*, or easy. Child's sickness, husband's irregularity of life, crustiness of old mother-in-law – every impediment to happiness will be removed at once. And what is the price to pay for this? One pice only!

RABINDRANATH TAGORE

The Nation

THE PEOPLES ARE living beings. They have their distinct personalities. But nations are organisations of power, and therefore their inner aspects and outward expressions are everywhere monotonously the same. Their differences are merely differences in degree of efficiency.

In the modern world the fight is going on between the living spirit of the people and the methods of nation-organising. It is like the struggle that began in Central Asia between cultivated areas of man's habitation and the continually encroaching desert sands, till the human region of life and beauty was choked out of existence. When the spread of higher ideals of humanity is not held to be important, the hardening method of national efficiency gains a certain strength; and for some limited period of time, at least, it proudly asserts itself as the fittest to survive. But it is the survival of that part of man which is the least living. And this is the reason why dead monotony is the sign of the spread of the Nation. The modern towns, which present the physiognomy due to this dominance of the Nation, are everywhere the same, from San Francisco to London, from London to Tokyo. They show no faces, but merely masks.

The peoples, being living personalities, must have their self-expression, and this leads to their distinctive creations. These creations are literature, art, social symbols and ceremonials. They are like different dishes at one common feast. They add richness to our enjoyment and understanding of truth. They are making the world of man fertile of life and variedly beautiful.

But the nations do not create, they merely produce and destroy. Organisations for production are necessary. Even organisations for destruction may be so. But when, actuated by greed and hatred, they crowd away into a corner the living man who creates, then the harmony is lost, and the people's history runs at a break-neck speed towards some fatal catastrophe.

Humanity, where it is living, is guided by inner ideals; but where it is a dead organisation it becomes impervious to them. Its building process is only an external process, and in its response to the moral guidance it has to pass through obstacles that are gross and non-plastic.

Man as a person has his individuality, which is the field where his spirit has its freedom to express itself and to grow. The professional man carries a rigid crust around him which has very little variation and hardly any elasticity. This professionalism is the region where men specialise their knowledge and organise their power, mercilessly elbowing each other in their struggle to come to the front. Professionalism is necessary, without doubt; but it must not be allowed to exceed its healthy limits, to assume complete mastery over the personal man, making him narrow and hard, exclusively intent upon pursuit of success at the cost of his faith in ideals.

In ancient India professions were kept within limits by social regulation. They were considered primarily as social necessities, and in the second place as the means of livelihood for individuals. Thus man, being free from the constant urging of unbounded competition, could have leisure to cultivate his nature in its completeness.

The Cult of the Nation is the professionalism of the people. This cult is becoming their greatest danger, because it is bringing them enormous success, making them impatient of the claims of higher ideals. The greater the amount of success, the stronger are the conflicts of interest and jealousy and hatred which are aroused in men's minds, thereby making it more and more necessary for other peoples, who are still living, to stiffen into nations. With the growth of nationalism, man has become the greatest menace to man. Therefore the continual presence of panic goads that very nationalism into ever-increasing menace.

Crowd psychology is a blind force. Like steam and other physical forces, it can be utilised for creating a tremendous amount of power. And therefore rulers of men, who, out of greed and fear, are bent upon turning their peoples into machines of power, try to train this crowd psychology for their special purposes. They hold it to be their duty to foster in the popular mind universal panic, unreasoning pride in their own race, and hatred of others. Newspapers, school-books, and even religious services are made use of for this object; and those who have the courage to express their disapprobation of this blind and impious cult are either punished in the law-courts, or are socially ostracised. The individual thinks, even when he feels; but the same individual, when he feels with the crowd, does not reason at all. His moral sense becomes blurred. This suppression of higher humanity in crowd minds is productive of enormous strength. For the crowd mind is essentially primitive; its forces are elemental. Therefore the Nation is for ever watching to take advantage of this enormous power of darkness.

The people's instinct of self-preservation has been made dominant at particular times of crisis. Then, for the time being, the consciousness of its solidarity becomes aggressively wide-awake. But in the Nation this hyper-consciousness is kept alive for all time by artificial means. A man has to act the part of a policeman when he finds his house invaded by burglars. But if that remains his normal condition, then his consciousness of his household becomes acute and over-wrought, making him fly at every stranger passing near his house. This intensity of self-consciousness is nothing of which a man should feel proud; certainly it is not healthful. In like manner, incessant self-consciousness in a nation is highly injurious for the people. It serves its immediate purpose, but at the cost of the eternal in man.

When a whole body of men train themselves for a particular narrow purpose, it becomes a common interest with them to keep up that purpose and preach absolute loyalty to it. Nationalism is the training of a whole people for a narrow ideal; and when it gets hold of their minds it is sure to lead them to moral degeneracy and intellectual blindness. We cannot but hold firm the faith that this Age of Nationalism, of gigantic vanity and selfishness, is only a passing phase in civilisation, and those who are making permanent arrangements for accommodating this temporary mood of history will be unable to fit themselves for the coming age, when the true spirit of freedom will have sway.

With the unchecked growth of Nationalism the moral foundation of man's civilisation is unconsciously undergoing a change. The ideal of the social man is unselfishness, but the ideal of the Nation, like that of the professional man, is selfishness. This is why selfishness in the individual is condemned, while in the nation it is extolled, which leads to hopeless moral blindness, confusing the religion of the people with the religion of the nation. Therefore, to take an example, we find men more and more convinced of the superior claims of Christianity, merely because Christian nations are in possession of the greater part of the world. It is like supporting a robber's religion by quoting the amount of his stolen property. Nations celebrate their successful massacre of men in their churches. They forget that

Thugs also ascribed their success in manslaughter to the favour of their goddess. But in the case of the latter their goddess frankly represented the principle of destruction. It was the criminal tribe's own murderous instinct deified – the instinct, not of one individual, but of the whole community, and therefore held sacred. In the same manner, in modern churches, selfishness, hatred and vanity in their collective aspect of national instincts do not scruple to share the homage paid to God.

Of course, pursuit of self-interest need not be wholly selfish; it can even be in harmony with the interest of all. Therefore, ideally speaking, the nationalism which stands for the expression of the collective self-interest of a people, need not be ashamed of itself if it maintains its true limitations. But what we see in practice is, that every nation which has prospered has done so through its career of aggressive selfishness either in commercial adventures or in foreign possessions, or in both. And this material prosperity not only feeds continually the selfish instincts of the people, but impresses men's minds with the lesson that, for a nation, selfishness is a necessity and therefore a virtue. It is the emphasis laid in Europe upon the idea of the Nation's constant increase of power, which is becoming the greatest danger to man, both in its direct activity and its power of infection.

We must admit that evils there are in human nature, in spite of our faith in moral laws and our training in self-control. But they carry on their foreheads their own brand of infamy, their very success adding to their monstrosity. All through man's history there will be some who suffer, and others who cause suffering. The conquest of evil will never be a fully accomplished fact, but a continuous process like the process of burning in a flame.

In former ages, when some particular people became turbulent and tried to rob others of their human rights, they sometimes achieved success and sometimes failed. And it amounted to nothing more than that. But when this idea of the Nation, which has met with universal acceptance in the present day, tries to pass off the cult of collective selfishness as a moral duty, simply because that selfishness is gigantic in stature, it not only commits depredation, but attacks the very vitals of humanity. It unconsciously generates in people's minds an attitude of defiance against moral law. For men are taught by repeated devices the lesson that the Nation is greater than the people, while yet it scatters to the winds the moral law that the people have held sacred.

It has been said that a disease becomes most acutely critical when the brain is affected. For it is the brain that is constantly directing the siege against all disease forces. The spirit of national selfishness is that brain disease of a people which shows itself in red eyes and clenched fists, in the violence of talk and movements, all the while shattering its natural restorative powers. But the power of self-sacrifice, together with the moral faculty of sympathy and co-operation, is the guiding spirit of social vitality. Its function is to maintain a beneficent relation of harmony with its surroundings. But when it begins to ignore the moral law which is universal and uses it only within the bounds of its own narrow sphere, then its strength becomes like the strength of madness which ends in self-destruction.

What is worse, this aberration of a people, decked with the showy title of "patriotism", proudly walks abroad, passing itself off as a highly moral influence. Thus it has spread its inflammatory contagion all over the world, proclaiming its fever flush to be the best sign of health. It is causing in the hearts of peoples, naturally inoffensive, a feeling of envy at not having their temperature as high as that of their delirious neighbours and not being able to cause as much mischief, but merely having to suffer from it.

I have often been asked by my Western friends how to cope with this evil, which has attained such sinister strength and vast dimensions. In fact, I have often been blamed for merely giving warning, and offering no alternative. When we suffer as a result of a particular system, we believe that some other system would bring us better luck. We are apt to forget that all systems produce evil sooner or later, when the psychology which is at the root of them is wrong. The system which is national today may assume the shape of the international tomorrow; but so long as men have not forsaken their idolatry of primitive instincts and collective passions, the new system will only become a new instrument of suffering. And because we are trained to confound efficient system with moral goodness itself, every ruined system makes us more and more distrustful of moral law.

Therefore I do not put my faith in any new institution, but in the individuals all over the world who think clearly, feel nobly, and act rightly, thus becoming the channels of moral truth. Our moral ideals do not work with chisels and hammers. Like trees, they spread their roots in the soil and their branches in the sky, without consulting any architect for their plans.

JAWAHARLAL NEHRU

The Tribal Folk

Mr chairman and friends, this audience is more or less a select one since it consists largely of experts. I am not an expert and I am afraid I shall not be able to contribute much if we were to sit down and discuss your problems.[1]

I suppose you have invited me here because I happen to occupy the office of Prime Minister, but I think I have another, and possibly greater claim to participate in this Conference. The claim is that I have always – long before I became Prime Minister – felt very strongly attracted to the tribal people of this country. This feeling was not the curiosity an idle observer has for strange customs; nor was it the attraction of the charitably disposed who want to do good to other people. I was attracted to them simply because I felt happy and at home with them, I liked them without any desire to do them good or to have good done to me. To do good to others is, I think, a very laudable desire but it often leads to great excesses which do not result in good to either the doer or the recipient.

In the tribal people I have found many qualities which I miss in the people of the plains, cities, and other parts of India. It was these very qualities that attracted me.

[1] Speech delivered at the opening session of the Scheduled Tribes and Scheduled Areas Conference held in New Delhi in 1952.

The tribal people of India are a virile people who naturally went astray sometimes. They quarrelled and occasionally cut off each other's heads. These were deplorable occurrences and should have been checked. Even so, it struck me that some of their practices were perhaps less evil than those that prevail in our cities. It is often better to cut off a hand or a head than to crush and trample on a heart. Perhaps I also felt happy with these simple folk, because the nomad in me found congenial soil in their company. I approached them in a spirit of comradeship and not like someone aloof who had come to look at them, examine them, weigh them, measure them and report about them or to try and make them conform to another way of life.

I am alarmed when I see – not only in this country but in other great countries, too – how anxious people are to shape others according to their own image or likeness, and to impose on them their particular way of living. We are welcome to our way of living but why impose it on others? This applies equally to national and international fields. In fact, there would be more peace in the world if people were to desist from imposing their way of living on other people and countries.

I am not at all sure which is a better way of living. In some respects I am quite certain theirs is better. Therefore, it is grossly presumptuous on our part to approach them with an air of superiority or to tell them what to do or not to do. There is no point in trying to make of them a second rate copy of ourselves.

Now, who are these tribal folk? A way of describing them is that they are the people of the frontiers or those who live away from the interior of this country. Just as the hills breed a somewhat different type of people from those who inhabit the plains, so also the frontier breeds a different type of people from those who live away from the frontier. My own predilection is for the mountains rather than for the plains, for the hill folk rather than the plains people. So also I prefer the frontier, not only in a physical sense but because the idea of living near a frontier appeals to me intellectually. I feel that it would prevent me from becoming complacent, and complacency is a very grave danger, especially in a great country like India, where the nearest frontier may be a thousand miles away.

We should have a receptive attitude to the tribal people. There is a great deal we can learn from them particularly in the frontier areas, and having learnt, we must try to help and co-operate. They are an extremely disciplined people, often a great deal more democratic than most others in India. Even though they have no constitution, they are able to function democratically and carry out the decisions made by elders or representatives. Above all, they are a people who sing and dance and try to enjoy life; not people who sit in stock exchanges, shout at each other and think themselves civilised.

I would prefer being a nomad in the hills to being a member of the stock exchange, where one is made to sit and listen to noises that are ugly to a degree. Is that the civilisation we want the tribal people to have? I hope not. I am quite sure that the tribal folk, with their civilisation of song and dance, will last until long after stock exchanges have ceased to exist.

It is a very great pity that we in the cities have drifted so far away from the aesthetic side of life. We still have a good many folk-songs and dances when we go to the villages, because modern civilisation has more or less left them untouched. The progress of modern civilisation in India involves both good things and bad. One of the things we have lost is the spirit of song and dance and the capacity for enjoyment and this is what the tribal people so abundantly have. We seem to pay too much attention to the cinema: it is undoubtedly an excellent medium for many good things, but unfortunately it has not proved to be particularly inspiring. We must imbibe something of the spirit of the tribal folk instead of damping it with our long faces and black gowns.

For half a century or more, we have struggled for freedom and ultimately achieved it. That struggle, apart from anything else, was a great liberating force. It raised us above ourselves, it improved us and hid for the moment some of our weaknesses. We must remember that this experience of hundreds of millions of Indian people was not shared by the tribal folk. Our struggle for freedom did influence the tribes in Central India to some extent but the frontier areas of Assam, for instance, remained almost unaffected by it. This was partly due to the inadequacy of the means of communication available to us in the old days. Of course, there were other reasons too.

One of the reasons was that the city people were a little afraid to leave their familiar haunts and go into the mountains. The Christian missionaries went to various tribal areas and some of them spent practically all their lives there. I do not find many instances of people from the plains going to the tribal areas to settle down. Apart from our own lack of initiative, we were not allowed to go there by the British authorities then in power. That is why our freedom movement reached these people only in the shape of occasional rumours. Sometimes they reacted rightly and sometimes wrongly, but that is beside the point.

The essence of our struggle for freedom was the unleashing of a liberating force in India. This force did not even affect the frontier people in one of the most important tribal areas. The result is that while we have had several decades in which to prepare ourselves psychologically for basic changes, the tribal people have had no such opportunity. On the contrary, they were prepared the other way round through the efforts of the British officials and sometimes the missionaries.

The missionaries did very good work there and I am all praise for them but, politically speaking, they did not particularly like the changes in India. In fact, just when a new political awareness dawned on India, there was a movement in north-eastern India to encourage the people of the north-east to form separate and independent states. Many foreigners resident in the area supported this movement. I do not understand how it could be considered practical or feasible from any point of view. My point is that the people of the north-east frontier had been conditioned differently during the past generation and even in more recent years: the fault lay partly with us and partly with circumstances. These factors have an important bearing on any genuine understanding of the tribal folk.

They are our own people and our work does not end with the opening of so many schools and so many dispensaries and hospitals. Of course, we want schools and hospitals and dispensaries and roads and all that but to stop there is rather a dead way of looking at things. What we ought to do is to develop a sense of oneness with these people, a sense of unity and understanding. That involves a psychological approach.

You may talk day after day about development programmes in regard to schools and other matters but you will fail completely if you do not touch the real core of the problem. The need, today, is to understand these people, make them understand us and thus create a bond of affection and understanding. After the achievement of independence, the basic problem of India, taken as a whole, is one of integration and consolidation. Political integration is now complete but that is not enough. We must bring about changes much more basic and intimate than mere political integration. That will take time, because it is not merely a matter of law. All we can do is to nurture it and create conditions where it finds congenial soil. So, the greatest problem of India today is not so much political as psychological integration and consolidation. India must build up for herself a unity which will do away with provincialism, communalism, and the various other "isms" which disrupt and separate.

As I said, we must approach the tribal people with affection and friendliness and come to them as a liberating force. We must let them feel that we come to give and not to take something away from them. That is the kind of psychological integration India needs. If, on the other hand, they feel you have come to impose yourselves upon them or that we go to them in order to try and change their methods of living, to take away their land and to encourage our businessmen to exploit them, then the fault is ours, for it only means that our approach to the tribal people is wholly wrong. The less we hear of this type of integration and consolidation of the tribal areas, the better it will be.

We ought to be careful about appointing officers anywhere, but we must be doubly so when we appoint them in tribal areas. An officer in the tribal areas should not merely be a man who has passed an examination or gained experience of routine work. He must be a man with enthusiasm, whose mind, and even more so whose heart, understands the problem it is his duty to deal with. He must not go there just to sit in an office for a few hours a day and for the rest curse his fate at being sent to an out-of-the-way place. That type of man is completely useless. It is far better to send a totally uneducated man who has passed no examination, so long as he goes to these people with friendship and affection and lives as one of them. Such a man will produce better results than the brilliant intellectual who has no human understanding of the problem. The man who goes there as an officer must be prepared to share his life with the tribal folk. He must be prepared to enter their huts, talk to them, eat and smoke with them, live their lives and not consider himself superior or apart. Then only can he gain confidence and respect, and thus be in a position to advise them.

The language problem is almost always exceedingly important from the psychological point of view. The best of solutions can come to nought if misunderstood or misinterpreted by the party concerned. It is absolutely clear to me that the government must encourage the tribal languages. It is not enough simply to allow them to prevail. They must be given all possible support and the conditions in which they can flourish must be safeguarded. We must go out of our way to achieve this.

In the Soviet Republic we have the example of a country that has adopted such a policy with success. Lenin and other leaders in his time were exceedingly wise in this respect. Regardless of their ultimate objective, they wanted to win the goodwill of the people, and they won it largely by their policy of encouraging their languages, by going out of their way to help hundreds of dialects, by preparing dictionaries and vocabularies and sometimes even by evolving new scripts where there were none. They wanted their people to feel that they were free to live their own lives and they succeeded in producing that impression.

In the matter of languages there must be no compulsion whatever. I have no doubt at all that the West Bengal government must have built special schools in places like Darjeeling and Kalimpong for the Tibetan-speaking people. If the tribal people have a script we must, of course, use it. But normally they do not have a script and the only script they have thus far learnt, to some extent, is the Roman script. It is a good script no doubt; and because many people have learnt it, I would not discourage it.

But if we are to evolve a script – here I do not speak with any assurance but am merely saying something that has occurred to me – it might be better, for the future, if we were to use the Devanagari script. It is a relatively easy script, apart from the fact that it can put the tribal folk more in touch with the rest of India than any other script. In areas where a majority of the people know the Roman script, I would not suddenly force them to abandon it because I do not want them to feel compelled in any way.

I find that so far we have approached the tribal people in one of two ways. One might be called the anthropological approach in which we treat them as museum specimens to be observed and written about. To treat them as specimens for anthropological examination and analysis – except in the sense that everybody is more or less an anthropological specimen – is to insult them. We do not think of them as living human beings with whom it is possible to work and play. The other approach is one of ignoring the fact that they are something different requiring special treatment and of attempting forcibly to absorb them into the normal pattern of social life. The way of forcible assimilation or of assimilation through the operation of normal factors would be equally wrong.

In fact, I have no doubt that, if normal factors were allowed to operate, unscrupulous people from outside would take possession of tribal lands. They would take possession of the forests and interfere with the life of the tribal people. We must give them a measure of protection in their areas so that no outsider can take possession of their lands or forests or interfere with them in any way except with their consent and goodwill. The first priority in tribal areas, as well as elsewhere in the country, must be given to roads and communications. Without that, nothing we may do will be effective. Obviously, there is need for schools, for health relief, for cottage industries and so on. One must always remember, however, that we do not mean to interfere with their way of life but want to help them live it.

HASAN SHAHID SUHRAWARDY

Tagore at Oxford

In 1913 when Rabindranath Tagore received the Nobel Prize I was a student at Oxford. In those days we were not many Indians, but we had amongst us a fervent, energetic band of young men, passionately patriotic, inclined to the extreme brand of nationalism and intolerant of moderation in all its forms. Scientific Marxism, the creed of the modern Oxford Indian, was unknown to us, though we also called ourselves socialists, meaning by socialism, in the manner of many contemporary Indian nationalists, a liberal and loosely mystical devotion to the idea of the Motherland. It was in 1912 that this group took over the Oxford Indian Club, a vague institution for tea and cakes on a Sunday afternoon founded some time previously by Har Dayal, and transformed it into the Oxford Majlis, which became not only the centre for all kinds of revolutionary debates at Oxford, but a powerful organisation upon which, because of our habit of voting solidly, depended the results of the election for the presidentship of the Oxford Union. To our meetings there came all the prominent orators among the students of the University, who sought our approval and suffrage by tempering their views on India according to our liking. We had indeed become a force in University politics, and Oxford Indians of the time were very conscious of their position as they sauntered down the High after dinner and exchanged uncomplimentary remarks and often blows with English students, who would reply to their anti-British slogans by asking them to go back to their black country. One can understand to what an extent there was an increase in our self-opinionated insolence when the rumour came to our ears that the highest prize in literature was going to be awarded to one who belonged to us. It is difficult now for me to recapture the elation and the ecstasy of those days, but I still remember distinctly that look of awe which was in my landlady's eyes when she brought in the breakfast with the morning paper containing the scoop, of which we had come to know earlier from "Mullickda" (Basanta Kumar Mullick) who had somehow already met the Tagores in London. Outwardly we, of course, took this sudden rise in our status for granted, but I must confess to a sense of relief that for the first time, after centuries, the India in whose past greatness we profoundly believed, without having much knowledge about it, had been placed once again on the map of the world. Till then we Indians were being looked upon as the degenerate descendants of those who had composed the Vedic hymns (in Max Müller's translations), or as snake-charmers or theosophists or, at best, terrorists from the banks of the Ganges.

I am ashamed to say that owing to defective upbringing I was then, as I am now, ignorant of Bengali except of the most debased kind, and so I had heard with a certain amount of scepticism of the great popularity of Tagore's verses, which were being sung, I was told, in every village home in Bengal. Therefore to me, as to those who first came to know of him through translations, the first renderings of his verses in English, not only because of their novelty but for their high personal literary flavour, came as a great revelation. I must confess, however, that during that first period not a little of that unbounded appreciation of the newly initiated which I had for the Poet's works was due to my knowledge of the association and collaboration with him of Rothenstein, Sturge Moore and particularly Yeats, a name draped in our fancy with magic raiments. About

Santiniketan I knew a little more. That year among the newcomers at Oxford there was a particularly chubby youth with a great deal of personal attractiveness, who had been brought up there and who described it to us in glowing colours. This was Apurva Chanda. After Santiniketan he had gone to the Central Hindu College at Benares and had come up to Oxford with a number of young men from that institution. They were all vegetarians, extremely devout, long-haired and soft-spoken. During weekends their number would become larger by the arrival from Cambridge of similar young men, notable amongst whom was Sri Prakash whom I came to know well afterwards, and it was said of them that in the early morning they gathered under a tree and chanted Vedic hymns. I did not believe there was any vestige of truth in all this except that they all lived in a house in Wellington Square and that behind locked iron-railings there actually was a tree in that square. Notwithstanding, with that thoughtless irresponsibility which is the charm and the most irritating quality of Oxford undergraduates, I too helped in the diffusion of this legend. The only thing which might have sustained the story was that Apurva with a beatific expression had the habit of half-reciting and half-chanting a few of the Poet's songs and we used to see in them through our burning imagination a beauty such as never was on land or sea. Apurva's singing not only took us in, which was easy, as we had no competence except our enthusiasm, but even Philip Heseltine who later on under the name of Peter Warlock made such a name for himself in English music.

The Oxford Majlis used to invite all prominent Indian politicians, who happened to be in England, as well as a great many English public men with interest in India. In fact, it was a loved game of ours to get hold of a well-known Indian political leader, cajole and flatter him, lavish hospitality upon him, invite him to the Majlis meeting and then skin him alive, proving to him that he was a worthless worm, who, in spite of his nationalistic pretensions, had done nothing else all his life but lick the boots of British imperialism. For, in those days if there was one thing we hated above everything else, it was experience. Naturally Indian public men in England used to dislike us, because of our bad name, yet they always came, almost afraid of annoying us by refusing our invitation, which would usually be entrusted to me as I had developed a gift for treacherous blandishment. I used to arouse their interest in us by mock humility, pretending that we were thirsting to be taught, while all along I knew what fate awaited them once they walked into our parlour. I could give a long list of distingusihed Indians who were thus brought to Oxford by me; only one person tamed us, that was Sarojini Naidu, another was consistently obdurate and that was Jinnah. Even in those days he was a difficult person.

So it is quite intelligible, if, given our reputation, we were a little afraid that the Poet might not accept our invitation. I was asked to proceed to London and explain to him, should occasion arise, that as far as he was concerned, we had transformed ourselves into a domesticated herd of antelopes.

Whilst I was casting and recasting the speech I was to make, posturing in the presence of my closest friend in my rooms, two circumstances made my task easier. Firstly, we heard that the Poet had already been invited by Manchester College to come and address a gathering there and that he had consented. So I had only to request him to divide his time between them and us when he came over. Secondly, the Poet's son and daughter-in-law were visiting Oxford and some of us were asked by "Mullickda" to luncheon to meet them.

"Mullickda" was the doyen of the Indian student community not only in years, but also in material prosperity. He did not live at college or in digs, as all of us did, but in a large boarding-house on Woodstock Road, where, according to report, he was being cruelly rooked. He was the naivest and best of men, exceedingly generous to all of us, paying up our debts and spoiling us with gifts. Nevertheless, his lunches were extremely boring because of that flair of his, which he has retained till this day, of gathering round an abundant table men and women the most incompatible in taste and temperament. He was already promulgating some sort of a philosophic doctrine of his own backed by lavish hospitality and no wonder in that city of large leisures he was drawing to himself people of widely divergent types. In spite of the great affection we all, and particularly I, had for him, I accepted his invitation with an inward fear at the prospect of being wedged in, as had happened before, between a lean clergyman from Pusey House bent on saving my soul and the fast-extinguishing charms of the widow of a defunct professor. Therefore this particular luncheon turned out to be such a delightful surprise. Incongruous people there certainly were present but the grace of Pratima Devi and the spontaneous urbanity of Rathi Babu gently smoothed down all the angles and for a short while we were happily enveloped in the kindly atmosphere of a Bengal home. I shall always be thankful to "Mullickda" for the opportunity he gave me of knowing these noble persons for whom my affection has since then ever been on the increase. Coupled with the gratitude which I like many others feel towards them for their unchanging kindness and goodness is my great admiration for that fine and rare talent for decorative art on the stage which makes Pratima Devi unique among our artists.

On arriving at Paddington station I took a taxi to Chelsea where the Poet and his suite were putting up in a big house. I was introduced into a large-sized room where I first saw the

Poet. He was sitting on a divan and along the walls there were many chairs occupied by men and women, Indian, British and continental, who sat in rapt silence, as in a prayer-hall. In one corner of the room an Englishwoman was modelling the Poet's head in clay whilst in another a fierce young man, a Pole perhaps, was sketching, as I saw from a corner of my eye, the fine folds of his robe. The windows were wide open on to the Embankment and I do not now remember if incense was burning in that room, but if it was not, it ought to have been because the atmosphere was so charged with awe and admiration. My visit was formal as the Oxford programme had already been fixed upon by Rathi Babu. Disconcerted as I felt at the collusive silence of the place, I was a little relieved at the thought that the invitation I had brought need not, by being communicated in words, strike a harsh note in that stillness. At that time I thought that the Poet's immobility and his closed eyes were due to his posing for the artists in the room, but since I have understood better for he possessed the rare quality of being able to withdraw within himself at will and relapse without effort into the statuesque. That capacity for complete aloofness in the midst of contacts, that sudden communion with the inner life in the intervals of spoken words, that faculty of abstracting oneself from one's surroundings, he shared with the prophets and the visionaries. Such men one may come to know very well and yet never be familiar with.

I have seen him later once in Paris after a lively conversation in a company of which he was the very soul, for he could be humorous, playful, almost childlike, chill into a beautiful stone mellowed with age, making me think of what Hammurabi would have looked like had that great Babylonian law-giver ever had the chance of being modelled by a Grecian master. On that occasion I was maliciously amused to see the consternation of the charming and exuberant Comtesse de Noailles, who was sponsoring the exhibition of the Poet's paintings in Paris and was treating him before all the assembled artists and writers as her special preserve.

I am not sure who was the president of the Majlis that year, whether it was Shaheed (the writer's younger brother H.S. Suhrawardy),[1] or Kiran Sankar Roy, but he was of short stature, for I remember how the Poet in his flowing robes loomed large above him as he alighted from the train at Oxford station. Beside the entire Indian colony on the platform there were a number of English people headed by Estlin Carpenter, vigorous and bearded, who was to be the Poet's host. The arrangement was that our visitor was to dine that night with the committee of the Majlis at the Randolph Hotel, breakfast in my rooms the next morning, deliver his address at Manchester College in the early afternoon and then attend the large reception the Majlis was giving him at a hired hall in the city. The whole of that morning we were busy fixing up details, the most important of which to us was to arrange to garland the Poet when he arrived by train. We gave, interrupting one another, instructions to the best florist at Oxford as to what kind of garland one uses on such occasions in India, carefully suppressing the fact of the sharp wire, which has lacerated the breast of many a distinguished Indian, and we were promised that a suitable object would be delivered at the station in time. Our horror can be imagined when the president turning to the florist's assistant,

[1] The reference is to the essayist's younger brother, Huseyn Shaheed Suhrawardy, who was at Oxford at the same time. This younger brother was Prime Minister (the post now called Chief Minister) of Bengal in 1946, and Prime Minister of Pakistan, 1956–7. Due to the two brothers having similar sounding names and the same initials, the writer of the present essay, Hasan Shahid Suhrawardy, was generally known as Shahid Suhrawardy. (He should also not be confused with his uncle, Sir Hassan Suhrawardy.) – Ed.

who had arrived breathless just at that very moment, unpacked the thing from tissue paper and held aloft in the air before the Poet's bowed head a funeral wreath, stiff in wire frame, decked with wide-staring white flowers.

One could not find anywhere a happier set of young men as during that evening in a private room at the Randolph Hotel. The Poet was in great form. He was talking to us all the time, commenting on the changes that had taken place since his last visits to Europe. He spoke of India, now solemnly and now playfully (we were too intense about India to enjoy that particular mood of his) and then listened with comprehending indulgence to our wild talks, in which we attempted to outshine one another. He ate little of the food, the menu of which I had prepared after careful thought, and I was a little glad to see how he banished one after another those culinary inanities which go under the name of vegetarian dishes in England. Rabindranath was a great connoisseur of the fine things of life, and also understood good food. In fact, he was not of those who glorify their failing digestion with reference to the high ideals of our traditional asceticism. I have always received encouragement at his hands for my frivolous advocacy of gastronomy. I remember him once at Santiniketan as he sat reclining on a low armchair and listened with smiling attention to a long confession of mine as a glutton in many lands. He was so interested that I am told it was one of those rare occasions when he did not order the meeting to be interrupted for the sake of the evening prayer, which it is customary to offer there.

The Poet came a little late to breakfast to my place the next morning as he had lost his way in Christ Church meadows and was full of the enchantment of Oxford. His visit had taken place during the summer term when Oxford was in her most beautiful month with laburnums hanging down in full bloom and the ivies on the old walls of colleges a mass of scarlet flame. It was a delight going round with him down the narrow lanes and along the broad stone thoroughfares and sharing in his joy at the sight of so much squandered loveliness. Only we were never alone as his unusual appearance attracted a large crowd that followed us about. That evening my landlady's little daughter told me she had seen me in the streets with Father Christmas. She did not know what treasures he had brought into our lives that year. Before luncheon, propped up on bright cushions, he sat on a punt, as we took him down that part of the river where it narrows under overhanging branches. He sat stone-still all the while in his shining garments of white and in the noon-haze I fancied to myself Orpheus, sculpted on the prow of some Hellenic boat, mirrored in the waters of the Ionian seas.

One thing I noticed that afternoon in the vast hall of Manchester College, cram-full with a brilliant and awe-inspired crowd of professors, dons and undergraduates, that the Poet's voice was ill-suited to large audiences. When he first spoke to me, I was struck by a certain discrepancy between his appearance, on which nature had showered her most exquisite gifts of beauty and dignity, and his voice, which did not seem to belong to his magnificent exterior. In itself the voice was melodious and expressive but it might have belonged to anyone else. It possessed a fine timbre but lacked in tonality. I have always wanted to ask members of his household whether a voice like his was capable of being raised in discussion or reprimand. I suspect, were he ever moved to anger, which I doubt, he would probably employ the subtler instruments of irony and humorous innuendo. I hope the newly baked fanatics of the Poet will not accuse me of disrespect towards him for these observations of mine. That would be very unfair because my love and reverence for him, since I first met him, has bordered on adoration. I am trying with difficulty to delve into my memory and I am faithfully recording my first reactions to him before more frequent contacts made me get used to his ways.

I do not remember either the subject or the gist of the Poet's lecture; I was too much under the influence of his enchanting personality, as he sat slightly bowed on his high chair reading out from a manuscript, detached and patriarchal, to listen to his words. My eyes have always given me greater pleasure than my ear. I know that evening I felt serenely peaceful as I hurried along after the meeting to catch up the fast-striding figure of Robert Bridges, who had come all rigged up in his full academic robes to do honour to the Indian poet, and walked part of the way with him. Bridges did not speak, he evidently did not wish to share his impressions with me. He was a curious old man, garrulous on occasions and then suddenly silent. When parting from me he asked me in that kindly curt tone, which was so characteristic of him, to come to tea the next afternoon when he had invited Tagore to his house.

Robert Bridges lived in a large house on a hill six miles from Oxford. In those days the road to it was long and difficult and to come to him one had to traverse meadows, pass by farmsteads and then climb a wood within which ensconced lay his house. This gave to each visit to him the flavour of a pilgrimage. During his lifetime he had already become legendary. There were plenty of stories about his whimsicality and crankiness and though he was the kindest of men, as some of us Indians had occasion to know, he had a reputation for being abrupt and rude. Of all men I have met he acted up to the injunction of Christ to his Apostles to be wise as serpents and harmless as doves. He would be often seen, like some large bird, ranging the hillside with his broad-brimmed hat closely set over his head and his loose black cloak flapping behind him. He rarely came down to Oxford, and when he did, people would stand about watching his tall figure slouching from the larger roads to the quiet lanes. He sometimes stood for hours before a bookstall in the street, reading a book he had picked up unmindful of the crowd behind him. He and Rabindranath Tagore were the two most beautiful old men I have ever seen. And yet I thought that afternoon when I saw them together how different they were in the quality of their attractiveness. There was nothing of the sage, rather of an overgrown schoolboy, about Bridges. With his splendid face marked accurately with wrinkles, like a perfect autumn leaf, his healthy complexion and spare figure he looked as one who had always lived the outdoor life in touch with fields and animals. There was manly energy in his large frame and even in his long unkempt hair. In other ways too there could be no greater contrast than he and Tagore and I thought that there in that house for once, physically, the East had met the West. For no poet in England was so indigenous as Bridges, so un-exotic, so classically free from the touch of the Orient. And Tagore in my eyes represented the melody, the abundance, the grace of the East; to him Beauty came as she flowed down streams or awoke on the sprays of the breeze-tossed corn; she came to him naturally as the cherished one to her lover. Whereas to Bridges she was a burden; with him there was a constant struggle to reduce the conflict between language and mood to the counterpoints of harmony, to force Beauty into the fierce shackles of tone and rhythm. I know this is not saying all. There is probably no deep difference after all between the East and the West, but it is true that each moulds in its own manner human passions and temperaments. Anyway, it is good that Beauty has many moods, she yields to him who fights for her as to him who succumbs to her.

I have seen Rabindranath Tagore at Chilswell, Bridges' home, twice, once then and about a dozen or so years later. I cannot quite disengage in my memory the incidents of the two occasions. I remember, however, one evening when the two sat together on a jutting hillock in the corner of the garden, which commands a superb view of Oxford. In fact, in 1914, Bridges had once said to me that were Germans ever to occupy his house, what a wonderful emplacement that hillock would afford to artillery reared to destroy completely with one shattering shot the eternal beauty of Oxford. For it is true that from the bench on which the two poets sat all the ugly accretions of modern Oxford were hidden by rolling uplands and one could only see the proud towers and spires against the sunset. Such must have been the vision of the lovely city that first burst upon the sight of Erasmus as he trudged along the road from his distant home to find in her the solace of faith tempered with reason.

Tagore had come over in a hansom-cab and I was going back to Oxford on foot. After he had left, Bridges excitedly spoke how that evening, more than he could from his works, he had come to understand Tagore's wise spirit. Then turning brusquely he added: Tagore is an extraordinarily good-looking fellow. There is something Assyrian, Old Asiatic. Do you think he puts gold in his beard? When I suggested that it was the colour of the sunset that had been playing on their faces, he broke into a loud schoolboy laughter and said: You cannot know the vanity of poets. And striding to the mirror on the wall of his vast study he carefully combed with his fingers his hair and beard tousled by the wind.

SÁLIM ALI

The Indian House-Crow

THE INDIAN HOUSE- or Grey-necked Crow is unquestionably the commonest and most ubiquitous bird in the city of Bombay and in the more densely populated of its suburbs. He is universally and perhaps justly reviled, but it is impossible to overlook his usefulness in keeping the city clean of refuse. However much one may resent his practices or deplore his morals, one cannot but admire his masterly finesse and cunning in invariably getting the better of his fellow-citizens, not excluding Man himself. Whether he is manoeuvring to deprive you of your *chota hazri* toast, or shadowing your movements to despoil a well-concealed nest as soon as your back is turned, there is in his tactics the same well-calculated shrewdness that places him without dispute in the front rank of avian intelligentsia.

The Crow is a born opportunist. His capacity for discriminating between a harmless person and one not to be trusted, and between a stick and a gun is truly uncanny. Climb up to his nest and handle the eggs or young and for weeks afterwards you will be singled out from among your fellows for special attention, even though you appear differently attired on each occasion. Execrations will be lavished upon you at sight and you will even be subjected to assault and battery by the bills of the outraged owners.

Much has been written about the Crow, but the subject is still far from exhausted. Indeed, as long as human ingenuity persists

Co-authored by Humayun Abdulali.

so long will the Crow continue to afford matter for study and amazement as he will continue to devise counter-measures to deal with any new situation that may arise in order that he may still get the better of Man and profit by his concerns.

In the matter of diet the Crow is omnivorous and not exacting. It is this that makes him a blessing – albeit a mixed one – to civic life and confers on him the patronage and protection of our City Fathers. No species of garbage comes amiss to him and he seems to thrive on everything. But while being a staunch ally of our health authorities in the maintenance of an efficient sanitary standard on the one hand, he also helps to promote disease on the other. In Chaupati Road, Sálim Ali once watched a crow hop into a milkman's shop while the owner was away in a back room. The bird sidled up and on to the rim of a vessel containing the stock-in-trade, already popular with the fly community of the neighbourhood, and inserting his head into it took several long and refreshing draughts! As the bird had quite possibly been feeding the moment before on the entrails of a sewer rat, or maybe something still more gruesome, it is not difficult to imagine his potentiality for the dissemination of disease germs.

With all this, however, it must be said that Crows are cleanly birds outwardly, and punctilious about their toilet. They never miss the opportunity of a bath and runnels of water or ornamental ponds such as there are in the Victoria Gardens always have their quota of regular bathers. We have also observed them frequently washing themselves by shuffling among the dense and dripping foliage of trees like Gulmohor or Karanj after a shower of rain.

They are amongst the regular habitues of *Erythrina indica, E. stricta* and *Bombax malabaricum* in bloom and revel in the nectar of the blossoms. Specimens shot off them show a considerable quantity of pollen adhering to their forehead and chin, and the birds undoubtedly play an important part in the cross-pollination of these flowers. Parties frequently indulge in hunting winged termites as they emerge from the ground on monsoon evenings, often till well after dusk. The birds either post themselves on the ground near the hole and tick off the insects as they appear, or else launch aerial sallies after them from rooftops and the like, often going through remarkable evolutions in the chase. We have seen one take a complete somersault loop-the-loop – in the air! One of their favourite hunting grounds is fish-markets where they cause endless annoyance to the fish-wives, sneaking up to the baskets and pilfering from them, both on the ground and off the women's heads, and just managing to keep out of their irate reach.

With a high wind blowing, numbers of these birds frequently indulge in aerobatics involving considerable agility, for no apparent reason except the mere fun of the thing.

Breeding: House-Crows breed abundantly within town limits and also about the local railway line, and all through the better populated suburbs. The season proper may be said to last from May to August, although in some years it may begin considerably earlier and last till about the middle of September. The earliest date on which we have observed a bird tugging at and breaking off a dry twig from a growing branch is 18 February (St Xavier's College compound). On 21 February we have a record of a half-built nest in the Victoria Gardens and on the 23rd of the same month another was nearing completion in a roadside tree opposite the Royal Opera House. The earliest date for young we have is 9 May when two were being fed in a nest near the Andheri railway station.

During the season almost every roadside tree in the town holds a nest, often two or more. The locality about the B.B. &

C.I. Railway line between Grant Road Station and Dadar seems particularly favoured, as also that in the neighbourhood of the docks. Here a large number of nests are composed more or less entirely of iron wire or scraps of hoop iron filched from the neighbouring goods yards. This propensity to utilise iron wire in the structure of the nests was responsible for great interruption and delays in the suburban electric railway service when it was first inaugurated in 1922. The engineers had reckoned without the Crow which soon discovered that the overhead brackets holding the power wires provided admirable nesting sites and took to them wholesale. The iron used in many of the nests caused short-circuiting and brought traffic to a standstill. Thus in one week forty-four trains were held up, and it was with some difficulty that the cause was finally discovered. Not until a specially designed insulated or crow-proof bracket was introduced was this nuisance finally eradicated.

The nests are mostly placed in trees – Mango, Tamarind, Albizzia, Casuarina, Polyalthia, Palms and others – from a height of about 12 ft up, mostly between this and 20 ft. In structure they do not differ from those of the Jungle-Crow except that owing to its greater availability in town, iron wire etc. is more employed in its construction. There is the almost classic example of a nest built entirely of gold and silver spectacle frames pilfered from an optician's shop in the Fort. About Rs 100 worth of frames disappeared before the culprits were run to earth!

Three to five eggs are normally laid and the largest number of young we have seen in a nest is four. In our experience two is the largest number of young being tended by the parents out of the nest, and it appears that the mortality in the nestling stage is heavy. The Koel habitually foists its eggs on the nests of the House-Crow. On 9 June 1931, Humayun Abdulali found a nest with Koel eggs of two different types which appeared to have been laid by two different females. There were no crow's eggs in the nest, but signs of a broken egg which may have belonged to the latter. We have usually seen a single young Koel being tended by its foster-parents out of nest: only on one occasion two. Never have there been any young crows about, and it might be questioned as to what becomes of them and whether like the European Cuckoo the young Koel also heaves its foster-brothers over the edge of the nest.

Various stages of albinism have been noted and described in the House-Crow in and around Bombay city. One that occurs more frequently than others is the isabelline phase of which an example bred for two years at least in the Government Dockyard (1921 and 1925). For those who still believe in the popular notion that crows mate lying on the ground with their vents apposed, it may be mentioned that we have now observed them mating in the usual manner of birds – "treading" – a sufficient number of times to dispel this fallacy. Popular belief also credits the crow with exceptional longevity or even immortality. The argument advanced is that in spite of its abundance one seldom comes across a crow that has died a natural death; a fact that is indeed true enough of most wild animals.

The Crow has few natural enemies and but for the heavy mortality in its nesting stage and other periodic checks, its numbers would soon become unendurable. A few years ago a mysterious disease appeared among the crow population of Bombay which evoked a good deal of correspondence in the local press at the time. Large numbers of adult birds were found lying dead in many parts of the city and suburbs, in a stiffened condition, beneath their perches. The Haffkine Institute investigated the matter but as far as we are aware without elucidating any clue to the mystery.

This account of the House-Crow has become inordinately lengthy, but there is so much of interest in the life of this pre-eminently urban bird that it could not be compressed further without doing him an injustice.

NIRAD C. CHAUDHURI

Apologia Pro Scripta Sua

THE HEADING OF this piece is a variation on a theme of Newman, an adaptation of the title of his famous autobiography. Thus it will be an apology, not for my life, but for my writings. Indeed, it may be taken as an apology for all writers.

Why do writers write? My acquaintances often ask me: "How did the idea of writing come to you?" I give them an answer which could be regarded as flippant. I ask in my turn: "Why don't you ask a tiger: How did the idea of hunting come to you?"

But I mean it seriously. To my thinking, no writer writes from choice; he writes because he cannot help it. He is under an irresistible compulsion to write.

The compulsion however is different for different kinds of writers. It is of one kind for those who may be called "vocational" writers, and of another kind for those who proclaim themselves and are recognised by the great majority of readers as "professional" writers. They, of course, far outnumber the "vocationals".

The obvious fact about the motivation of vocational writers is that they have no motive at all. They give expression to what comes to their mind without thought of money, position, fame, or even attention. In stark contrast, the professionals want all these. I shall indicate their social affiliation by citing the great Bengali novelist, Bankim Chandra Chatterji (1838–94). He created an eccentric character, very much of a wag, who was summoned as a witness. The plaintiff's lawyer asked him: "What is your profession?" He retorted angrily: "Profession! Am I a prostitute or a lawyer that I should have a profession?"

He was an authentic traditionalist in his brusqueness. As Kipling wrote in his story "On the city wall":

> Lalun is a member of the most ancient profession in the world, Lilith was her very-great-grandmamma, and that was before the days of Eve.

Over and above, writers can be classified zoologically. Actually, all vocations and professions may be placed within the zoological taxonomy. Members of each one of them can be regarded as an animal of a distinct species – say, a lion, a horse, a dog, or cat.

There is, however, a fundamental difference between the zoological correlatives of writers and those of all other professions. Members of all professions are one animal, differing among themselves only by their standing as that particular animal. For instance, a successful barrister in a High Court may be an Arab horse, while lawyers of lowly rank in a court of the lowest jurisdiction will be hackney.

But writers, zoologically classified, are not one animal: they are different animals. This is to say, if one writer can be regarded as a lion or horse, another will be a bullock, or donkey, or a monkey, or even a skunk. Therefore no one can form a correct idea of what a particular writer is or does by simply considering him as a writer. This is a very vague description and too wide in its scope to be of value for particularisation.

I shall not proclaim myself as any particular animal as a writer, but leave it to the reader to place me in the zoological hierarchy. I shall only describe how I write and what conception I have of the business of writing.

First, considering myself as a "vocational" writer, I certainly set down in writing whatever comes into my mind. But I do not regard it primarily as a product of my own mind, i.e. as an idea or a sense impression of my own.

I try to convert my mind into a camera to take the impression of whatever to which it is exposed, and thus create an exact equivalent of a photographic negative. My personal work is to develop this negative and then make a print. I do not allow anything of what was not present in the untouched negative to be in the print for the sake of pictorial effect.

I have next to explain the methodology of my writing. The basic realisation which dictates my method is that language is something to be heard, not merely to be looked at. Thus I consider what is written by way of literary work to be the exact equivalent of a musical score, and when writing I always behave like a musical composer, I never write without sounding what I am writing in my ear.

I did not learn English from Englishmen nor heard it as spoken by natural speakers of the language till late in life. Till 1910 I learnt it at my birthplace, Kishorganj, a small town in East Bengal, from my Bengali teachers. From 1910 to 1914 (when I passed the Matriculation examination) I learnt it in Calcutta, also from Bengali teachers. This gave me a sound mastery of English syntax, idioms, and also an adequate vocabulary, so that when I entered university life in 1914, I did not have to consult dictionaries for the meaning of words, and concerned myself with the subject matter of what I had to read, both as to information and to ideas.

Therefore, an acute anxiety troubled my mind when I was writing my first book, *The Autobiography of an Unknown Indian*, in 1947 and 1948. I asked myself whether what I was writing would sound like English to those who were born to the language. I knew, unless it did, no English publisher would accept my book.

I adopted a special method to rid myself of the worry. I read what I had written loudly (incorrectly of course) and then also read a passage from some great book of English prose (in the same way). If the two sound effects agreed I passed my writing.

The prose writers I selected were very diverse, e.g., from Joseph Hooker (sixteenth century) to George Moore (twentieth century). There is no such thing as one standard rhythm of English prose, and despite T.S. Eliot Milton's prose is as English as is Newman's. English prose rhythms are bewilderingly diverse, but all are authentic English rhythms. There is diversity even in one writer. No one (unless totally deaf to sound) will say that Sir Thomas Browne's *Religio Medici* is in the same rhythm as is his *Hydriotaphia*. Dryden in his prose (which I admired) as well as Gibbon in his, were equally authentic to me, in spite of the latter's assertive gallicisms. I might add George Moore in his *Esther Waters* was not the same writer as he was in one of his latest books, *The Brook Kerith*. His *Hail and Farewell* I found to be captivatingly limpid.

This method proved itself. When after the publication of this book in England on 8 September 1951, the BBC read out certain passages from it, I said to myself: "That was the sound I had in my mind's ear."

The habit of writing by sounding has led me to another basic discovery in regard to diction. I have found that the mood and temper created in me by anything I see or feel control the rhythm and tempo of what I write. For instance, if my mood is excited and dramatic my diction at once becomes staccato in rhythm and allegro or even presto in tempo; whereas when I am contemplative these become legato and adagio or even lento.

All these correlations are spontaneous and unselfconscious. No self-conscious striving after effect succeeds in moving readers.

Another realisation which has come to me is that the substance of a piece of writing cannot be separated from its style. There is no such thing in literary works as good substance spoilt by a bad style, or poor substance undeservedly accompanied by a good style. To believe in such theories is to have the stupidity which is dead to matter and the vulgarity which is dead to form. A great French writer said that the style is the man himself. I would say that the style is the subject itself.

With all these explanations, I have done with my methodology. But method is only a means to an end. Does my method have any end in view? I shall try to answer that very natural yet baffling question.

At the very outset, I have to give the preliminary information that my writing life has extended so far over seventy-one years from 1925 to 1996. I am sure it is the longest in history. In its course, I have written fourteen books in English as well as Bengali, and poured out hundreds of articles and broadcasts. I have been more a journalist than a man of letters. But to what end? My countrymen have left no room for doubt as to their view of it. They have ceaselessly proclaimed that my purpose has always been to settle my score with them, the score of an unsuccessful, embittered and soured life, by denigrating them, their life, and their civilisation. I have never contradicted them in words.

At first I did not understand why there was such a hostile reaction to my book from my countrymen. But Sir John Squire who as publishers' reader reported on the book expected this. In a letter written on 5 December 1950 to an Indian friend of his he wrote: "If the book comes out it may put India into an uproar, and he might possibly find a refuge in England . . ." etc.

This has come true and after considering the question deeply I have understood why the Indian reaction was ferociously adverse.

The dedication to the "memory of the British Empire in India" did not provoke them. But that was due to their failure to understand its significance. It was really a condemnation of the British rulers for not treating us as equals. It was imitation of what Cicero said about the conduct of Vewes, a Roman Pro-consul of Sicily who oppressed the Sicilian Roman Citizens, although in their desperation they cried out: "*Civis romanus sum*".

As to the effect of British rule on us, what I wrote at the end of the dedication was a paraphrase of what Swami Vivekananda, the creator of New Hinduism, said in plain words.

Next, I gave offence to fellow Indians writing objectively about the personality of my parents. No Hindu does this, he utters hagiographical platitudes.

Last of all I wrote in an English style which was not accessible to the general run of educated Indians. Sir John Squire detected this. He wrote: "His English is so good that one is tempted to think that he must have had a translator; but a translator as good as that would never have bothered about translation, but written great works of prose on his own."

I think all this explains the hostility.

But I have contradicted my detractors by my actions. I have been, so to speak, a man of action through my writings. I have always been what is called an *engagé*. I have never shrunk from getting involved in all that I have seen and experienced and reacting to them in writing.

Furthermore, I have frankly admitted that in the last stage of writing I became a dogmatist and theoriser. I have written two books which are clearly dogmatic. I admitted that by describing the subject of one book in one borrowed phrase: *De Rerum*

Indicarum Natura. I also confessed my dogmatism by quoting the following biblical passage:

"I will pour out my spirit upon all flesh; and your sons and daughters shall prophesy, your old men shall dream dreams, your young men shall see visions."

Thus I have been something other even than a journalist, I have really been a preacher. I have said to myself: "I applied my mind to know wisdom and my mind has great experience of wisdom and knowledge."

But my countrymen have not taken my preaching at my valuation. They have set it down as mere *bavardage*. Perhaps it is so in form.

Nonetheless, I would say that all this *babil* of mine shows no absence of clarity and honesty, and also no absence, if not of courage, at least of boldness.

Here ends the apology for my writings.

23rd November 1996

On stepping into the 100th year of my life.

SUDHINDRANATH DATTA

Calcutta

AMONG MY MORE fabulous friends is an infuriating philosopher who used to claim that the only way of knowing a place was never to visit it. He is the most single-minded person I have yet encountered; and his paradoxes are the natural product of a speculative intellect that would compose the differences of the real and the negative in related multiplicity. Or such is my guess after looking at the titles of the formidable books he has published since he deserted his native Bengal to return to Oxford; and though that is as far as I have gone in understanding his basic ideas, I now admit the converse of his proposition. For I belong to a family which had lived where Fort William was built after the Battle of Plassey; and removed thence to the centre of the town, it has remained rooted to Calcutta ever since. But I who was born here at the turn of the century, and have spent most of my years in the city, cannot define its character; and when a newcomer asks me what he should see, I am struck dumb.

I see no connection between such failure on my part and the fact that Calcutta is an upstart hardly two centuries old, whereas the rest of India measures antiquity by millennia. At any rate, cities in other parts of the world can be young and attractive at the same time; and even in this immemorial land the populous sections of every town are seldom more ancient than the first capital of the British Raj. Besides, if Calcutta lacks archaeological sites, it can boast of lanes as dingy and buildings as mouldy as those of Muttra, Delhi, and Benares, to mention only three out of perhaps a hundred names; and the east has the advantage over the north in possessing a truly disintegrating climate that generates ruins in record time. This the Bengalis seem to have realised early in their history; and so until, say, two hundred years ago most of them not only lived in mud houses with thatched roofs, but likewise worshipped clay images which, once their day was done, went back to rest in the beds of superabundant rivers and ubiquitous marshes.

But until the eighteenth century the sacred Ganges considered the Hooghly her principal outlet into the sea; and consequently, on both banks of the latter, urban communities pullulated right down to seven or eight miles north of what is now Calcutta. Beyond stretched mangrove swamps dotted with obscure villages; and because the English who had already obtained a foothold farther upstream found themselves in constant difficulty with either the ruling power or their European rivals, they moved down to three of the larger fishing settlements. Thus in the seventeenth century was born the second city of the British Empire; and if its infancy passed amidst peril and pestilence, its nurses could find resignation in the thought that it was obviously under the influence of Siva's bloodthirsty consort whose shrine at adjacent Kalighat had been drawing pilgrims from at least the fifteenth century. It is conceivable that Calcutta does not owe its name to that destructive goddess; but I, for one, am convinced that she alone is responsible for its initial indifference to the past and subsequent avidity for the future.

In other words, however haphazard the preliminary choice, no site could be more appropriate for founding an exotic empire; and though Calcutta's indigenous residents were first attracted to it because it was a haven of security in a sea of anarchy, they stayed on for the sake of the new horizons they could glimpse from there. So long as they remained on foreign territory, they were free from traditional restraints; and the voluntary exile filled their pockets with easy money, as it stuffed their heads with strange ideas. In time the last became the most lasting of Britain's gifts to India; and for years Calcutta was their distributing centre. But, to start with, nobody felt rooted here: those who profited by the city's commerce bought estates elsewhere; and even after absentee landlords had ceased to be exceptions to the rule, they considered themselves less as members of a coherent community than as opportunists competing with others of their kind. The result did not conduce to the growth of economic classes; but it reduced the importance of caste by making the family the hub of all activity.

Meanwhile the fashion of living in storeyed houses of brick and mortar had caught on; and even the would-be rich had to build mansions which their descendants could pretend to own so long as they could keep usurers at bay by promises or litigation. Thus arose the self-styled city of palaces; but it was altogether devoid of planning and civic conscience. Perhaps the pattern was set by the surrounding marshes with their solid protuberances; and stately homes soared over agglutinations of unspeakable hovels. Through them meandered lanes that changed from dunghill to cesspool during the monsoon; and though by the time I was a small boy they had been replaced by metalled roads in the better quarters, yet once, after a particularly heavy downpour, half the main streets remained under water for a whole week. Nor was any architectural sense discernible in individual buildings; and if the pillared residences of the Europeans were spaciously colonial, the public edifices were uniformly hideous. The Government House, the Museum, and perhaps the Victoria Memorial are exceptional; but the mock-Gothic High Court must be seen to be believed.

The corresponding achievement of the private sector is a Scottish castle constructed by a great patron of Indian culture; and since the most pungent of Calcutta's fish and vegetable markets had to be crossed to reach it, the juxtaposition is nightmarish enough to belong to the city of dreadful night. Other instances of bad taste were only a little less eccentric; and the rich Bengali could almost never conceive of a house in which Ionic supports and cast-iron balustrades did not go together. Walled grounds cut some of the palaces off from outside squalor; and within were lawns and flower-beds and ornamental waters, Greek-style vases and rococo fountains and nudes of imitation marble, all focused around sprawling structures containing several courtyards, many halls overflowing with chandelier, console furniture, and mirror; and countless small rooms where men and women led their separate lives, only to come together at night to produce yet more life. Among the less wealthy the garden was reduced to potted palms, only two courtyards had to suffice, and while bedrooms were numerous, public rooms were few and fly-blown.

Facing the principal court stood a single-storeyed pavilion; and the number of its arches, as also of its inner compartments, was a fair index to its owner's pretensions. In it took place the religious festivals; and these were said to be at least thirteen in twelve months. The foremost among them occurred after the rains; and for four days a benign manifestation of Kali was worshipped under the name of Durga. On the tenth day of the full moon the ten-armed image was consigned to the river; and for the rest of the evening everybody had to embrace everybody else. The only other occasion when barriers were customarily lowered was Holi – a spring feast unashamedly erotic in content; and then not only did the streets turn into a riot of colour, but even homes suffered invasion from Bacchanalian crowds. At all other times people kept to their particular orbits; and respectable women were never admitted to them. There was, however, no dearth of nautch girls; and while they danced and sang in the great halls, the head of the house sat about with his friends and hangers-on drinking champagne or sipping brandy.

Less intimate, if more ostentatious, parties were occasionally graced by the family's British patrons; but though on arrival they were obsequiously received, their segregation was soon contrived; and for an hour or two the condescending untouchables remained on exhibition, draining Gargantuan tumblers and nibbling Indian sweets. A wider circle was invited to the musical soirees, operatic performances, and readings from the epics and religious classics, which took place in the big courtyard; and for the frequent weddings of sons and daughters, nephews and nieces, every court and corridor and terrace had to be given over to banqueting, as no acquaintance could be excluded from the list of guests. But before the European stage could be adapted to Bengali conditions, Calcutta knew no public entertainment or, for the matter of that, public life. Bengalis did not frequent clubs; food taboos prevented the growth of restaurants; and drinking was a sin that could be indulged in apparent secrecy. So until organised sports, like racing, football, and cricket, in that order, began to draw crowds of fifteen to twenty thousand, Calcutta's only communal amusement was public meetings.

The Bengali's love of grandiloquence is coupled with vehemence in argument; and though the first public gatherings were convened to voice the well-recognised need for social and religious reform, the resultant debates emphasised, instead of mitigating, the factionalism inherent in the life of Calcutta. If, nevertheless, the native society did not soon reach maximum entropy, the reason was the increasing weight of the "White Man's Burden". A handful of strangers in a teeming land, the city's rulers could not help suffering from some agoraphobia; but after they had managed to survive the Mutiny, their aloofness turned to arrogance of surprising blatancy. In that touch-and-go affair the Bengali had been wholeheartedly on their side; and he did not agree that insolence should be his reward at its conclusion. Even so he was prepared to make allowances for an alien's poorer nerves; and it was only when Ripon's proposal to let Indian magistrates try European criminals had almost unleashed a British mutiny that he grew too indignant to remember his differences with his countrymen.

In their treatment of one another more snobbish than he was in his daily life, the foreigners presented to him a serried front more solid than the walls of his ancestral house. Whatever his station, he could not visit their homes except as a suppliant carrying propitiatory gifts; if business demanded his attendance at their clubs, he could only enter by the servants' door; he was not allowed to stray into the part reserved for them in the best public park; and to eat in their restaurants he had to borrow their clothes, or be thrown out. Macaulay had, of course, considered him indispensable to the administration; and to teach him a modicum of English, his own system of education had been deliberately suppressed. But because his proficiency had exceeded his mentors' intention, he could be called a Babu by even his near-illiterate superiors, provided they possessed a paler skin; and as a sedulous ape mouthing polysyllabic words whose meaning presumably eluded him, he was denied admission into the ranks of the Indian Army.

No wonder that before the last century was over, political agitation had become the vocation of most able Bengalis; and for this some credit must go to the Bengali law of inheritance which, by insisting that all assets of a deceased father be equally divided among his sons, prevents concentration of wealth for more than three generations. The old families were therefore declining fast; and a new prestige was beginning to attach to professional men who rose in the world without any obvious favour from the British. The majority of them were in legal practice, though numerically doctors came next; and quite a few edited newspapers which carried great influence. They realised that their success depended on their personal qualities and not on family connections; and inevitably they were loyal to their professions. Many of them had, moreover, learnt their trade abroad; and if, incidentally, they had returned with esoteric affectations that provoked the uninitiated to rude laughter, they received, at the same time, homage as national heroes because they claimed absolute equality with the European.

The savagery of Kipling's repetitive satire proves how furiously he and his community hated the Anglo-Bengalis; and there is no denying that at times they were quite insufferable. Even after years of eminence in their professions they spent their leisure recounting their juvenile pranks at Oxford or Cambridge, London or Edinburgh; and if they objected to being termed "wogs", their only exclusive club was open to oriental gentlemen who were too obviously westernised. Yet when a British Chief Justice wanted to show his liberalism by asking to be a member of the institution, he was promptly told that he could join as soon as a leading Bengali barrister was admitted to the Bengal Club; and though, more British than the British in their immaculate frock-coats, the patriots worded their annual resolutions in mellifluous English they demanded self-government for the whole of India. For by then they had counterparts everywhere in the country; and behind those figures, often distorted by the twilight, were ranged so many educated Indians that Curzon himself, for all his Olympian haughtiness, was shaken to the core.

Otherwise he would not have misused his position as Chancellor of the University of Calcutta to attack the Bengali character; and at least a decade earlier British officials had learnt to equate the Hindu intellectual with the scum of the earth. Its salt was, of course, the rural Jath and the retrograde Pathan, who, being Muslims, had hitherto been openly discriminated against as former rulers of India; and since one of the declared aims of the Mutiny had been restoration of the Mughal imperium, the uprising made their situation worse. They too, on their side, had so resented the rise of the new order that they had shut their eyes to its merits; and in keeping with their isolation their religion had turned revivalist. But, now suddenly, the Civil Service discovered their old-world charm; and though their qualities were supposed to derive from their avoidance of modern education, even those among them who had been seduced by the example of the Hindus were somehow given the benefit of the doubt.

In the meantime Hindu reformers, whether mystic or rationalist, had been denouncing bigotry; and because by a natural transition they began to dream of an Indian nation, Curzon's successor forgot himself so far as to put down in black and white that the British Raj must follow a policy of divide and rule. Fortunately the Calcutta Mohammedans were a small minority – mostly petty traders with a sprinkling of decrepit aristocrats who lived on partible pensions which grew tinier and tinier from generation to generation. So while the indefatigable Mr Beck continued his work at Aligarh as the nurseryman of Islamic intransigence, pending its transplantation throughout India, Bengal was partitioned to give the Muslims the status of a majority in a region where they were undoubtedly subject to Hindu exploitation. But, to start with, the earnest failed to clinch any contract; and if few Muslims shared the exaltation of the Hindu terrorists, both exulted equally when, as the outcome of the latter's deeds of dramatic violence, the so-called settled fact was unsettled, and the province became again one.

The "sun-dried bureaucrats", as they were popularly named, hated the humiliation; and to show their resentment they shifted the capital of the Indian Empire from Calcutta to Delhi. Or so at least the Bengali thought; and while the Northerner's approval of the move seemed to him lying propaganda designed to hide the same diabolical policy of divide and rule, he was quick to remember an old saying that no throne set up in Delhi would stand for long. Recent events have certainly confirmed the prophecy if it can be so described; and yet in 1911 the dissolution of the British Raj was but a patriot's dream, whereas the emergence of Pakistan was a nightmare which even the worst pessimist could never have invented. For all that, Calcutta's equilibrium was rendered unstable; and though the city continued to grow as the centre of the country's commerce and the largest port in Asia, the territories it directly fed upon were reduced to less than half by the new boundaries of reunited Bengal.

Undoubtedly the old province had been too big for efficient administration; and the separation of some regions could now be justified on the ground that if what is culturally one may not be disrupted, then tracts which are linguistically different must also receive their due. But those who were thus hoist with their own petard continued to believe that large areas were taken out of Bengal so as to make Hindus and Muslims equal rivals for British favours; and the fact remains that the rift between the two communities widened as the years passed. At any rate, religious riots became specific to Calcutta soon after the First World War; and their climax was reached in August 1946 when history came full circle and Pax Britannica, together with the empire which was supposed to be founded on it, ended ignominiously in the very city where it had been born in such glory hardly two hundred years before. With it disappeared the unity of India that was considered the greatest achievement of the

British rule; and perhaps the special destiny of Calcutta was thus fulfilled.

Formal independence came a year later; and what happened in the Punjab immediately thereafter rightly overshadowed the Great Calcutta Killing, as the local carnage was rather infelicitously named by the newspaper I worked on at the time. All the same, our orgy of death must receive its due honour as the first of its kind in India's history; and since the number massacred was at least ten thousand, it was a sizeable affair. For three days the corpses lay in the streets of the country's largest city, exposed to the sun and rain until they had become black and bloated and too putrid for even rats and vultures to feed on; and the bodies thrown into the river collected where it bent under the window of a young girl who went raving mad watching the accumulation. Those in possession of their senses kept their doors bolted; and if thus they missed the fine glow imparted to the monsoon sky by houses blazing away at night, nowhere was there any escape from the stench of rotting carcasses.

Death, sudden and violent, was, of course, no stranger to Calcutta; and apart from earlier riots which took their regular, if smaller, toll, Japanese planes killed nearly a thousand dock-workers in the one and only daylight raid on the defenceless city. There was also the 1943 famine; and at its height as many as two thousand dead and dying were picked up daily from the indifferent streets. But callousness, inefficiency, or complacence did not explain the Manichaean outburst of 1946; and those who participated in the mass murders were literally without number, and came from all classes of Indian society. In any case, when at last, through the good offices of an English friend, I could visit my mother, the first thing I heard was how a neighbour of hers, an alumnus of a British university, had incited a mob to finish off a dozen Muslim hawkers whose decomposing remains I had passed to reach my mother's house; and so, on returning home that day, I destroyed the draft of a booklet I had contracted to write, proving that my countrymen, as a whole, were allergic to physical violence.

Full twelve months had to pass before all the city streets were again safe for every denomination; and if their comparative tranquillity in subsequent years derived largely from the withdrawal of the British, the creation of Pakistan, and the resultant slump in the stocks of communal militancy, the real miracle of Calcutta was wrought by one indomitable man who, more than any other, had brought about the first, disregarded the second, and threw his life away in passive resistance to the third. When it became clear that he had failed to persuade India to remain one, Gandhi decided to return to East Bengal where he had spent many months, trying to end the state of anarchy that had developed there soon after the Calcutta Killing, and from the same cause. But on his way back he found Calcutta in the throes of yet another religious riot; and he could not very well refuse the request of the Muslim head of the local government to stay here for at least a few days to control the Hindu rowdies.

He started unpromisingly enough; his first prayer meetings were attended by hecklers; and the climax came when a violent mob surrounded Gandhi's house demanding that he deliver to them Mr Suhrawardy, the execrated Chief Minister. But Gandhi offered himself to the crowd; and though high praise is certainly due to Mr Suhrawardy's courage in joining him not long afterwards, he had by then won the day. Thus on the night of independence a little later, the same streets that had borne the burden of so many dead a year before filled magically with a multitude of celebrants; and while Gandhi, all by himself, mourned the end of Indian unity, Hindus and Muslims indulged in spontaneous fraternisation. The sight was as unforgettable as the earlier terror; and if it reinforced the moral that the Bengali is volatile, it disturbed me more as showing how his constructive capacity had declined. Nor did the balance-sheet improve on a non-parochial view; and even after admitting that the Gujarati saviour was the greatest of his country's sons since Akbar, the fact remained that the scapegoat was the last and the least of British Governors.

Gokhale, Gandhi's political guru, used to say that what Bengal thinks today, the rest of India will think tomorrow. But that was when Calcutta was the capital of the Empire; and since the seat of the central power was moved to Delhi, the Bengali has lived withdrawn into himself, bitterly resenting the unwillingness of others to take him at his own valuation. The ghosts of Calcutta's past citizens, like Surendra Nath Banerjea and Chitta Ranjan Das, continue to haunt his waking hours; and unable to repeat their performance as national figures universally acknowledged as such, he refuses to change the mentality he developed as the leader of the permanent opposition in the heyday of British rule. The civic commotions of which he has been a witness or participant in the intervening years have also left their traumatic mark; and with or without just cause he is ready to join violent demonstrations that fail in their undefined object only because authority has learnt to be tactful and to provide, once or twice a year, a few tramcars to burn.

For all that, he is essentially ungregarious; and at least in 1946, and for quite a while later, Calcutta was as fragmented as it had been at the end of the eighteenth and the beginning of the nineteenth century. By the time of independence the old families had, of course, gone for ever; and even the great houses built by men successful in the learned professions were in decay. Yet the "new poor" are no less fanatically loyal to the quarter they inhabit than were their ancestors; and except when they congregate to fight for their chosen side during the football season, or to applaud any demagogue in all seasons of the year, they split into small groups which collect every evening in the roomiest house of the neighbourhood. The old and the young naturally keep apart; and women are almost never present. But the talk is incessant; many cups of milky tea with large quantities of sugar are drunk; and the meeting breaks up only after all reputations outside the circle have been reduced to tatters.

The more sophisticated gather in clubs where the syrupy tea is replaced by weak whiskies; and occasionally there are "ladies' nights" with interludes of inept dancing. Otherwise the pattern of amusement is much the same; and even at cocktail parties that tend to become the one social event universally repeated in the life of the rich, the same faces smile at the same gossip. But, given time, the observant is bound to notice defections; and he needs only to be comparatively non-attached to discover that the absentees are busy creating their own cliques. Indeed this fissiparous tendency is ubiquitous in Calcutta; and whether it be a school or a college committee, the board of directors of a bank or an insurance company, the presidium of a learned society or an academy of art, would-be dictators are ever faced with potential insurrectionists. Coteries form and dissolve in the literary world as everywhere else; and no Bengali writer, apart from Tagore in his last fifteen years, has yet been able to exist without the plaudits of his own camp and the sneers of opposing factions.

The one good point of all this is that it makes for individuality, with the concomitance of a lively mind and a boundless curiosity; and once things at hand seem unworthy of admiration, there is enchantment in the distance. Thus even if the Bengali intellectual of today reads fewer foreign books than, say, his Bombay counterpart, he reads with more passion and penetration; and when he speaks of his own literature he speaks of technical experiments, of use and abuse of language, rather than of ennobling themes whereby contemporary Hindi writers claim to judge one another's work. At least one quality of his forefathers has not deserted him: he loves disputations; and years ago, on his return to Calcutta, a friend of mine who had witnessed the beginning of the Russian Revolution, and did not escape until 1921, used to repeat that Bengalis were exactly like Russians. A French resident, on the other hand, never tired of maintaining that this city reminded her of Paris; and a discriminating American once told me that only after reaching Calcutta did he feel that he was in India.

The similarities, if at all real, do not obviously reside in the landscape, architecture, or weather, although the last is, in general, hardly worse than that of Washington; and the "atmosphere" of Calcutta must be allowed to seep slowly in before the eyesores can be disregarded. In 1911, when a start was made with modernising the town, the population envisaged was two millions at the end of time; and already between four and five millions sleep here, while another million come to work for the day. Consequently, as the city has crept southwards, turning localities once inhabited by the nabobs into swarming slums, the living space available per head has shrunk to be the smallest in the world; and yet prospects of improvement are dim, because rent control and an adequate building programme accord ill, whereas nothing regulates the flow of newcomers from all directions. Calcutta is specifically Bengali; but nearly thirty-five per cent of its residents are foreign, including ten thousand Europeans; and even among the rest only twenty per cent belong to families which may be described as "cockney" at least metaphorically.

In any case, Calcutta resembles London in the proportion of its population to the total population of West Bengal. About a fifth of the people live in this metropolis; and since the creation of East Pakistan the province has not enough resources to support such a monstrosity. The Hooghly too is dying; except in the rainy season, it is a tidal reach which cannot expel the silt it receives at high water; and perhaps one day Calcutta will revert to the malarial swamp it once was. Meanwhile it attracts all and sundry; and that not only because it is the one real city in Eastern India, but also because its inhabitants, notwithstanding native peculiarities, are so individuated that strangers are at home in their midst. Most foreigners do not, of course, cease cursing the climate, and complaining exaggeratedly of the filthy streets; and they blame their lack of company on the Bengali's clannishness. But they spend their lives here without learning a word of the local language; they keep to circles narrower than the endemic ones; and after having been here awhile, they want to stay on.

As for the tourist in a hurry, Calcutta has nothing to offer except its explosive vitality; and even this contrasts incongruously with the leisurely self-indulgence of the sacred bulls who sit ruminating in the middle of the busiest streets, completely disrupting the traffic, and desolating the man already late for his appointment. Nevertheless the thronged bazaars are an everlasting testimony to its irrepressible energy; and the largest of them, the New Market, is, as a whole, perhaps the biggest emporium in the world, although individual shops with their separate owners may sometimes be no more than a small booth or kiosk. The nearest approach to it, in my limited experience, was the Old Market in Istanbul if that be its name, and some of the North African *souks* must also belong to the same genus. But undulled by long familiarity as my response to the latter was, I did not find them as exciting as the New Market; and before import control was extended to include even consumer goods, almost everything produced anywhere in the world could be bought there.

Restriction of foreign exchange has likewise forced out of business the big departmental stores owned by British companies; and high taxation, coupled with the rising cost of living, has so reduced the clientele that smaller bars and chop-houses, especially those which sprang up during the war, have closed down. The foreign clubs are also in difficulty, because their members no longer spend money on the old scale; and though European meals of good quality can still be had at a reasonable price in the bigger restaurants, drinking is a costly luxury. The Calcutta hotels have always been unattractive; and in four or five cabarets dated stars continue to create an illusion of provincial Europe. The Chinese restaurants have generally declined; and the Indian ones, apart from providing hot curries, give a poor account of the country's food which, as in England, is best only in private homes. But the winter racing is still exciting; the tennis tournaments reach a high standard; and if the Eden Gardens now sprout the shoddiest fairs, the great Maidan persists in spite of excrescences and encroachments.

Calcutta's environs are quite dreary. Barrackpore used to be a fine cantonment, as military stations are named in India; and the park with its old trees was worth an afternoon. But the war ruined it; and the still magnificent Botanical Gardens on the other side of the river cannot be approached except through dreadful streets, now that the ferry does not run regularly. Chandernagore, also across the Hooghly, was until lately a French possession full of a faded and yet exotic flavour. However, since what may be termed its integration, even the Gallic esplanade has lost its nostalgic quality; and the road, though the only arterial one in Bengal, is merely overcrowded and tortuous up to Chandernagore. The other historical highway leading out of Calcutta ends at Jessore in Pakistan; and its avenue of ancient banyans has ceased to allure. Nevertheless, as Jamini Roy loves to say when in his denigrating mood, Calcutta alone can become a village without a moment's ambivalence; and a motorist with time to waste will discover scenes of pleasant rusticity all by himself.

So a short visit to Calcutta need not bore; but those who prolong their stay find in the cinema their chief entertainment; and while Indian films are seldom rewarding, perhaps a third of the better British and American pictures comes here sooner or later. In other words, the pleasures that this city offers are not refined enough for a connoisseur bemoaning his enforced exile; and a dilettante out on a quick discovery of India must begin elsewhere. For, as I said at the outset, Calcutta is devoid of archaeological interest; its upstanding buildings are not even endearingly ugly; the Bengali stage, once its pride, suffers from recurrent depressions; though classical music attracts enormous crowds, its local travesty is so sentimental as to be tiresome; and Bengal never took to Hindu dancing. Mercifully, however, there is Jamini Roy's studio where a great painter can be seen reinterpreting his inheritance in an idiom all his own; and if his conversation is paid the attention it deserves, more can be learnt about the Indian ethos than from the superb collection of sculpture housed in the Museum.

Calcutta's secret charm must, however, escape the impatient; and only an amateur of history will really love it. For nowhere else in the modern world has a new culture emerged from the deliberate intermingling of two older ones – the peripheral culture of rural Bengal and the cosmopolitan culture of English Whiggery; and to my mind it is the finest legacy of British rule.

Initially the hybrid was bound to appear ridiculous; and there is no doubt that its make-up was largely utilitarian. But just as pure altruism often informed the other side, so also the best among us were possessed by intellectual integrity. Or such at least is the impression created in retrospect; and the essence of what was accomplished has not been lost today. Bengali prose, at any rate, originated in the impact of Western ideas on Ram Mohan Roy and his contemporaries; and Michael Madhusudan Datta remodelled Bengali verse as a memorial to English literature. Extending their discoveries, Rabindranath Tagore evolved a seemingly fresh language; and gradually in the last fifty years it has become the speech of every educated Bengali.

All three of them, and scores of others almost equally great, were either born or nurtured in this metropolis; and that is why throughout the present article I have made no distinction between Bengal and Calcutta. Of course, the former existed long before the people who called the latter into being were known in history; and if Alexander the Great did not penetrate far into India, it was because even he feared the famous war elephants of the Gangaridae, to give the Bengalis their Greek name. But during the last two hundred years the capital has so dominated the province as to become one with it; and this is untrue of another city in the country. Hence the dispute about whom Bombay belongs to; and while Maharashtra and Gujarat can conceivably prosper without Bombay, Bengal will die when parted from Calcutta, as indeed will Calcutta separated from Bengal. Conversely, Bombay, deprived of the Gujaratis, or for that matter of the microscopic Parsi community, may lose its international character; and Calcutta is no less cosmopolitan now that its founders, the British, have abdicated.

VERRIER ELWIN

Do We Really Want to Keep Them in a Zoo?

ONE OF THE CURIOUS criticisms passed almost automatically in India on anthropologists is that they want to keep the tribesmen in zoos or museums for their own purposes. This suggestion was first, as far as I know, made in the Legislative Assembly in February 1936 in a debate on the Excluded Areas, when a number of speakers attacked anthropologists as wishing to keep the primitive people of India "uncivilised" and "in a state of barbarism" in order to add to their "blessed stock of scientific knowledge". And although India has now recognised the importance of anthropology for any intelligent and planned advance of tribal peoples, there are still many who repeat the infantile complaint: indeed if one was to give a word-reaction test to almost any politician of a certain colour, his response to "anthropologist" would certainly be "zoo".

Now it is true that there are, and always have been, people who consider that primitive folk are better than we are, and are therefore better off as they are. They would like to segregate them from the contaminating influences of civilisation and would protect them not only economically, but culturally, from outside exploitation.

But this attitude has nothing to do with anthropology, and in actual fact few anthropologists hold it. Today, indeed, the fashion in anthropology is to study developing rather than static societies, and the blessed stock of scientific knowledge is thus more likely to be augmented when the doors of the zoo are thrown open than when they are kept closed.

It is interesting to find that the correct attitude to tribal peoples was keenly debated hundreds of years ago, long before scientific anthropology was ever thought of, and that precisely the same arguments were used as are used today. Is Man better in a state of Nature or of Art? Is the untutored "savage" happier, more moral, in a word "better" than the sophisticated and urban product of the modern world?

Boswell and Johnson discussed this question several times. Boswell, who after all had personally visited Rousseau, was all for the Noble Savage. Johnson was not. "Don't cant in defence of savages," he exclaimed, and when Boswell attempted to argue for the superior happiness of the savage life, he retorted, "Sir, there can be nothing more false. The savages have no bodily advantages beyond those of civilised men. They have not better health; and as to care or mental uneasiness, they are not above it, but below it, like bears." He thought that the (American) Indians had no affection; had he been born one, he must have died early, for his eyes would not have served him to get food. One evening he poured scorn on those who preferred living among savages. "Now what a wretch that must be, who is content with such conversation as can be had among savages!"

But long before this, the discovery of the New World, with its exciting populations of primitive people, had set all Europe thinking about the problem. Opinion, then as now, was divided. Some were in favour of leaving them alone. Of these Montaigne is an example. He considered that the inhabitants of the "unpolluted and harmless world" of the hills and forests were naturally virtuous as compared to civilised man. In his essay, *Of Cannibals*, he declares that the Indians are only wild in the sense that wild flowers are wild, but that in them are "the true and most profitable virtues and natural properties most lively and vigorous." Civilisation has "bastardised" these virtues, "applying them to the pleasures of our corrupted taste." He regrets that Plato did not live to see the discovery of primitive America, for he might then have given a better picture of the Golden Age.

Many other writers took the same view. Spenser has a gentle noble tribesman in *The Faerie Queene*; Drayton enthused over the reports from America; Beaumont and Fletcher write of "sunburnt Indians, that know no other wealth but Peace and Pleasure." And many deplored the corrupting influence of the first colonists and planters; Fuller spoke of Christian savages who went to convert heathen savages.

Other reporters, however, took a less optimistic view. We find the Indians spoken of as "human beasts"; they are "perfidious, inhuman, all savage"; Sandys says that the Indians, like the Cyclops, are "unsociable amongst themselves and inhuman to strangers." Nowhere is the divergence between the two views set out more plainly than by Shakespeare in *The Tempest*.

In this play, Caliban (whose name has been derived from Carib, an aboriginal of the New World, and cannibal) stands for the Indian, and Prospero for the colonist or planter, and the conflict between them reflects the current controversies about the character and status of primitive man.

Caliban, who is of a "vile race", the product of witchcraft, "a freckled whelp hag-born", scarcely human in appearance, "as disproportioned in his manners as in his shape", is the aboriginal owner of the island on which Prospero and his daughter have been marooned. His own description of the process by which he loses his rights makes rather uncomfortable reading.

> This island's mine, by Sycorax my mother,
> Which thou tak'st from me. When thou cam'st first,
> Thou strok'st me, and made much of me; would'st give me
> Water with berries in it; and teach me how
> To name the bigger light and how the less,
> That burn by day and night: and then I lov'd thee,
> And show'd thee all the qualities o' th' isle,
> The fresh springs, brine-pits, barren place and fertile:
> Curs'd be I that did so!

Yet in taking over tribal territory, Prospero does not neglect some measures of social uplift and education, and in this his daughter Miranda is a keen and efficient assistant. Even though they reduce Caliban to a mere slave and woodcutter, she "pities" him, takes pains to make him speak, teaches him each hour one thing or another.

This is not altogether successful. As Mr Frank Kermode has recently pointed out, "Caliban's education was not only useless, but harmful. He can only abuse the gift of speech; and by cultivating him Prospero brings forth in him 'the briers and darnell of appetites' – lust for Miranda, discontent at his inferior position, ambition, intemperance of all kinds, including a disposition to enslave himself to the bottle of Stephano." Such is, of course, the very common result, even today, of a too-rapid acculturation.

Yet Shakespeare, so much more universal than Johnson, sees also the other side. Caliban is not wholly without virtue; there is a suggestion that he has been wronged; above all, he has an ear for music and, like tribal people elsewhere, he has poetry at command, and for a moment speaks words of sublime beauty. And the representatives of civilisation who follow Prospero to the island are in their way no better than Caliban himself. Stephano and Trinculo are drunken buffoons; Antonio is a malicious degenerate; the life of Alonso is deeply stained with guilt. It is under the inspiration of these representatives of the modern world that Caliban takes to drink and turns treacherously upon his master. It is surely not without significance that Shakespeare shows us this primitive man becoming a "footlicker" of a drunken butler.

And it is interesting, in view of methods that have since been attempted to win the confidence of tribal people, to find Stephano claiming to be descended from the moon in order to impress Caliban.

Shakespeare's view, then, seems to be that, although primitive man is not much good, contact with civilisation can only make him worse.

Throughout the seventeenth century, however, this realistic attitude was obscured by a widespread sentiment in favour of the innocent shepherd, the happy husbandman, the Hortulan Saint. So rich indeed is the poetic material of this period that a Norwegian scholar, Dr Rostvig, has required nearly five hundred pages to exploit it in her recent work, *The Happy Man*. The pastoral tradition of European poetry derived its ideas of the Golden Age from the classical poets, Horace, Virgil and Hesiod, and even from such Latin prose writers as Cato, Varro and Columella who wrote so enthusiastically in praise of agriculture and farming. The life admired by these authors was not altogether "primitive"; it had its elements of comfort and decorum; but it was simple, obscure and self-contained, in sharp contrast to the degraded, mercenary and unhealthy life of the towns. A score of English poets extolled this kind of existence in some such terms as those used by Cowley in a translation of one of the Horatian Odes:

Happy the Man whom bounteous Gods allow
With his own hands Paternal grounds to plough!

Like the first Golden Mortals happy he
From Business and the cares of Money free!
From all the cheats of law he lives secure,
Nor does th' affronts of Palaces endure.

Under the stress of the Civil War and the prevailing Puritanism of the Roundhead movement, "Nature" and the country life became more and more idealised; it was here alone that man could commune with God; it was here that the purest virtues could be practised. The most famous of the writers who infused the classical ideal of the Golden Age with a mystical enthusiasm was the Polish poet Sarbiewski, to whom the Biblical motif of the *Hortus conclusus* or Earthly Paradise was a living reality. He seems to have influenced the Welsh Vaughan and the English Marvell, especially in the latter's garden-poems.

Along with this belief in the innocence and beauty of the uncorrupt life of Nature went the theological doctrine that Adam and Eve, the first of all the tribals, were created perfect – Aristotle is but the ruins of an Adam. Before Darwin, the course of history was commonly supposed to have been steadily downhill, and civilisation was a steady corruption of what had originally been perfect. This led logically to Rousseau's back-to-nature movement in the following century.

One result of this was the emergence of an attitude to life which has been called primitivism, and which has been studied in great detail by a number of American scholars, Lovejoy, Boas and Margaret Fitzgerald. This has been divided into cultural primitivism, which regards modern "uncivilised" societies as being, in all the fundamental values of life, better than civilised populations; and chronological primitivism, which holds that the earlier, pre-civilised periods of human life were the happiest and best. Adam and other tribals are better and happier, partly because they are earlier in time, partly because they lived beyond the Inner Line that circled Eden.

Seventeenth-century primitivism led to an increased interest in primitive peoples, and Mr R.W. Frantz, in an important study of the travellers of the period, has pointed out that "certain voyagers discovered, or thought they discovered, traces of a universal and fixed morality and the prevalence of three cardinal virtues – piety, benevolence and self-control – which seemed to be fundamental to all peoples, whether semi-civilised or totally savage." The idealist was easily able to persuade himself that "the good and noble life was to be lived not in towns and cities, but in the solitude of the American forests or the South Sea Isles."

An interesting result of this was that, unlike later Imperialists who justified themselves as having to bear the white man's burden of native superstition and ignorance, the first colonists tried to encourage immigration to the tribal areas by painting their inhabitants in glowing colours. Thus when Walter Hammond wrote his pamphlets on Madagascar, he called the first of them (published in 1640), "A Paradox, proving that the Inhabitants of the Isle called Madagascar, or St Laurence, are the Happiest People in the World." Who then would not jump at the chance of going to live among them?

Primitives were further divided into "hard" and "soft". In antiquity, says A.O. Lovejoy in his *Documentary History of Primitivism*, "the men of the Golden Age under the Saturnian dispensation were soft primitives, and the imaginary Hyperboreans were usually soft savages; on the other hand, the noble savages par excellence, the Scythians, and the Getae, and later on the Germans were rude, hardy fellows to whom 'Nature' was no gentle or indulgent mother; they were extolled for the fewness of their desires and their consequent indifference to the luxuries and even the comforts of civilised life." In more recent times, the soft, sensuous and elegant primitives of Tahiti or Bali have excited the admiration of artists and poets, while the virile hardy primitives of, let us say, the North-East Frontier of India have won the respect of soldiers.

Even at this comparatively early period, there is evident, in the attraction felt for the "soft" primitives, a delight in the erotic freedom, the lack of inhibitions and the sexual innocence supposed to have been enjoyed by man before he was corrupted by modern society and its rules. It is significant that the expression "the Noble Savage" did not originate, as is so often thought, with Rousseau, but with the astonishing Mrs Aphra Behn, that ardent missionary of free love, whose poems, plays and stories constantly compare the advantages of the simple rural life with the frustrations of sophistication.

In that blest Golden Age, when Man was young;
When the whole Race was vigorous and strong;
When Nature did her wondrous dictates give,
And taught the Noble Savage how to live . . .
When every sense to innocent delight
Th' agreeing elements unforc'd invite.

The hero of Mrs Behn's *Oroonoko*, though a "native" of Surinam, is a great gentleman who found happiness by refusing to be "civilised". Mrs Behn was no anthropologist and she assumed, of course quite wrongly, that primitive man had no need for external government (which only existed to curb the greed and ambition of educated persons) and enjoyed all the raptures of free love. Or as Thomson was to put it later: "The romp-loving miss is hauled about in gallantry robust."

Other poets of this century who exalted the "savage" were Thomas Heyrick, whose poem, *The Submarine Voyage*, describes the people of the South Sea Islands as "happy in ignorance", and "strangers to care"; Waller in his *Battle of the Summer Islands* draws an idyllic picture of the inhabitants of plantain-shaded atolls of sensuous beauty and ease. And the great Dryden himself, in a famous couplet, spoke of the happy days

> Ere the base laws of servitude began,
> When wild in woods the noble savage ran.

The last thing that the poets and travellers of this period wanted was to "improve" or "uplift" these aboriginals; what they desired was to go and share their lot. There was no question of keeping them in a museum; they wanted to enjoy their earthly paradise.

In the following century, the voyages of Captain Cook and other explorers provided factual support for these sentiments. According to Captain Cook, the "savages" of Australia may indeed appear to be the most wretched people upon earth, but in reality "they are far more happy than we Europeans, being wholly unacquainted not only with the superfluous but with the necessary conveniences so much sought after in Europe; they are happy in not knowing the use of them." And visits to Tahiti and the Friendly Islands confirmed this picture of the Noble Savage.

This fitted very conveniently into the more advanced thinking of certain philosophers and revolutionaries, especially in France. The doctrine of original sin, it was supposed, was discredited by what Bougainville found in the Pacific. The child is happier and better than the man. The existing state of modern society appears decadent and corrupt before the peaceful and truthful civilisation of the islanders; it must therefore be overthrown. Mr Christopher Lloyd epitomises the views of Diderot, whose article on Savages was so subversive that it was omitted from the Paris edition of the French Encyclopaedia. In a remarkable dialogue, which he pretended was a supplement to Bougainville's Tahiti journal, Diderot "accused his countrymen of acting the part of the serpent in this new Eden. He makes an old islander beg him to go away and leave the natives in peace. Otherwise such men as he will return with a cross in one hand and a gun in the other to enslave their bodies and poison their minds. For civilisation, according to Diderot, was indeed a kind of poison injected into the mind of natural man, thereby creating a sort of war within ourselves which lasts all our lives. Natural man is at odds with artificial man, and the best description of the unhappy product was, in the words of his friend Buffon, *Homo Duplex*."

But now came the new European Imperialism and with it a great expansion of the missionary movement. Colonists and missionaries alike had to justify their existence by showing how necessary they were to the heathen world. From now onwards primitive man was painted in the darkest terms. Even in Java, as Bishop Heber suggested, though every prospect pleased, man was vile, blind, benighted.

Can we whose souls are lighted
With wisdom from on high,
Can we to men benighted
The lamp of life deny?

We have come a long way from Cook and Hawkesworth, from Boswell, Rousseau and Diderot. To them primitive man was not fallen, he was *better* than modern man; we had much to learn from him; and the best thing we could do for him was to leave him alone. To the missionary and the colonist, however, primitive man seemed to exemplify the ancient doctrine of original sin, and it was above all necessary that he should be saved.

Even in recent times there have been men, such as Gauguin, R.L. Stevenson, Pierre Loti, and Herman Melville, who have insisted that the "aboriginal" is no mere Caliban, but in many ways has the advantage of us. A typical, though now unfashionable, view is expressed in the words used by John Collier of the English peasants of the northern hills of Hampshire: "These are the best people I have ever met in my life, far and away the best, better than any I know among artists or writers, or any rich people, or any of the proletariat. You would laugh if I were to describe the stringent measures I would take, had I the power, to preserve them from the wanton fools who would degrade them, or the insolent, presumptuous fools who endeavour to improve them."

It is surely evident that, whether the idea of the tribesman's superiority is right or wrong, the suggestion that he should be left alone in his peace and happiness has nothing to do with the anthropologists.

In modern times in India there have been three different attitudes to the problem. The former British Government tended on the whole to leave the tribesmen alone, partly because the task of administration, especially in the wild border areas, was difficult and unrewarding; partly from a desire to quarantine the tribes from possible political infection; and partly, I think, because certain officers sincerely held the Rousseau–Diderot doctrine that the people were better and happier as they were.

In sharp distinction to this is a policy of "assimilation" which has become very popular since Independence. Both Christian missionaries and Hindu social reformers have, in their different ways, desired to see the primitives civilised, their "inferior" social customs and ideas eliminated and their identity assimilated either into the Christian Church or into the general framework of Hindu society.

The Christian missionaries have had striking successes in some tribal areas, though they have failed in others. Especially in Assam, they have converted a high percentage of such tribes as the Lushais, Khasis and the so-called Naga groups. The Christian Khasis have preserved their matriarchal social structure, and the Lushais and Nagas have retained certain aspects of their life (in particular their very beautiful hand-weaving), but in the main they have lost most of what is distinctively tribal and have adopted a semi-Western culture.

Similarly, the ambitious programmes of education, reform and change now being initiated by most of the State Governments, while bringing many economic and social benefits to the people, are likely to bring to an end the older values, good and bad alike, of tribal life. For though a sincere desire for tribal welfare is now everywhere apparent, this is not matched by an equal interest in or respect for tribal culture. You cannot make an omelette without breaking eggs, and the continued existence of the tribes as tribes is regarded as of less importance than the march of civilisation. This policy has already created many examples of the *Homo Duplex*.

Between these two extremes of doing too little and doing too much there is a third policy, with which the name of the Prime Minister, Mr Nehru, is associated. This may be summarised as one which approaches tribal life and culture with respect and the tribesmen with an affection which eliminates any possibility of superiority. It would bring the best things of modern life to the tribes, but in such a way that these will not destroy the traditional way of life, but will activate and develop all that is good in it. In a number of remarkable speeches, Mr Nehru has spoken of the strong attraction which he has for the tribesmen and has described how he approached them "in a spirit of comradeship and not like someone aloof who had come to look at them, examine them, weigh them, measure them and report about them or to try and make them conform to another way of life." He has given serious warnings of the dangers of the "assimilation" approach. Pointing out the disastrous effect of "the so-called European civilisation" on tribal peoples in other parts of the world, "putting to an end their arts and crafts and their simple ways of living," he declared that "now to some extent, there is danger of the so-called Indian civilisation having this disastrous effect, if we do not check and apply it in the proper way."

"I am alarmed," he said, "when I see – not only in this country, but in other great countries, too – how anxious people are to shape others according to their own image or likeness, and to impose on them their particular way of living." He declared that he was not sure which, the modern or the tribal, was the better way of living. "In some respects I am quite certain theirs is better." "They possess a variety of culture and are in many ways certainly not backward." "There is no point in trying to make of them a second-rate copy of ourselves." He emphasised the importance of encouraging the tribal languages, so that they would not only prevail but flourish. He insisted that a measure of protection must be given so that "no outsider can take possession of tribal lands or forests or interfere with them in any way except with their consent and goodwill." He hoped that the high sense of discipline, the power to enjoy life, the love of dance and song would endure among the tribesmen. Schemes for welfare, education, communications, medical relief were no doubt essential, yet "one must always remember, however, that we do not mean to interfere with their way of life, but want to help them to live it." "The Government of India," he said again, "is determined to help the tribal people to grow according to their own genius and tradition."

The same policy has been admirably stated by Mr Jairamdas Daulatram, Governor of Assam. "Each section of our large population," he has said, "contributes to the making of the nation, in the same manner as each flower helps to make a garden. Every flower has the right to grow according to its own laws of growth; has the right to enrich and develop its own colour and form and to spread its own fragrance to make up the cumulative beauty and splendour of the garden. I would not like to change my roses into lilies nor my lilies into roses. Nor do I want to sacrifice my lovely orchids or rhododendrons of the hills."

We do not want to preserve the tribesmen as museum specimens, but equally we do not want to turn them into clowns in a circus. We do not want to stop the clock of progress, but we do want to see that it keeps the right time. We may not believe in the myth of the Noble Savage, but we do not want to create a class of Ignoble Serfs.

Now this attitude poses a serious problem to the administration. The assimilation policy which holds, broadly speaking, that there is not very much to be said for tribal life; that if it disappears it will not matter greatly; that the "backward" must be brought forward and that the low are to be "uplifted", is simple and straightforward; it is logical, and it brings many benefits – at a price. So did the British policy of leaving well alone – though at a different price.

But the new attitude, the Nehru attitude, has complex implications. For, unhappily, tribal culture is the most delicate thing in the world. Of it we may say what Oscar Wilde said of innocence: it is a delicate, exotic fruit – touch it, and the bloom is gone. Tribal social organisation in India has to some extent managed to survive, though many acculturated tribal communities have suffered a tragic moral decline. The tolerant influences of Hinduism have enriched tribal religion with a loftier ethic and vitalised it with a nobler conception of deity, but at the same time they have often brought the more dubious accretions of new gods to be placated and new taboos to be observed.

The contact of civilisation has generally had an adverse effect on tribal art and culture. His exquisite taste for design and colour disappears when a tribesman enters a shop in the bazaar. The splendid tribal dress and ornamentation is rapidly abandoned in favour of a parody of Western clothing. The tribal languages have shown an alarming lack of vitality when confronted by a system of education in another tongue. In some areas the dance has died out altogether, in others it has become woefully debased. The tribal craftsman does not seem able to maintain his standards before external competition.

The task set by Mr Nehru, therefore, is no easy one, for it involves several ideals that have rarely been found compatible. The first is to preserve, strengthen and develop all that is best in tribal society, culture, art and language. The second is to protect tribal economic rights. The third is to unite and integrate the tribes in a true heart-unity with India as a whole, so that they may play a full part in her life. And the last is to develop welfare and educational facilities so that every tribesman may have an equal opportunity with his fellow-citizens of the open country and the plains.

This original, indeed unique, conception, at once scientific and humane, steers a middle path between the two older ways of approach and, if properly applied, should have the advantages of both and avoid their dangers. It is difficult, but it is surely right. It is supported both by the findings of anthropological science and the warnings of history. It is a charter of religious, social, economic and cultural rights. It is the embodiment of the spirit or reverence. It is a gospel of friendliness and equality.

Here, for almost the first time in history, the conflicting attitudes of Boswell and Johnson, of Rousseau and Bishop Heber are reconciled. The new knowledge that anthropology has brought has enabled us to see tribal people without sentiment, but equally without prejudice. Isolation in the modern world is impossible; it would not be desirable even if it was possible. The old controversy about zoos and museums has long been dead. We do not want to preserve tribal culture in its colour and beauty to please the scientists or to attract the tourists. But we see now that the tribesmen will be of the greatest service to India if they are able to bring their own peculiar treasures into the common life, not by becoming second-rate copies of ourselves. Their moral virtues, their self-reliance, their courage, their artistic gifts, their cheerfulness are things we need. They also need the comradeship, the technical knowledge, the wider world-view of the plains. The great problem is how to develop the synthesis without destroying the rare and precious values of tribal life.

R.K. NARAYAN

Elephant in the Pit

At dawn we motor to a village about fifty miles from Coimbatore and reach a lonely farm-house in the shadow of the Anaimalai Hills. From there we travel in a bullock cart towards the hill, bumping over boulders and wading through little streams. Columns of people are seen moving along under the bright sun to the foot of the hill. Presently we find that a camp has grown up where the vendors of plantains, oranges and coloured aerated water are carrying on a brisk trade. The aerated water is being manufactured on the spot – the available water (in the puddles and cesspools) is strained through old, discoloured Turkish towels into large pans, then bottled and given a dozen turns on an aerator riveted to the edge of a wooden handcart, and sold at once to thirsty customers besieging the handcart: the only difference between this and the water in the nearby pond being that this is coloured and you have to knock off a tinsel lid before drinking out of the bottle.

People are crowding around a pit into which an elephant has fallen. I have never seen an elephant looking more bewildered and miserable. We are generally used to seeing an elephant in a better state – walking majestically with calmness and assurance in its eyes. But here it is in a most undignified position, thrust into a pit and made to look up at a vast, curiosity-stricken crowd.

The people in these parts seem to have perfected the technique of elephant-catching. All along the foot of the hills they have dug circular pits about fifteen feet deep, covered with bamboo, camouflaged with leaves and grass. Away from these pits they have cultivated many acres of *cholam*, whose green, waving stalks tempt the elephant in the hills to come down when he looks about for something to munch at dusk. Treading the ground anywhere here is risky and sooner or later he goes down. The moment he has fallen, hundreds of persons, who have watched his movement from the treetops, surround the pit and get busy. Heavy logs are drawn over the pit and lashed together in several cross-layers. The elephant is now bottled up. They then manage to pass down ropes and loop them around his neck and feet. Presently heavy ropes, thick as temple-chariot tugs, emerge from the pit and go up a hundred feet or more, out into the hands of nearly two hundred persons ranged about the mouth of the pit. They have the appearance of a tug-of-war team. They are now able to steer and turn the elephant in any direction they please. They are able to prevent his getting entangled in the ropes and also his attempts at knocking down the sides of the pit with hefty kicks. Yelling, shouting human beings, running hither and thither, gaping at him, and interfering with every movement of his, must seem to him peculiarly monstrous creations of God.

They keep throwing at him pots of cold water, not only to keep him cool but also to create enough mire to make his foothold slippery. In a short while, his head and trunk are covered with clay, his feet are in a mess.

Very soon the information spreads to all the surrounding villages that an elephant has "fallen". A vast crowd turns up in buses, bullock carts, cycles, and jeeps, and spreads itself about in picnic groups.

Now the next big event is the arrival of a trained elephant from a jungle eighteen miles away. Everyone knows it by name and mentions it with respect – a famous elephant named Ayyapan. They expect him to arrive at ten a.m. but he is really sighted at three in the afternoon. He presents a perfect picture of an elephant, very tall and slightly arched on top – the prototype of the one we used to see on the covers of illustrated journals of old times. Matters get brisker now. A most elaborate roping of the captive goes on. It is tethered on all sides.

Ayyapan comes up and in a businesslike manner unties the logs, lifts them and puts them away in a neat pile. The excitement and shouting are tremendous. People are ordering and directing and making a deafening uproar. Most of the logs have now been removed. In a moment the captive will be out and will try to run away, but Ayyapan will pilot him into a steel enclosure in the farm-house, where two veteran trainers, whose equipment seems to be unlimited elephant lingo and a thin cane, will cajole and bully the captive into entering the world of man and living on good terms with him. But unfortunately just when the climax is reached, there comes a sudden lull. Ayyapan is driven away in haste a furlong off, the swarm of workers withdraw from the pit, and the tug-of-war team slacken their hold. All shouting ceases and a silence falls on the gathering. The sun is going down. The captive elephant is dead. In the melee of instructions and counter-instructions, the rope was tugged too violently in a wrong direction: it wrenched the neck of the elephant and probably snapped its spinal column. It raised its trunk a moment ago in readiness to come out, but the next moment dropped down dead. I shall never forget the fixed stare in its eyes as it lies back half-submerged in the mire, its trunk lying limp across its tusk. The crowd turns back and files away across the *cholam* fields in a solemn silent mood as the night comes on.

BUDDHADEVA BOSE

To Remember Is to Live Again

THERE WAS A TIME in my life when I was marooned in a women's college in Pittsburgh. I lived on the campus and ate my meals at the school where they said grace and sang "Happy Birthday". On Fridays there was execrably cooked fish; Sunday "suppers" were the equivalent of high tea. For lodgings I had a couple of rooms in an attic reached by a flight of steep stairs. It yielded views of rosy skies in evenings in autumn, but as winter came and the heating system revealed irremediable flaws, I nearly froze in bed, trying to read Thomas Mann or listening to the howling of boreal winds. I was alone, I scarcely knew anybody in town, nor was I inclined to go out of my way to make casual acquaintances. The girls I taught twice a week were remarkable for good looks but showed no signs of that high scholastic ability which I was later to find among American students. Reading my copious mail and answering it was my chief diversion. Thus I survived week after week, dreaming of a time when I would be able to see a little more of America, venturing outside steely Pittsburgh.

By a happy turn of events, that time came sooner than I expected. The prisoner was freed; he was even enabled to make a coast-to-coast tour. It was during this period of exhilarating freedom that I took the unusual step of visiting Henry Miller at Big Sur. Unusual, because by nature I am hesitant about

he had painted. Within the next five minutes I became one of his family.

Never, as long as I live, will I forget the few days I had spent with the Millers, days snatched out of a somewhat hectic lecture tour, during which my brain had stored more impressions than it knew what to do with – faces and places which dissolved one into another, friendships ended when scarcely begun, landscapes whose message I hadn't yet deciphered. Repose I found with the Millers, something more than pleasure, something humanly shared and assimilated into experience. Henry, turned sixty, slim, straight, grey-haired, his face kind yet austere; Eve, his wife, full-lipped, fresh-complexioned, a model of mature beauty; Tony and Val (Henry's children by an earlier marriage about whom he has written so often and joyously), both blue-eyed, flaxen-haired, charming, amiable. Miller gave me the impression of being loose-limbed, relaxed, capable of hours of inaction, hours of reverie, slow and gentle in speech, careful in the choice of words, a marvellous listener, graceful in the gestures of his hands. I enjoyed the points of contrast between him and Eve. Henry had the "un-American" habit of writing his letters in longhand (what was more, with the nearly demoded fountain-pen instead of the "ball-point" which had already started on its triumphal march), whereas Eve never "penned" a line except on a typewriter. Before I had known her for one hour, Eve urged on me to call her by her first name (quite a usual procedure in America and one which I since learnt to appreciate), but Henry, while drawing me into the warmth of his friendship and affection, never used any form of address except "Mr Bose", which revealed a certain temperamental affinity between him and us of the Old World. No doubt his long expatriation in Europe had left its mark on Miller; he seemed world-weary, rather reserved, whereas Eve, so far as I could make out, had all the charm, the frankness, the vivacity, and the exuberance of the modern American woman.

Even more remarkable was the contrast between Miller's literary style and his personality: the latter, impressive in a quiet, subdued way, reticent almost, marked with a certain "holding back" of himself, meditative, part-Oriental; and the former a torrent of energy, a tide of American vigour, a medley of ideas, quotations, narratives, allusions, reflections, and memories, a gust of enthusiasm which showed no respect for "form" and dispensed with those undertones, nuances, and convolutions which constitute the French idea of "le style". How bold and direct and straightforward was everything he wrote, and how restrained his conversation!

What did we talk about? Books and writers, Henry Miller's joustings with life, Big Sur, India, America. "You won't find a single home in America where someone will say to you, 'This was my grandfather's chair.' We are becoming a race of nomads." Reflecting on my flat on Rashbehari Avenue where one room served me as bed-living-room-cum-study, I said that to most people today ancestral furniture might be an embarrassment rather than a valued possession. "There is much to say for the dynamism of American life," I added. "But one needs some centre, after all," Miller replied. "Something one can hold on to, some idea of home." I recalled a passage in *The Colossus of Maroussi* where Miller says how he taught himself to "feel at home at home". I asked him if he had read Tagore. No, he had not, but his temple had a niche for Ramakrishna. He wanted to go to India, just to see a real saint. "Oh, no," I protested with some alarm, "saints are rare everywhere. One of the misfortunes of India is that anyone who claims to be a saint is regarded as one by the multitude." The transition from Ramakrishna to Rimbaud was easy enough and Rimbaud led to

Blaise Cendrars and his (Miller's) life in Paris. When Eve joined us after washing the dishes I asked her what she thought of life at Big Sur. Well, it was sort of fun, with the nearest shopping centre in Carmel, not even a drug-store anywhere near, and no telephones. (This was in 1954; I do not know about later.) One had to drive miles for the smallest necessity, one had to stir out in any weather to fetch one's mail. "This is also the American way, isn't it?" I suggested. "The spirit of the pioneers." "That's true." Eve nodded, maybe without much conviction. "But I do miss the telephone. I've never lived without one, and sometimes I can hear it ringing even here."

As the night deepened and we re-filled our glasses, Miller let fall a few words on a topic he has written about so movingly: the time of his youth and hardship. There was a time when he worked with Western Union in New York, a time when he was unemployed and did not want to be employed, when he went about hungry and traded his topcoat for a taxi-ride at the end of winter, but never a time when he did not devour books and gaze at art-dealers' windows, never a time when he did not want to be a writer. "I became one," he added with a wry smile, "but even now there may be days when I can't spare a dime to write a friend abroad." I realised his situation was like certain middle-aged Bengali authors whose work had brought them fame but very little money – a most embarrassing combination.

Miller and I parted for the night at the door of the log-cabin which he had rented for me to sleep in. Near it was the Pacific Bend, famed for its hot sulphur springs. In a glimmering moonlight the ocean was faintly visible. I gave the landscape a few minutes before turning in. A thin moon hanging over the sea and flattened by the sea-fogs; above it, towering darkness reaching up to the zenith, perforated by stars. My cabin lay in the shadow of a huge hill of which I could make out but the barest outline. There was a rippling breeze, not a cat in sight, not a whirr of a passing automobile; only a faint swish of the ocean and the breathing of the voiceless trees. As I switched off the light, the darkness grew as black as a mother's womb and in my ears the silence began to buzz like cicadas. I had an intense feeling of the reality of the night – deep, dark, mysterious, overwhelming, a flood on which my consciousness was rocked, not to slumber, but back and forth between memories of loves and friendships, from one dream to another, dreams of happiness found and lost, and regained but to be lost again. What I felt was in fact an incipient poem, faintly tapping at my door, like a waif left out in the cold. I wanted to let it in; a first line formed itself in my mind, a vague shape, shadowy stanzas, ghostly rhythms, but before I could get any further the night itself was obliterated in sleep. The next thing I remember is the Pacific, sharply curved like a half-moon, clinging as it were to the earth with two arms outstretched, seen in the morning light from a window of the restaurant perched on the edge of the ocean. Miller came round just as I was finishing breakfast.

Big Sur evokes in my mind vivid splashes of colour, emanating from the redwood forest where green and purple shadows darkened the hour of noon; from the Big Sur river, moss-green and translucent, slowly gliding among boulders, overhung with vegetation more lush and green than I had ever seen alongside the creeks in East Bengal; from one or two oceanic sunsets which seemed to have come out of Baudelaire and Rimbaud. I visited that bend of the Pacific where the water was steaming hot and one could smell the sulphur from a mile away; I went through the ritual of the sulphur bath; I saw an open-air exhibition of local paintings. But of people I saw no one except the Miller family, and I saw them all the time, eating my meals with them and going about in their station wagon, but not going out much.

It was this circumstance, I think, which gave a peculiar quality to this visit, a roundness which the years have not blurred, a savour which I can still distinctly recall.

From the moment of my arrival to that of my taking off for Portland, there was never an hour when Miller made himself unavailable, although I am sure he had lots to do. Nor did he let me spend a single dollar; he paid for the log-cabin and even my breakfasts, frustrating all my efforts to prevent him. All his time he gave me, all his attention. And yet he had known me only through a few letters and very brief presence; he did not know my language and had no idea of the books I had written and wanted to write; that part of me which I cannot but regard as my real self was completely hidden from his view. But I had read some of his works and was familiar with his background and ideas; even before meeting him I had known him in a way in which there was no possibility of his knowing me. And this I thought was the most touching aspect of his friendship – that he had accepted me on trust, as though he had discerned the worth which exists, if at all, not in me, properly speaking, but in what I write in Bengali.

For quite some time Miller remained one of my strongest links with America; his letters reached me in Paris and Rome, then in Calcutta followed by parcels of his books with touching inscriptions. A second meeting did not take place, despite my subsequent travels in the Occident; the correspondence naturally flagged. Even so, I occasionally heard from him, at intervals of months or years, through some magazine or clipping he had mailed, or a phone call from one of his friends passing through Calcutta. And I heard about him, too, from mutual friends in New York, who told me he was separated from Eve, had abandoned Big Sur, returned to Europe but had an alternative home in Pacific Palisades, California. I rejoiced over his soaring sales and his legal and moral triumph with *Tropic of Cancer.* In one way or another I have felt close to him, despite distance and silence, always, since the time of our meeting at Big Sur. It no longer seems very likely that I shall see him again, but I know I shall remember him as a friend, as a good, wonderful, big-hearted man, and a writer of significance.

As I finish writing these words, Henry Miller arrives at the age of seventy-five. Comes the time for an "appraisal" of his works, for the tiger to be put into an academic cage. The American zeal for research did not leave him alone even during his Big Sur days, and latterly I have heard his name mentioned in hushed tones by Harvard undergraduates. Soon the professors will have their hooks on him in right earnest; he will be dissected, labelled, anatomised, atomised. Some will say (perhaps this has been said already) that he represents that phase of twentieth-century literature which was nihilistic, perverted, anti-art, that in his novels the concepts of character and situation are demolished, that his novels are not novels at all, but long, rambling monologues of a non-professional philosopher, that his essays could be anthologised to make a Henry Miller novel. Others, because of his explorations into the mysteries of sex and his flouting of formal conventions, will make him a precursor of Robbe-Grillet and the "new novel". Perhaps he will be described as an American D.H. Lawrence – and a writer whose mania was confession.There will be some truth in all this. True, he is one of the least "objective" of writers, breaks through the distinction between reality and fiction, the "true" and the "invented" story. In a sense everything he has written is about himself; his Rimbaud is another incarnation of Henry Miller, his Big Sur is an overflow of Henry Miller, even his Greece is an extension of his eccentricities. It is also true that this is one of the reasons why his books give us such a delicious sense of freedom, of release from our oppressive analytical intellect. But I hope the American tone of his writings will also be noted, despite his avowed "anti-Americanism". He has a sense of wonder, a receptivity, a sponge-like quality of mind, and a love of Nature, which links him with classical American writers, especially Whitman and Thoreau. (I think a very profitable comparison may be made between *Walden* and Miller's *Big Sur and the Oranges of Hieronymus Bosch*; they belong to the same indefinite genre and have a similar philosophy.) It seems to me that Miller retains the essence of the Brooklyn boy who ran away from home and finally made good; I perceive in him a certain innocence, reflected in his wide-eyed, open-armed attitude to life and the verve with which he plunges into it, which distinguishes him from his European contemporaries, such as Aldous Huxley and Jean-Paul Sartre. What Miller said of Whitman may as well be said of him, that he liked a great many things and disliked very few. His books make us feel that it is still possible to be happy – in Brooklyn, Big Sur, Paris, Greece, Tibet – anywhere. And just because this feeling comes to me very seldom, I value Henry Miller and his books, as I admire the Brahmanical fastidiousness with which he has abjured all temptations – money, drugs, politics and suchlike – that are likely to bedevil a writer in our time.

G.V. DESANI

The Benares that Was

I RAN AWAY FROM home thrice and for many years the major conflict with myself was concerned with a compelling wanderlust. I can, *ergo*, find my way about in Cairo or Jerusalem, Mombasa or London, Athens or Istanbul.

Growing up in places, some cities become your cornerstones. Varanasi – which is the new name for Benares – is such a cornerstone for me. The two men whose *vidya* (secret craft) caused me the greatest (temporary) suffering and brought me the greatest (temporary) happiness, I met in Varanasi.

Here is a contrasting view of the city from an equally widely travelled man: "Laughter! People laugh, don't they? I used to laugh. But nobody in this holy hovel of Hindu hokum laughs unless he cackles like a maniac. Only death here, yapping monkeys, cows on your porch, and crazy people drinking sewer water, or praying to a concrete lad with an elephant's head . . ." (*Sewer water:* water from the river. Sewage is discharged into the Ganges. *Concrete lad:* Varanasi's exalted elephant-headed god Ganesha, the *siddha* Vinayaka.)

Gordon Sinclair, the author of the above impression (John Murray, London, 1933), arrived in India during Holi,

> . . . on a day set aside to honour the feminine biological function called menstruation. A hundred thousand Hindu hooligans ran right through the streets and bazaars squirting red ink, purple dye and green acid on every moving thing, from Brahmani bull to ruling

> rajahs. That night of the menstrual holiday, eclipse stood over the moon of India and found a hundred million shrieking ignoramuses lining the sacred river, rhythmically clapping hands. I crowded among ascetics, yogis, sadhus and other smelly saints to the steps leading to water. The priests were moaning and groaning up and down the ghat, telling the wide-eyed hooligans that the moon was being eaten by the demon. This world would be eaten, too, they said, unless the mob kicked in with silver . . .

Perhaps you have noticed, too, that mice don't like drafts. Birds like drafts. Why? Rats hate light. Birds love it. Why? I am bothered by several such questions these days.

Human behaviour is comparatively easy to explain. For instance, I know why Varanasi disagrees with the blasé traveller. But here is a mature judgement from the psychologists: Desire – attraction, liking; and distaste – revulsion, dislike – are cultivated emotions. Adult humans teach such things to the young. Explaining, rationalising, justifying, comes *after*. And the testing procedure for such group behaviour is near enough scientific. A scientific hypothesis is tested on an accurate prediction test. Water would boil at so many degrees F. And one can – near enough – predict the emotional response of a group of adult non-Hindus and adult Hindus to Varanasi and the river. To wash off one's sins, no more potent means than the Ganges exists. Incidentally, one cannot make accurate predictions about individuals.

I went to live in Varanasi for personal reasons. I was searching for a healer. *Please* – I don't want to bore anyone, but I was terribly unhappy. (*Who isn't?* Anyway, I did not know then that to be unhappy is rather necessary: as it is to die, if you would go to heaven.) I also wanted to know how miracles are performed. The position I have taken up today is that to skip, to doodle, or to laugh, are miracles.

A few days after arriving in Varanasi, I visited a pretty, private ghat. The two feet or so wide platform and the steps leading to the river were small because the good widow could not afford a larger ghat. It was a moonlit night and a heap of saffron flowers – offering to the river – on the resplendent marble, and the flickering lamps floating down the river, the utterly *noble* lustre upon the swords of silver – so I fancied the waves – overwhelmed me. The throaty, strangely alliterative hymn of praises, the *arati*, offered at the Visvanatha temple, heard a day or two after, affected me deeply too: "*. . . Tan dhik tan dhik . . . dhinaka dhinaka . . . Hariharaho! . . . Trisuladhariho! . . . Halahalaho! . . . Kailaseho, Kailase! . . . Gangadhariho, Gandadhari!*" In spite of the warnings – of blindness, paralysis, permanent deformity – I spent a night alone inside the Visvanatha temple: a *most* generous and unprecedented gesture by the Chief Priest, the *mahanta* of the temple. Such emotional occurrences result in enthusiasms.

Within a year, though I was deeply involved in the life of the city – I saw it a shade too close – and with the problems, conflicts and antagonisms, which must be, wherever human beings in such numbers have house and hearth and those things – speaking as an addict of the poetic, the beautiful and the strange – disenchanted me.

And before I learnt the learned trick of describing *all* propositions as equally valid, *all* views as *one* and the *same*, *all* doctrines as *one* and the *same*, *all* religions . . . I happened to be on the plane of ignorance, *māyā*, duality – *dwaitam* – you see, and duly discriminated between *health* and *disease*, *beauty* and *deformity*, *boys* and *girls*, *poverty* and *plenty*, *hunger*, *thirst* and *satisfaction*, and the stages *surfeit*, *glut*, *hogging*. I was also preoccupied, pardon, with the notions of the *useful* and the *non-* (to whom?).

With such dim ideas, the only thing to do was to study *evil* – some call it occultism – and the author whereof. No apology is needed as far as the enlightened – the sages, the *jnanis* – are concerned. *All* Good and Evil being *one* and the *same* apart, it was Milton – was it not? – who described Satan as the Prince of Intellectuals. Well, that is flattering to us sons of Satan, and Satan is *fun*.

I have hundreds of pages of notes on Varanasi. It wasn't easy. To begin with, the environment.

My first summer at Varanasi's suburb Sarnath – for a year I lived in a cottage generously conceded to me by the reverend *bhikhus* of the Mahabodhi Society – was memorable for an unforeseen reason: a sudden and violent advance of living things. It all started with the birds.

As the summer heat swelled upon us as a curse, a bad kind of madness came over them. The noise they made was – hundreds of alien, immigrant crows among them – *insufferable*. Then came the mango fleas. I did not know such creatures existed. These suck your blood. Everyone slept in the open and the noise made by jackals at night – prowling and toting around paltry *shikar* – made (uninterrupted) sleep impossible. White ants arrived soon after. These could – did – lick off the ground heavy and venerable books in a matter of hours. There were scorpions and cobras, too, and the magpies. These things – in hundreds and fifties – would settle down on grass for gossip and hops, and it all started with a chatter, in the morning (yes) and sometimes earlier, if they were fooled by a lighter sky and themselves lost sleep. Because of them, I broke down twice and cried. ("For God's sake, shut up, will you!")

At 115 F. in the shade – without ice, fans, humidifiers, air conditioners, no electricity was supplied to Sarnath those days – to say nothing of the dust storms, the fiery *loo* winds, the cholera epidemic, and water from open and infected wells, *and* the mosquitoes, it was a challenge. You needed faith of a fiend to remain alive and put.

In the month of June, one morning, the first thing, I found the floor of the cottage black and grey and *moving*. I happen to be used to horror – Edgar Poe and others apart, I happened to have seen freak accidents and people's arms torn off from a blast – and I do not frighten easily. And the stirring floor – the genial Postmaster of Sarnath, Kalida Chakravarti, who is learned in such matters, explained, answering an urgent summons – was hundreds of thousands upon thousands of ants moving in: and the grey part, he explained patiently, was an optical illusion caused by the eggs. ("Can't find my glasses. What eggs?" "Those that they carry in their mouths.") *And* this sort of thing. You happen to be a guest at a feast and ceremoniously fed a rare and expensive fish: a man-eater. The genus feeds on the corpses floating down the river: of lepers, cholera cases, all kinds of casualties. This sort of tidings, passed on to you casually by your host during the meal, can bring on an attack of urticaria – even though the living black-and-grey pall on the floor merely shook you.

The next year, I quit. I moved over to Sigra, to the Buddha Mandir – the alcove, pantry and the parlour generously conceded by the Ven. U. Kittima of the Burma Kuti.

In the Buddha's day – citing the venerable *Ambattha Sutta* – there were about professional people, with pretensions to holiness, who used to practise fortune-telling, reading marks on hands and feet, divining omens and auguries: and they interpreted dreams, read the gnawings of mice, dealt in charms, laid ghosts, knew poisons, acted the marriage broker, predicted rain, specialised in secret medicine, and pursued similar other – thus the Buddha – "low arts". They still do. And there are people who specialise in *fascinating, immobilising, causing enmity* – between friends, husband and wife, lovers, partners – and *pulling* (*akarsana*, calling into submission persons from far and near). Both men and women adepts – *siddhas* – are involved professionally in these matters and such necessities as cotton carded by a virgin (a *kumari*), vomit of the crow, droppings of the monkey, and *mahisa rudra* – buffalo blood – are available to order. It was in Varanasi that I learnt, among other unrevealed things, to identify by sign and smell genuine lard – human, not hog: and *not* the stuff that can be gathered from the oozing half-cremated bodies at the Manikarnika Ghat but – my friends taught me – got from the grocer. Human fat, needed for the ritual lamp in certain magical work, is procurable.

Magic is practised for all sorts of reasons: to banish an enemy, to exile a client's creditor, landlord, or moneylender, to cause blindness, to set fire to a man's house, to starve his cattle (the animals would refuse fodder and die of starvation), to hold a man or woman in subjection (*vasikarana*), to make anyone *nirlaja* (without a sense of shame), to astound (to make *chakita*), to make flavourless (*gandhahina*) a man's meat and drink (to spoil it for him), to break a man's pots and pans, to kill his horse, to make him sleepless, to madden him, to make him impotent.

A number of Varanasi *siddhas* specialise in finding buried treasure. I did not see any alchemists although I had heard of them. I met some exponents of *kaya-kalpa* (rejuvenation). I learnt in Varanasi to be buried underground for half an hour. It is a trick. There is ample air inside the pit but your breathing must be shallow to the point of no-breathing. This is achieved by concentration upon a fixed image. (I found it easy to concentrate on the image of a former girlfriend. The guru, in the next pit, was concentrating on "God", he said.) The fear of darkness, suffocation, cramps, of snakes drilling through to you, of rats gnawing their way to you, and losing confidence in the hirelings up the pit to lift the lid on time, and the potent anxiety of being bounded, in duress and landlocked, can only be overcome by watching a man go through with it and doing it yourself. The same guru, incidentally, offered to teach me to eat with antidotal impunity a snake – a cobra, hood and all.

There are masters whose crafts – to meet face to face your *chhaya purusha*, the *hamzat*, your *etheric* Double – demand such exclusive disciplines as vowing never to look at your privy parts. Such a vow, as soon as breathed – this is a law – would lead to a terrific struggle to keep it. Try this known test: say to yourself, "I vow not to think of a horse for two minutes." See what I mean?

There are experts living in this city who can guarantee to murder anyone unseen, and within the stipulated period, for so much down payment and the balance on conclusion. They would offer you a darling, a trusting month-old kid for a trial. Those who can kill instantaneously – the *siddhas* of *tatkala marana* – are rare. If anybody has trouble with his conscience, thus the *Maheswari Tantra:* "He who aspires to supremacy (*aisvariya*, power) should practice *māranā* (killing). He must practise *māranā* with this view, 'All is *Brahman*'. Otherwise sin adheres to one." In Varanasi, moreover, both the victim and the transgressor are recompensed: the victim has the satisfaction of having repaid a debt – of a murder committed in a past existence – and the thug, the remission of his sin by *Ganga snana* – bathing in the Ganges.

Māranā – murdering by psychic means – is the greatest and most feared *siddhi*. Incidentally – speaking as someone interested in techniques and crafts – it is not possible to kill anyone by these means. The victim kills himself. The method used is – it is a most guarded secret – to visualise the victim as bleeding from every pore, as horribly mutilated, as wounded in the head and his vitals. If this is done for an hour or so a day, for two or three days, a person – or the proxy, the trial animal – so imagined kills himself or manages to get run over. People can be made to have terrible dreams, given fixed images of fearful disease, by similar devices, and a *tar* – a telegram, a message – is another form of unspoken suggestion and it is effective at any distance. A message is sent to the victim, while he sleeps, and suggestions of illness, disaster, given. "You have sinned. Your arm will be broken." "Your limbs are paralysed." For these practices, it is necessary to have a highly developed concentration. It is a mistake to believe – most people do – that a concentrated mind is a prerogative of saints. The suffering caused by such means can be "healed" by a *sadhu* for a consideration (*seva*) and, of course, caused again. I am won by St Paul's insight: ". . . *The love of money is the root of all evil.*"

My access to these people, who practise in secret, was assured from the fact that I accepted several as subjects for hypnosis, and treated them for such habits as tobacco-chewing and certain functional disorders, and was in turn accepted as a brother magician.

The saints of Varanasi – not counting the genuine, the unknown and the anonymous – are legion. Among them are the men and women who claim to be incarnations of God, the *tatwa jnanis* – the knowers of Essence who do not discriminate (*"Sivoham! Bhairavoham!"* "I am Siva! I am Bhairava!" and "All is *one* and the *same*"), the *katha* reciters (minstrels who claim deference due to holiness, by retailing stories written by others), the verbal specialists – the people who can explain *Brahman*, *Atman*, the *Kundalini*, the *Gita*, Yoga, the highest *samadhi*, Gurdjieff, the *yang* and the *yin*, the Sufi view, the Subud, Zen, the *I Ching*, E.S.P., the dark night of the soul, the lot, without themselves feeling obliged to attain, or to practise: *talking* being their *sadhana*, and the worshipped irresponsibles who break your heart because they go about blessing, granting boons, and gleefully promising wealth, cures of diseases, husbands and male progeny to the needy, success in litigation, *abhaya* (freedom from fear) everything. And there are those who have realised the Ultimate Truth. A sane question asked by a distinguished professor of a famous European university was promptly answered by a female adept with, "Sit near the tree!" (Wrong! This is not a Zen quick-fire question and answer, the *mondo*.) The ardent devotee, the head of a department of the nearest university, interpreted it. "The Holy Mother wants you to keep company with good people – that is what is meant by 'sitting near the tree'!"

One or two incarnations, with charming ways, whose company I have kept, were addicted to *bhang* – *Cannabis i.*, hemp, which is the ritual drink offered to the presiding deity of Varanasi. It used to be sold at the cold-drink shops, round about Godaulia and the Chowk. Eight other ingredients added to it – including traces of arsenic and copper, you rub these two on the curry stone and add the wash to the drink – makes a nail-in-your coffin called *Nava ratna* – the nine gems. Unconsciousness is attained within ten minutes. If still conscious after the draught, it is not difficult to declare oneself the Ruler of the World (a *chakravarti rajan*), or Siva (*"Sivoham!"*), or *Sa* (She, the Creatrix, hence *"Saham!"* "She, I am!") without assuming the burden of proof. It is a form of *licking the world.* To reach yet greater heights – to identify oneself with the inconceivable Absolute – might take a bolus or two of opium, downed with sugared milk.

During the winter – when the grass poacher and the petty thief were not abroad – I have sat out in the afternoons, in the mango grove, at Isipatana, where the Buddha first preached the *dhamma*, and found stillness blended perfectly with the deep sound of the Vihara gong – and now and then heard, as if for love – a bird singing. It must have been so in the Bhagava's day, so I have fancied. One day, J. Krishnamurti came to see us, I remember. (The magpies taught me to chatter.) Asked by a sceptical *samanera*, a novice, about what did he teach, a member of his party, with a movie camera, subdued him (the novice) with, "Reality". At lunch, a day or two after, I told him (Krishnamurti) about it. When you are up against "Reality", I suppose, there is nothing more to be said.

After my return from Australia, not quite a year ago, I visited Varanasi again. It was no longer my kind of place. Particularly saddening was the change at Sarnath. There were about hawkers, beggars, stall-keepers selling snacks, and noisy crowds, picnic-makers – all sorts – people who obviously had no respect for the sanctity of the earth, the Jain temple included.

Although one can truthfully describe the Varanasi town centre as about the most insanitary in the country and visiting it a health hazard, this city surprises. Mr Sinclair – whom I have quoted at the beginning – has noted that although he was literally eating dirt, and quenching his thirst with – as he said – sewer water, he had never enjoyed better health. I would cite a similar experience. (Reacting rather sharply, on my third visit, a municipal officer took me on a tour of inspection of the hospitals and charitable dispensaries. Full. Overcrowded.)

Yet, in spite of everything, Varanasi is my *guru sthana*, the place where two of my most compassionate and revered teachers lived – the aforementioned dispensers of the greatest (temporary) suffering and the greatest (temporary) happiness. A traditional obligation accruing from this fact is that I must always regard not only the *puri* – the city proper – but several *yojanas* nigh and beyond, as *sacred* ground. That I do. That I try to do.

AUBREY MENEN

My Grandmother and the Dirty English

My grandmother, like Michelangelo, had *terribilita*. She had a driving will; she would not be baulked and whatever she did was designed to strike the spectator with awe. She was also something of a stick. She rarely spoke to anyone who was not of her own social station and she received them formally: that is to say, with her breasts completely bare. Even in her time women were growing lax about this custom in Malabar. But my grandmother insisted on it. She thought that married women who wore blouses and pretty saris were Jezebels; in her view, a wife who dressed herself above her waist could only be aiming at adultery.

When I was twelve she demanded that I be brought and shown to her. I was incontinently taken half across the earth, from London to south of the town of Calicut. My mother came with me.

The last part of the journey was made by dugout canoe (there being no railways and no good roads near our family estate) and in this we were poled on a moonlit night up the Ponani River. The river was lined with palm trees and crocodiles.

My mother taking fright at these beasts, I sang to keep them away from the boat. I sang a song I had been taught at school called "Drake's Drum". This had been written in the reign of Queen Victoria and told how, if the Spaniards should embark on the unlikely project of attacking nineteenth-century England, Drake would come back to life and drum them up the Channel "as he drummed them long ago". I had been taught many songs with similar sentiments but this was the noisiest. I sang it with a will because my young heart (especially in such very foreign parts) glowed with the sentiment. The crocodiles yawned and, like the Spaniards in the Victorian age, showed no signs of attacking.

This singing marked a stage in my life. Shortly afterwards I lost my innocence. My grandmother took me in hand and I never thought the English were perfect again.

When our boat journey was done, servants with flaming torches led us along narrow paths between tall trees, and finally conducted us to a house. This house was large and smelt of paint. It was (my father said) not my ancestral roof.

When my grandmother had heard that my mother intended to make the visit as well as myself, she had given orders for a special house to be put in repair for my mother's accommodation. It was on the furthest confines of the family property. This was her solution of a difficult problem. My mother was ritually unclean, and therefore whenever she entered my family house, she would defile it. The house would have to be purified and so would every caste Hindu in it. It followed logically that if my mother stayed in the house, it would be permanently in a state of defilement and permanently in a state of being ritually cleaned. Since this ceremony involved drums and conch shells, my mother's visit foreshadowed a prolonged uproar. All this was avoided by my grandmother's decision to put her up in a separate building.

I cannot say that my grandmother was ever rude to my mother. She never referred to her by name but always as "the Englishwoman". This was not necessarily an insulting expression, but my mother had Irish blood and what with this, and the house, and some other pin-pricks, her temper rose. She ordered a quantity of medical stores from Calicut, and when they arrived she set up a free dispensary on the verandah, to which the peasants flocked. It was an admirably devised answer. My grandmother had shut the door in my mother's face. She now had the galling experience of seeing my mother industriously cleaning up the doorstep. As my mother well knew, each drop of iodine that she dispensed stung not only the grateful patient, but also my grandmother's conscience.

My grandmother brooded on this for a while and then sent my mother a bag of golden sovereigns. My mother, taking this to be a bribe at the worst, or at the best, a tip, sent it back. But she was wrong. It was a peace offering. It was sent again next day, accompanied by the family goldsmith who sat, slept and ate on the verandah for one week while he made the sovereigns (with tweezers and a charcoal fire) into a great gold collar which my mother still, on occasion, wears.

When, fourteen years before my trip, my father had written from England to say that he was getting married to a white woman, my grandmother had been far from giving the union her blessing. But it would be wrong to say that she had objected to it. If an English boy of twenty-two wrote home from foreign parts to say that he had taken to cannibalism, his parents would not object. They would be so revolted that a mere objection would never meet the case. So with my grandmother.

She had never met the English but she knew all about them. She knew they were tall, fair, given to strong drink, good soldiers and that they had conquered her native country. She also knew that they were incurably dirty in their personal habits. She respected them but wished they would keep their distance.

It was very much the way that a Roman matron looked upon the Goths.

My eldest uncle had been to England for two years and he spoke up for the English. He said that while the Hindus were undoubtedly the most civilised race on earth and had been civilised a thousand years before the English, nevertheless, the English were now the masters of the Hindus. My grandmother's reply to this was that the English were masters of the Hindus only because "nobody would listen to *us*." By this she meant that our family, along with others of the same caste, had strongly objected to Vasco da Gama being allowed to land in Calicut. They had, in fact, done their best to get him and his sailors massacred. But the country was not behind them and he escaped. Everything, my grandmother argued (and not without some reason), had started with that.

But her chief complaint was that the English were so dirty, and this was rather a poser for my uncle. When my grandmother asked if, like decent people, they took a minimum of two baths a day, my uncle, who could not lie to his mother without committing a disgraceful sin, said that, well, no: but a few took one bath and the habit was spreading. He could go no further than that. But he added that my grandmother should remember that England had a cold climate. This she loyally did, and when she discussed the matter with me she was able to treat the matter lightly, as one does the disgusting but rational liking of the Eskimos for eating blubber.

As for the question of eating, she did not have the expected prejudices. She did not think it strange that the English ate ham and beef. The outcast hill-tribes (called Todas) who made the family straw mats and cleaned the latrines, ate anything. She was not disturbed, either about their religion, because my uncle assured her that they had practically none. Their manners, however, she abominated. If she did not mind them eating meat, she considered their way of eating it beyond the pale of decent society. In my family home, each person eats his meal separately, preferably in a secluded corner. The thought that English people could sit opposite each other and watch each other thrust food into their mouths, masticate, and swallow it, made her wonder if there was anything that human beings would not do when left to their own devices.

She was not surprised to hear, after this, that in England a woman could have more than one husband, particularly (and this was the crowning paradox) if she had been a widow. To the day of her death my grandmother could never understand how people could call themselves civilised and yet allow widows to marry again. For her the very foundation-stone of society was that a child should have one father, and obey him. Nobody ever dared her wrath sufficiently to explain the position of women in English society. She was intensely proud of the standards of her house and she permitted no lewd talk to defile them – certainly never in her presence.

With this background, then, my grandmother's peace offering of a bag of sovereigns was a considerable victory for my mother, particularly since the gold collar which the goldsmith had been told to make from them was the characteristic jewellery of a Malabar bride.

I had many meetings with her. I used to visit her in considerable state. The distance from our home – the isolation wing, so to speak – to the main family mansion was too far for walking in the Malabar sun. I used to go by palanquin. It was a hammock of red cloth with rather worn embroidery of gold thread, and it was swung on a black pole which had silver ornaments at either end. Four virtually naked men, two in front and two behind, carried the palanquin at a swift trot. There was considerable art in this. If the four trotted just as they pleased, the hammock would swing in a growing arc until it tipped the passenger out on to the road. To prevent this, the men trotted in a complicated system that I never really understood: watching them and trying to trace it out was as difficult as trying to determine the order in which a horse puts its hoofs down. They kept their rhythm by chanting. I used to fall asleep on the way, listening to them. It must have presented an interesting spectacle – a red palanquin, the sweating men, and a sleeping schoolboy wearing an English blazer with its pocket sewn with a badge gained by infantile prowess at some sport that I do not now remember.

The family house was vast and cool and, in my view, unfurnished. But to my grandmother's eye it was very elegant. There was nothing but the floor to sit on. She disliked chairs and thought them vulgar. What use were they, except for ostentations? She approved of beds but insisted that the mattress be made of taut string – nothing else was considered clean. She also had a taste for handsome brass-bound boxes. So beds, boxes, and oil-lamps were the sole furniture of the innumerable rooms of the house. There were no tables and no tablecloths. In my grandmother's house, if anybody dared eat in any fashion but off a fresh plantain-leaf, his next meal would have been served in the kitchen, where the servants were allowed to eat without ceremony.

My grandmother usually received me sitting by her favourite box in her boudoir. She made an unforgettable picture. She had great black eyes, a shock of white hair, and lips as lush and curved as a girl of eighteen. The skin of her bosom, bare as I have said, was quite smooth. I used to sit on the floor in front of her in my school blazer and since my father had never taught me Malayalam (wishing me to be brought up like any other English schoolboy), we talked through one of my uncles.

The things my grandmother told me were a puzzle at the time. But I have come to understand them better. Much as she looked down on the English, I think that had she met some of them, had she overcome her well-bred fastidiousness and actually mixed with them, she would have found she and they had much in common. Her riding passion, like theirs, was racial pride. She believed – and this made her character – that she belonged to the cleverest family of the cleverest class of the cleverest people on earth. According to Lord Russell, this was also the firm faith of Mrs Beatrice Webb, who used to repeat it to herself in moments when, otherwise, she might have felt inferior, such as when she made her entry into a distinguished party. Though my grandmother never went to parties I'm sure that she, too, repeated the formula as a stiffener of her already formidable morale.

She felt that she was born of a superior race and she had all the marks of it. For instance, she deplored the plumbing of every other nation but her own. She would often say to me, through my uncle:

"Never take a bath in one of those contraptions in which you sit in dirty water like a buffalo. Always bathe in running water. If you have servants to pour it over you, that's best. But otherwise you must stand under a tap and pour the water over yourself. A really nice person does not even glance at his own bath water, much less sit in it." Here she would laugh to herself, while my uncle translated; not an unkind laugh, but a pitying one, as she thought of the backwardness of the white man's bathroom.

Another mark – and I have met it in many nations – was that she believed that English sexual morals permitted and encouraged all sorts of abominations from which a civilised person shrank. She spoke to me with great freedom on this point: I was after all at puberty. I could not always follow the drift of her remarks, but I did gather that she felt strongly on one point. Why, if the English wanted their offspring to grow up decently and not lewdly, did they omit to marry them off when they were children? There was something sinister in the neglect. A child should grow up knowing quite well that all that side of his life was settled according to the best available advice and in the best possible manner for his welfare. When he was eighteen or twenty the marriage would be consummated. Till then, he did not have to worry his head about women – or if he did worry, he knew he was morally slipping.

History, I have discovered, is on my grandmother's side. The great majority of civilised peoples have always agreed with her. Romance and love and such things were, in antiquity, things for slaves. Respectable families arranged their marriages as my grandmother arranged those of her offspring. To take a single example, my grandmother and Brutus would fully have understood each other. She felt hurt that she had not been consulted over my father's marriage: while among the many sidelights that we have on that honourable man who assassinated Julius Caesar is a letter in which he complains at being left out of the bargaining that went on during the betrothal of "my dear little Attica", who was nine years old.

But a grandson was a grandson, even though her permission had not been sought to bring him into the world, and she set about being a mother as well as a grandmother to me. She knew that soon I would go back among the heathen to finish my education, and she wanted me to go back knowing who and what I was. On one of my visits she gave me a small book in which were written all my duties and privileges as a member of my class. The book was written on dried palm-leaves, strung together with a cord between two covers of wood. It began with a prayer to God thanking Him for creating us – our caste, that is – so much superior in every respect to the great majority of other human beings.

My grandmother explained what followed several times and with much emphasis, for she wanted to imprint it on my memory. Our family belongs to the caste – or class – called Nayars. The Nayars of Malabar are as old as Indian history and therefore, it can be assumed, a good deal older. My grandmother told me that traditionally we had two obligations to society. We were warriors when there was fighting to do, and when there was not, we had the duty, on certain holy days, of carrying flowers to the temple.

I remember that I thought this very romantic at the time and could not understand why my grandmother took it so prosaically: to me, warriors, flowers and temples conjured up a picture of some Oriental Round Table. But my grandmother was right. Our caste is a commonplace, it exists everywhere. In England it is scattered all over the countryside. The men are what is called "Army" and the women take not only flowers, but fruit to the temple on the occasion of the Harvest Festival. It is curious, and inexplicable, that the combination of these two activities, whether in the Shires or in the coconut groves of Malabar, produces the most ferocious snobs.

My grandmother explained to me that, as a Nayar, I should always be very careful to keep my dignity when dealing with Brahmins: Brahmins are priests. The priests who have the cure of souls in my family are treated as domestic chaplains. Since their temples were on our property my grandmother had several "livings", so to speak, at her disposal, this side of religious affairs always being left in the hands of the older women. Priests were therefore expected to make themselves agreeable, in return for which they were regularly fed. They were expected to mind their own business, which was to perform the weekly ceremonies and to direct their preaching at the lower orders, particularly the servants. The Anglican Settlement in England was much more elaborate, but reduced to what it meant to the average priest-in-the-vestry it came to much the same thing, and provides one more reason why I wish my grandmother had visited the country of my birth.

But my grandmother was quite ignorant of these striking resemblances and begged me when moving among the English to remember myself. "They will look up to you, as a Nayar, to set an example," she used to say. "They know that you have two thousand years of advantage over them and they will be willing to learn. Show them this book. They will be very interested. It was written when they still went about naked. And I will give you some trinkets which you can hand out as gifts: some amulets which we use and some things made of sandalwood, which is very rare in England, so I am told, and much sought after. They will help you make friends. But remember, it is your *example* which will count more than anything."

She gave me all the things she promised and as she had foretold, they were much admired. Some of them, I believe, are still in my school museum. She also gave me her blessing, which was what I had been brought across the world to get.

I thought over her advice but I was in some confusion. My headmaster, wishing me goodbye and good luck when I had set out on my trip, had said much the same thing. "Let them see," he had said, "by your example that you have been trained in an *English* school. Wherever you go, it is for *you* to set the tone." He did not give me any sandalwood, but I was very impressed. I was also very impressed with what my grandmother had said.

In my dilemma I remembered that I had another grandmother. She had been born, as I have said, in Killarney, but had come to England to live – briefly enough, for she had died before I was born. I asked my mother about her. She told me many things but one stood out in my mind.

"My mother," she said, "was never really happy among the English. She longed to go back to Killarney. Sometimes when things had become unbearably tiresome, she would heave a long, deep sigh, shake her head and gently close her eyes."

M. KRISHNAN

The Jellicut

IT IS A LONG TIME since I saw a Jellicut, but I am not likely to forget it.

The Jellicut is the southern bull ring. There are no horses and lancers here, no flashing matadors with blooded swords. No one waves red cloth at colour-blind bulls; such cloth as there is may be of any colour and is swathed around the bull's horns. The men are unarmed and unprotected, and their aim is not to kill the bulls, nor even to infuriate them.

All the same this rustic sport does not lack spectacle, or excitement, or risk.

Each bull that enters the ring – a circular stockade – has a piece of cloth, often brightly coloured, wound across and around its horns in a loose bandage, and the game consists in the men snatching the cloth clear of the horn as the bulls are driven down a fenced lane. That is, basically, the Jellicut, and explained this way it seems a tame pastime. Let me give a fuller account.

Around Madura, and elsewhere in the South, an active, medium-sized breed of cattle, compact and powerful, is to be found in varying degrees of purity. The Jellicut bulls come from this stock, and are specially reared for the ring. The best type of fighting bull is a beautifully balanced beast, not running to exaggerated dewlap or hump, light and quick-muscled. It is so evenly made, without frills and fancy touches, that its power is not apparent at first sight, except perhaps in a certain arrogance of carriage and gait. A well-trained bull will suffer no stranger to approach close, and is wickedly fast on its feet and with its horns. White, laced with front-grey or a rusty fawn on the head, fore quarters, and legs is a much-fancied colour and is said to indicate fighting blood.

Not all the bulls that enter the Jellicut ring are pure-bred or have the fighting temperament; even steers get in, at times. Some specially dangerous bulls are widely known and respected, and are taken around the countryside for the sport. These are known by the names of their villages, or by the number of years for which they have held their own, unconquered, in Jellicuts. A Jellicut is a major event in rural areas. Men and beasts come to it from all around, sometimes from considerable distances.

The crowd gathers right from the morning for the afternoon's sport. The bandaged heads of the bulls give them a deceptively complacent and domestic look, as their owners lead them in. A number of bulls are driven into the circular stockade – at the farther end is a long, narrow, fenced lane, leading out to open fields.

The spectators crowd around the palings thickly, and the men who enter the arena take up strategic posts in the lane, the frequent gaps in the bamboo fencing allowing them a ready, squeezed, acrobatic exit, should the need arise.

The fun begins with the first batch of bulls – any number up to a dozen – entering the stockade. A terrific din is set up, with the aid of drums and tin cans and loud voices. The bulls careen round the ring, the dust rises in a red ground-mist under their hooves and they are off, with waving tails and low heads, down the lane. They are not allowed to enter the lane all together, but one by one, so that the waiting men have a chance.

The men hug the fence, and as a bull goes lumbering past one of them steps in and deftly snatches the cloth from off its horns. A cool head, smooth-moving limbs and perfect timing, rather than bravery or brawn are what make for success in this game, as in all sports of skill. But it is not always that the bull goes tearing blindly past, allowing its crown to be lightly snatched – close holds, and courage too, are often needed.

The Jellicut begins modestly, and the first few batches to enter the stockade hold no really dangerous bulls: some of them are just overgrown, mild-eyed calves still. The bulls with the worst reputations come later; they are reserved for the time when body and spirit have been sufficiently warmed.

At the last Jellicut I saw, staged in a village a dozen miles or so off Madura (I have forgotten its name), there was a notorious bull, a beast that had not been routed in five years, and with the name of a killer. This bull entered the stockade late in the afternoon, when we were tired of watching the sport and were about to turn home. A wave of excitement spread down the close mass of watchers, and five bulls entered the lane in quick succession, giving the men near the lane mouth no opportunity to single out any of them.

I asked my neighbour (never are neighbours nearer) to point out the killer to me, and he waved an obliging hand at the oncoming bulls. There was the bull, right in front, a big fawn-and-white animal with rolling eyes and a large, massive head held threateningly low. As it trotted past, a man leaned out from the fence, side-stepped the sweep of the horns, and plucked the cloth casually off its horns. Joining in the spontaneous applause, I felt my neighbour poking me in the ribs. "Not that one," he said. "Do you see that grey bull behind all the rest? That's the one." The grey bull was well behind the others, sauntering down the lane and keeping to the middle, the down-held head swaying from side to side to the rhythm of movement. I must say I felt disappointed at the killer's looks and leisurely manner – there were many bigger and more defiant bulls in the Jellicut that day.

A splendid young man, who had distinguished himself earlier, stepped lightly down the lane as the grey bull passed him, and reached out for the cloth. The bull turned in a flash, the young man leaped back from the quick, sideways toss of the horns, and the bull continued its sauntering way down the lane. Only when the man collapsed on the fence, and was helped out of the lane, did we realise that the bull had scored. I had come up to this Jellicut with a doctor from Madura, and we hurried round the stockade to the casualty. The horn had pierced and torn the abdominal wall, and the man was in obvious pain, but I was told that it was not so grave an injury as it looked. We tried, long and ineffectually, to persuade the young man to go with us in the car to Madura, where he could have proper attention: he would have none of our help and was sure that the aids and medicines available in the village would do.

A week later, meeting a man from a nearby village, we learned that the bull had claimed another victim.

AMRITA SHER-GIL

Modern Indian Art: Imitating the Forms of the Past

It seems to me that I never began painting, that I have always painted. And I have always had, with a strange certitude, the conviction that I was meant to be a painter and nothing else. Although I studied, I have never been taught painting in the actual sense of the word, because I possess in my psychological make-up a peculiarity that resents any outside interference. I have always, in everything, wanted to find out things for myself.

With this tendency it is rather fortunate that in 1929 when our parents decided to take my sister and myself to Paris for the study of music and painting respectively, the great French professor Lucien Simon took a fancy to my work and admitted me to his studio at the Ecole des Beaux Arts. Before leaving for Europe I had worked entirely from imagination, and, although I went through an academic phase in the first few years of my stay in Paris, I had never imitated nature servilely; and now I am deviating more and more from naturalism towards the evolving of new, and "significant" forms, corresponding to my individual conception of the essence of the inner meaning of my subject.

Lucien Simon never "taught". He made us think for ourselves and solve technical and pictorial problems ourselves, merely encouraging each of those pupils whose work interested him, in his or her own individual forms of self-expression.

I worked for some time at the Ecole des Beaux Arts and got prizes at the annual portrait and still-life competitions for three consecutive years. My work in those days was absolutely Western in conception and execution except for the fact that it was never entirely tame or conventional.

I had not in those days learnt that simplicity is the essence of perfection. One sees with such exuberance, uncritically, when one is very young that one is liable to sacrifice the artistic whole to unessential detail, if it happens to be pleasing to the eye. One lacks the faculty of discrimination, so essential to the production of true art.

Towards the end of 1933 I began to be haunted by an intense longing to return to India, feeling in some strange inexplicable way that there lay my destiny as a painter. We returned at the end of 1934. My professor had often said that, judging by the richness of my colouring, I was not really in my element in the grey studios of the West, that my artistic personality would find its true atmosphere in the colour and light of the East. He was right, but my impression was so different from the one I had expected, and so profound that it lasts to this day.

It was the vision of a winter in India – desolate, yet strangely beautiful – of endless tracks of luminous yellow-grey land, of dark-bodied, sad-faced, incredibly thin men and women who move silently looking almost like silhouettes and over which an indefinable melancholy reigns. It was different from the India, voluptuous, colourful, sunny and superficial, the India so false to the tempting travel posters that I had expected to see.

Before leaving for Europe as a very young girl I had been so wholly an introvert that I had never really seen or observed anything round or outside me. I worked entirely from imagination in those days, and living on pictures instead of reality I conceived India through the medium of those unutterably mediocre specimens of fifth-rate Western art that still abound in the local exhibitions, providing doubtful if not harmful aliment to the artistically under-fed and undeveloped mind. And I regret to say that, not satisfied with the production *ad infinitum* of this type of painting by the Europeans here, it is perpetuated, in blissful ignorance as to its artistic demerits, by a number of Indian artists! I say "regret" because the paintings can no more be accused of being true interpretations of India than they can be accused of being works of art! When pursued as a form of recreation by amiable foreign amateurs of both sexes, or tourists who wish to conserve, in the form of oils or water-colours that have no pretensions whatsoever of art, souvenirs of their various travels, it is pardonable; but when the essence of mediocrity is adopted to found a school of art to give impetus to a new Indian artistic movement, then it is to be deplored in the extreme. I call this tourist painting, because it has all the characteristics of the tourist mind, being absolutely superficial, both pictorially and psychologically, impressions of impressions, where there is no room for artistic conception, penetration or insight.

Those so-called paintings that depict an India where the sun shines with an inevitability only equalled by the mediocrity of conception and execution of that sunlight as it plays on flesh tints of standardised grey-browns and gives opportunity to the ambitious artists to exploit the possibilities of orange reflected "lights" and blue "half-lights": cheap tricks of the trade that have to be learnt but that must be forgotten before one can think of producing true works of Art. Those serene or sun-flooded landscapes, consciously naturalistic, with authentically Indian ruins in the "middle distance", that serve as trademarks, conclusive, irrefutable proofs as to the genuineness of the article (manufactured in India), not one brushstroke of which conveys India really. Those futile views of snowy mountain ranges (where ultra-marine blue laid on in neat washes represents shadows) have succeeded in destroying any aesthetic enjoyment that might otherwise have derived even from the actual view of snowy mountain ranges! Those portraits of beggars, of the miserable, the poor of India, viewed as objects of topographical interest, without an atom of either artistic or human understanding.

My violent reaction to both the pictorial and psychological conventions of this type of painting and my own mode of pictorial expression will be understood to some extent when viewed in the light of my first impression of India as opposed to the picture I had mentally made of it, thanks to the above-mentioned form.

And now I shall proceed to explain how one is to approach a picture to derive from it the maximum aesthetic enjoyment. In the first place, a Picture must be a Painting, which means that the picture of a chair or of a pair of boots must be aesthetically as satisfying and interesting as the portrait of a remarkably handsome man or charming woman. (The aim of art being the derival of aesthetic emotion from abstract beauty, the beauty, the vitality, of line, form, colour and design, as opposed to the pleasure derived from the prettiness of the object depicted in the picture.) I cannot stress this point enough, as it is of vital importance in the appreciation of works of art. It is the alpha and omega of all artistic and aesthetic knowledge.

I am aware of the fact that this form of appreciation being on a much higher level than the more obvious one of mere sensual interest, is much more difficult to attain, particularly for the infinite majority of those who have never even seen real paintings (painting "per se", for instance the Ajanta and Bagh cave paintings, perhaps the highest forms of pictorial art ever to be evolved in any country or civilisation), and when given the opportunity of looking at them, are not taught how to see them.

Left to their own initiative (except a few who are blessed with an exceptional artistic sensibility), the great majority of people lapse into the common error of trying to discover in pictures emotional pegs on which to hang their feelings (usually sentimental or romantic), and imagine that what they derive from the process is synonymous with the ecstasy of the real aesthetic emotion which the initiated derive from the contemplation of sheer pictorial beauty. Painting is the primary factor and the subject only the secondary factor in a picture. In the highest forms of art mere human interest of the spectator is not played upon either by grimaces or physical contortions of the men and women that are depicted, nor yet by the human incidents or descriptive elements in a picture (in fact these things do not usually appear at all in good art and are peculiar to that abomination "the picture that tells a story"), but by those experiences that, having stirred the artist emotionally, are transmitted by him to canvas, not on the descriptive plane, but on the plane where there is no room for cheap emotional appeal, the plane of deep emotional significance – Line, Colour and Design. That beautiful phrase of Vincent Van Gogh's, "I want to express, want to express, with Green and with Reds, the terrific, the terrific human passions", conveys so exactly what I want to say, that I cannot resist quoting it here. Clive Bell, in his excellent book on art, says: "If in the artist an inclination to play upon the emotions of life is often the sign of flickering inspiration, in the spectator a tendency to seek, behind form, the emotions of life is a sign of defective sensibility always . . ."

The fundamental idea of that form of Indian Art which drew its inspiration from Ajanta (that really great and eternal example of pure painting) was right to begin with because it started with the principle of the primordial importance of "significant form", but unfortunately, except for a few men of talent who have wrestled successfully with the coils of mythological convention, this Art has developed an illustrative tendency that has gone to the detriment of the fundamental principles and tends to devitalise and render it effeminate in execution. It has committed the mistake of feeding almost exclusively on the tradition of mythology and romance, and no Art can do that with impunity for any length of time. Art cannot imitate the forms of the past (because, for one thing, imitation is a form of debility and so the work thus created will necessarily be feeble); it must draw its inspiration from the present to create the forms of the future.

I am an individualist evolving a new technique that, though not necessarily Indian in the traditional sense of the word, will yet be fundamentally Indian in spirit. With the eternal significance of form and colour I interpret India, and principally the life of the Indian poor, on the plane that transcends the plane of mere sentimental interest.

SANTHA RAMA RAU

With Shivan and Kitty in New Delhi

THE TRAIN MOVED slowly into Old Delhi. We had left behind the advertisements for Players cigarettes and Chrysler cars which looked so strange with their Hindi captions. We had passed the dingy washing hanging in slum yards, the solitary men staring out of windows. Now we drew into the outdated and gracious but dirty station. The coolies woke from their inter-train naps and fussed their way down to the train, winding their turbans as they ran shouting for attention.

We were to stay with my uncle and aunt, Shivan and Kitty, in their house in New Delhi. Ever since Mother had explained the plan to Premila and me, we had felt a little uncomfortable. We were going to spend the whole winter in Delhi and it seemed suspiciously like sponging on our relatives, but Mother told us that it was considered very poor form to stay at a hotel when members of the family lived in the same city. It would give strangers the impression that our family was feuding. Accordingly we searched the platform from our carriage window trying to catch a glimpse of Kitty and Shivan, for they did not follow my grandmother's custom of sending a servant to find the arriving guests.

When Mother and Premila and I climbed down from the train we found that apparently only Kitty had come to meet us. She wore a pale silk sari and was peering doubtfully into the carriages. In the painful glare of the station lights she looked incredibly pretty and gentle. I had not seen her for several years – since the time when she and Shivan used to pay brief visits to London and take Premila and me for ecstatic afternoons at what we used to call the "Sixpenny Bazaar" – Woolworth's. Kitty would give us each ten shillings to buy all the perfume bottles shaped like begging dogs, jigsaw puzzles with guaranteed interlocking pieces, and yo-yos that we could carry. Shivan was our favourite uncle partly because we knew him so much better than the others and partly because he always seemed to be in some sort of scrape with the rest of the family and would tell us about it in a rather guilty and completely charming way. He wasn't exactly the black sheep: he was the "unconventional one".

Kitty saw us surrounded by coolies, each shouting his particular claim to our luggage. She came to us smiling and joining her hands in the Indian greeting. She kissed us all composedly and ordered the coolies away.

"Shivan," she explained, "is making his usual tour of the book-stands to see if they have his book."

"His book?" Mother questioned carefully.

"Oh yes, about industrial labour and such. If they have it he says, 'Good.' If they haven't, he says, 'What!' and looks shocked."

Shivan came up looking worried but obliging, followed by his bearer and a procession of coolies. His appearance is anything but that of the conventional black sheep of the family. He has a kind vague smile, horn-rimmed bi-focals, and thinning hair; somehow he looks like an unsuccessful scientist. He always wears the traditional Indian dress – a long Russian-collared tunic over white cotton jodhpurs crushed into wrinkles around the ankles and open Indian sandals – even though two of his brothers and many of his friends have adopted the more easily obtained Western costume.

Men's clothes in India change relatively little from province to province. The women's sari is worn in a number of different ways; basically the plan is similar, but the details of the drapery vary according to the part of India from which the women come. The Maharatta women, for instance, wear their saris draped between their legs because in the more warlike days of Maharatta history the women used to ride to battle with their men and needed to be able to sit astride their horses. But the men all over India wear, as their informal dress, a cotton loincloth with a long shirt over it; sandals for their feet and a Gandhi cap – rather like a soldier's overseas cap – at all times, indoors or out.

The Gandhi cap has replaced the more unwieldy turban very widely in the cities. Now for the most part only the very rich, maharajas and their entourages, and the very poor, peasants who have to carry things on their heads, and railway porters, wear turbans. Depending upon the wearer's circumstances, turbans are of cloth and gold and brocades covered with jewellery or of cotton; the latter seem always to be in the process of being rewound.

Shivan was wearing the formal dress for Indian men. The formal shoes that should go with that dress are long peaked sandals that look like gondolas with a curling tail in front. Sometimes the uppers of these shoes are embroidered with gold thread or different coloured leathers, but most people nowadays wear open sandals instead. The formal clothes of the princes are, of course, more elaborate, but the added decoration is not in actual design but more usually in the substitution of real jewels for buttons, or gold-embroidered collars on the coats, and jodhpurs made of silk or satin.

My uncle's coat was made of thin gray Kashmir wool. One button was undone, and his hair was beginning to stand on end. He looked quite charming.

He greeted us as though he had left us only a few minutes before. He showed no surprise and only a polite interest.

"Kitty and I have just been to the wedding. Really very exhausting. How lucky you were to miss it."

"What wedding?" I asked. Shivan had the curious habit of assuming that everyone knew exactly what he was talking about with no explanations on his part.

"One of the Viceroy's daughters. Didn't you know? She married one of the A.D.C.'s. So all of us poor innocuous citizens are ordered to mingle with the empire-builders all afternoon at some kind of reception. We grasped iced-coffee in one hand and the local caterer's bun in the other and smiled at each other for hours. Facial fatigue is what I'm suffering from, it's practically – "

"That's easily remedied," Premila interrupted briskly. "Just give me a raw egg and a jar of cold cream . . ."

"Well," said Shivan, "at least there are only two more to go."

"Two more what?" I was getting confused again.

"Viceregal daughters. The suspense is something shocking."

Kitty was looking desperate. "We really must go home," she said. "Shivan is quite capable of standing here talking about nothing all night."

We drove through the bright and noisy bazaars in Old Delhi where it was necessary for the chauffeur to sound the horn almost constantly. The car crept along while beggars peered inquisitively in the windows, pushcarts were rushed to the side of the road to make room for the car, and Shivan talked happily about the Indian newspaperman's life. Eventually we reached the dark, empty street leading to New Delhi.

A few miles later we found ourselves in a strange geometrical world – New Delhi. A flashily gauche city of straight streets and carefully trimmed grass circles at every crossroads. All the houses there must be painted white, with white or brick walls separating the gardens from the streets. The centre of the town is an enormous circular plaza from which confusingly similar residential roads radiate. We drove through this maze of red and white, through the shade of trees planted at regular intervals on each side of the road. Soon we passed the monstrous wedding cake of an Assembly building with its statues of former viceroys. There seemed to be no cars on the roads and no pedestrians on the sidewalks. It was a frighteningly lifeless place.

Shivan looked at the moonlit gardens and silent houses belonging to the hundreds of diplomats and government workers who compose so large a part of Delhi's population.

"You know," he commented at last, "they say that the only sound to be heard in Delhi at night is the grinding of axes."

Kitty and Shivan's house was low and white, with deep verandas, a rose garden in front and a tennis court and mango trees behind. The servants were lined up on the front veranda when we arrived. They bowed quickly, looking embarrassed and interested, and vanished before we could say a word to any of them. They were just curious about the "strangers", Kitty assured us. As we walked in I saw a crowd of small children peering round the corner of the house. They giggled and ran back to the servants' quarters when I turned.

Inside, the house was furnished in a surprisingly successful mixture of Indian and Western styles. Kitty had chosen only Indian materials for her slip-covers, curtains and bedspreads, but the furniture itself was European. The draperies were of heavy khadi cotton with borders of unfamiliar stylised animals marching in a solemn procession, and the Kashmiri carpets of winter had just replaced the rope *daris* – made in the Indian jails – which covered the marble floors in summer.

It was late and we were all tired so we went in to dinner at once. On the centre of the table was a simple but imaginative reproduction of a train made in sugar icing. From the funnel on the engine came a streamer of spun brown sugar – the smoke. The curtain across the door leading to the kitchen bulged suspiciously. The cook was obviously waiting for our admiring gasps. Kitty put her hand over her mouth to keep from laughing.

"He gets rather carried away by his work sometimes, I'm afraid," she said in English.

Premila was staring at it in fascinated horror. Mother, as usual, took everything in her stride. She called the cook, congratulated him on his ingenuity as well as on his astonishing mechanical knowledge, asked him to remove it very carefully so that he could display it to the servants' children in the morning, and sat down to her soup.

Kitty's meal, like her house, was a mixture of East and West. After the soup a typically Indian curry was served with rice, *chapatis, daal*, and all the accessories to which we had grown accustomed in my grandmother's house. But it was served on plates and eaten with knives and forks. The dessert was the cook's invention. Inspired by the character of the rest of the house, he had blended both the cooking styles he had learned during his experience with English and Indian families. He produced something that tasted like a very rich and very popular Indian sweet – *halva* – yet was made like a souffle. He wouldn't tell even Kitty how this miracle was accomplished.

In incongruous contrast to the Indian silver and enamel on the table, the carved Indian chairs and Indian ornaments was the large, shiny Kelvinator refrigerator in one corner of the room. Kitty saw me staring at it several times during the meal.

"I know it looks funny here," she said at last, "but we had to take it out of the kitchen because the servants were so fascinated with the idea of a machine that could make ice in an hour or so that there was never any left for our drinks. Sometimes the children would put their clothes in the refrigerator during the summer heat. They found that this cooled them off wonderfully for a little while."

I had always thought of Shivan in the way one remembers people one has known only for the summer – irresponsible, living always in the sun and surrounded by a distant glamour. In our spasmodic glimpses of him in Europe he seemed to be perpetually involved in improbable schemes. We met him once in a theosophical camp in Holland. "I'm living in – ah – Aerda Castle," he explained, "for a few weeks anyway. No . . . no, I have no immediate plans." Then he added with a happy smile, "We wash our own dishes." To my seven-year-old imagination this seemed like a wonderful way to live; splendour and squalor all mixed up together.

My grandmother likes to think that he has "settled down" now that he is established as a journalist. She can tell her friends that he works on the staff of the *Hindu* – a prominent Indian paper – and corresponds for several American and British papers. She never says a word about his extensive political activity, or about his work for the Indian trades-union movement.

When Shivan announced his engagement to Kitty, no member of the family had courage enough to tell my grandmother about it. Before her sons went abroad to college she had made perfectly clear to each of them her attitude toward foreigners. They hesitated to find out about her attitude toward foreigners in the family.

Kitty was Viennese. But worse than that, Kitty, whose major interest was child psychology, had started an experimental kindergarten school in Benares: she worked for a living. The family was so amazed at the prospect of one of its members marrying such an unusual person that my oldest uncle is reported to have said to Kitty, "Either you misunderstood Shivan, or else you proposed to him." Kitty telegraphed Shivan frantically to reassure herself.

My grandmother's attitude on this occasion was wholly unexpected. Since she could do nothing to alter the fact that Shivan was going to marry a foreigner, she decided to re-model the foreigner as well as she could. Kitty found herself learning Hindustani – she now speaks it fluently. Her European clothes mysteriously disappeared when she was staying with my grandmother in Colaba, and in their place she found new saris and "family" saris (ones that have belonged to other members of the family) which are the traditional equipment of an Indian bride. Indian jewellery and sandals appeared in the same way and all her Western cosmetics were replaced by Indian ones: henna for her fingernails, *ghaza* as rouge, sandalwood oil for her skin, attar of roses as perfume, and *kajal* – a black paste that smells of herbs and is used as mascara. The only item that was omitted was the *tika* for the caste-mark which my grandmother felt that Kitty should never wear.

All Hindu women wear in the centre of their forehead a coloured mark which, in the old days, denoted their caste and sub-caste. Nowadays the wearing of the *tika*, a tiny circle of red powder, is a formality, a decoration rather than a badge having particular meaning. The *tika* is made from a mixture of powders and spices; I remember, as a child, opening Mother's little silver box of the powder and sniffing its unfamiliar heavy perfume. Some Indian women find a red-paste *tika* more suited to an active life for it does not blow off as easily, but Mother still puts a small smear of cocoanut oil on her forehead every morning and presses the powder *tika* on to it with her finger, making the circle without the help of the nailhead Premila and I have to use. Nowadays the traditional red *tika* is often replaced by one to match the sari – it may be black, orange or even a piece of gold or silver tinsel. But my grandmother, preserving the old ways even in a matter as small as this, wears the entire complicated *tika* which was meaningful in her childhood. Hers is a long smear of red running across her forehead, a pear-shaped splotch of saffron between her eyebrows, and above that the dab of ash from the shrine fire. Altogether these denote that she is a Saraswat Brahmin – that is, her religion is Hindu, her caste within that religion is Brahmin, and her branch of that caste is Saraswat.

Under my grandmother's guidance Kitty became Indian; my grandmother forgot that she had ever been anything else. She still points out to her friends the astonishing fairness of Kitty's skin and how unusual it is in "this new sports-loving generation" of Indian girls.

Kitty allowed herself to be moulded with admirable grace and now, like all the other members of the family who do not live in the family home, she keeps up a pretence of conforming to the old rules in my grandmother's presence. She wears no lipstick at Colaba, keeps her sari over her head whenever she is in the presence of her elders, and addresses only those who are younger than she is, unless she is spoken to.

Her life in Delhi, however, is far from that of the conventional Hindu woman. She and Shivan are not only informed and interested observers of current political and social events in India, but feel themselves inextricably involved in those events. To Shivan every political setback is like a sickness in the family. He worries about countless things – say, the failure of an interview between a Congress Party leader and the viceroy. He will see people, spend hours on the telephone following every step in the proceedings, he will interview the leaders of all the parties to assess their reactions. He neglects his own writing and seldom shows up at meals. Often he will call Kitty at ten-thirty or so at night saying, "I thought I had better let you know in time that I won't be in to dinner tonight." She never has the heart to tell him that it no longer occurs to her to wait meals for him.

On our first morning in their house Shivan got up as usual about six and spent a couple of hours dictating to his secretary. He expected to be out of the house the rest of the day and had to finsh his work for the *Hindu* before he left. Premila and I came in to breakfast just as he was finishing.

At sight of us he threw up his hands. "Go away!" he said. "I'm eating Quaker Oats!"

Premila looked first amazed, then understanding, began to laugh. "Don't worry," she said. "We are older now, and I hope more controlled."

Shivan was thinking of the time when neither Premila nor I could eat Quaker Oats because they reminded us too strongly of the car trip from Delhi to Simla. Infallibly we would both be car-sick and after long experience Mother used to take along dozens of empty Quaker Oats cans so that the journey would not be delayed indefinitely.

All three of us began at once on a flood of reminiscence which might well have gone on all day if Kitty had not come in and reminded Shivan of his appointments. When he had gone she smiled at Premila and me with a characteristic tilt of her head.

"And what are you two planning to do with your time from now on?"

"Well," said Premila, "I am going to begin job hunting and I am going to start as soon as I can talk you into giving me some names and introductions and things."

"I see that you have already learned that everything in India is done through friends of friends," Kitty said. "I dare say that Shivan's secretary would be of as much help as I could be. We'll consult him after breakfast." She turned to me. "Would you be interested in visiting a village school with me?"

"Of course, I'd love to. I'm not very sure what it is."

"I'll tell you about it on the way there. We should be leaving fairly soon and we'll probably spend the day. It's out in Okhla."

I wondered how and when Kitty did her housekeeping. She couldn't have as large a staff of servants as my grandmother, yet she seemed not to give the house a second thought. I was about to ask her about it when the cook came into the dining room followed by four other servants. Kitty did not even turn around but went on buttering her toast while she called off the menus for the day, specifying the maximum price the cook was to pay for fruit and vegetables. The bearer was told what special jobs were to be done in the house – the marble had to be polished and the verandas watered; the gardener was instructed what flowers he was to cut and how often they were to be changed; the chauffeur was informed that he could have the day off, and the dhobi was taken to task about some torn sheets from last week's laundry.

Kitty's housekeeping had taken her exactly twenty minutes. When she looked up she saw that I had been watching her.

"It's a fascinating procedure, isn't it?" she asked. "But you've only seen the first instalment. Now the servants will go back and tell their apprentices what to do." I must have looked puzzled. "For instance, the cook has taken on a pupil who pays him perhaps a rupee or two a month [about 50 cents] to learn his trade from him. This boy does all the marketing, peels the potatoes, shells the peas and so forth. Meanwhile I pay the cook about 20 rupees a month and keep my eyes closed to all these backdoor transactions, on the assumption that as long as the meals arrive on time the rest of it is none of my business."

"And all the other servants do the same thing?" I asked.

"I suppose so." She pushed her chair back from the table. "Come," she said with her singing Viennese inflection.

Premila and Shivan's secretary went into a conference as Kitty and I walked out of the house. We met Mother at the front door.

"Good morning, darlings," she called. "I'm off to do my errands."

"What errands?"

"Oh . . ." Mother's voice trailed off, "I have to look up old friends and sign my name in the Viceroy's Book . . ." Then she hurried off.

"What book?" I asked Kitty.

Kitty laughed. "You have to leave your name at Viceregal Lodge when you first arrive in New Delhi if you are anything even remotely diplomatic. I think they have to be sure to invite all the appropriate people to the receptions there, and this is the only way they can keep track of their comings and goings."

NISSIM EZEKIEL

Naipaul's India and Mine

To begin at the beginning for those who do not know: Mr V.S. Naipaul published a book a few months ago entitled *An Area of Darkness* (André Deutsch, 1964), with the explanatory subheading "An Experience of India". It describes a year's stay in this country. After a dramatic opening chapter, which narrates how the author was harassed by the Bombay customs officials, he tells us some important things about himself in relation to India. It was the background of his childhood, the country from which his grandfather had migrated, to settle down as an indentured labourer in Trinidad. The family became West Indian but retained some of its Indian customs and ways of thinking, retained in particular objects brought from India. These were "cherished because they came from India" but they were allowed to disintegrate without regret.

This kind of sterile continuity Mr Naipaul recognises as typically Indian, a continuity without cultivation. Even at this early stage in the book we recognise Mr Naipaul's special gift for the telling detail and the penetrating observation based on it. We see the point of his mentioning the grimy, tattered string-bed, the straw mat, the brass vessels, the wooden printing blocks, the coarse, oily books, the ruined harmonium, the brightly coloured pictures of deities, the images, the stick of sandalwood.

For Mr Naipaul as a child, the India of such artifacts and of the persons related to them, a few of whom he portrays, was "featureless". It was an area of darkness. After his journey he found that "something of darkness remains, in those attitudes, those ways of thinking and seeing, which are no longer mine." His darkness is peopled, packed with a kind of life which is death, a negation, distortion and degradation from which he is glad finally to escape. He says at the end of the book that he is sorry to have had the experience, that it has broken his life in two. Even the menials of Beirut, first stop of his return flight, seem to him "whole" compared to the caricature and mockery of all that is human which he observed in India.

The grandfather, characteristically Indian, "carried his village with him" from Uttar Pradesh to Trinidad, joining others like him in re-creating his ageless environment in another setting. The generations that followed could not do the same. They accepted the West Indies but continued for long as Indians in a multi-racial society, giving the matter no further thought.

Mr Naipaul outlines precisely what it meant to live in that state of innocence, relying "on the old, Indian divisions, meaningless though these had become." The family was Hindu Brahmin, the outside world was not. The first experiences of boyhood involved savouring the difference without questioning it.

But even before the questioning began, a temperamental advantage was already secure. Mr Naipaul "was born an unbeliever" and in addition "remained almost totally ignorant of Hinduism." Examining himself with that peculiar honesty of his, he writes that what survived of Hinduism in him was a "sense of the difference of people . . . a vaguer sense of caste, and a horror of the unclean."

Turning these Hindu weapons against Hindus, he wins his spectacular victories, metaphorically speaking, against the Hindu way of life. He speaks with the virulent sharpness of one who has "contracted out". The attenuation of his childhood culture began in the family when he was six or seven, was complete when he was fourteen. A few ambivalent attitudes of course remained, and Mr Naipaul acknowledges them freely. But essentially the older, Hindu, traditional Brahmin side of him was dead or existed in a new way. The newer and truer side of his nature kicked against what he noticed in India, a multitude of evils flowing from "the smugness . . . the imperviousness to criticism, the refusal to see, the double-talk and double-think . . ."

That was the monstrous reality compared to the India which was an area of his imagination, compared again to the India of the newspapers and books, the political speeches and the cultural exchanges. The apprenticeship for rejecting this Monstrous India, as it may be called, was long and radical. If the Indian community in the West Indies seemed self-defeatingly static, the Gujarati and Sindhi merchants who came out to settle there appeared "foreign". From Mr Naipaul, the word does not sound chauvinistic because his cultural base is not national but humanist, not a territory or even a culture but a complex of values which cuts across all historical divisions. Of the Gujaratis and Sindhis, he writes, "They lived enclosed lives of a narrowness which I considered asphyxiating. They were devoted to their work, the making of money; they seldom went out; their pallid women were secluded; and all day their houses screeched with morbid Indian film songs. They contributed nothing to the society, nothing even to the Indian community. They were reputed among us to be sharp businessmen." Moreover, they maintained their static relations with India, built up none with their new environment.

The picture is a clear one and its justice cannot be denied, except that it would be equally true of most other Indian communities. Considered as a whole, and allowing always for individual exceptions (a small percentage, but running into huge numbers[1]) the communal way of life in India is hidebound, inimical to personal development, fantastically ignorant and prejudiced about the world outside the community, and hopelessly uncreative in every conceivable area of life.

My quarrel with Mr Naipaul, which I hope to conduct in a way that will be understandable to him, is not because of these condemnatory judgements of his, so fiercely, so blazingly expressed. My quarrel is that Mr Naipaul is so often uninvolved and unconcerned. He writes exclusively from the point of view of his own dilemma, his temperamental alienation from his mixed background, his choice and his escape. That temperament is not universal, not even widely distributed, that choice is not open to all, the escape for most is not from the community but into it. To forget this is to be wholly subjective, wholly self-righteous, to think first and last of one's own expectations, one's extreme discomfort. If only Mr Naipaul could have realised how utterly unreasonable this attitude is! It nearly undermines the validity of his arguments.

"To be in Bombay was to be exhausted. The moist heat sapped energy and will . . ." From that starting point, nothing can be done; the evidence of Indian bureaucratic stupidity becomes suspect. In *A Passage to India*, which Mr Naipaul quotes from admiringly, Adela accuses Aziz of having tried to rape her. Later, she confesses that her behaviour was like that of certain women who honestly believe that they have received offers of marriage when none were intended. Forster too makes much, and rightly, of the heat and the exhaustion, but his book is a novel. He has to make the situation plausible, both psychologically and circumstantially. Mr Naipaul's is a travel book, though an

[1] "In a country like India, so vast and so populous, the individuals who form the exceptions may well run into millions." Nirad C. Chaudhuri, *The Autobiography of an Unknown Indian.*

unorthodox one. Dealing with the same material, he would probably relate how an Indian took two English ladies to see some caves and tried to rape one of them there. It would not be an impossible story, only an appalling one.

Mr Naipaul suggests over and over again that appalling stories don't appal Indians. He keeps running into obtuse, unsympathetic Indians, bland, silly and incapable of understanding his simplest problems. It may be true, but somehow one feels that Mr Naipaul's aloof, sullen, aggressive manner contributed to his difficulties, accentuated them. What is to be thought of a man who writes, "I stood in the shade of Churchgate Station and debated whether I had it in me to cross the exposed street to the Tourist Office?"

Mr Naipaul will no doubt be bitterly scornful if it is hinted that some of his experiences seem self-flagellatory. He will take it as further evidence of the Indian unwillingness to see. But I am not in fact doubting his veracity, only his approach towards the discovery of the truth. He makes the truth about India seem simple. I don't believe it is simple. Honestly and frankly, he exposes his state of mind. I cannot believe that in such a state of mind, truth can be discovered. The truth about Mr Naipaul, certainly, but not the whole truth about India. He asserts loudly that in India for the first time in his life he was one of the crowd, and that it upset him to be so.

What, in God's name, is there to be upset about that unless one has abandoned humility altogether? "There was nothing in my appearance or dress to distinguish me from the crowd eternally hurrying into Churchgate Station." Why should there be? In what way is it reassuring to be different in dress and appearance? "In Trinidad to be an Indian was to be distinctive . . . To be an Indian in England was distinctive . . . Now in Bombay I entered a shop or a restaurant and awaited a special quality of response . . ." Is this so much as intelligent, is it fair? "And there was nothing. It was like being denied part of my reality. Again and again, I was caught. I was faceless. I might sink without a trace into that Indian crowd. I had been made by Trinidad and England; recognition of my difference was necessary to me. I felt the need to impose myself, and didn't know how."

This fear, this anxiety, this feverish insistence on being different, this frequent assertion of what and where he had been "made", this irrational urge to "impose" and the rage at being unable to do so, this constitutes the mirror Mr Naipaul holds up to India. This is the source of his curses, the cause of his raving and ranting. I hasten to add that it does not, for me at least, decrease the impact of his criticism. Perhaps it is even increased. Mr Naipaul's book has the moral authority of hysteria, the interest and value of a suffering impotence. "I was too tired to go back, to talk in a voice whose absurdity I felt whenever I opened my mouth."

A pathetic rather than a tragic situation. Unfortunate Mr Naipaul. Unfortunate India. That much I feel. But now: How right Mr Naipaul. How wrong India. And that is what, no doubt, he expects the reader to feel. It is a pity. For I share most of his ideas and problems. But I see India in my own way, a way I would like to take this opportunity of clarifying and developing by contrasting it with Mr Naipaul's.

Not that my way of seeing India is important, least of all to Mr Naipaul. He is a brilliant and successful novelist whose writing I greatly enjoy and admire. I know him personally, too, a little. A friend introduced him to me soon after his arrival in India. He was friendly and open but said nothing about his first painful encounters with Indian life, which he describes in his book. Then he wrote to me from Srinagar to ask if I knew anyone in Bombay willing to adopt a stray dog (or was it a cat?)

he had rescued from ill treatment and starvation. When I met him a second time, at a party in Bombay, he freely expressed his revulsion against certain aspects of Indian behaviour. Since those aspects are revolting, I had no difficulty in agreeing with him.

The third meeting was more than a year later, in London, again at a party. He left early. The others present talked about the distinguished writer's conversational performance. I was struck by the fact that he had aroused their malice. It was not the first time I had occasion to reflect that a hypersensitive person is quite capable of trampling on the sensitivities of other people.

So, in Naipaul's India, "the clerk will not bring you a glass of water even if you faint." In my India, a clerk will do virtually anything for you if he is treated humanely. I know those clerks, their background, their problems, their conditions of work, their income, how they are transported to and from their places of work, their educational and cultural limitations, their sense of dignity and worth, their humanity, in short. Mr Naipaul is both right and wrong about them as he is on many other points in his book. I admit that for Indian readers the core of rightness in his complaint ought to be taken seriously. It is more valuable than his reckless generalisation, his grotesque exaggeration, his nagging, irritable manner. On the other hand, why should he be allowed to get away with all that? It would only confirm and deepen his contempt for the "'spiritual' humility" of Indians – the inner quotes of "spiritual" are his.

Mr Naipaul shows little humility, spiritual or other. His response when he meets an American lady during his pilgrimage to Amarnath is, "she attracted me. But I had grown tired of meeting young Americans in unlikely places . . . there were too many of them." The "Eastern hospitality" they receive outrages his sense of propriety. He accuses them of "exacting a personal repayment for a national generosity," which is the most caddish anti-American sentiment I have ever read.

The lady was of an unbalanced, disagreeably foolish kind. Mr Naipaul could not have met any other kind of American lady in India. If he had, he would not have written about her. This piece of female fantasy suits his pen ideally. She is blind to the squalor of India, and a "seeker" attracted to Hindu philosophy. Observing that "her breasts were good and full" he remarks that she would not "remain a seeker for long". It turned out that he was right, but he does not realise that it was not worth being right. The unavoidable implication that she represents the typical American woman in India does no credit to Mr Naipaul. That long story about her is amusing in itself, but in a book purporting to explore India, it is worthless.

Similarly, there is a long story about Ramnath, a clerk in a government department, who is happy until Malhotra joins it. Malhotra is an Indian from East Africa, "educated at an English university." He dictates a letter to Ramnath which the latter takes down in shorthand but does not type out. In Mr Naipaul's story, there is also Hiralal, the typist. Ramnath passes on the shorthand notes to Hiralal who is too busy to type from them that day. Malhotra orders Ramnath to type all letters dictated to him. Ramnath says it is not his job, he is a steno, not a typist. Malhotra insists. Ramnath keeps silent, takes more dictation, passes on the notes to Hiralal. Malhotra, furious, dictates another letter to Ramnath, after making no impression on the head of the department. This letter is to request that Ramnath be sacked for insubordination and insolence.

Ramnath was defeated. He typed all Malhotra's letters that day. He also "dropped to the floor and touched Malhotra's polished shoes with his clasped palms." Then he sobbed, "embracing the shoes, polishing them with his palms."

That is the kind of thing that happens in Naipaul's India. In my India, stenographers type out the letters dictated to them.

Is the story, then, a fabrication? Unlikely. There are so many questions I would like to ask about it. Was Ramnath, perhaps, the only steno in the department? From how many persons did he take dictation? Could he have typed all the letters dictated to him? Had he been instructed to make himself available only for dictation? I don't know. Since the head of the department was pusillanimous and evasive, was he concealing something about the terms on which Ramnath had been hired, a man capable of taking down fast dictation from one who has been "educated at an English university"?

There was undoubtedly some misunderstanding. A young Englishman of my acquaintance in Bombay used to speak bitterly to me about his Indian office assistants, claiming that they invariably misinterpreted his simplest instructions. I could barely follow the general tenor of his argument, to say nothing of grasping the details, so clipped and jerky was his manner of speech, so pronounced his Oxford accent. Needless to say, based on his experience, this gentleman tended to doubt the intelligence of all the unfortunate Indians who worked under him.

In the office of a weekly for which I worked, I once heard the Irish editor thundering at a sub-editor, concluding with the words, "You haven't the intelligence of a rabbit." The sub came up to me sadly and said, "What information does the editor want me to obtain about rabbits?" It is often the arrogance of the whites in India, and of those "educated at an English university" that makes me despair, not the intelligence of clerks, stenos and subs.

Mr Malhotra interests me. It seems that earning only Rs 600/- a month "his place was therefore with 600-rupee-a-month men." This somehow makes him an outsider, and at his level "there were no outsiders, no one who, like Malhotra, had rejected the badges of food and caste and dress." (The reference to dress indicates how careless Mr Naipaul is about the unquestionably narrow and closed compartments in which most of Indian life is lived. Even when they preserve the restrictions of food and caste, urban Indians dress as they please, in the Western or Eastern styles, often in a curious compromise between the two.) Mr Malhotra wishes to marry and, notwithstanding his English education, applies for advertised brides whose parents or brothers want a higher salaried man. "No marriage, then, for him." Mr Naipaul is very sorry for Malhotra.

That is the kind of thing that characterises Mr Naipaul's India. In my India, the Malhotras marry by the million, and not always by answering advertisements in the matrimonial columns. They move rapidly from 600 a month to twice that sum and more; even on the starting salary their friendships are not confined to those with the same or similar salaries. With his English university background, Malhotra need not have had any inhibitions.

Does this mean that Mr Naipaul has invented Malhotra? Not necessarily. He has swallowed Malhotra's story as he swallowed many others. These stories enabled him to believe what he wanted to believe. Perhaps Malhotra expected a higher starting salary. That was his fault. He does not seem to have much confidence in his ability to rise. His applying for brides suggests that his education had done him little good. "No marriage, then, for him; and the years were going by, and his parents were breaking their hearts." Rubbish, Mr Naipaul.

After Malhotra, Malik. He is an engineer returned from Scandinavia, earing Rs 1200/- a month. European engineers less qualified than he earned thrice as much. This is true, alas, and shameful. As an Indian, I am ashamed. But Malik's story too is suspect in my eyes. He claims, and Mr Naipaul believes him, that he is not given the superior jobs for which he applies because he has no car. "Do you own a car? Malik didn't. The probing was abandoned; no one was even interested in his parentage."

That in Mr Naipaul's India. In my India, engineers trained abroad, provided they have what it takes, advance rapidly, buy a car before they can afford it because advancement is certain, land superior jobs even if they don't have a car and are given one by the firm, with an allowance for maintenance.

Malik failed to get a bigger job because his personality and abilities did not measure up to his qualifications. Indians do tend to think that qualifications are enough, particularly if they are foreign. They explain their failures in many ways. Malik believes it is because he has no car, though he could easily buy one and sail over the alleged obstacle. He has "a well-appointed flat in one of the finer areas of Bombay" and on the bookshelves there is Ibsen in the original. Malik is stuck and Mr Naipaul is sorry for him. At every interview, "Do you own a car?" Malik didn't. "The probing was abandoned." Rubbish, Mr Naipaul.

It is my turn now to tell a story, a true one which does not cast any dark reflections on much-maligned India. The overtones are purely human. We were five executives in a business firm. One of us never succeeded in getting a woman to go out with him. We teased him about it. "A modern Indian woman," he said, "will not go out with a man unless he has a car." We laughed heartily. None of us had a car at that time – and we had no problems in that delicate area where our colleague was unsuccessful. He was merely unattractive to women, and still is, seven years later. He has had a car for a long time. But he is always alone in it.

I would like to meet Malik, though, and discuss Ibsen with him.

If true-blooded Indian *mores* make Mr Naipaul sneer, westernised Indians make him snarl. Their nicknames annoy him and he quotes their "dated slang". If the slang had been up-to-date, he wouldn't have liked it either. He laughs at the Indian army officer because he is "at a first meeting a complete English army officer." If he had been a complete Indian army officer, he would have laughed even more loudly. Indian Anglo-India is of course vulnerable. What is detestable is Mr Naipaul's refusal to see it in human and historic terms. Bunty, the uneasy mixture of West and East, is condemned merely by description, so to speak. His grandfather conducted his business over a hookah, reclining on bolsters. Bunty "discusses business over drinks at the club or on the golf course." If he returned to hookah and bolsters, Mr Naipaul wouldn't approve either.

In Bunty's home, a Jamini Roy painting is hung beside a Picasso, which is, of course, infuriating. If he had only Jamini Roy he would have been provincial, if only Picasso, a snob. Bunty can't win, though he "sees himself as every man's equal and most men's superior." He speaks English fluently, which maddens Mr Naipaul. If he had spoken it badly, Mr Naipaul would have despised him.

Mr Naipaul saw a banner in Bombay on his first day there, advertising the Oxford and Cambridge Players' production of *The Importance of Being Earnest*. He finds it funny, an example of confused values. Wilde's witty comedy to be produced in Bombay, city of slums, hutment dwellers, pavement sleepers and beggars, appears to him absurd, fantastic, part of the mimicry of English life. The fact itself I don't find absurd; any pretension attached to it is. Mr Naipaul doesn't make the distinction. The very announcement of the production he thinks symptomatic of a profound cultural disease. It is actually a symptom of a natural and inevitable division in Indian society as a result of British rule. English was made the national language of India by the British, and the medium of education. For obvious reasons it could not be immediately and entirely removed. If it had been, there would be no banner in Bombay advertising in English to upset Mr Naipaul. He would then have commented, no doubt, on the disappearance of all that intellectual activity in English which was the natural accompaniment of English education in India.

To understand the situation, one does not have to be for or against the continuance of English. It was, is and will remain part of the Indian scene for many years to come. There is an "Indian withdrawal and denial", there is a "confusion of Indian Anglo-India", but Mr Naipaul is too subjective to analyse it meaningfully. He argues too exclusively from revulsion and anger to *see* (his favourite word) the problem in the round.

In the chapter entitled "The Colonial", Mr Naipaul uses Gandhi in an original way to reinforce his attack on Indian culture. He quotes Gandhi against the kind of "misplaced charity" which consists in organising free meals for beggars or giving them money. He then says that Gandhi "Of course in this matter of beggary . . . failed." If begging continues in India only because of misplaced charity, Mr Naipaul would be right. No doubt there are beggars in India capable of earning a living but who beg because it is easy and pays. But surely the overwhelming majority begs because there is no alternative. Beggars will disappear in India not when Indians heed Gandhi and other reformers but when economic progress makes begging unnecessary for anybody.

Mr Naipaul calls Gandhi "the least Indian of Indian leaders" because of his attitude to sanitation, physical labour, service, inefficiency and untouchability. In these matters his attitude was indeed different from the ordinary run of Indian leaders. Nevertheless it can with equal truth be said that he was more Indian than most in his attitude to sex, his advocacy of prohibition, his asceticism, his food fads, his opposition to modernism in every field. His ideal society was of self-contained villages, an economy based on the spinning wheel (the use of which, he claimed, would "cool one's lust"), altogether a pre-medieval society of holy poverty and otherworldly absorption. I think Mr Naipaul is not interested in the truth about Gandhi, one way or another. He cites him merely to criticise "the whole diseased society" which Gandhi criticised, except that the phrase is not Gandhi's but Naipaul's. This does not seem to me particularly honest, since Gandhi may be and has been criticised for innumerable characteristically Indian vices, including doublethink.

Let me pause to explain again that I see India in most ways as Naipaul sees her. All that he says against the grossness and squalor of Indian life, the routine ritualism, the lip-service to high ideals, the petrified and distorted sense of cleanliness, and a thousand other things, all this is true. My dissatisfaction is with his mode of argument, his falsifying examples.

The top bunk in a railway sleeper is avoided in India, Mr Naipaul writes, because it "involves physical effort, and physical effort is to be avoided as a degradation." Well, I avoid the top bunk because it brings me too close to the fan which is attached to the ceiling. Turning the fan away causes the bunk to be rather airless; in the heat of India, this makes it very uncomfortable. In Europe and elsewhere, as Mr Naipaul points out, the favoured bunk is the top bunk. It is cool. It offers greater privacy. The top bunk in Indian railways often has no ladder leading up to it. One has to swing up, placing the feet on the arm-rest of the lower bunk. So I have sometimes given up my reserved lower bunk to a lady or an elderly person.

As for the Indian unwillingness or reluctance to do physical labour, the charge is justified. Nevertheless, in all my train journeys I have seen people roll out their bedding on the bunk, then roll it off again. This job is not done by porters. The incident Mr Naipaul describes, in which he changed his lower bunk with a passenger and found himself doing "the porter's job" without assistance from the person he had obliged, made me raise my eyebrows. I quote:

> His bedding had been spread for him on the top bunk by the porter, and he was waiting until we got to the next station, two hours' distance, so that he might get a porter to take it down for him . . . I wished to settle down. I began to do the porter's job. He smiled but offered no help. I lost my temper. His face acquired that Indian expressionlessness which indicates that communication has ceased and that the Indian has withdrawn from a situation he cannot understand. Labour is a degradation; only a foreigner would see otherwise.

Here is truth told in such a way that it becomes falsehood. I do not say that all or even the greater part of Mr Naipaul's argument is vitiated in this way. A great deal is, far too much is, and given the unrelenting irritability, this is not surprising. The publisher's blurb on the dust jacket of *An Area of Darkness* refers, startlingly, to Mr Naipaul's "Vision distorted by indignation or fear." I can only concur. The blurb goes on to praise the honesty with which Mr Naipaul records his indignation and fear. Even if I concur again, that distorted vision does not dissatisfy me less.

Most of the persons Mr Naipaul met in India were grotesques, contemptible or pathetic creatures. He writes about them at great length as though they are important illustrations of his argument. Mrs Mahindra of New Delhi, whose "craze for foreign" sprawls over several pages. M.S. Butt, proprietor of Hotel Liward in Srinagar, and his assistant Aziz, the boy from Bombay who comes to stay in Hotel Liward, are others of the same kind. Mr Naipaul treated them with a mixture of impertinence and condescension, converting himself into a grotesque in the process. Abandoning his culture and his manners, he seems to act out of pure, unreasoned hostility and records it all with his usual "honesty".

The utter triviality of some encounters doesn't bother him. "I had loathed the boy from Bombay on sight." Naipaul loathed him. The boy is listening to Radio Ceylon. Mr Naipaul "ran downstairs", turns the set to Radio Kashmir because he wants to listen to the news. After the news, the boy switches it back to Radio Ceylon. No words are exchanged. "And so now it went on, morning and evening." It is the boy who eventually calls on Mr Naipaul, who has fallen ill. "Thereafter courtesy was imposed on both of us. I offered him Radio Ceylon; he offered me Radio Kashmir." Our sympathies are supposed to be with Mr Naipaul! He is a sensitive man. The boy from Bombay, in his eyes, is set "against a background of swarming Bombay slums."

The reader does, in fact, sympathise with Mr Naipaul when he describes what he sees, the scenes of callousness, coarseness and suffering, the everyday degradation of the human image not only among the poorest of the poor but among the middle class and in Indian society as a whole. All or almost all that he writes about the effects of British rule in India is subtle and suggestive. The comparison with the colonial consequences in the West Indies is illuminating. The fact that the British had possessed the country so completely, that the Indian subjection was so thorough and her resistance so puny, is related to the age-old "Indian ability to retreat, the ability genuinely not to see what was obvious." It was not merely, as with others, a "foundation of neurosis" but part of "a greater philosophy of despair, leading to passivity, detachment, acceptance."

Few Indians are willing to believe that the roots of their failure go deep into history. They believe in their high ideals, attribute failure to not living up to these. That the ideals are false and stultifying is never clearly perceived. Hence the contradiction between words and behaviour which is virtually universal in India, the insensitive contradiction between belief and way of life. The story of the village politician, austerely dressed, lauding Gandhi publicly and having seventeen people murdered during an election contest, may be exaggerated but basically it is quite plausible.

Mr Naipaul has only to describe certain Indian phenomena to make them suspect. Some of them are easy targets but need to be hit over and over again, until they are eliminated. The pious family of wealthy Indian merchants from East Africa and their adoption of a holy man in Delhi provides occasion for a sharp look at the most popular and influential kind of saintliness in India.

It is seen to be simplicity of a primitive kind, "cooking on stones, eating off leaves, fetching water from the spring." Gandhi believed in that too, though he was opposed to the casualness and disorder which often and typically accompany Indian holiness. The belching and spitting, the unaesthetic dress, the ritualistic and arrogant cleanliness coexisting with dirt, the decadent veneration – all are indicated merely through the accumulation of concrete detail. How much better this is than the self-chosen situations of extreme anguish, compelling confessions of "that deep anger which unhinges judgement and almost physically limits vision!"

A recurring theme in *An Area of Darkness* is public defecation in India, with the waste left exposed on the surface of the earth. Gandhi is quoted – his words deserve constant reiteration – "Leaving night-soil, cleansing the nose, or spitting on the road is a sin against God as well as humanity, and betrays a sad want of consideration for others. The man who does not cover his waste deserves a heavy penalty even if he lives in a forest." It is some consolation that the educated, on the whole, and those above the lowest economic life cease to be guilty of these loathsome practices. Unfortunately, even so, their sanitary habits remain careless. Indians tend to spurn it as an unpleasant subject.

A distressing episode in *An Area of Darkness* concerns Mr Naipaul's involvement with an alienated, violent-minded and ferociously prejudiced Sikh. They are in a third-class air-conditioned compartment of a train travelling south. The compartment is full of South Indians, whose way of eating their liquidised food is pictured with more than malice. But, humour is humour. The Sikh is a different proposition, an uncultured communalist who strikes a man for staring at him. Mr Naipaul admits his mistake in being friendly with the Sikh, but the mistake is significant. When they fall out, the Sikh calls Mr Naipaul "a dirty South Indian swine." Earlier, he refers to the South Indians in the train as "punks" and "blackies". Did Mr Naipaul really meet no decent Indians? He fell once too often into the trap of his own general revulsion.

In the India which I have presumed to call mine, I acknowledge without hesitation the existence of all the darkness Mr Naipaul discovered. I am not a Hindu and my background makes me a natural outsider: circumstances and decisions relate me to India. In other countries I am a foreigner. In India I am an Indian. When I was eighteen, a friend asked me what my ambition was. I said with the naïve modesty of youth, "To do something for India." My friend who was a Muslim and wanted India divided (he left for Karachi soon after Pakistan was created) laughed, though not unsympathetically, as I remember. India is simply my environment. A man can do something for and in his environment by being fully what he is, by not withdrawing from it. I have not withdrawn from India.

In one of the rare positive moments in *An Area of Darkness*, Mr Naipaul writes, "Anger, compassion and contempt were aspects of the same emotions; they were without value because they could not endure. Achievement could begin only with acceptance." As always, Mr Naipaul overstates the case. I believe in anger, compassion and contempt. They are not without value. I believe in acceptance that incorporates all three, makes use of them. I am incurably critical and sceptical. That is what I am in relation to India also. And to myself. I find it does not prevent the growth of love. In this sense only, I love India. I expect nothing in return because critical, sceptical love does not beget love. It performs another, more objective function.

In a very small, even negligible way, this objective function may bring results which have eluded the prophets and reformers of India, or so it suits my sardonic conceit to think. Mice may gnaw through the ropes of bondage where the roaring of lions makes no impression. It is at least an experiment worth trying.

Not being Hindu, I cannot identify myself with India's past as a comprehensive heritage or reject it as if it were mine to reject. I can identify myself only with modern India, a place with more things in it than are dreamt of in Mr Naipaul's philosophy. I am neither proud nor ashamed of being an Indian. I am neither proud nor ashamed of being westernised. History is behind me. I live on the frontiers of the future that is slowly receding before me. Contempt for background impresses me as little as pride in background. Both are distorting. Tormented, self-regarding resolutions of cultural conflict create new, tormenting problems. Poise, a sense of proportion and that irony which Mr Naipaul finds lacking in Indians, must be maintained if one wants to help. Otherwise, criticism is self-indulgence. It must attack, even denounce, but it must not deny human beings their humanity.

In *An Area of Darkness* Mr Naipaul comes dangerously close to doing that. The South Indian way of eating he mocks, but he does not seem to have met these people who eat so coarsely. I don't know if he is serious or merely guilt-ridden when, surprisingly, he writes near the end of the book, "Nowhere were people so heightened, rounded and individualistic; nowhere did they offer themselves so fully and with such assurance. To know Indians was to take a delight in people as people; every encounter was an adventure." I distrust that "nowhere". Excessive moralising on the incongruities of Indian life has betrayed him into an excess here. He who exaggerates blame will exaggerate praise.

My concern with Mr Naipaul's criticism of India has been to analyse the way the job is done. I have made it clear that it is an unsatisfactory way, from my point of view, and heavily flawed in detail. All the same, I am on the side of the criticism against the myriad Indian and foreign evaders of Indian reality. Culture doesn't consist only of literature, and philosophy and art, and it is certainly not acquired by adhering to the beliefs of the past and conforming to its institutional demands. Its living presence is indicated in behaviour, by rich and poor alike, and there are universal human standards by which it may be judged. Mr Naipaul is right to see us as we are in the streets, in buses and trains, in our kitchens and lavatories.

Mr Naipaul's conclusion is negative. "Shiva has ceased to dance." It would be too facile to say that He may dance again.

Certainly, that is the hope and the endeavour. There is some endeavour too, in modern India, which need hardly be mentioned as evidence for hope. It is at least as obvious as the poverty and the squalor, physical, social and moral. A book could be written about it which would not have to falsify or exaggerate anything. It might well point the way out of the present Indian confusion.

F.N. SOUZA

Nirvana of a Maggot

SOME YEARS AGO I spent a few months in an almost deserted village in Goa, which is my native country. I was living in an old half-dilapidated house. The village, quite a primitive one, was scantily populated. The tentacles of the monstrous civilisation spreading on the outskirts beyond were gradually strangling it. Most of its able-bodied inhabitants had left to seek their fortunes elsewhere, in the larger towns and countries, if there were any fortunes left to find. But the village somehow still survived, even without a post office. Every few days I rode my bicycle twelve to fourteen miles to the next village to post my letters and collect my mail.

The house was furnished with an infested bed and a broken chair. There was no table. I had to squat on a mat to write and paint and eat my food. The floor was overlaid with a thick paste of cow-dung spread manually in a pattern of semi-concentric circles. There were little toads in nearly every hole in the walls, and the corners seemed to be tied together by cobwebs. Two holy pictures hung close to each other: Christ and the Madonna with their hearts in their hands. Placed on corroded nails, a worm-eaten plant made a simple oratory. Some dead flowers, a candlestick with its socket burnt off, and a small wooden image of St Thomas with a hole in the head for fixing a halo which happened to be missing . . . A crude, baroque arabesque painted on the faded, falling wall in red and green distemper . . .

In a little almirah I found a book. I took it out and dusted it. It was full of silverfish, some of them nice fat ones which had devoured the leaves with a diligence which reminded me of some of my learned professors. The book was an outdated edition of collected English essays by authors as ancient as itself. I wondered who the recluse reader previously occupying the house could have been. Perhaps he was one of those Englishmen who go about in the midday sun and have been to the far corners of the earth, even to cobwebbed corners. There was no one in the village who was literate except the vicar of the church, and he didn't know English. I read one of the essays in the remains of the book: "On Wild Flowers", by Richard Jefferies. I don't know how old man Jefferies stands in English Literature or whether he was a horticulturist or a mystic; but his essay induced me to examine with great delight the wild flowers in the vicinity, on knolls and in thickets.

Our servant Salu had accompanied me on this bit of exploring an uncivilised Goan countryside. In those days I painted peasants and rural landscapes. I painted them with broad strokes, heavily outlining masses of brilliant colours. Peasants in different moods, eating and drinking, working in the fields, bathing in a river or a lagoon, climbing palm trees, distilling liquor, assembling in church, praying or in procession with priests and acolytes carrying the monstrance, relics and images; ailing and dying, mourning or merry-making in market places, and feasting at weddings.

I used to write a lot too. But whenever I write, I get a feeling of incompetence. Not so when I paint, for then I feel I am the master of the situation. Words, however, are very elusive little things to me and they fail me. Nevertheless, there's an urge to express myself with them. What I'd like to do first of all is merely to articulate freely and easily. I have never learnt grammar and I can't spell correctly. Yet I want to say something, to make just a sound, even a guttural sound or a grunt, an onomatopoeic sound emitted with a clearance of my throat. What I'd want to do is to suspend my vocal cords on the nib of my pen, like a mouthful of food on the end of a fork; to throw my voice like a ventriloquist's, but over a page; to emit sounds with gummed backs like postage stamps which stick firmly on paper; to make the split point of my pen the sensitive needle of a seismograph, as I can easily do when I draw. But it is difficult for most Indians to articulate by word of mouth or pen. There is an innate paralysis in us; a kind of latent paralysed force . . .

I'd want my language to ooze out of my mouth naturally, pure like a bubbling spring, a fountain spouting out, its source embedded deep within the crevices of pristine music, echoes of which we still hear at times in a poet's voice and in the voice of the turtle. Such a language may have no orthography, no solecisms. It is ecstasy, emotion, groans, sighs, everything a man feels and endures, and it comes from the heart. We call it *vachana-bala*, that is, the power to make a sound. It is only when we hear the palpitations of a man's heart vibrate on the membrane of his vocal cords that we consider him to have spoken well. He may not have uttered a word that is comprehensible or intelligible. He may have said something which doesn't mean anything – it does not matter, so long as he has delivered himself to the wind and the clouds and falling fruit – as long as he has united himself to the sight of flowers, the song of the bird, and rustle of rice, the smell of mangoes, the taste of good food and the feel of flesh, playing his counterpoint in the polyphonic orchestra of the cosmos with his phonetic instrument. Inside the cosmos, semantics is a word inaudible because the cosmos itself is meaningless or reveals no meaning.

I myself read, write and think in a language alien to me: English, a language not my mother tongue but spoken to me by my mother since my childhood. But the difficulty in expressing myself arose from the very start. For how can one articulate in Anglo-Saxon with a jewelled mandible that was fashioned by the ancient Konkan goldsmiths of Goa? It bewilders me to think that my inarticulation was due to England having possessed a lot of boats which had netted India into its vast Empire.

The Portuguese, too, on the other hand, had colonised Goa and had converted its inhabitants to Christianity, and this also again divided my tongue and minced my words. (St Thomas the Apostle, according to legend, had landed on our shores and preached the Gospel five centuries before it was heard of in Portugal. In any case there were Christians in India called the Nestorians, much to the surprise of the Portuguese conquistadores, but whom they later stoked into the incendiary Inquisition.)

Salu cleaned up the house thoroughly and made it habitable enough for me. He had destroyed all its creeping inhabitants. The toads, white ants, silverfish, cockroaches, spiders, lizards, and snakes he swatted ruthlessly, brutally. He pierced them with a pointed stick like a Hannibal, and burnt them alive like an Inquisitioner.

In the mornings I swam in a lake across the fields, quite near the house. The lake was luminous and flat, of an unbelievable blue, descended as it were from the blues. It looked like a piece of sky fallen on earth and embedded there in a miraculous moment of sublime tranquillity, when earth and sky yearned to unite, not lip to lip as they do at the horizon, but in a ventral unity, in a cosmic copulation. Sails of small fishing boats gleamed white, sharp as the wings of herons on the harp-shaped lake. Light on water, sound, movement, ripple, glitter; a rise, a splash of fish or green water-snake taking sudden fright and darting away towards the opposite shore. More sound, noise of leaves, of thunder, of rain on water . . . and in the cool of the blue distance beyond rose a range of monstrous hills shouldering monstrously changing shapes in the sky, all the time being born anew and renewing again in the dark water of monsoon clouds. Kingfishers, mynas, parrots, bluebirds sat on submerged water-buffaloes, pecking at gnats on these enormous immobile torpid pachyderms who looked like the black hulks of Viking ships. The edge of the lake was ornamented with rushes, waterlilies, lotus, coral, barnacle; and its great deep auriferous glittering bed was a playground for God's incarnations or for Fisher Kings. I doused pleasantly in the cool fresh water for an hour or two every day and returned to the house very hungry. I swallowed a fiery alcohol and ate gluttonously a heavy meal of boiled rice, red-hot curry, fried fish, served all in a heap on a brass plate. Salu was a good cook, a primitive sort, but it was more the swim, the salubrious air, and the liquor that gave me a tremendous appetite. Then to bed for a siesta; or under the shade of a mango tree I dozed off in an easy-chair which I had borrowed from the vicar.

One hot afternoon I was lolling on my bed, half-drunk and naked to the waist. Through my window, I saw the vicar with the sacristan walk down the path, carrying Extreme Unction for someone in the village who was dying or had probably died. I could not tell exactly because the church bell had not begun to toll.

A drunken state is when humility escapes and remorse sets in. Remorse about everything. But it is really a state of humiliation more than anything else, and at such times, truth comes crawling like a maggot out of the dung. If I didn't have such setbacks as I did have, I said to myself, I'd be so and so. Well, but I'm no less I said again. Everyone I want to emulate has come of good stock, not of bad straw like me. What was I originally? I was a blooming maggot on a dung heap. That's exactly from where I originated. That has been my breeding ground. My childhood has been insipid: like an undigested bit of straw. I have still the taste of dung in my mouth. Where I come from, they worship the cow. But nobody worships the maggot which I think might even be a venial sin against Baal-Zebub the Lord of Maggots. But now, if they whom I want to emulate were originally maggots, would they have been the ones I now want to emulate? I suppose not. But I, I was a humble little maggot. And now, look what a big proud brute I've made of myself. My mother, she's a strapping, handsome woman. She smells richly of the womb. I have the nose of a foetus. My father died when I was born, like a beetle that dies having laid the egg. Then I caught the small-pox and my mother vowed to God that should I be spared, she'd send me to a seminary to become a priest. But I go about giving a damn to everything. Life was just one big orgasm, like my father's. Then finished. I know. I have the memory of a foetus. I can never forgive him for having died just like that, and having left me in the lurch. How could I get into the church after that? . . . It takes a lot of money to serve the Heavenly Father with vestments on, and an earthly father is needed to take care of it.

Then my mind began to wander into the city I was bred in: Bombay with its rattling trams, omnibuses, hacks, railways, its forest of telegraph poles and tangle of telephone wires, its flutter of newspapers, its haggling coolies, its numberless dirty restaurants run by Iranis, its blustering officials and stupid policemen, its millions of clerks working clock-like in fixed routines, its schools that turn boys into clerks in a mechanical, Macaulayan educational system, its bania hoarders, its ghatine women carrying a million tiffins to the clerks at their offices during lunch hour, its lepers and beggars, its panwallas and red betel-nut expectorations on the streets and walls, its stinking urinals and filthy gullies, its sickening venereal-diseased brothels, its corrupted municipality, its Hindu colony and Muslim colony and Parsee colony, its bug-ridden Goan residential clubs, its reeking, mutilating, and fatal hospitals, its machines, rackets, babbitts, pinions, cogs, pile-drivers, dwangs, farads, and din.

As a boy, I had to attend school like any other, the difference being that schoolboys in Bombay were crammed by rote with a wretched system of education, the Macaulay system, intended as everybody knows to provide clerks and bureaucrats for maintaining what was a vast imperial racket. I had tried to escape it for more than ten juvenile years of my life, often successfully by playing truant day after day, or by malingering.

I spent nearly four months happy as a barbarian in this little village. I patted the earth and thanked heaven that there was at least a small plot of land left on this planet which had not been poisoned by our ghastly civilisation, if it can still be called that, with its mechanised fangs which were simply and surely sucking the life out of us. Four months of peaceful celibacy but without any hermit's temptations. I had put on some flesh on my otherwise emaciated body. I was lying on the bed blissfully indolent, without cares and hopes.

Under the oppression of the whites, the black man had cried out in blues. But we, from the diamond-pointed Bharat with its pearl-like pendant; we of Aryan descent browned by the sun, if we were oppressed we took it with a stolid, austere resignation. If somebody squeaked, he was quickly smothered and gagged. The rest of us were all tongue-tied and dumbfounded, four hundred million of us. For three hundred years under a powerful foreign rule, and with two petty foreign powers on our coasts, we presented a vast spectacle of human endurance, drudgery, poverty, undernourishment, sickness, humiliation, imbecility, intolerance, fanaticism, caste and proselytism, tuberculosis, pus and open sores, primitive farming, erosion and famine, infant mortality, moribund living, mendicant families, dirt and squalor, lice, ticks, fleas, nakedness, and death. We lived lividly in a state known to us as "tamas" which could be described as the stupidity of the poor for sleepily clinging to poverty, and the stupidity of the rich who connived at whatever happened as long as their slumber was not disturbed. The yogis too went to sleep on a bed of nails. To rouse such an inert state one could do nothing but scream one's guts out, but as I said, we were all tongue-tied and dumbfounded.

Then, all of a sudden, there came a mastermind and dwelt amongst us and he made this horrifying inertia of ours work according to a definite plan of his own, if inertia could be made to work at all, except scientifically or miraculously. That man was Mahatma Gandhi. To the few zealots and Communists who were urging him to wake the nation to battle with the enemy, he gave a listless ear and admonished them to be silent. Resist not Evil, he told them, quietly quoting a dictum of Christ. The enemy, who was by the way Christian, was all the more baffled. It is a long history of tension between a great active force and a great passive force, the like of which never before occurred in the history of the world. The Western Christian world has never understood this truly oriental dictum of Christ's. It voluntarily resorts to terrifying might against whatever it considers is evil and at times even to mean spite. But Gandhiji did not budge. He was in no hurry to retaliate even with the peaceful weapon of his great idea. He had an astonishing certitude, and a precision of timing his move in a stagnant land where time is taken in terms of eternity and eternal rebirths from maggots to Nirvana. But by the time the ultimatum, or what is called the political crisis, came, the Mahatma had already converted our national paralysis into an army of non-violence. We won the battle.

The vicar of the village church was a man of great religious fervour, unlike those others one meets in Goa who take to priesthood and make it a mercenary end. The sacerdotal profession is a lucrative business there. The vicar and I became friends despite some of our ideas which were almost diametrically opposite; very much like those of a saint and a sinner, and yet, a sinner could really be a good friend of a saint and the saint must necessarily be a friend of the sinner. On Sunday evenings, the vicar invited me to dine with him in the sanctity of the little parochial cottage allotted him by the Holy See in Goa. A laundered tablecloth was spread only when he had guests, a luxury he permitted himself with touching simplicity. (Occasionally he'd remove his biretta and wipe his sweating cropped head with a soiled handkerchief.) Compared to Salu, the vicar's cook was sophisticated. Stuffed cock, roast pigling, sausages, turtles' eggs, snails and *butch*, a heavily spiced dish of pig's intestines, comprised some of the Sunday dinners. Portuguese wines and a kind of cocktail which the vicar himself made, called confecao, flavoured with fruit kernels and sweetened with sugar, was one of his specialities.

Then he would discuss theology with me and I would roll aesthetics into it and my side of the argument would seem to him almost sacrilegious for I'd discuss the possibilities of the Creator on the basis of being a creator myself.

If you ask God to show you the cause of His whole Creation, this infinite universe, the entire cosmos, you will see that the cause itself is not as big as the Creation, in fact, it is something very small, for He will show you in the palm of His hand a tiny little thing which could perhaps be a drop of water, a speck of some sort, a nucleus maybe, or a germ of some kind: something which is impossible for us to grasp, both with hand or mind, but sometimes grasped at rare inspired moments by the heart. Therefore, we have called that little thing "Nothing" or "the Word", "Matter and Energy", "Om", "Breath", and what not. But all the same, it is that tiny thing which is the cause of the whole Creation.

In the same way, my own activity in matters of paint and words, I am trying to make one of creation within Creation. My drawings and paintings, for instance, are made of a little structure: two parallel lines cross-hatched on either side, e.g.

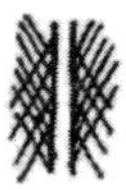

All my work – still-lifes, landscapes, portraits, and compositions – are based on this principle, or perhaps it is a drop of water or a germ of some sort . . . because, if man is made in the image of God's likeness, his creative activity must also be in the likeness of a hypothetical activity of the Creative God.

QURRATULAIN HYDER

My Aunt Gracie

NASIR CHACHA WAS a pirate-catcher. When he was a young man, he used to take his gun and go out into the dark night in his high-powered speedboat. He returned in the early hours and slept till noon.

He was my father's boyhood friend and was the son of a Nawab of Patna but never deigned to use the title. Only his son's Goan ayah, Gracie Pereira, insisted on addressing him as Nawab Saheb.

We had come from Lucknow to spend a month in Bombay with Nasir Chacha and were being looked after with tremendous enthusiasm by Gracie, who had styled herself the Nawab Saheb's housekeeper. She was about thirty-five, had been widowed at the age of twenty, and had devotedly served Nasir Chacha's wife who had died a few years ago, leaving little Asghar in her care.

Gracie mothered Asghar to distraction and bossed over the servants. She spoke polyglot English and reigned over the house like an autocrat.

Gracie, the battle-axe, certainly had a presence. She wore saris of bright colours, which made her look darker. She was sturdy and plain but looked attractive when she grinned from ear to ear, flashing her pearly white teeth. Now, my ayah back home was different. She was thin and languid and was always dressed in a snow-white, starched *ghaghra*. She spoke better English and was very very pucca and polite. Gracie was short-tempered, quarrelsome and a chatterbox.

One morning she volunteered to recount to my mother the story of her life. "My husband," she began, wiping her face, "was a big man, Mem Saheb. He was assistant cook at Taj, working under English head cook. He died in accident."

She stopped for a while and continued.

"My brother Patrick, steward on P.&O. liner. He also died. My papa, mama, both dead long long time. I had very bad time after my Joe died, Mem Saheb. When I came to my Mem Saheb's service here, I got roof on my head first time after my Joe's death." She sniffed and wiped her tears with the corner of her purple sari.

"My Mem Saheb, she God's own angel. For her sake I going to look after Asghar Baba and Nawab Saheb till I kick the damn bucket."

"Grace," said Nasir Chacha that afternoon to my mother, "has a heart of gold. But the trouble is that she has become terribly possessive about Asghar. And have you heard the atrocious language he speaks? I send him to the best English school, but at home he has poor old Gracie as his mentor. I could get a highly refined Mughlani-bi from Patna to look after him, but I just don't have the heart to turn Gracie out. Begum, may her soul rest in peace, on her deathbed literally entrusted the child to Gracie. I don't know what to do."

Frankly, I had no sympathy with Asghar. I could not get along with him, although he was about my age. Gracie had turned him into a thoroughly spoilt brat and a bully.

Nasir Chacha and I had become great friends.

"Tomorrow," he would say in a feigned conspiratorial tone, "we go to Juhu. There you wallow in the sea and have lots of ice cream afterwards."

In the evenings all of us strolled down to the Taj which was not far away. Nasir Chacha bought me stacks of Mickey Mouse comics.

Nasir Chacha had a majestic personality. He was a Brown Saheb with the dignity of an old-world Nawab. He also had a tremendous sense of humour.

Nasir Chacha had a habit of saying: "So, Saheb, this too has come to pass." In the morning, as he went through the newspapers, he would suddenly look up, address nobody in particular and announce: "So, Saheb, this too has come to pass . . . "

Once in a while I slipped down to the flat on the ground floor where Chacha's Jewish assistant lived with his wife and many children. There, on a Friday or Saturday evening, I watched, in fascination, as the *kashta*-clad Mrs David Khandekar (the whole thing was very mixed up: they were Jews but also a kind of Marathas) lit a lamp while a pictured Moses led a motley crowd across what I thought was a dried-up Suez Canal.

The same day I happened to read in a book upstairs: "You were good to me like Moses but I was ungrateful to you like a Pharoah and was lost in the desert . . ."

I asked Nasir Chacha what it meant.

"You will understand when you grow up," he said casually. I used to pester my father with all manner of questions which he always patiently answered. But not Nasir Chacha. Once he said, rattled: "Don't ask too many questions. Their answers will sadden you."

"Why?" I asked.

The world certainly was most intriguing. The fire temple with its Assyrian bulls. The bearded men in longcoats and golden turbans. The ancient, hawk-nosed Parsi who sold ice cream in a roadside kiosk. The distant lighthouse of Colaba.

I stumbled upon Gracie's little mystery quite accidentally. One morning, as I went to her room to call her for some errand, I had to stop outside as the door was half closed and she was angrily talking to someone.

"Look here, you Virgin Mother, if you not find me store-room keys by eight o'clock Indian Standard Time, breakfast late, Nawab Saheb cut off my head. What do you know. You never done work as ayah."

Gracie, I discovered, was actually quarrelling with a statuette which she kept by her bedside.

Gracie is mad, I decided. How can she talk to a statue and expect it to find her the lost keys?

Then I remembered that only last week, when Nasir Chacha went out on a tour of inspection, Gracie had rushed to her room, quickly lit a candle, and mumbled something before the china figurine of the Virgin.

The mystery deepened. One morning three equally hefty ladies came up the stairs, panting, and entered the drawing room with great solemnity. Their Lucknow-style *ghararas* trailed behind them. They carried velvet boxes like the Three Kings of the East bearing myrrh and gold and frankincense.

Nasir Chacha came into the drawing room. The leader of the delegation opened a velvet case and, with a flourish, produced a photograph. He glanced at it indifferently. Whereupon all three ladies said in a chorus that the engagement ceremony was to take place the next evening at the girl's place. Thereafter, one of the Three Wise Women opened a jewel box and produced a ring they had bought on Nasir Chacha's behalf.

Gracie was ordered to go to the market and buy eleven seers each of sweetmeat and fresh and dry fruits. She was also told to be ready with everything by five o'clock next evening. After which they left.

The three ladies were the wives of Nasir Chacha's colleagues and friends. They had finally persuaded him, for the sake of

Asghar's proper upbringing, to get married again. And for the purpose of reforming poor Asghar's deplorable language, they had selected a beautiful girl whose wealthy family was not only of Persian extraction but had lived for many generations in Lucknow.

"This is ridiculous," Nasir Chacha growled when my mother came home after shopping at Whiteway's. "Jamila Bhabi insists on performing all the stupid rites . . ." Then he noticed me and chuckled: "So, Saheb, this too has come to pass . . ."

The next morning my parents left for Poona to visit some friends. In the afternoon Gracie went to the market and bought home the required stuff. Then she asked me to come to the box room.

Inside the box room she opened a Chinese chest and brought out an engraved, Mughal-style *seeni* or round silver tray. Next, she unlocked another trunk and took out round tray-covers of silver and gold work. "My Mem Saheb had made these herself," she sniffed. "I have locked up everything for my Asghar's bride." (She was always saving things for Asghar's bride.) After selecting a red *khwanposh* Gracie went to her own room and put on a sari of printed georgette. ("My Mem Saheb give it to me.") Then she adorned her jet-black hair with a fresh *veni* and plastered her shiny black face with white powder. Our Gracie was ready for the engagement party.

Gracie dressed me up in one of my frilled party frocks of pink organdie, tied a big pink bow on my hair, and made me wear my socks and shoes with the expertise of a born nanny.

We piled into Nasir Chacha's chauffeur-driven Buick and set out for Omar Park. The Three Wise Kings followed in their own motorcars.

On reaching the double-storeyed house of the bride-to-be, we ascended the broad wooden staircase in the form of a procession. We were led by Jamila Bhabi. Gracie came in the rear, carrying the silver tray. Two servants carried the baskets of fruit and sweetmeat.

We were received at the door by our hosts. After much *salaaming* and social pleasantries they led us inside.

The drawing room was stacked with furniture, photographs, vases and embroidered cushions. In a corner stood a tall "showcase" which proudly displayed a miniature Taj Mahal, Japanese dolls, Bidriware, cups and trophies, and other bric-a-brac. On the top stood an elongated saki pouring wine into the cup of a dreamy-eyed Omar Khayyam. The walls were adorned with framed parrots, swans and tigers embroidered on black velvet by the Daughter of the House.

In no time the room overflowed with gorgeously attired guests and their wailing infants. I began to feel suffocated in the strange surroundings and looked for Gracie. She stood outside in the gallery, along with the other ayahs. I wondered why she looked so grim.

Suddenly the electricity failed and the ceiling fans stopped whirling. The overcrowded room became unbearably stuffy. But I bore it all courageously, waiting eagerly for the bride-to-be.

After half an hour Nasir Chacha's fiancée was ushered in. She was a tall, ungainly looking lady of about thirty. Her face was chalk-white. She almost hopped into the room and sat down with a thud on the sofa. Then she glanced around rather foolishly.

I was sorely disappointed. The brides I had seen were always very young and shy and never lifted the *ghunghat* from their blushing faces.

Jamila Bhabi and the other two ladies looked a bit unnerved. However, Jamila Bhabi quickly took control of the situation and ordered Gracie to bring in the tray.

Arjumand Apa uncovered the tray with great finesse, gingerly picked up a piece of rock sugar and placed it in the girl's mouth. The girl began to chew the rock sugar with considerable gusto.

Jamila Bhabi tied the velvet band of "Imam Zamin" to the girl's arm, entrusting her to the Twelfth Imam's care, and slipped the diamond ring on her finger. The girl watched the proceedings with keen interest. Suddenly she began to giggle uncontrollably, got up, and strode out of the room.

Her mother and aunt quickly followed her. The room was too crowded for the guests to notice anything.

The Three Wise Women of the East began a hurried whispered conference.

"We have been duped."

"Bland like a turnip."

"Can't be less than forty."

"How she giggles! Shameless woman!"

"Can't be less than forty-five."

"Are you daft? She is only twenty-four. I know for certain," whispered Arjumand Apa who was mainly responsible for arranging the match. She looked very upset.

"And anyway," Jamila Bhabi tried to be an optimist, "Our Nasir Bhai is not a kid. He is past fifty. She is all right for him. He is a good man. He will treat her like a Rani."

The girl's mother and aunt returned to the room and tea was served hastily. The terms of *mehr* (dowry money) were discussed.

"We always fix rupees one lakh," declared the girl's aggressive aunt.

"Whereas we always fix the sum strictly according to the rules of the Shariat," Jamila Bhabi replied sweetly.

This led to a general discussion in which all the ladies present vigorously took part. The infants began to howl with greater might. The fans were still stationary. I suddenly felt dizzy and terrified.

Gracie noticed my plight and marched forward: "Mem Saheb," she announced in a firm voice, "my Baba want to go home."

The Three Wise Women had got so deeply involved in the controversy over *mehr* that they too thought it best to make an escape. The discussion was postponed to another date.

We returned home.

Nasir Chacha sat in his armchair engrossed in a Persian classic. The three ladies swept in and brazenly announced:

"Congratulations, Bhaijan. The bride is like the Moon of the Fourteenth!"

"They will give her a brand-new Opel in the dowry."

"There is a little hitch about the *mehr*, but they will come round. They cannot get a boy like our Bhaijan here."

Nasir Chacha flicked the ash off his cigar and smiled. As usual he seemed greatly amused. Gracie had gone straight to the box room to put the silver back.

Late that night, long after Nasir Chacha and Asghar had gone to bed, I was awakened by a strange inhuman voice coming from across the corridor. I got up and rushed out to call Gracie.

The voice was coming from her own room. I went to the window which opened in the back verandah and looked in.

Gracie squatted on the floor and addressed the holy image hoarsely: "I made the Novena and broke my legs climbing your shrine. Telling the rosary my head turned round and round. Praying-praying – my head turned round and done this *four-twenty* with me . . . You never become widow at twenty. You never slept in lonely verandahs . . . Your son never got a step-mother . . . *Deva che Mai* . . . *Deva che Mai* . . ."

All of which convinced me that our Gracie had gone round the bend. I tiptoed back to my room.

The next morning my parents came back. I told them about the hilarious engagement party. Gracie sulked and remained busy in her work. She never spoke a word.

A couple of days later the three good ladies arrived again, panting. They sat down on the cane chairs in the verandah facing the sea and called Gracie to give them some water. Nasir Chacha strolled up and down, cigar in hand. He did not look amused.

Arjumand Apa was saying: "Thank God we wasted only one-two thousand rupees. I hope they will return the diamond ring. Disaster has been averted. Suppose the *nikah* had been solemnised? Then?"

"Now I understand," Jamila Bhabi put in, "why her mother insisted on rupees one lakh. It would have made the divorce so difficult."

"And they gave us a ten-year-old photo!" Arjumand Apa wailed.

"Thank God," repeated Jamila Bhabi, shuddering. "We happened to discover this only today. Through a neighbour of theirs . . . And she did look odd, didn't she? Chronic hysteria, Good God!"

"Bland like a turnip. Walked like a camel," said the third lady.

All three continued to cluck like fat leghorn hens.

In the evening my parents and Nasir Chacha went out for dinner. Gracie decided to entertain me. After putting Asghar to bed she took me to her little room and opened an old suitcase. It was full of knick-knacks and trinkets her steward brother Patrick used to bring for her from various ports of call. Toby mugs and willow-pattern dishes of Staffordshire. Holy souvenirs from Rome. Also a print bought in a backstreet of Liverpool, of an early-nineteenth-century painting. It showed a moonlit graveyard with a slanting tombstone which read: "Good times and bad times and all times get over."

Gracie showed me the Woolworth trinkets she had carefully stored away for "Asghar's bride". Then, with great tenderness, she took out a musical box. "Patrick bring it for me from Glasgow," she said, winding it. I recognised the tune as "The Bluebells of Scotland".

While I listened to the musical box Gracie looked at her wrist-watch and announced: "Ten o'clock, Indian Standard Time . . . Now I pray."

"Shall I go, Gracie?" I asked politely.

"No, no, Baba. You sit right there and see this album." She passed on to me her brother Pat's Nestle chocolate pictures of old Hollywood filmstars. While I got lost in the world of Tyrone Powers and Bette Davises, Gracie lit a candle and began mumbling her prayer in Konkani.

Then in a sudden burst of confidence she turned to me and said: "Baba, in Mahim. There is a big Dewal. There is photo of Our Lady. It does miracles. I made Novena there. Our Lady heard me . . ." As quickly she checked herself and said: "It is very late now. Go to bed." She escorted me back to my bedroom and said a happy "Goodnight". Her pearly white teeth flashed as she vanished in the dark corridor.

Many years after Partition I met Nasir Chacha in Lahore. As soon as he came to know that I was in town, he sent Asghar to my cousin's place to fetch me.

Asghar arrived in a huge car borrowed from a friend. He had grown into a flashy man-about-town. He had not studied beyond Senior Cambridge and was trying to "do business". He dropped me at the gate of a small, desolate-looking bungalow in Model Town and whizzed off, whistling.

Nasir Chacha sat in the sun under a bare tree. A few books and Urdu magazines lay before him on an unpolished table.

He looked up and blinked. Somehow, I expected him to say: "So, Saheb, this too has come to pass!" But he merely pointed to a wicker chair, indicating that I sit down.

After some minutes he looked at me and said accusingly: "Your father let me down." Then he hung down his head again. The wind rustled in the poplars. An enormous Persian cat appeared on the verandah and began sunning itself.

Abruptly, my uncle Nasir announced to nobody in particular: "Left without prior notice. Must be happily living in Heaven."

"Is there a Heaven, Chacha?" I asked, trying to make conversation.

He slipped his horn-rimmed glasses on to his forehead and squinted at me. "You continue to ask questions. Don't ask questions," he growled angrily.

He had grown very old and grouchy.

It was a dreary winter morning. The wind was chilly and an anaemic sun floated listlessly behind the clouds. Nasir Chacha looked ill. He had covered his legs with a worn-out blanket. I was vastly depressed.

All of a sudden he grunted again and said: "I hear you have become a writer. Do you also write this? . . . This balderdash . . . this piffle . . . this . . ." He pointed angrily at an Urdu magazine which published terribly avant-garde contemporary literature. "Remember," he continued grumpily, "Your father never wrote such . . . such . . ." He became too angry for words. In the same breath he shouted: "Gracie, come here! See who has come." The next moment a grey-haired old woman came out of the bungalow, wiping her hands on a duster.

She came close, bent a little and opened her eyes very wide.

"Stupid woman. Can't you recognise this child?" Nasir Chacha roared.

"O my goodness gracious me . . . My little Baba grown big lady . . ." Gracie started sniffing and broke into her fantastic English which had not improved with the years.

She took me into her neat little kitchen and began lighting the stove. She seemed house-proud as ever, although there was nothing much in the cold, bleak cottage to be proud about. It was obvious that Nasir Chacha was in a bad way. Also, Asghar had been a bitter disappointment to him.

"Gracie, you have become old," I said.

Gracie turned towards me and said: "Call me Aunt Gracie, please, my *bachcha* . . ."

"Oh," I said happily. "Oh, Gracie, I mean . . . Aunt Gracie, you really deserve this!"

"Yes, dear. God has been good to me." She got busy preparing the lunch and continued: "We *banaoed* marriage when we came here. Nawab Saheb in strange land. No friends. No *sagawalla*. Only me to look after him. My Asghar got into bad company. Nawab Saheb's pension still *phansoed* in India. His property and all lost in his *muluk* . . . Our *bachcha* insisted he come to Pakistan to do business. Nawab Saheb wanted to settle in his *muluk* – Patna – after pension. But because of Asghar Baba we had to come here.

"Big big *ghotala* going on here in this country. But what to do? And your uncle's health very bad. He become very short-tempered on account of his high blood pressure. This pressure. Asghar got into real bad company. All kind of worries. I have promised Imam Hussain to present one silver candlestick in his Imambara, and told the Virgin also. One candlestick to Her, one to Imam Hussain . . ."

"Gracie Chachi, you are incorrigible," I said, laughing.

That was the last time I saw the sad old couple. The very next year I came to know that Nasir Chacha was dead. After his death Asghar started some kind of shady business in which he prospered in no time and married a society girl. His wife was deeply ashamed of acknowledging an ordinary Goan ayah as her mother-in-law. Asghar was embarrassed too. He shipped her back to India.

It was impossible to hunt for my Aunt Gracie in Bombay. But I thought of her especially when one day I went to the Mahim Church to take photographs for an illustrated article. The church was empty except for a few worshippers who dotted the pews.

A bedraggled old man was whispering the Hail Mary.

Ave Maria
Cheia de graca
O senhor e comvosco,
Bendita sois vos entre as mulheres . . .

A humble woman knelt before the sacred image and muttered tearfully: "*Santa Morye Deva che Mai, ami papiya khatir vinti dar* . . . Amen!"

Perhaps her husband had died. Perhaps she had been turned out by her stepson. She made the sign of the cross: "*Bapache navem Putrachem ani Spirita santche Amen!*"

Perhaps she had nowhere to go to and no roof over her head . . .

As she got up, I looked around, unconsciously searching for my Aunt Gracie. The devout started pouring in.

So, Saheb, this too had come to pass.

ASHOK MITRA

An Ordinary Man

HOME IS THE SAILOR, home from the sea. He was an ordinary man, belonging not even to a species, but a genus. He had his early schooling in Santiniketan: but that was a mere episode, long forgotten, even by him. An ordinary man who, a while ago, had crossed his sixtieth year, with archetypal Bengali Hindu middle-class affinities and alignments, hopes and aspirations, scuttled beyond redemption by the rampaging inflation. A homoeopath by profession. He died last week.

An ordinary death. The homoeopath was suffering, for the past few months, from various ailments common to hard-placed, undernourished old men. He shuttled between hospital and home a number of times, his health did not improve; despite medication and care, the complications grew, and his general condition continued to deteriorate with every week. Last week, he died. It was an ordinary funeral. A small circle of friends gathered. They remembered the hundred kindnesses rendered to them by the man, spanning over many, many years; they remembered his warmth, his generosity, the magnificent grace which defined his personality; it was a moment of empathy and commiseration, mutually shared and offered. But a moment like this is always brief. It was an ordinary funeral, the funeral of an ordinary man, it did not take long. The friends dispersed. The family is now left to its loneliness. It is not just the loneliness which follows the departure of a close and dear one. There are, inevitably, major economic implications of the death of the head of the household. The vacuum left by an ordinary man's passing can indeed assume extraordinary proportions.

An ordinary man. Even as a homoeopath, he was perhaps just about ordinary. Till his very last days, he remained somewhat overawed by the skill and proficiency of better-known eminences in the profession. He had, besides, that innate modesty: deference to the views, and sometimes idiosyncracies, of others was second nature to him. An ordinary man, who never asserted himself, whose professional opinions too were always expressed mutely. An ordinary man who was professionally popular, but not "successful". Success is measured in terms of rates of return. The homoeopath could barely make enough for his family. In more recent years, as his health began to fail, his state of finances became increasingly more precarious. But this again identified him as being only one of a genus. The number of professional men, whether in medicine or law or teaching, for whom in this clime living is an unceasing struggle to scrape a minimal of income, is legion; Calcutta and the *mofussils* are literally strewn with such specimens. You can spot them by the pallor of their faces, by the trace of chronic malnutrition in their physique, by the cynicism and bitterness which keeps intruding into their vocabulary.

The homoeopath, until a few years ago, kept the bitterness within himself. He succeeded in discovering sources of serendipity. Call it love for your neighbours, call it social conscience, he considered it great fun to medicate, free of charge, for the poor and needy in working class slums. The coarseness of commerce never intervened. There was no fanfare. The homoeopath's chamber was bare, commonplace. It would have been atrocious had it been otherwise; an excess of dazzle would have put off his clientele. Sometimes he would be paid a token fee; most of the time there was no question of a fee. Odd calls here and there, now and then, would fetch some income; these were chancy and altogether too infrequent. But you telephone him, he always had time for you and your problems; he could not afford a car, but he would trudge on foot, or push his body into the frighteningly overcrowded public transport and arrive where you wanted him to be, tired but cheerful, full of solicitude and courtesy. Doing a good turn to others was for him a cerebral impulse. The sum of such impulses was his life. And, all the while, money would continue to be short. But you would never guess by looking at him: graciousness had little to do with the presence or absence of money.

Even an impoverished homoeopath, though, has his dreams. Perhaps our quiet, gentle man had a greater claim to dreaming dreams. Most of the time, he dealt with the down-and-out; percentage-wise, there are more honest and good human beings amongst the tramps and the destitute than amongst the filthy rich who travel to private nursing homes for the treatment of their maladjusted egos. The kingdom of the poor ought to come, and soon, the homoeopath must have felt. But you have to work for it, the filthy rich deserve to be dispossessed, there will never be a voluntary abdication on their part; there must be a movement, a political movement, a movement which begins at the grassroots, so that the kingdom of the poor comes.

The homoeopath was an ordinary man, a quiet man, but he had his passion, his own convictions. These were not quite explicitly stated in all seasons. Here was a polite man; despite the fact that the crowd he treated consisted mostly of the poor, the Bengali Hindu middle-class tradition made it inevitable that he straddle a wide enough social spectrum in the course of his daily perambulations. He was firm in his views, but rudeness did not come easily to him; who knows, perhaps he considered it better strategy to camouflage his political predilections when visiting the camp of the enemy. But the devotion and allegiance remained. He was not exactly a part of the political movement; yet it would be preposterous to suggest that he was not. He and his like have always been around, giving flesh, ever since 1905 or thereabouts, to deep-stirring political concepts. They have shunned the limelight, but no movement worth its name could have developed without the sustained spadework put in by them. All along, they have acted as catalysts between people and ideas. A dream has to be brought home; a star has to be cajoled to make a landing. An enormous amount of anonymous perseverance is called for in this task: hard unobtrusive slogging, day after day, in different spheres of social existence. Party leaders and party cadres play their parts, but an almost equal contribution is made by a handful who remain outside the domain of established party structure – genuine volunteers, who shun prominence, do not sign manifestoes, refuse to join a delegation or, for that matter, a procession, but for whom the dream remains no less the real thing. Lawyers, doctors, teachers, they constitute the great tribe of catalysts, the moulders of mass sentiments, the non-loquacious, non-demanding organisers. They do not proclaim it from the housetops: their identification with the cause is nevertheless total. For its sake, they sacrifice their time, their opportunity for money-making; completely integrated individuals, they perceive straight away the link between the context of the dream and their mundane, immediate chores. The rainbow of a bridge joins their life with their dream. The great silent army of dreamers marches along.

The homoeopath was one such dreamer. He was an ordinary man; ordinariness defined his being. He had no great personal ambitions. He remained loyal to his friends, loyal and affectionate and generous. But, alongside, he remained loyal to the cause of social and political change. He was a sympathiser, not a cadre. But the grammar of nomenclatures can be a pretentious portmanteau: instead of revealing, it can obfuscate. In his modest, silent way over the years he signed in his contribution. In such matters, there is always a problem of toting; once the memory of a few people is obliterated, none will remember the specifics of his sacrifice. Those who seek anonymity easily come to it. It is a superior choice in most cases. The more civilised do not want their names to be bandied about. So it happens. Through the ages, the silent ones remain the silent ones, unknown, unacknowledged, unlisted. But the law of human dynamics would have been immobilised without them. History does not inscribe their names in its scrolls, but history will hardly ever dare negate them.

The homoeopath, kind, solicitious of the welfare of neighbours, did not suffer from any crisis of identity. He loved to tend others, including the large number of the poor who were unable to pay him, either for his visit or for his medicine. There was a certain community of affection between him and those whom he treated, free. Maybe because he loved them, they also came to love his cause; they came to the awareness – more by instinct than by tuition – that his cause in fact was theirs: he would not even have bothered to work for the cause were it not for them.

A hero in his own manner, but there will be no record of his heroism. The last few years made a sombre chapter. Suddenly the cause seemed to be more distant than ever; externalities came to loom large in the calculus of possibles and probables; confusion rent the air. These were years of a certain sadness; it was as if while the cause remained as it ought to be always, some unscrupulous elements had walked away with the props of one's faith. Disease and illness one can put up with; it is much harder when one's zest for life is gone.

An ordinary existence. The ordinary life of an ordinary man. And now an ordinary death. But all these do add up, otherwise history would be a fraud. It is the ordinary men who shape the modalities of history, despite the fact that the scrolls do not mention them. Ordinary men, great in their particular manner. The homoeopath, Amal Sen, slipped away, last week; an ordinary death, the hunter home from the hills. Amal Sen, an ordinary man, nevertheless a great man. His greatness will enrich history, even though history will be barely aware of it.

DHARMA KUMAR

108 Varieties

WHY A HUNDRED and eight? Because it is a large number, and a classical one, and because the other alternatives, fifty-seven and infinity, the usual symbols of variety, are both inappropriate, for different reasons. Fifty-seven, with its reference to Heinz advertisements, is too Western, and the number of Indians is not yet, thank goodness, infinity. The first point to be made, simply, is that there are a large number of varieties of Indian English, even though, to the English themselves (and other foreigners), all Indians sound alike: whether it is the Nawab of Pataudi in *Bodyline* or Professor Godbole in *A Passage to India*, they all imitate Peter Sellers imitating an Indian.

It is obvious why there are so many varieties of Indian English and that is the varieties of Indians themselves. Take education for instance. Indians educated at Oxford speak and write English very differently from the alumni of Banaras and Agra, and Doon School boys from the products of municipal schools (the Doon School boys probably use "*yaar*" more frequently). The subdivisions can be made finer: the stamp of Cambridge (Eng.) differs from that of Cambridge (Mass.), and far larger numbers of Indians now study in America.

These differences may be reflected in the English of upper-class occupations – Indian Foreign Service trainees are still sent mainly to England, while Indian universities are full of American graduates. So one often hears in university seminars those two American academic cliches – "That is a hard act to follow", and "That was the good news, now for the bad news". Presumably business correspondence too is full of American cliches, and much worse than academic cliches at that, but fortunately I do not have to read it.

Education, occupation, income, mother tongue, class (but not caste?) – these and many others account for the varieties of Indian English but I will comment mainly on the mother tongue. Moreover, I will confine myself to a few languages or language groups, and will base my remarks on, to use that economists' excuse for wild generalisation, casual empiricism.

It is hardly worth stating that the rhetoric of Indian English, rooted as it generally is in Sanskrit or Persian, is not Anglo-Saxon: the differences within the species are more interesting. Is my impression correct that Bengali English and Tamil English are more elaborate and varied in their rhetoric, and more grammatical than other forms of Indian English, and that these differences are (or were) more marked the lower one travelled down the social scale? The longer Indians are educated abroad, the less their regional origins count, and some Indian institutions, too, such as the Doon School and St Stephen's College, are powerful homogenisers. But in Bengal and Tamil Nadu, people who may never have travelled outside their districts reveal a knowledge of English life and literature which the smartest products of Delhi University will not attain, however often they go abroad (the early Nirad Chaudhuri is an extreme example: he is indeed *sui generis* – but here are a few other examples).

In 1946 I went to the Reserve Bank office in Madras to get an exchange permit for study abroad. The official I saw was not very senior, and he asked me where I was going.

"Newnham College, Cambridge."

"You know what they say about Newnham women?"

"No."

"There is Abishag the Shulamite and Shabby Hag the Newnhamite."

A Maharashtrian friend looking into district records in a small town in Bengal revealed to the clerk at the archives that he was studying at Oxford. "Oh, then you will have heard of Mr X, our former Collector. He was the fine flower of Eton and Balliol."

The Bard was apparently particularly popular in Bengal and the South. Elderly relatives of mine, who had never been abroad, could recite Shakespeare by the hour. And here is Desani's Mr Bannerji: "Excuse me, despite, as your well-wisher, I have chosen a married woman, I am aware, he has said, Oh, hell! To choose love by another's eye. But excuse me, he has also said, Hamlet speaking, Angels and ministers of grace defend us!" (Incidentally, "Excuse me", to express apologetic dissent, is commonly used in many parts of India, and indeed by other foreign English speakers too.)

Again, can one imagine the following funeral oration for a professional bodybuilder in the North: "With his bulging biceps and tremendous triceps he was unparalleled on the parallel bars?"

That, of course, was meant to rouse tears, not laughter. But all English-speaking Indians make jokes about Indian English. One common element in our oral humour is that every Indian language group finds the English pronunciation of every other group irresistibly funny – the Punjabi who goes to the "satation" to meet a "luyyer" and the Bengali who hears the "bhard" "shing" unite in roaring with laughter at "yevery" Tamil. This of course annoys or surprises the Tamil who, like all the others, finds *his* English accent natural, indeed correct.

When I told a Tamil that a Malayali friend had mocked the Tamil English accent, he could not believe it. "That is not possible," he said in the ripest of accents. "Our pronunciation is perfect though our intonation may be a bit peculiar." And all Indians except the England-returned find an upper-class English accent odd – but that amuses other Englishmen too. And here too there are regional differences. At one end there is the Sardarji joke:

"Are you Milkha Singh?"

"No, I am relaxing."

At the other, there is the man who my Bengali friends swear is not wholly apocryphal, who gets his proverbs hauntingly wrong. "All roads to Rome were not built in a day."

These regional differences are signs that English was better taught and for a longer period in Bengal and the South than in the North. But language chauvinism has probably swept most of these differences away. All Indians will be equally ignorant of English literature, so that regional differences will mainly reflect the differences in structure and style of the mother tongues. Maharashtrian English will continue to be drier than Bengali English; Tamils will be alliterative when they want to make a flourish, and terse otherwise. Kamaraj is the paradigm with his "Parkalam" in Tamil, but Tamil English examples abound. Only tepid goodwill is conveyed by the English exchange:

"How do you do?"

"How do you do?"

But Tamils convey more goodwill, as well as information, in their exchange.

"How are you I hope?"

"Oh yes."

Again, when two Tamils meet in the interval of a concert, all they need to say is:

"Yenjoing?"

"Simply." (Tamil English for "absolutely".)

Apart from language groups, there are many other forms of Indian English (a very useful principle of sub-division is according to occupation). One main category is official Indenglish – indeed it deserves an article to itself, if not several volumes, of which one should trace its development from the first East India Company minute. Why is it that all communications from juniors to seniors must be in the third person, "Secretary may please see?" Does this reflect eighteenth-century English or present-day Indian notions of respect?

There is a marvellous volume to be written on the evolution of GOI English – *babu* English is not the right term, partly because it is not restricted to clerks. Some changes can be easily dated. Certain locutions are clearly post-1947, such as, "This file may be sent to the concerned ministry." And the rude Anglo-Saxon never wrote, "For Secretary's kind perusal, please." Perhaps development came to be invariably linked with "stresses and strains" after 1951, as in "The five-year delay is due to the stresses and strains of development." But one cannot be sure of this – the historian is often surprised to find in past official records a phrase he had thought peculiarly modern.

On the other hand, some sentences can be firmly dated. It is only in the era of foreign aid that every Finance Minister who went on a begging expedition reminded an increasingly bored Western audience that no man is an island. (As a very junior government official in the Finance Ministry I tried in vain to introduce another quotation, of far greater domestic relevance – Sam Weller's, "But it's over and done with, and that's one consolation as they sez in Turkey when they cut the wrong man's head off." I quote from memory.)

The English of PAs is a special sub-class, and being almost entirely oral it is important to record. "May I know your good name, please" appears to be particularly North Indian; the extra polite ask one for one's "good number". (A charming variant is the Delhi child's, "When is your happy birthday?") My favourite PA-ism is the following. I had rung up a close and very proper friend in the Finance Ministry; his PA, recognising my voice, said doubtfully. "He is on the sofa with a foreigner, madam. Should I disturb him?"

Dance programmes have a special jargon of their own, and an excruciatingly limited one. By the time one has been to one's sixth Bharata Natyam performance one should be able to recite by heart the descriptions of the *alarippu* and *tillana*; the *tillana*, we are everlastingly informed, is a sequence of intricate pure dance steps where the dancer displays her dazzling virtuosity. But there is the occasional variation – baffled by the difficulties of translation. One programme I treasure said the dancer would describe "the sweet *chhed-chhad* of Lord Krishna."

Other occupations too have their peculiar forms. It is obvious that lawyers and doctors and dentists will each have a special jargon, much of it doubtless international. But the "English" of some occupations is peculiarly Indian – where else do motor mechanics charge you for "denting" your car (i.e. removing the dents)?

Again, Indian economists never refer to "the poor", but only to "those below the poverty line", which they seem to feel is more scientific. Planners too are made uneasy by the poor – "the weaker sections" are less disturbing. This repellent phrase occurs in the Constitution too, perhaps in the unconscious realisation that while we may abolish poverty, the weaker sections will always be with us.

Indian sociologists have eagerly adopted the jargon of the West – everything is "mediated" if it is not "encompassed". Instead of visiting the 10,000th village to tell us for the umpteenth time that villages have factions (so unlike departments of sociology), why do they not analyse the language of marriage advertisements, or New Year cards, or wedding invitations or, indeed, even visiting cards? Consider the poignancy of one Nizamuddin landlord's description of himself – "ex-aristocrat". Indian English may bring to the surface aspects of our social psychology hidden in Indian languages.

But it is time to bring this rambling essay to an end or it may have to be retitled "The 1008 Varieties of Indian English".

SHEILA DHAR

Baua

THE SADDEST AND most mortifying secret of my life and that of my two brothers when we were still infants was that our father did not like our mother, whom we called Baua. He treated her with the utmost disdain and usually did not speak to her or even answer her if she asked a question. Strangely, he made no effort to cloak this state of affairs from anyone, not even from his children.

The living arrangements reflected the situation between my parents with a depressing finality. Ever since I can remember, my father had a sort of bachelor establishment in an annexe of the sprawling colonial house we lived in while my mother was allotted a small room in the main house where she lived with her three children. My brothers and I were very close to our mother and felt instinctively that our father's rejection of us was something to be ashamed of and to hide from everybody. We also felt guilty because somehow it seemed to be our fault. We envied our cousins for being able to approach their fathers and clamber up on their knees, prattling and laughing happily. They seemed to us to belong to a superior breed, privileged in a manner we could not even dream of.

We were too young to give a name to these feelings, but Baua understood and shared them, though she tried constantly to erase all negativity from our minds with her spirited optimism and warmth. Even so, an undercurrent of anxiety that she was deprived and troubled in some serious way was always present, even when we were enjoying our otherwise happy childhood. I remember an occasion when I tried to banish the pain I felt at Baua's unfortunate position in the household by telling totally unnecessary lies to my school friends about a visit to the circus with my "mummy" and "daddy". I invented the fiction that I had sat on my father's lap when things had got too exciting. I went on about it until I realised that to my friends such a detail was nothing out of the ordinary and so not worth mentioning. For my older brother, the main motivation for growing up was that he would be able to take care of Baua, me and his younger brother. We also began to wait for this day. We were sure that there was a golden future in which our mother would be cherished as she deserved to be.

The room my mother was given was an odd one in the centre of the house. It was probably never meant to be lived in as it had no bathroom attached to it or even close by. This was rather difficult for Baua, specially because her children were still small. She had to use the primitive facilities in a block of structures outside the house. My grandfather had had these built with his characteristic forethought in order to take the pressure off the attached bathrooms in the main house if need be. I remember my mother ferrying us across the veranda and the courtyard in the morning one by one to get us ready for school. When any of us were sick, or when it was too hot or too cold to carry us to the outhouses, which were a longish walk away, it used to be even more of an ordeal for her. But her hand when she woke us up was always cool and fragrant because she was already bathed and dressed.

A widowed aunt we called Shammo Bhua had made her home with us after her husband died. By nature she was not a particularly powerful personality but the joint family politics generated by my father's attitude of active indifference to his wife and children gave her an irresistible handle to exercise authority over us. She was always there to say "no" to whatever any of us wanted or needed. Gradually this tendency hardened into a sort of instrument with which she thought she was giving shape to her brother's wishes.

Shammo Bhua had a huge, high-ceilinged room with six skylights which could be opened or closed by pulling at thick cords attached to the shutters above. Every time one tugged, the appearance of the room and the colour of the walls used to change in a magical way. It was a game we longed to play, but we knew, just from the way Shammo Bhua tightened her lips every time one of us reached for the inviting cords, that this was forbidden territory so far as we were concerned. Her bathroom was spacious and modern by the standards of those days and even had a bathtub and shower. She also had a dressing room almost as large as the room allotted to my mother and her children.

Shammo Bhua's domain accounted for nearly one-fourth of the main bungalow and had been set aside for my grandfather's daughters whenever they or their families were in Delhi. However, Shammo Bhua was the most permanent and often the sole occupant of this accommodation. She also considered herself the local representative of what was thought of in the family collectively as "The Sisters" and faithfully guarded the "sisters' rooms" against encroachments from undesirables like my mother, even when the other claimants were not in town.

Although Shammo Bhua couldn't openly turn down her own mother's good-hearted suggestion that she share her bathroom with Baua, who was after all her own sister-in-law, she would make a sulky, sour face which my grandmother couldn't always see, partly because of her bad eyesight and partly because of her stubborn view that every member of her family was a decent person. But Shammo Bhua's hostile emanation punctured us, even when we were too young to be able to describe her attitude.

Baua, on the other hand, never lost her robust optimism and had a sunny temperament which was practically egoless. She asked Shammo Bhua when she might use the bathroom without clashing with her timings or putting her out in any way. My aunt said "seven o'clock" with a sullen face, but went out of her way the next day to keep the bathroom occupied at the very time she had given to Baua. She probably had to sit in the bathroom for several hours at considerable inconvenience to herself to make sure that it did not become available to Baua. The affair of the bathroom stretched out for about ten days in which my mother was given and vainly tried various timings – five o'clock, six o'clock, eight o'clock and nine o'clock. I remember her leaving our room, her towel and fresh clothes draped over her arm, and coming back almost at once because "Shammo Bibi" was in the bathroom. This happened at least a dozen times before she finally gave up. Although my grandmother wanted everyone to be accommodated and accommodating, she usually didn't go into details. Baua never dreamt of complaining or making an issue of it, so things remained as they were.

Like a good dependent in a joint family, Shammo Bhua was going with the flow, not taking any individualistic position of her own. Her instinct was to reflect the attitude of the real centre of power in the family at this time, which was my father. It was usual for him to make pointedly unkind remarks about my mother's bulk, her lack of elegance and polish, about the unrefined family she came from, about the backwardness of Agra, her birthplace, about the way she talked, walked, or did anything at all. Most of the time he did this to entertain his fawning sisters, and of course to let the household know that she was no part of his life and therefore not worthy of consideration. When there was no audience, he just ignored her. The monthly allowance to run the kitchen and pay the servants' salaries was handed to Shammo Bhua, not to Baua. This was an unmistakable signal, if one were still needed, for the servants to know who the real boss was. Baua didn't protest or fight back or feel resentful. I know that this was not out of weakness but because of an extraordinarily generous disposition, and an inexplicable, unquestioning devotion to my father. Whether this last was a personal emotional condition or an entrenched cultural attitude, I was not able to tell.

My grandparents exercised a benign but loose control on things, but the actual running of the house was the financial responsibility of my father. Consequently Baua was expected to be physically responsible for all the family meals as well as for all hospitality. She was always in the kitchen supervising and assisting the servants and planning the next meal for the enormous household. I remember her as slightly out of breath from her exertions, her face pink and beaded with sweat, her white cotton sari which had been fresh and starched when she woke us up in the morning crumpled and stained with turmeric for most of the day. The other women of the house sat in cane chairs, sipping nibu-sharbat and generally being animated members of my grandparents' durbar, which admitted a constant stream of droppers-in from the neighbouring houses.

Baua would work hard and creatively in the kitchen trying to devise dishes to suit my father's delicate stomach and demanding palate. The special cup of soup before dinner which the family doctor had recommended for him was a major challenge that she took up every day. Even as a child it used to make me nervous because I felt my mother was on trial and might be sentenced to death. The steaming cup would be placed ceremoniously at my father's place on the table. When he lifted it to his lips there would be a hush in the dining room. All eyes were riveted on him as he took the first sip. My father was a deeply political being and quite simply relished the sensation of exercising power, especially psychological power, over people. So he would prolong the suspense of whether the soup had passed or failed by deliberately keeping his face expressionless for as long as he could. Then, after what seemed like ten minutes but was probably much less, one of three things could happen. He could nod his acceptance of the liquid and put it down, sipping it at intervals through the meal, causing my mother to glow with happiness. Or he could push it away and leave the room in a huff. The worst scenario was when he refused to take cognizance of it at all and acted as though neither the cup nor my mother who was responsible for it existed. Baua always looked stricken and bewildered when he reacted like this. To her meek "Is something wrong with the soup?" she never got a reply. This business of her not getting any response at all from my father on the rare occasions when she ventured to speak to him made us anxious and miserable and dogged our entire childhood and adolescence. The rare occasions when he favoured her with a monosyllable in answer to a question such as "Will you be back for dinner?" made news in the household that everybody commented upon without feeling in the least delicate.

My father's refusal to talk to Baua was not only an emotional difficulty, but a serious practical one too. The personal spending money that she needed for herself and her three children was supposed to be provided by my father. She was expected to present a list of her needs and what they would cost to my father every month for his scrutiny. He had the reputation of being an extremely generous man with a very cavalier attitude to money. The world of music and Urdu poetry was abuzz with stories of wildly extravagant gifts my father was in the habit of making to deserving artistes, in grand gestures of admiration. But so far as we and our mother were concerned he grudged every penny, and resented being forced to address himself to our problems. I remember my mother painstakingly making her list in Urdu, because that was the only script they both could read, on a page torn out of my old school copybook. It had items like hairpins, toothpaste, soap, ribbons, cloth and buttons for the children's clothes, occasionally shoes, socks and knitting wool.

In the years between 1940 and 1950 the total was in the neighbourhood of sixty rupees. Her monthly journey along the long back veranda to my father's rooms with this document was always a trial. Sometimes he just took the slip of paper from her without a word, dismissing her with a nod before she had a chance to sit down, and sent the money through his valet, Jai Singh, the next day. But at other times he would remain a stone behind his newspaper and Baua would have to retreat in confusion, her list still in her hand. During our teens each of us individually tried to take up the cudgels on her behalf many times and confronted him with basic questions, unaccountably encouraged by our good school reports which my grandfather's legal clerk quietly publicised in the household. At the age of thirteen when I stood first in my class and won an arts talent prize, I also suddenly acquired the courage to address my father directly. Nothing worse than death could happen after all, and there were always my brothers to set right whatever went seriously wrong because of my foolhardiness.

Entering his rooms felt like being summoned by the principal of the school for a talking-to, or like going into a dentist's clinic for an extraction. Everything smelt different, and everything looked exclusive and intimidating. There were Chinese vases and a white marble sculpture of a tragic Greek female figure lying on her face, her stony tresses in artistic disarray on the mantelpiece. In a niche in the wall was a four-and-a-half-foot-high plaster of paris reproduction of the Venus de Milo whose torso Jai Singh used to cover decorously with a bath towel when there were visitors, even if it was someone like me. These and other artefacts, along with a good deal of crockery and cutlery, had been acquired by my father at an auction held by a hotel in Simla after it went into liquidation. He had been retained as a lawyer by the hotel during this process and the impression in the family was that for him the whole experience had been extremely advantageous in many ways. There were many reminders of this in the way his rooms were furnished. There was an upholstered three-piece sofa, with wood and chrome armrests of hideous design which proclaimed its modernity, a great assortment of occasional tables and knick-knacks, a roll-top writing desk and an antique dressing table. There was always a box of imported cigars and a jade-green pack of some special brand of English cigarettes for guests from the outside world since my father was not a serious smoker himself. All this together gave off an aroma which I still consider the smell of fear, though physically it was clean and pleasant.

About the time that I felt confident enough to seek an interview with my father in a just cause, his own attitude to me had undergone a slight change. My academic prowess was not the only thing that claimed some grudging attention from him but also my passionate interest in music which the extended family attributed to his genes. He began to regard me as territory to be conquered and brought on his side. At any rate, he could no longer ignore the rebellion which he knew had now become articulate. He would let me sit and wait for a few minutes before he joined me, with a long-suffering and questioning look.

"I want to talk to you about my mother and ask you why you don't give her any spending money," I'd blurt out heroically.

"How do you suppose you are all clothed and fed? You go to school, you play games, you even learn music. You all have everything you could possibly need. I do not understand what the problem is," he would say, stalling like a lawyer.

"But she has to come to you so many times. She is so unhappy. You don't even talk to her properly."

At this, a dark and tragic expression would come over his face and he would fall silent, looking as though he was trying to hold back his tears. I felt tremendous pressure from him to feel some sympathy but was just not able to.

"No one has control over happiness or unhappiness. I find myself in a predicament that is not of my asking."

This was the sort of thing he would usually say and I never knew what it meant or what to say next.

"But if you didn't like my mother why did you have children, why did you have us?" I once dared to ask.

"You are too young to understand these things. One day, when you are much older, you will have the answer."

The operative part of the meeting was over very quickly but then he wanted me to stay and listen to anecdotes illustrating his sensitivity, his humility, his love of beauty, music, poetry and justice, his loneliness, and his generosity. He spoke softly, in a voice surcharged with emotion, but I felt totally unable to respond or even to warm to any of the unaccustomed disclosures. All I wanted was for someone else to come in and interrupt the session so that I could escape into the fresh air.

Both my brothers were familiar with this phenomenon and experienced it regularly themselves, but singly, throughout their adolescence and youth. The three of us were never summoned together. My father preferred to take us on one at a time. We discovered later that he kept notes of his conversations with us in separate files in which he entered remarks about our states of mind so that he would know better how to tackle us on the next occasion. My older brother and I also discovered random scribblings which really were a sort of homework he did in preparation for any issues on the anvil between him and his children. For instance, "Am only criticising mother to fit them better for their own lives. If I say they are intelligent and can understand better than others their age, will they accept my bona fides? Can I tell Sheila that I want her to study medicine because she is not good-looking enough to marry well? R cannot have cartridges for his gun unless he demonstrates responsibility. Must ask them what is the purpose of life . . .", and so on.

By the time things took this kind of turn, we were already quite alienated from our father emotionally. Each session with him seemed an ordeal in which he was the stronger adversary, with nameless weapons whose impact we felt but could not describe or forgive, either then or even later when we were much older. My brothers and I were in our own individual ways overwhelmed by the quality of love and support that flowed constantly from Baua, so strongly, so unostentatiously and so selflessly. She really kept us alive and nourished our spirit as nothing else ever did. What she often had to undergo at the hands of our father only sharpened our awareness of what she meant to us.

Once, the family was invited to a wedding in New Delhi and my father was going to drive one of the cars to the event. Baua dressed us and then dressed herself and we all waited on the cane chairs in the front veranda along with Shammo Bhua for my father to appear. I remember the rare and wonderful sight of my mother in her only "going-out" sari, a pale pink Mysore silk with a dull-gold woven border of decorative leaves from Indore.

It was a luxurious feeling for me that her clothes did not smell of kitchen spices this evening but of sandalwood. She looked happy like a child in fancy dress going to a party. She hardly ever went out anywhere except for kitchen and household shopping. Finally, my father took the wheel and all the children piled into the car, followed by Shammo Bhua while Jai Singh obsequiously held the car door open. Just as Baua was getting in, my father made a gesture asking her to wait. He reached out, pulled the door shut and drove off, leaving her standing in the driveway with Jai Singh, her face red with embarrassment. I watched her from the back window of the car, my heart pounding, and felt waves of nausea. But I knew instinctively that if I did get sick my mother would somehow have to suffer even more.

The strangest thing was that no one blamed my father for this sort of behaviour. My grandparents certainly wished things had been different, but treated the situation as an ailment that had overtaken their son. It was common knowledge in the entire community that my father was not nice to his wife and children though he was such a good man and so kind to everybody else. It was true that he never spoke to me or to my brothers during our early school years but lavished all his attention on the much better-looking children of his younger brother and his sisters. He would pointedly leave us out of the many activities and outings he planned for the children of the family – walks by the Jamuna river, trips to the Qudsia Gardens, picnics at Okhla in the mango season, elephant rides on New Year's day in the Roshanara Club and rowdy, improvised games in our own front lawn. Once, he took all the older boys on a fishing trip to Kashmir but left my older brother behind, with no explanation. Nothing could have hurt my mother more, and as we reached adolescence we realised that that was precisely the reason why he did such things. It was only Tauji, my father's elder brother, who lifted us up in his arms, swung us around and hugged us, when he was there, which was at least once a year. When he went back to Patna, we felt like outcasts again. My grandfather's special consideration for us because we were neglected and needed compensation was somehow not visceral enough to count for much in our emotional lives, though it provided a much needed support and reassurance to Baua.

I don't know why we never rebelled. I think there was a powerful, unwritten code that we followed without question. However, the sorrow about our mother's predicament and our own helplessness created a lifelong bond among the three of us. I also don't know how and when the story of why my father treated Baua in this unaccountable fashion became coherent to me. Some of the pieces came together through chance remarks Baua made to me in her old age when I was married and in my mid-forties.

Apparently, my father had fallen hopelessly in love with a distant relative when he was twenty years old and declared his intention of marrying her. My grandfather was appalled. He considered it extremely impertinent of my father to say anything at all about his own marriage while his elders, who knew what was best for him, were still alive. The fact that he had been to England to study law and considered himself a person of modern views did not change this attitude.

"It's all because of the Parsee theatre and the romantic Urdu ghazals he has recently taken to. The boy has lost all sense of propriety," my grandfather had lamented. But he stood his ground. So my father stopped eating, grew a beard, and lay down on his bed, speaking to none and sighing in the approved fashion of the classical lover. Women of the household were afraid that he would die unless he was united with his lady love.

A kindly uncle intervened at this point and persuaded my grandfather to soften his position. Pundits were summoned to study the two horoscopes, and they gravely pronounced that this union was never to be because the stars of the girl were so malefic that they would kill the boy. The brief flash of hope was therefore quickly extinguished and my father took to his bed again, seriously prepared to die for love. Everybody watched helplessly. The kindly uncle said that since the boy was dying in any case, he had decided to take a second astrological opinion. This time the pundits peered at many more charts and came up with the same opinion, or almost the same opinion. The stars did not match, but the danger from the bad conjunction was to the girl, not to the boy. This slight shift in angle seemed to make a big and immediate difference to the attitude of my father's well-wishers in the family, though nobody said so.

In the mean time the news from the girl's home in Allahabad was not very different. She too was languishing, refusing to eat or speak and crying all the time. This was made out to be the immediate cause for the family's change of heart but the real clincher was of course that their own precious boy would be safe. The girl's parents didn't have much choice because her emotional state was already being whispered about in the community and physically she was already half dead. She was considered to be already committed and as such had virtually no better prospects to hope for. Both families kept their real feelings in their hearts but agreed with outward grace to celebrate the marriage as early as possible. My father left his bed, shaved off his beard and began to eat, drink, and laugh again. By the time he was dressed up as a bridegroom, the roses had come back to his cheeks. The rites were performed and a short, euphoric period followed.

Exactly as predicted, the bride fell ill six months after the marriage and died, reportedly of typhoid, within a year, leaving my father an inconsolable widower at the age of twenty-one. His parents couldn't very well allow him to weep away his life in sorrow. They badgered him unsuccessfully for two or three years and then forced an arranged second marriage on him. Reportedly, he abhorred the very idea but gave in to the relentless pressure in what must have been something like suicidal desperation: because of the structure of the joint family and because of the circumstances of the second marriage, he never felt personally responsible for his wife or children. Somebody or the other would take care of things, and it was not his idea anyway. He remained a sort of romantic, always thinking of himself as a victim whom life had caught in a web. He felt perfectly justified in taking his frustration and resentment out on his wife, my mother.

The most effective way of punishing her was to be harsh to her children and this was such an effortless exercise for my father that the three of us took it as normal and were never surprised. The more favoured children of the household took the cue from my father, who was a natural leader in all the fun and games and tended to gang up against us. They delighted in manufacturing secrets for the pleasure of keeping them from us and tried to block our entry into their play activity. In fact this became, both for them and us, an exciting game in itself. Though it definitely made life more interesting for our own age groups, I know that it tortured my mother.

My grandparents were aware of the situation but they never spoke their minds to their son on this matter. They felt that their miscalculation and bad judgement were to blame for everything and that their son should not have to bear the brunt of their mistake. This attitude fuelled my father's predisposition to see himself as a martyr. In fact, as time went on, he armed himself with more and more grievances against my mother and her simple, affectionate family. I am sure that some of these were purely imaginary, but he clung to his half-truths because they justified him in his own eyes.

At the time when the family was looking for a suitable match for my father, now a widower and therefore expected to lower his expectations somewhat, a "candidate" was pointed out by his eldest sister, whose comparatively humbler in-laws lived in Gwalior. This aunt of mine was an imperious and self-assured lady who considered that she had been married beneath her station. Possibly she did not see why she should be the only one in the family to whom this had happened. Her line of reasoning was that a humble background and low expectations or no expectations would be the best thing to seek in my father's second wife. She had sighted just such a person on the balcony across the road watching the Ramlila procession passing below and made enquiries about the family. Everything was satisfactory, so she sent word that her parents could go ahead with arrangements for the wedding.

Her word carried a lot of weight and it all came about as planned. Years later, when she saw that it had really not worked out at all and that perhaps her brother blamed her in his heart for her part in the affair, she took the easy way out to clear herself and told him privately that the person she had been shown on the balcony, by arrangement, was someone else, not my mother, the implication being that there had been some kind of fraud. Ours was a very "civilised" family and a matter like this could not have been brought out into the open, but my aunt's disclosure, which I am now sure was fictional, ensured that my father would never reconcile himself to his marriage or stop blaming my mother and his family for his misery. Baua would never have known this story but for a chance remark my father let drop much later in their lives. She put two and two together and reconstructed what must have happened. Although it was dreadful, it relieved her somewhat. She said it was better for her to know at least a part of what my father was simmering about than to be completely in the dark, always guessing, always trying and always failing to reach him behind his thick wall of emotional alibis.

Baua was fifty-three years old when my father died suddenly. Despite the kind of relationships that had existed between us, we were all devastated. There were big and bitter changes in our lives, including traumatic family partitions of property in which we had to give up the house where we had grown up and where Baua had lived ever since it had been built by my grandfather. She had to move to another old building which had fallen to our share, leaving Shammo Bhua behind in the main ancestral house. My husband and I decided to give up our quarters on the university campus and move in with her so that she would not be alone. This started a new phase in her life where she experienced freedom and respect for the first time.

My husband, whom most people thought cold and undemonstrative, developed a tender concern for her which I found miraculous and most gratifying. Soon he became her friend and confidant as well and the days soon began to pass happily and effortlessly for the three of us. The birth of my two sons enriched our lives even more and gave Baua great joy. Her presence was a tremendous support to me and I could pursue my music and my job without too much guilt or tension. She was a central figure in the lives of my children while they were growing up and they developed an independent and extremely close relationship with her.

Baua grew old as a part of my family. She had always been a most wonderful mother to me but at some point during this last phase of her life she and I became intimate friends. I felt I could tell her everything and ask her anything I wanted to. Once, when I had the use of a chauffeur-driven car, I asked her whether she would like to go out somewhere. She was most enthusiastic and said, yes, she would like to go and visit Shammo Bhua.

"Why on earth do you want to drive all those dusty and hot miles to see someone who tortured you for forty years?" I asked.

She made an impatient gesture and said that I had put my finger on it myself.

"In forty years, one can get attached even to a piece of furniture. She is a human being, not a table or chair. We have been associated for so long that I admit I am attached to her," she said with a shy smile.

It must have been about a month before she died at the age of seventy-two when Baua and I were talking about old times. I asked her a question that had troubled me the whole of my adult life. I had thought about it so many times that it came out with somewhat greater aggression than I intended.

"Baua, I really want to know why you stayed on in that house tied to my father's name when your life there was so unbearably humiliating. Were you afraid of what people would say if you walked out and went back to your parental home? Or were you afraid to hurt your parents with the disclosure that your marriage had not been a happy one after all? Or did you think that nobody except the house into which you were married would be willing to extend financial support to you and your children? Or did you want to ensure at any cost that your children did not lose the social and educational advantage of being brought up in a 'high class' family?"

She was a little alarmed at the intensity of my tone and the unrelenting manner in which I threw all the possible alternatives at her.

"If you really want the truth, I'll have to think about it. Then I'll definitely tell you," she said in a matter-of-fact tone.

Other things claimed my attention and there was no further talk on this subject for the next three days. One morning, when I was getting ready for office, she called me and said she had to tell me something important. At that moment our earlier conversation was far from my mind.

"I have been thinking about what you asked me. For three whole days and nights. You wanted the absolute truth. Today I think I can tell you," she said.

I put my files down on a table, abandoned the idea of going to the office altogether if necessary, and pulled up a chair near her.

"None of the reasons you suggested is correct. I made sure of that. I asked myself each of those questions many times most searchingly because I do want to tell you the truth about this."

"What was the reason then? Did you discover it?"

"Yes," she said. "The truth is that I loved him."

VICTOR ANANT

The Three Faces of an Indian

It is characteristic of people born, historically speaking, on a borderline and reared in a no-man's land of values to live lazily; and lazy living, in plainer words, means living by opportunism, treachery, cowardice, hypocrisy and wit. There is no effort implied in such a way of life, no awareness of a need to make a deliberate choice. It is a fact of nature – just as, in politics, the notorious unreliability of border areas may primarily be a result of their geographical situation.

I know this from direct reflection on my own situation. I am one of these people. My generation of urban Indians was born when the movement for independence was just gathering momentum, between 1925 and 1935. We were bred through an interregnum of frustration, dissension, prolonged suspense and struggle. We finally saw freedom arrive, not with an ideological bang, but with a whimper of political expediency. And we have lived through more than a decade of self-government.

The generic term for us is "Macaulay's bastards". Though the introduction of English as the medium of education in India is attributed to Lord Macaulay, we were, in terms of the assembly line, the first near-perfect products of this system. But this term means more than the simple truth that English is the language largely used by us, although we may be able to get by in one or the other of the many homespun Indian languages. It means that people like me are heirs to two sets of customs, are shaped, in our daily lives, by dual codes of behaviour. For example: my generation on the one hand declared its agnosticism and on the other tamely succumbed to hoary ritual; we yearned for romantic love but were reconciled to marriage, by the well-established method of matching horoscopes, to a girl selected for us by our parents; outside our homes we smoked, consumed alcohol, and ate meat when available, but at home we were rigidly puritan and vegetarian; we glibly talked about individual salvation although we belonged to a very closely knit joint-family system.

Until India became independent there was, in the minds of most of my generation, no dismay at the contradictions inherent in our way of life. This was due to moral inertia and flabbiness. If we had then tried to come to terms with our two influences we may have been able to see them as mutually antagonistic, and we would then have been compelled to make a choice. The flabbiness was also partly due to the general climate of our time. The majority of Indians were engaged in a struggle for political independence, but the method of warfare corresponded to our mental slovenliness and to our physical lack of energy. Freedom was a national enterprise and all our moral anguish could be contained in one word – slavery.

My generation was an enthusiastic body of freedom-mongers; many of us must have served terms of imprisonment. Because our patriotism was never suspected, not even by ourselves, we were able to feel fully integrated members of one vast community, sharing one purpose, creating one destiny. But was this not, simply, the laziest way out? When all that was demanded of us was to lie down in multitudes in front of trains or on the streets, and walk in chanting unison to crowd the jails, which one of us could fail to respond? Struggle usually means going through a violent experience, and when struggle comes with the end of one's period of youth then it means growing into manhood and self-realisation. But we did not grow through Indian independence. We were just sucked into a shuffling, sleepwalking mass and dreamed of waking up in some cloud-cuckoo land of bliss. We had all the grandeur and all the emptiness of a hypnotised people.

The obsession of those times can best be seen in the work of Indians who were then writing in English (with one exception, Mr R.K. Narayan). Indian novels published abroad before 1947 were essentially political. Their authors were propagandists for the cause of independence, for the strategy of non-violence and for the efficacy, not the morality, of passive resistance. Their whole vocabulary was derived from, and based on, politics. The word *satyagraha*, for example, literally means a search for – or a profound yearning for – truth. This is a word which could have generated motive power for endless depth-plumbing and intense self-questioning. But, by constant association with politics, there is no more magic left in this word and it is used today only to categorise a specific device, instrument or technique for political purposes. Until independence, therefore, contemporary Indian writing does not serve as a vehicle for adventurous imaginations. It stands only as a record of a phase in Indian history. Because that period in history is significant the writing is also significant; but because of the very nature of their preoccupations those writers all seem to be posing *one* problem of a nation, not the *many* problems of an individual. Not one Indian – or a type of Indian – but a whole community was the hero.

This emphasis on the community left deep marks on us. One of them was the need to create and worship living political personalities, or national heroes. And so our politicians and leaders automatically became repositories of our faith, our hopes and our values. My generation had three to choose from. It is, again, a sign of our sloth that we chose the one least likely to embarrass us, least likely to wrench us out of our opium dream. To begin with, there was Gandhi – a unique phenomenon, a saint. We knew that we would never measure up to his kind of greatness. Then there were the uncompromising radicals, like Subhas Chandra Bose. We did not possess the guts for their kind of extremism and shied away from them. Finally, Nehru. Here was a social democrat, adopting Gandhian means for "progressive" ends, a man of letters, a bit of a philosopher, agnostic, emotional, romantic, glamorously torn within himself, and for all that a natural sceptre-and-crown figure. We settled for him.

It was not possible for us to conceive of any heroism outside politics because none existed. Personality cult politics in emergent states, or in advanced states, reflect the poor quality of artistic imaginations at that time, or the loss in vigour of the exploratory mind. Bertolt Brecht has said: "Unhappy the land that has no heroes; no, unhappy the land that has need of heroes." To which an Indian of my time may add: "Unhappy the hero who has no nation; no, unhappy the hero who has need of a nation." Exclusive participation in the quest for nationhood thus stifled all desire to discover oneself, blinded us to the excitement and danger to be experienced in the search for selfhood. We went around like people without underwear, wearing just a large, communal greatcoat. We were completely devoid of any sense of intimacy with ourselves. There was no need to define oneself because questions of personal morality never even arose. Instead, one joined in a nation-wide moral mudbath. Or, alternatively, one simply left it to Gandhi who, by his periodic fasts, undertook to cleanse the national soul.

Another mark of this non-individual basis of our lives was the habit of turning into abstract terms any particular question. Nothing was specific. We used to sit around in coffee houses, those dens of communal phantasy-making, talking for hours about "democratic socialism and communism", "ends and means", "English or Hindi as the lingua franca"; or just talking; dabbling in the cosmos without knowing the ground on which we stood; drawing up charters for a world religion; or making various formulae for one world. In the evenings we would return to our suburban houses mentally too exhausted to observe the fascinating complexities of our bourgeoisdom, which should have been our only real starting point.

The result of this kind of abstruseness is best summed up by what happened to an Indian mystic friend of mine who commutes now between the pink gin and champagne salons of literary London and the cold, hard floors of a guru's ashram in India. He was commissioned by an American publisher to write a sociological study of India after independence. He was paid a large advance in dollars. About a year later he submitted a manuscript which began, "India does not exist and I do not exist. This being the Nature of Reality . . ." and elaborated upon this theme in a hundred thousand utterly incomprehensible words. The manuscript came back with a letter which said, "Since India does not exist and you do not exist, the contract does not exist, and the question of paying you the balance does not exist. We are so deeply moved by your revelation that from now on you may be assured we do not exist for you. In fact, at this rate we wonder how we could exist for anybody at all." My friend sighed as he said to me: "The West will never understand *maya*. It is too materialistic."

I have described all this in some detail to show why, with independence in 1947, my generation in particular was unable to respond heroically to the moral confusion that was soon to prevail. We were ready to disintegrate because we were wholly unprepared for the shock of self-recognition. It was as if a huge fog had lifted and in the dazzling clarity of the aftermath we saw ourselves as we had never imagined possible, each with distinctly separate, unrecognisable faces. Our pathetic inability to create a moral order to live by was brought into sharp focus by three catastrophic events which came soon after independence.

The first was when, as a result of Partition (never accepted by our leaders for what it was, a recognition of the British assumption that there were two Indias, Muslim and Hindu, but slurred over as a political compromise), the frontier areas between Pakistan and India erupted in savage scenes of murder, arson, loot and destruction unparalleled in Indian history. The second was the assassination of Gandhi, a man whom every Indian deified. The third was the shocking use of military force against the native states of Junagadh and Hyderabad and against the raiders in Kashmir. Suddenly we saw our nakedness. Our smug moral complacency (or national consciousness) was nothing more than a series of superficial lies. But what private means did we have of hiding our shame? What was the meaning of being an Indian?

For the first time we saw the cause and consequence of our laziness. The contradictions smouldering underneath the surface, the contradictions ignored by us, had already slowly drained us of all daring, of all creative impulses. We realised we had been living until then on an *ad hoc* basis, taking what we could from the "petty-cash boxes" of two different cultures and were suddenly confronted with our bankruptcy. Where could we find the cultural capital needed to respond to the challenge that freedom had brought in its wake?

It is after these events, in the early years of independence, that most of my generation begins to turn towards England, at first hesitatingly then with growing confidence and in a concerted fashion. A curiously self-analytical tremor may be detected in writers published abroad since 1947. The theme of national aspiration and a national cause is relegated to the background. We have instead, themes of individual aspiration and self-propaganda. There is, for example, the bizarre self-mockery and pungent satire against holy men in Mr G.V. Desani's "All about Mr Hatter"; there is the unexpected homage paid to dear departed British liberal humanism in Mr Nirad Chaudhuri's "Autobiography of an Unknown Indian"; the delicious drawing-room anguish incorporated into themes of Indo-British romance in novels by Miss Santha Rama Rau, Miss Kamala Markandeya and Dr Balachandra Rajan; but the important significant trend in this new range of articulateness is the *distance* now created between the individual Indian and India. Alienation has arrived in Bombay, Madras and Calcutta.

What is alienation? An alien is a stranger; and alienation, in a personal sense, therefore means estrangement from oneself. Sophisticated European writers – who have been for long friendly with this word and are conditioned to accept complexity as an index of a higher state of awareness – would hardly fall into the trap of formulating such a dreadfully simple definition. But in terms of my craft – the craft of writing, which, I believe, is a means to self-knowledge – I am far too young to take anything for granted. So the question that forces itself out from all sides, the question that begins with ominous drumbeats of doubt, until the temples begin to throb, until the rhythm becomes persistent, menacing, deafening, until there is no holding back the cry any longer, is – Who am I?

Who am I? From now on I must, perforce, part company even with my generation of Macaulay's bastards and speak for myself.

In 1952, when I left India for England, I was certain I was a Briton *even* in the colouring of my skin. (Did not my mother say she had found a "very fair" girl for me whom I should marry before I left?) If independence had resulted in self-consciousness, and self-consciousness in alienation, I was sure England would make me a whole man again. (I did not know it then, but I assumed there was some superior merit in not being split.) There were, of course, practical reasons which I did not deny myself; the difficulty of earning a living in India, with the prevailing grimly nationalistic mood; the numerous attractions of a Welfare State; visions of sexual freedom and completeness; good English beer. But this materialistic pill was coated with a liberal amount of ideological sugar.

First, I thought of my relationship with the English language. I had already begun to write when I was fourteen, and could not use any Indian language to express myself. My very first effort was a poem, and I mention it here because it has interesting psychological undertones. It was addressed to a girl who had turned me down for another boy and the poem was charged with sexual contempt for her, treating her as a prostitute.

About this time, too, I suffered a public humiliation in college. Again, English was connected. It was during our essay period, taken by a woman professor. She looked upon me as an undesirable element in class and was waiting for an opportunity to ridicule me. The trouble was that I was always first, and fast, with my essay. That day she found me brooding, chewing on the end of my pen. She asked me, "Have you finished your essay?" I stood up and replied, "My pen is leaking, madam." I was summoned to her table and made to stand facing the class. She pointed at me and said, not concealing her delight, "This boy has been learning English since the age of four. And yet, if I were to ask him a simple question like, 'Where are you going?' do you know what he'll reply? He'll reply, 'My grandmother is dead, madam.' [She waited for the class to stop laughing.] I ask him if he's finished his essay and he turns round and tells me his pen is leaking! When will you learn to speak in English, boy?" Everybody enjoyed my mortification. But the confusion in my mind was the result of something deeper than ridicule; it was the result of a painful discovery. I felt that evasion was an instinct native to me; precision had to be earned; precision was a sign of civilisation. I was speaking English, but not *in* English. The whole explanation of my inadequacy was to be found in that loaded preposition. This curious association of the English language with two women, one developing into inverted contempt, the other into self-pity, began, I believe, my *sensual* attitude to English, my looking upon it as an instrument of sensual analysis.

There is a morality inherent in a language, woven imperceptibly into the fabric of words. When you are born into a language you wear this morality with natural ease: it is your skin. But when you are forced to recognise the foreignness of a language then you are in the singularly terrifying position of being aware of a whole range of moral implications that have to be discovered step by step, you are aware of the urge to experience every nuance and shade of this morality and to create a relationship with words which may not be related to your native instincts. Every little whisper, every caress, becomes larger than life, frighteningly charged, and the deeper one goes the more hopelessly tongue-tied one gets, until one has ultimately either to kill the language or be killed by it. This is what, I think, Nabokov means when he calls *Lolita* his "love affair with the English language". His very sensual strangeness forces him to indulge self-consciously in every kind of exploration of a child love, and he sees depths the natives do not see. By a cathartic process his exploration of a language becomes a profoundly personal mode of sex, and he shocks even such wide-awake and liberal natives like Mr Philip Toynbee.

Secondly, I was disturbed by the fact that an imperial power, concerned mainly with economic aggression and not in the old sense with any proselytising purpose, should inspire religious awe in me, born and brought up as a Brahmin. In the fifth century AD St Thomas, a Syrian Christian, arrived in Kerala and founded a church. Today twenty per cent of the people of Kerala are Christians. Vasco da Gama came with the Pope's blessings on his voyage of discovery in the fifteenth century and landed on the West coast. Today Goa is still firmly Catholic and in the firm grip of Portuguese imperialism. But except for children of British parentage (and Naga tribesmen) there are no Christians to speak of in the rest of India. I wondered what strange power the Church of England possessed that it could make me feel Christian, stir in me a protestant conscience, even though I was not a convert in any ritual sense.

Thirdly, I could not help feeling that the political victory belonged to Britain and not to India. Thinking again of French and Portuguese possessions in India, there seemed to be a magnanimity of vision, and much human charity, in the manner in which Britain had transferred power to Indians. Only the moral, surely, recognise morality? Moreover, what better evidence of Britain's victory than that the new republic remained, of its own volition, within the Commonwealth, recognising the Queen as head of it?

It is only after seven years in London – broken by a one-year return to India – that I see how false my reasoning was, that I have never been, and can never be, a Briton, and that if I had then been able to look deeper into myself I could have seen my real motives. In these seven years I have lived largely in relationship to India, which means I have lived incestuously with myself, and am able to take Britain without false emotion and incorrect reasoning.

To mention the materialistic aspects first. Welfare State amenities are useless for a writer such as I am. I thrive on adversity. If I felt completely safe I would perhaps stagnate as a writer, because writing to me is fundamentally a rebellion against a sense of ancient security, a security that ultimately destroys the need to create, a security that lulls one into self-deception. I discovered, too, that I have a deep-rooted prejudice against doctors and curative drugs of any kind. I prefer to heal myself by my own devious ways and even simulate sickness when I feel too healthy. I have even cultivated my own nervous breakdown and gone away and quietly had it, and come through it by myself, with my sense of the comic (in this kind of a game with oneself) remaining intact.

If nationalistic India is grim, nationalism is even more deadly and smug in England. It produces pompous statesmen like Mr Harold Macmillan who leave Mr Nehru far behind. Retaining the H-bomb, in effect as a deterrent *against the United States of America*, wanting to form a non-nuclear club so that France (and the Europeans) may be blackmailed into not wanting the bomb, for hypocrisy of such a high order Britain still remains unequalled.

Sexual freedom: the kind that exists in London is only sexual hysteria. It bores me stiff. And again, I was startled to discover the range of perversities here, including an obsession with necrophily shown by young writers, and one case of a man who listened to the sighs made by a woman during an orgasm and recorded on a tape-recorder. At the same time sexual prudery, with all its attendant class inhibitions, on sale every week in at least three lots at five-pence a time – I mean the women's magazines. I cannot, therefore, like an Indian friend of mine, claim that the first time I held an English woman I felt "the whole of the British Empire crumbling in my arms." There seems to be no awareness of sex at all in England, no awareness that sex, like all the essentially simple things of life, is not sporadic, boisterous, haphazard, but is a slow, repetitive, educative process, to be savoured anew.

Nor do cultural interests hold me in thrall. I find I read more American or European writers than British ones, for to be British seems to imply that one does not ask fundamental questions. I read American reviews more seriously than I do British ones. And as for food, I mostly cook an Indian meal for myself and find that I cannot drink beer because it upsets my stomach.

What about the "intangible" advantages? It is mainly in my relationship to the English language that I find a curious change, a certain kind of revulsion at the way the language is used in England. During my early days here, walking down Soho, I was appalled when I was hailed by a prostitute with the words, "Want to come home, darling?" and a little further along, "Want a short time, darling?" Home – and a short time – what ghastly words to associate with going to a harlot! I am sure that if this is their vocabulary of sex there can be no genuine whores in England. My second shock was to hear a middle-class girl of reasonable intelligence describe a weekly picture magazine as a "book". My third was to see a debutante arrive at a party and announce, "I think I'll traipse over and perch on that seat." Mr Dwight Macdonald reproduced a classic English conversation in an article in *Encounter.* It went: "Is it raining?" "Not really." I have now decided that what I need to protect myself from is the danger of writing *in* English; I want to write English; I want to write *badly* in English. I think I shall succeed.

The Christian spell, my second main source of "intangible" anxiety, is, I now discover, one that was cast by the greatest Christian this age has produced, Gandhi. Influenced by Tolstoy, Gandhi modelled himself, as I now see, closely on the life of

Christ. His "miracle" – to make salt from seawater, the staff of life for India's multitudes – his days of silence, his abandoning the first civil disobedience movement to go into solitary retreat, all these were clearly derived from Christ's manoeuvres. His language was deliberately biblical. And I think the reason why Gandhi terrified Britain was that he strove with a Christian conscience against a power that was Christian.

Political disillusionment came with the understanding that there was not the slightest shred of charity in the manner in which India was partitioned, and that, if for any reason at all, it was because it was too expensive maintaining an Empire that power was transferred.

Why, then, did I come to England, and why do I stay here? The answer to the first part of this question is straightforward. The archetypal adventurer is Ulysses. There is a parallel to be found in the Indian epic, the Ramayanam. In both these stories the hero is exiled because of a suggestion that within his tribe he is a weak man. The process of going abroad, physical combat with forces unknown, long periods of isolation, reflection, and discipline, these make a weak man strong. And, finally, the exile returns a hero, ready to bend the long bow and to reveal himself as the strongest of the tribe. In the Ramayanam, Rama is exiled to a forest for fourteen years. His main task is the destruction of the demon king Ravana, who has kidnapped Sita, Rama's wife. Rama does this and returns to his home to claim the throne. The populace rises against Sita, who by now has two children. They suspect her of adultery – she remained for quite a period in Ravana's custody. It is then that Rama, once weak, reveals his moral fibre, his sense of dedication towards his people. Even though he himself believes in the infinite fidelity of his wife he disowns her and his two children in the interests of his people.

The second part of the question concerns a writer's instinct for survival. I must have known intuitively that it is in the nature of British civilisation to cherish people like me, homeless orphans. We are looked upon as children of conflict, born in transit, to be pitied. It is assumed that we will eternally remain torn within ourselves but that we can be taught to recognise our duality: the dear octopus of dichotomy never surrenders its victims. For nearly seven years, ever since I came to England, I have lived smugly and comfortably on the borderline, battening on the profits that derive from playing the role of cultural schizophrenic.

And why not? In such a singular position I did not have to go out and woo life. One is endlessly misunderstood, and, in terms of literature, misunderstanding pays dividends; in terms of life, misunderstanding provides one with a cloak under which the interior monologue may be conducted without any disturbance from outside. I did not have to endure the daily tyranny of living with one face: instead I could wear two eternally unconverted faces. I did not have to make an effort to walk the tightrope: instead, opposing winds conspired to keep me balanced there. To be a cultural split-personality is a useful occupation in Europe, where to be harmonious and integrated would be disastrous.

The other reason is fanciful, but nevertheless one which may be proved in time to have some truth in it. Assuming that it is possible to draw the outline of a national image, it is then possible to see, in these our other-directed times, a set pattern of love-hate relationships between never-the-twain-shall-meet nations. A few spring readily to mind: American and Japanese (with American interest in the mystique of Zen); French and Arab (with French interest in the mystique of Islam); German and Jew (with German interest in the Jewish myth); British and

Indian (with British interest in the mystique of Hinduism). These nation-pairs pass through all phases involved in a marriage, beginning with love and conquest, and then going on to exploitation, responsibility, an attempt at mutual destruction, a desperate anxiety to preserve identity, guilt, reparation; and will perhaps end only with the inevitable failure that must follow all such intense relationships. At any rate these nation-pairs have an exciting time discovering and discarding each other, playing coquettes in turn, going away and coming back, and producing beautiful half-castes. The new order may yet be in the hands of the new bastardy. I see that despite all the tales I will tell when I go back home, despite my cynicism, many Indians will still have to go through the same ordeal. It is an enriching ordeal. It is the source of all creativity.

It is this, which I hope to create, which I call the third face. For as long as there are two people they must wait for the third man to arrive.

Who am I? I can only give tentative answers. Or, in other words, it may be more valid to say what I hope to become. For in order to discover the meaning of one's life it is often necessary to speculate, to leap in the dark, to take off, so to speak, from the runway of reason and fly into the open vistas of the imagination. On the biological and sociological evidence thrown up by one's past it is possible to build a house of fact. But the human paradox is that the more seemingly self-protective such a house, the more torrential a slight leak in the roof appears, the more devastation to be read in a slight puff of wind. It is possible to live within reason, but ultimately is it possible to live by reason alone? Some of the sturdiest children are the result of a wild interplay between fact and fancy, and we have known generations to survive on the hopes contained in one idea. It seems to me that just as physical friction results in the ecstasy of an orgasm, so also mental friction, the constant leaping up and down from oneself to the other, can result in the ecstacy of a "vision".

I have often, in writing, mentioned my sense of being a Brahmin. This has been interpreted by many friends, especially by my Indian friends, as a harking back to reactionary days, to communalism, to exclusiveness. This is nonsense. The word Brahmin has no meaning today because it has been given too many meanings, like holy man, performing priest, yogi, mystic, faith healer, a superior caste, etc. This, too, is nonsense. Hinduism, like Judaism, repels many people because it has not been subject to perennial re-definition. I do not use the word Brahmin in any religious or narrow sense. I use it to stand for the most imaginative kind of living I know, I use it to indicate the function of an artist in Indian society.

What I hope to do, ultimately, is to re-define the word in a way as to make it seem more real, more a part of our times. The main difficulty in this is that Hinduism seems to be, unlike the life of ancient Greek city-states, a way of life derived from an all-peasant civilisation. There were really no castes, only crafts. It was, shall we say, a kind of highly organised and more dogmatic guild socialism. It is inevitable, of course, that modern India must industrialise, so that there would be no sense at all of talking of Hinduism today as a complete way of life for a nation. It is possible, however, that one of the ancient *crafts* may survive, the *craft* of being a Brahmin. This hope is based on the attitude of the Brahmin not to derive any profit from his work, his austerity, his aptitude for rigorous living, his sense of greater responsibility to the community. It will not be possible for an artist in India ever to aspire for profits from his art. One lives by myths, and an artist lives more intensely by myths because he makes new myths all the time. My myth is the myth of a

Brahmin artist as depicted in the story of Narada. He was a singing minstrel during the time of Krishna, one of the forms in which God was reincarnated. Narada was, I believe, the world's first dialectician, the first to use the theory that action and reaction set against each other would produce a synthesis. One day Krishna's mother asked Narada to sing to her the story of her son. Narada refused. He said, "Old woman, don't tell me to do this. You are not aware, but the time is not yet ripe for the deeds of your son to be extolled." But she begged and pleaded. Finally he gave way, but on one condition. He insisted that Krishna himself should not be given an opportunity to listen to a song in his praise. And so Krishna's two wives were stationed at the door as guardians to warn Narada if the child-god should enter.

Narada began singing, playing on his *veena* (a stringed instrument). The magic of his music was such that the mother completely lost herself in it. The two wives at the door completely lost themselves, too. Krishna walked in, past the guardians and stood beside Narada. He listened to the music and *he* began to lose himself. When God began to lose his sense of identity, his reason for having taken human shape, he started returning to an elemental state. He started dissolving, from the toes upward, into water.

Only Narada, the artist, still remained self-conscious. He stopped his song. There was only one way to call God back to his purpose, he realised. Although he was the sort of person who did not appear to be very religious, he began plucking at the strings of his instrument, and chanting the name of God, *narayana, narayana, narayana*. When Krishna heard the cries of a devotee, he shook himself out of his trance and once again realised his sense of mission. He had by then already half-dissolved into an oceanic state. (This is known as the half-man half-water incarnation.)

But this, alone among all Indian stories, is the one that portrays what it means to be an artist. An artist has, it is implied, to remain ceaselessly vigilant, so self-conscious that even sensuous pleasure in his craft may have to be forsaken, and so vigilant that he must be ready even to wake up God from time to time.

Narada was a mischief maker, of course. Perhaps he had a vision, all along, of what was to take place. He had three faces: the face he showed Krishna's mother, the singing face; the face he showed Krishna, the face of a devotee; and the face he showed to no one but himself – the harmonious face?

ARUN KOLATKAR

House with Nine Rooms

I GREW UP IN A house with nine rooms that were arranged, well almost, like a house of cards. Five in a row on the ground, topped by three on the first, and one on the second floor.

The place wasn't quite as cheerful as playing cards though. Or as colourful. The rooms had mud floors which had to be daubed with cowdung every week to keep them in good repair. The walls were painted, or rather distempered, uniformly in some indeterminate colour which I can only describe as a lighter shade of sulphurous yellow.

All the six doors on the ground floor were so aligned (as if the rooms had been skewered through, from one end of the house to the other) that anyone standing in the front door could not help seeing through all of them, all the way through to the back door as a matter of fact, and into the modest backyard.

Which consisted of: a split-level craporium, with an access opening in the back at street level, for the masked municipal scavenger to stick his hand in and clear the load of crap, or for the occasional freewheeling and freeloading pig to stick his snout in, and give quite a start sometimes to the man upstairs, the preoccupied labourer; a woodshed, with stacks of firewood and coal sacks, and undermined by a resident bandicoot, where I loved to watch my uncle chop a bit of wood, and might even on occasion have gone so far as to actually pick up an axe; and a peru tree, as I prefer to call it, by its Indian name, rather than guava tree, that was a stopover for hysterical parties of passing parrots and the refuge of venerable white-haired caterpillars.

I loved to watch those caterpillars, but they were rather reserved, you know, and I soon got bored.

When I got bored of watching the caterpillars, and whenever my father was not in the house, I repaired to his room on the first floor, which was the only one with any kind of furniture in the whole house: the only table in the house, a simple study table, small and unpretentious but solid stuff, made by a competent carpenter rather than a cabinet maker; a straight-backed wooden chair to go with it; two cane chairs and an easy chair. A balcony, or should I say gallery, ran the whole length of the room and overlooked the road outside, in front of the house.

The rooms even had some pictures on the walls. No ancestors, no family members; it was all art.

The most imposing of the lot was a black-and-white head, in outlandish headgear, more like a bird of some kind than anything else on earth, a profile of what could've been a Greek god, but whom we thought could only have been Alexander the Great, or Sikandar as we called him, rendered beautifully in charcoal by a local artist called K. Vasudeo, whom we had never seen, but who, we believed, was out there somewhere in the big world, making a name and a fortune for himself. It was an antique study, presumably, or, more likely, copied painstakingly from a photograph reproduced somewhere, with charcoal powder and paper stubbs.

We were all very proud of our Alexander; but there was something about him that disturbed me. Our Alexander was blind in the only eye that he presented us.

Which is how the human eye is always rendered by great sculptors I'd been told by the highest authority on art I knew:

our drawing teacher. But I didn't know whether to believe him or not. For he himself had a good part of his left ear missing. A rat had got to it when he was a baby.

We also had a small, unsigned watercolour, another original, though as much a copy of a copy, of someone we thought of as another superhero, Napoleon, who was bareheaded and whose hand was swallowed up not by his coat but by some kind of muff, and whose arm was raised as if he had a good mind to take a backhanded swipe at the viewer.

Then there was a reproduction of Gainsborough's *Blue Boy*.

And one was a reproduction of a painting which showed a fair, helpless, and presumably shipwrecked woman, in some kind of a diaphanous garment that left her shoulders and arms bare, leaning backwards against an outcrop of rock, her arms flung wide on either side, her head thrown back, a mass of blond ringlets tumbling over her bare shoulders and on the rock surface, with waves dashing at her feet, and an expression of inexplicable ecstasy on her face.

I didn't have a name for her but she could've been Andromeda. Because, well, after I wrote that description I happened to open the dictionary to look up some word and I came across Andromeda; and it said "daughter of Cassiopeia, rescued by Perseus from the sea monster, for whom she was fastened to a rock", and come to think of it, that woman on my father's wall did appear to have been kind of "fastened" to the rock, though neither her rescuer Perseus nor a sea monster was anywhere in sight.

The only other work of art in the house, displayed on a wall, though not in my father's room but downstairs, was the first thing you saw as you entered the house; and it was my mother's handiwork, a mixed multimedia showpiece with woolly birds with sequin eyes among clusters of glass grapes and embroidered, crewel I think, leaves on a black velvet ground.

That wasn't the end of all art in the house though. There was a hidden treasure in one of the drawers of my father's desk, which consisted of three or four packets of glossy black-and-white picture postcards showing the monuments and architectural marvels of Greece, as well as sculptures from the various museums of Italy and France.

As I sat in my father's chair, examining the contents of his drawers, it was inevitable that I should've been introduced to the finest achievements of Baroque and Renaissance art, the works of people like Bernini and Michelangelo, and I've spent long hours spellbound by their art.

But at the same time I must make a confession. The European girls disappointed me. They had beautiful faces, great figures, and they showed it all. But there was nothing to see. I looked sadly at their smooth, creaseless, and apparently scratch-resistant crotches, sighed, and moved on to the next picture.

The boys too; they let it all hang out, but they were hardly what you may call well hung. David for example. Was it David? Great muscles, great body, but his penis was like a tiny little mouse. Move on. Next picture.

I looked helplessly at the statue of a muscular old man and two young men – who did not seem to be of much use in a crisis – struggling heroically but entangled hopelessly in the seemingly endless coils of – was it one? or two I think – two very determined and relentless serpents, each one almost as thick as the old man's thigh. It was of course the statue of Lokoon as I still pronounce the word, and still do not know whether that's the right way or, as I suspect, not.

I might've wondered then who the old man was and who the clean-cut kids were, and how they had managed to get themselves in such a fix. And I also might've wondered if Krishna, had he found himself in that situation, would not have been able to straighten out the two serpents and come out on top, the way he battled and subdued Kaliya, the serpent king, in the river Jamuna, as I had heard my grandmother tell so often.

You probably don't know what a grandmother is. Never had one, did you? Oh dear, this is going to be difficult, I can see that.

Even in India, they've all been wiped out you know, eradicated as they say, like malaria or smallpox.

I mean you do get them, but not the real thing. Only *analogues* imported from Korea in completely knocked down condition and assembled locally.

The one I owned was always switched on. We never had to push any buttons or anything. She responded to an oral command, the human voice, and she had a phenomenal 640K memory. And although she didn't give any printouts – she could neither read nor write – she actually talked. Mmmm, I think it's about time; somebody will soon just have to go around reinventing them.

We usually kept her in the third room on the ground floor, from where she could keep an eye on all the comings and goings, since from that position she could keep the front as well as the back door in her sight, which meant that no stranger could come in without her knowledge, and that's the other thing: she operated as a burglar alarm as well.

At any given moment she knew which ones of the dozen or so family members were in and which ones were out. She could always stop me whenever she saw me running out the front door barefoot, and remind me to wear my chappals, which I found such a tedious thing. And since the room she was installed in was the one next to the kitchen, she could also keep her two daughters-in-law on their toes, and ensure that there was peace in the kitchen.

She was a multipurpose grandmother. Quite versatile actually. Quite an expert at little things like making cotton wicks for brass lamps, for example. Or big things, like planning and supervising the annual pickles and preserves project. She also provided banking services to my father who handed over his pay packet, intact, to her at the beginning of each month and she balanced the budget for him.

And she acted as the family doctor to us all. It's to her that we went for all minor ailments, for which she had a ready supply of various herbs and roots and barks and leaves and bulbs and berries and nuts. And she played a major role in the family decision-making process. Phew!

It does sound rather like a lot of things for one grandmother to do.

I used her mainly in her storytelling mode. Hooked on her, like all the other children in the house. It was usually at night, after the day's work was done and everyone was relaxed after dinner, that she functioned best, with the children hanging on to every word she said and the grown-ups too plugged in, not missing a word.

And every time she was in danger of running out of stories, all she had to do was go to listen to the katha or the kirtan in the Murlidhar temple in the other lane to pick up and stock up on a few more, like she did every evening, rain or shine.

Fortunately, she was kind of water-repellent you know. Rain. Never touched her. I know, because she told me herself.

"Why don't you carry an umbrella when you go to the temple?" I asked her once, and she said, "I don't need one." "But you'll get wet," I said, horrified at the thought. "No," she said, "I won't. God sees to it that it doesn't rain where I walk." "Really?" I asked. "Really," she assured me.

That's nice of him, I thought. Her goodness created a force field around her you see. I realised that and wasn't surprised in the least when she came home dry.

And you too, if you're good, you too will never need a raincoat or umbrella or anything.

Apart from the obvious attractions like the easy chair, the bottle of Eno's Fruit Salt in the top drawer, the picture postcards, and the gas mask in the bottom drawer of the table (my father was in charge of civil defence in my hometown during the Second World War and may have been an air-raid warden) there was something else in my father's room that drew me to it: a small cupboard built into a wall that contained most of the books my father owned.

As thick as a brick *The Wonders of the World*; *The Mysterious Universe* by Sir James Jeans; *Nature of the Physical World* by Arthur Addington; *What is Beauty?* by I.A. Richards; *On Politics* by C.E.M. Joad; *The Kathopanishad* and the *Kenopanishad* in English translation; practically all the plays of George Bernard Shaw and his *Intelligent Woman's Guide to Socialism, Capitalism and Communism*; *Gitanjali* by Rabindranath Tagore; Tennyson's *In Memoriam*; and the *Oxford Book of Modern Verse* edited by W.B. Yeats, pronounced Yeats, as in Keats, then, and for a good many years afterwards.

I also remember *Vangmayin Mahatmata* by Ba Si Mardhekar; *Gitarahasya*, a commentary on the *Bhagawat Gita* in Marathi by Bal Gangadhar Tilak; *Jyotirvilas*, a book on astronomy; *Trikhanda Ramayana*, the story of Rama retold in Marathi; *Yadhodhan* and *Yashogandha*, two collections of poems by the Marathi poet Yashwant; and a huge dictionary of Marathi phrases and idioms which didn't shy away from four-letter words, and had the largest number of entries under arse and balls, all hilarious.

I used to take all these books out of the cupboard one by one, settle down in a chair, open them reverently, flip through the pages, ponder over the print, shut them, and put them back, regretfully, in their respective places, in exactly the same positions and angle of inclination as I found them, since . . . oh, even before I could read any of them. In the same way that, on mornings when it was my turn, I'd sit cross-legged at almost ground level on a small red-lacquered patla or wooden seat before the mini temple in one corner of our kitchen and, one by one, take out the household gods (little thumb-sized brass figures, the baby Krishna for example, crawling on hands and knees), wash them, bathe them in a copper vessel, dry them, anoint them with sandalwood paste, and put them back in the respective places in the little doll's house of a temple.

Of course, I had to purify myself first before I was allowed to touch the gods, which meant having a bath myself and wearing a special-purpose dhoti, magenta it was, and silk, because cotton, considered impure for some reason, was taboo.

But tradition was of no help when it came to approaching the books in my father's cupboard. It was silent on the subject of what procedures I was required to follow before I could touch them. I realised I was on my own and evolved my own set of rules.

First, as a routine precaution, I fortified myself with a spoonful of Eno's Fruit Salt, for the heck of it I guess, for the sheer effervescence of it, or perhaps because I'd discovered very early that it was generally good for my soul and increased my resistance. It seemed to be the most sensible thing to do, at the time anyway.

Next, I took my father's gas mask out of the bottom drawer of his desk; and it was only after I had donned the mask that

I felt I was ready for the books. Although no word of warning was printed on any them, I must've understood, at some level, that I was about to handle dangerous substances. And, if I was contaminated in spite of all the precautions I took, it must have been because, somewhere along the line, my frequent and rough handling tore the black rubber of the mask, or maybe I just grew careless, and, at some point, stopped wearing the mask altogether.

The *Oxford Book of Modern Verse* had always been one of my favourite books from my father's collection. That's where I first came across names like Thomas Stearns Eliot ("The Hollow Men"), Wystan Hugh Auden ("It's no use raising a shout"), Ezra Pound (Canto 17), Gerard Manley Hopkins ("The Caged Skylark"), and of course William Butler Yeats ("Sailing to Byzantium", "An Irish Airman Foresees His Death"), and I didn't know whether that stuff was poetry, but I knew it was pure poison. Dangerous micro-organisms were bound to escape from the minute configurations of printing ink and invade my system, as soon as I opened the book.

I fail to understand how my father, and he an educationist and all, could've been so careless as to leave it lying around, within easy reach of children. Not knowingly, I'm quite sure of it. I suspect the poor guy had no idea what was inside that book. In fact, I'm ready to bet he had never read the darn thing himself.

The size was handy, almost as if it were a prayer book; it was beautifully printed on the whitest and the finest paper I'd ever seen, Bible paper I imagine (or could it have been onionskin?); gilt-edged; beautifully bound in cloth (midnight blue I think), and the gold embossed letters, inside a simple gold embossed border said THE OXFORD BOOK OF MODERN VERSE. And I'll be damned if it didn't come complete with a royal blue satin ribbon with a cloven end for a bookmark.

It had fewer words per page than almost any other book I'd ever seen (except *In Memoriam* which had just four short lines floating in the middle of every page), and it was obvious, even to me, that they had to be very important words indeed to have been allowed to sit on one of those pages. They had to be; if they were anywhere like worth the paper they were printed on.

Having described the book in such vivid detail (a book I haven't set my eyes on for god knows how many years), I thought it would be a good idea to sneak another look at it, for old times' sake, and in the interests of veracity. I didn't want anyone to get up and say, "Ha! The book had a shocking pink candy-striped cover you know."

So I quietly borrowed it from a library and, as I write this, it's right in front of me. And I must say that the book, like Walter Pater says in his piece on Mona Lisa on page 1, does kind of look as if it has been dead many times and knows the secrets of the grave.

The gilt is gone from the edges; there is just a faint glimmer of it, topside; and there's still some gold left in the downstroke of the embossed V from the first letter in the last word of the title.

The cardboard shows at the corners of the hard covers, where the cloth, a dull black though it might've been midnight blue once, has worn through, and the gauze lining is laid bare along the spine, from where the cloth has disappeared altogether, and where the book has been patched up, inexpertly, by the library staff.

The back cover, somewhere along the top edge, has received a severe blow with a blunt instrument, and the tough cardboard is dented.

But on the whole the book, first published in 1936, which makes it practically as old as me, has weathered the onslaught of years much better than I have, and suffered much less than the reputations of the majority of the ninety-nine poets between its covers, which of course is a tribute to John Johnson, who printed it at the University Press, Oxford, and whose name appears on the last page, rather than to the literary judgement of W.B. Yeats.

But what I find most shocking is the strange fact that the book seems to have put on quite a bit of weight over the years. It's twice as thick and twice as heavy as the book I remember. It looks positively bloated, and is an affront to my memory of it.

It's the pages, you see; what bothers me is not that they're yellowed and freckled with age, but the fact that they're so thick; not Bible paper at all. And no royal blue satin bookmark either.

I can only conclude that somehow or other my father must've managed to lay his hands on a deluxe edition, regardless of whether it had been issued or not.

MADHUR JAFFREY

The Dining Room – Winter Evenings – Dining at the Long Tables

On winter evenings in Delhi, we all gathered in the drawing room where Ishri, my grandfather's manservant, had already lit a fire. "It must have snowed in Simla," we would say, rubbing our cold hands and pulling shawls, cardigans, and coats closer to ourselves. Simla, that much-loved Himalayan hill town where my sister Kamal had been born, was in the very distant north, but whenever it snowed there, icy blasts made sure we got the news.

No-one in the Number 7 household had been blessed with much sense of style so furniture, bought wholesale at auction, was shoved against all four walls. As you entered the drawing room from the gallery end, there was the radio around which we huddled to hear Hindi movie songs at midday and cricket commentaries in the afternoons. Beyond it, on the same north side, was a big sofa, above which hung a large framed print of Hope sitting, head bent, on top of the globe, playing a lyre. In the corner was a kind of piano that could only be played by pumping wind into it with a pair of foot pedals. Then, as you turned the corner to the east side, there were overstuffed chairs galore of disparate designs. Above them on the wall, attempting to give the room some cohesion, was a tinted, rather nicely framed photograph of my grandfather, looking quite Edwardian – Raj Narain, Barrister-at-law. Next, on a stand and enclosed in glass, was a miniature marble reproduction of the Taj Mahal and a potted palm on a stand. On the south side, the fireplace held a rather lovely Chinese cloisonné urn with dragons. On the mantelpiece was a print of a young, free-spirited lady (European but with an Eastern abandon), gazing into a fish bowl.

Surrounding the fireplace was an upholstered bench. Farther into the room was another large sofa where my grandfather sat and more overstuffed chairs. There was a Persian carpet of exquisite workmanship on the floor, which was also used as seating. The drawing room was, basically, a functional room that had been designed – or not designed – to hold a lot of people.

The evening routine in winter hardly varied unless there was a religious festival, wedding or music recital.

As sunset gave way to dusk, the air slowly filled with the perfumed smoke of *uppalas*, dried cow-dung cakes, being burned in braziers throughout the city. This was, and to some extent still is, the winter smell of Delhi. As the cows mostly ate hay, that was what their dung smelled like.

When the soft haze of the *uppala* smoke began drifting through the glow of the setting sun, squawking birds by the hundreds, propelled by their own clocks, would begin circling our trees in flocks: green-feathered parrots with red beaks, sparrows, yellow-beaked mynahs and also the dreaded crows. They would fly round and round above the mighty tamarind, the umbrella-shaped jujube, the mulberry near the gate, the medicinal neem and the mangoes. As they circled, they would come lower and lower, disappearing, as night fell, into the darkness of the foliage. You could still hear them for a while, though, chattering noisily, and then there would be quiet.

Ishri would light the fire in the fireplace then hobble off to prepare my grandfather's hookah, his hubble-bubble water pipe, a fairly formal, floor-standing version. I would follow Ishri because the odour of that wet, dark, manly-but-sweet tobacco drove me wild. Ishri would make a ball of the tobacco and deposit it in the top section, the *chillum*, of the hookah. Over this he would arrange small pieces of burning charcoal and blow on them repeatedly until they glowed, his cheeks puffing like a toad as he did so.

My white-bearded grandfather, supporting himself with his cane, would come through the door that connected his room to the drawing room and settle down in his accustomed place on the right side of the sofa. However old he may have been by this time, he was still king of the household. Ishri would put down the hookah and set a whisky and soda on a small table near it. Babaji would draw on the hookah. A roll of gurgling sounds would follow as the air went through the water in the pipe. He would then take a sip of his whisky. It was the start of another winter evening at Number 7.

The women, freshly washed and changed into their evening sarees, would follow, coming in from various doors, one after the other. The first two were generally commandeered by my grandfather to sit at his feet on the Persian carpet and play chess, or more often *chaupar* (a form of Parcheesi), a game using three long, rectangular dice. He directed the game and the women played it, more to please him than each other.

The children, having finished their sports or their homework, wandered in as well. If we passed my grandfather, he would dip a finger in his glass of whisky and give us a lick. We were known to queue up for these licks. The men returning from work would start dribbling in as well. If Shibbudada happened to come through the door, which was rare as he was generally out at musical events, bridge parties or at Roshanara Club, the air in the room would immediately become supercharged. He nearly always came in demanding our immediate attention.

"Look what I have for you! These are dates from Iran. Sweet, sweet dates. Embedded in each one of them are the best walnuts you can ever hope to eat. Take a bite. Just take a bite." Yells and shrieks of delight would follow. Taiji would look up at Shibbudada with fresh hope, forgetting for a moment the years of unfulfilled expectations.

This was the social part of our day and we never knew who might visit. No-one needed to call before showing up. Mostly it was relatives, both close and distant. There was no formality, only familiarity. Om and Shant, green-eyed sisters, and granddaughters of Babaji's younger brother next door, might walk over to regale us with their wit or impersonations. Prema and Krishna, from Number 10, the daughters of my father's eldest and most beautiful sister, Bhuaji, could stop by. Prema and Krishna were about Lalit's age and identical twins. One wore glasses, the other did not. They were born as triplets but only two had survived. I remember once, Prema and Krishna arriving without Prema's customary glasses on. As we looked quizzically, they told us they had been to a guru who had given Prema special eye exercises to do at dawn every day while gazing at the rising sun. She had done the exercises religiously and now she was cured! She was indeed.

Other than the unassailable family rule that you always gave your chair to anyone older than you, seating was very much a grab-what-you-can arrangement. Generally, the grown-ups settled into all the plump sofas and upholstered chairs while we cousins draped ourselves where we could, on the arms of the sofas, the carpet and the bench by the fireplace.

All social occasions are fuelled with food and drink, and our winter evenings in the drawing room were no exception. The men were offered whisky sodas, the women tea, and the children squashes and lemonade. Squashes were fruit concentrates sold by the bottle. You poured some into a glass, added water and ice and you had a tolerable drink. I disliked squashes intensely. The Glacier brand we drank was manufactured in the Himalayan foothills by close family friends. My father had once wrested a superb marmalade recipe from them. Even that refused to endear these lifeless squashes to me. Now, lemonades were another matter.

In the mornings as we sat sunning ourselves in the front verandah, we would hear the sound of hooves and the cry of a hawker, "Lemonade-wallah . . . Lemonade-wallah." We would plead with our mothers to get some cases for the evening. A servant would be dispatched to the gate to signal to the lemonade-wallah that his wares were desired, and the lemonade-wallah, sitting atop his laden horse-cart, would come clip-clopping in.

Lemonades had nothing to do with lemons. They were carbonated drinks, sodas really, that came in special, to-be-returned glass bottles with marbles in their narrow necks. It was the marbles that held the fizz inside. Once the marble was pushed down with a stopper-shaped gadget, red, green or clear lemonade was there for the taking.

With the drinks were served the inevitable nuts. Nuts were warming, according to my mother, grandmother, and all the ladies of the house, and winter was the best time to eat them. They were freshest then too, having been harvested in the autumn.

These were not nuts you could grab by the fistful and shove into your mouth. No, you had to work for each and every one of them as they came in their shells. The shells could be tossed into the fireplace, which was fun, but the peeling was sometimes harder.

Chilghozas (pine nuts) demanded the most time and concentration and I liked them the best, especially the raw, untoasted ones with their soft white flesh and green inner core. My preference then ran to walnuts, especially the *kaghzi akhrote* or "paper-shell" variety. These could be crushed between two hands without help from a nutcracker. As I picked out the flesh from the mess of crushed shell, my mother would remind me, always eat walnuts with raisins or you will get . . ." "I know, I know," I would answer, "a sore throat." There would be peanuts too, freshly roasted in *karhais* (woks) filled with sand, and pistachios from Iran, the best in the world.

The nuts were not always enough, so a servant would be dispatched to the distant kitchen for plates of *pakori* (vegetable fritters) made by dipping vegetables or slices of them in a spicy chickpea flour batter and deep-frying them. We would shout in the general direction of the servant's departing back, "Ask the cook to make extra green chilli *pakori*s." The *pakori*s were eaten by most with fresh green mint chutney but for those of us who wanted to set our mouths ablaze, a bite into a hot chilli *pakori* after a bite of a sliced potato *pakori* was the perfect pairing.

Soon all the guests who did not live at Number 7 would begin to depart: My grandfather would take his last sip of whisky and say to no-one in particular, "Have the food put on the table." After a while the servant who had taken the order would return, salaam my grandfather and announce, "*Sa'ab,* the food is on the table." We would all get up and start ambling towards the dining room annexe in small groups.

In the dining room was a long, formal dining table. Joined to it were two other dining tables of decreasing quality. There was a chair for my grandfather at the head of the formal table, a chair for my grandmother to his left, and more chairs for the grown-ups on either side. Further down, at the tables of lesser quality generally reserved for the children, chairs gave way to benches. We children were so far away from the head of the table that I did not know until I was told years later that my grandmother was a vegetarian and had invented the East-West dish, spicy cauliflower gratinéed with cheese, that we all loved so much. We could hardly hear or see what was going on at my grandfather's end. We made note of Babaji's bobbing white beard but we were too busy with our own discussions to pay the upper end of the table much heed. I did know one thing though. My grandfather didn't drink water with his meals. He drank Club Soda. We saw it being poured.

Whatever was cooked in the kitchen's large *pateelas* (pots) came to the dining room in recurring serving dishes, two or three to each of the tables. There was hardly a question of courses. Everything savoury was part of the main course and came to the tables at the same time. Fresh fruit and sometimes carrot *halwa* in the winter followed.

Winter dinners often included game, as the men were avid hunters. There might be duck, partridge or quail, some with pellets still inside them, cooked with rich, cardamom-flavoured sauces. My father's favourite was leg of wild boar, cooked for a whole day in beer, but most of the time it was the usual goat and potato curry, a standard and much loved staple. Accompanying it might be cauliflower with peas, carrots with fenugreek, greens and some spinach, all to be eaten with *phulka*s, little puffed whole-wheat breads. We rarely had rice at night.

Special needs were catered for as well, such as soup for a sick child. Once, when Taiji was on a diet to control her ballooning weight, her meat was boiled, and instead of eating it with Indian bread, she wrapped each morsel in lettuce leaves.

I began to notice a disturbing pattern. Very often, choice pieces of meat were missing. Marrow bones, pieces of fish-shaped muscle (the best meat), where were they? I would look around in the serving dish and find nothing I wanted. Then I would see Taiji come in from the kitchen with a small bowl and quietly spoon out these very pieces to just her own three children, Raghudada, Sheila, and Rajesh. Indignant and unable to deal with what I perceived as unfairness, I would look up at my mother but she would blink her eyes, suggesting I be quiet.

At night, as I undressed for bed, I would complain bitterly to Bauwa but she would hush me up – Taiji's room was just next door – and say something like, "You had enough to eat, didn't you?" or "Once we get back to Kanpur you can have whatever you want."

If Taiji was trying to compensate her children with choice foods for their emotional deprivations, this could be written off as one of the smaller ripples created by Shibbudada's behaviour towards his family. As we all got older, the ripples would reach further and further and enmesh Shibbudada's family and ours in the worst tangle of human relationships.

RUSKIN BOND

The Last Time I Saw Delhi

I'D HAD THIS OLD AND faded negative with me for a number of years and had never bothered to make a print from it. It was a picture of my maternal grandparents. I remembered my grandmother quite well, because a large part of my childhood had been spent in her house in Dehra after she had been widowed; but although everyone said she was fond of me, I remembered her as a stern, somewhat aloof person, of whom I was a little afraid.

I hadn't kept many family pictures and this negative was yellow and spotted with damp.

Then last week, when I was visiting my mother in hospital in Delhi, while she awaited her operation, we got talking about my grandparents, and I remembered the negative and decided I'd make a print for my mother.

When I got the photograph and saw my grandmother's face for the first time in twenty-five years, I was immediately struck by my resemblance to her. I have, like her, lived a rather spartan life, happy with my one room, just as she was content to live in a room of her own while the rest of the family took over the house! And like her, I have lived tidily. But I did not know the physical resemblance was so close – the fair hair, the heavy build, the wide forehead. She looks more like me than my mother! In the photograph she is seated on her favourite chair, at the top of the veranda steps, and Grandfather stands behind her in the shadows thrown by a large mango tree which is not in the picture. I can tell it was a mango tree because of the pattern the leaves make on the wall. Grandfather was a slim, trim man, with a drooping moustache that was fashionable in the twenties. By all accounts he had a mischievous sense of humour, although he looks unwell in the picture. He appears to have been quite swarthy. No wonder he was so successful in dressing up "native" style and passing himself off as a street-vendor. My mother tells me he even took my grandmother in on one occasion, and sold her a basketful of bad oranges. His character was in strong contrast to my grandmother's rather forbidding personality and Victorian sense of propriety; but they made a good match.

But here's the picture, and I am taking it to show my mother who lies in the Lady Hardinge Hospital, awaiting the removal of her left breast.

It is early August and the day is hot and sultry. It rained during the night, but now the sun is out and the sweat oozes through my shirt as I sit in the back of a stuffy little taxi taking me through the suburbs of Greater New Delhi. On either side of the road are the houses of well-to-do Punjabis, who came to Delhi as refugees in 1947 and now make up more than half the capital's population. Industrious, flashy, go-ahead people. Thirty years ago, fields extended on either side of this road, as far as the eye could see. The Ridge, an outcrop of the Aravallis, was scrub jungle, in which the blackbuck roamed. Feroz Shah's fourteenth-century hunting lodge stood here in splendid isolation. It is still here, hidden by petrol pumps and lost within the sounds of buses, cars, trucks and scooter-rickshaws. The peacock has fled the forest, the blackbuck is extinct. Only the jackal remains. When, a thousand years from now, the last human has left this contaminated planet for some other star, the jackal and the crow will remain, to survive for years on all the refuse we leave behind.

It is difficult to find the right entrance to the hospital, because for about a mile along the Panchkuin Road the pavement has been obliterated by tea shops, furniture shops, and piles of accumulated junk. A public hydrant stands near the gate, and dirty water runs across the road.

I find my mother in a small ward. It is a cool, dark room, and a ceiling fan whirrs pleasantly overhead. A nurse, a dark pretty girl from the South, is attending to my mother. She says, "In a minute," and proceeds to make an entry on a chart.

My mother gives me a wan smile and beckons me to come nearer. Her cheeks are slightly flushed, due possibly to fever; otherwise she looks her normal self. I find it hard to believe that the operation she will have tomorrow will only give her, at the most, another year's lease on life.

I sit at the foot of her bed. This is my third visit, since I flew back from Jersey, using up all my savings in the process; and I will leave after the operation, not to fly away again, but to return to the hills which have always called me back.

"How do you feel?" I ask.

"All right. They say they will operate in the morning. They've stopped my smoking."

"Can you drink? Your rum, I mean?"

"No. Not until a few days after the operation."

She has a fair amount of grey in her hair, natural enough at fifty-four. Otherwise she hasn't changed much; the same small chin and mouth, lively brown eyes. Her father's face, not her mother's.

The nurse has left us. I produce the photograph and hand it to my mother.

"The negative was lying with me all these years. I had it printed yesterday."

"I can't see without my glasses."

The glasses are lying on the locker near her bed. I hand them to her. She puts them on and studies the photograph.

"Your grandmother was always very fond of you."

"It was hard to tell. She wasn't a soft woman."

"It was her money that got you to Jersey, when you finished school. It wasn't much, just enough for the ticket."

"I didn't know that."

"The only person who ever left you anything. I'm afraid I've nothing to leave you, either."

"You know very well that I've never cared a damn about money. My father taught me to write. That was inheritance enough."

"And what did I teach you?"

"I'm not sure . . . Perhaps you taught me how to enjoy myself now and then."

She looked pleased at this. "Yes, I've enjoyed myself between troubles. But your father didn't know how to enjoy himself. That's why we quarrelled so much. And finally separated."

"He was much older than you."

"You've always blamed me for leaving him, haven't you?"

"I was very small at the time. You left us suddenly. My father had to look after me, and it wasn't easy for him. He was very sick. Naturally I blamed you."

"He wouldn't let me take you away."

"Because you were going to marry someone else."

I break off; we have been over this before. I am not there as my father's advocate, and the time for recrimination has passed.

And now it is raining outside, and the scent of wet earth comes through the open doors, overpowering the odour of medicines and disinfectants. The dark-eyed nurse comes in again and informs me that the doctor will soon be on his rounds. I can come again in the evening, or early morning before the operation.

"Come in the evening," says my mother. "The others will be here then."

"I haven't come to see the others."

"They are looking forward to seeing you."

"They" being my stepfather and half-brothers.

"I'll be seeing them in the morning."

"As you like . . ."

And then I am on the road again, standing on the pavement, on the fringe of a chaotic rush of traffic, in which it appears that every vehicle is doing its best to overtake its neighbour. The blare of horns can be heard in the corridors of the hospital, but everyone is conditioned to the noise and pays no attention to it. Rather, the sick and the dying are heartened by the thought that people are still well enough to feel reckless, indifferent to each other's safety! In Delhi there is a feverish desire to be first in line, the first to get anything . . . This is probably because no one ever gets around to dealing with second-comers.

When I hail a scooter-rickshaw and it stops a short distance away, someone elbows his way past me and gets in first. This epitomises the philosophy and outlook of the Delhi wallah.

So I stand on the pavement waiting for another scooter, which doesn't come. In Delhi, to be second in the race is to be last.

I walk all the way back to my small hotel, with a foreboding of having seen my mother for the last time.

ANITA DESAI

A Secret Connivance

LIKE MANY WRITERS, I am a member of PEN, the international club which seeks to protect and promote the rights of authors. I regularly read their newsletter about imprisoned writers in various parts of the world and sign protests and appeals on their behalf to various governments. I am aware of the price writers have to pay for their freedom of speech in countries with tyrannical or totalitarian regimes. Lately, with the upsurge of peaceful revolution in many such countries, one has been made aware of how their triumphs have been won by the courage and suffering of writers.

I come from a country which prides itself on the fact that ever since it won independence from a colonial power in 1947, it has been a democracy. Elections have been held at regular, lawful intervals and they have been won, by and large, by those candidates for whom the people voted. I do not know of any writers who are in prison for the views they hold. It is true that briefly, for a period known as "The Emergency", only those writers and artists who agreed to praise the regime received government patronage, or could expect to have their films screened or appear on television. But when I, among others, declined their invitation, we were not punished and nothing worse happened than that we were ignored. A writer is free to air his views in print – some win approval, some do not, but it is not a matter of risking one's life or courting death.

I cannot, however, claim that there is no suppression in India; that there is freedom for all of speech and expression. There is a subtle, deep-rooted form of suppression, a secret connivance at the taking away of freedom for which I cannot blame the present or even the past regime, and for which a whole society, and its entire history with its burden of custom and tradition must be indicted. All who belong to PEN and subscribe to the ideals of PEN will know what Saul Bellow meant when he said: "Everybody knows that there is no fineness or accuracy in suppression. If you hold one thing down, you hold down the adjoining."

One form of imprisonment in India is that created specifically for women. Like other countries where women are traditionally suppressed, India deified its women. In many Catholic countries, there is the cult of the Virgin Mary. In India, which tends in everything to plurality and excess, there are 100,000 such cults built around the Mother Goddess in one form or another – that fecund figure from whom all good things flow – milk, food, warmth, comfort. Her ample bosom and loins, her enticing curves and buxom proportions make her not merely the ideal mother but the ideal woman – consort, lover, plaything. She is the richest source of art in India – sculpture, painting, dance and poetry. Around her exists a huge body of mythology. She is called by several names – Sita, Draupadi, Durga, Parvati, Laxmi, and so on. In each myth, she plays the role of the loyal wife, unswerving in her devotion to her lord. She is meek, docile, trusting, faithful and forgiving. Even when spirited and brave, she adheres to the archetype: willing to go through fire and water, dishonour and disgrace for his sake. As Sita says when she offers to accompany her man into exile for fourteen years: "Surely your fortune is also mine . . . We will be together. The water will be nectar, the thistles milk, the rawhides many-coloured blankets. I cannot be cast away like water left in a cup. Dear Rama, I am the humble dust at your feet, perfectly happy."

An Indian girl is brought up from her infancy on these legends, she is as well acquainted with them as a child in the West with Goldilocks or Cinderella. She must not fall short of them. Even if in reality she is nothing but a common drudge, first in her father's house and then her husband's – a beast of burden bearing an endless string of children, putting up with any brutality or disloyalty or failing of her husband's – she has no alternative: she must live as Sita did, as Draupadi did; she is Durga incarnate. The myth keeps her bemused, bound hand and foot. To rebel against it, either in speech or action, would mean that she is questioning the myth, attacking the legend, and that cannot be permitted: it is the cornerstone on which the Indian family and therefore Indian society are built.

To say that this situation is created by men to serve their own purposes is simplistic. The truth is that it is connived at by women who in some perverse way insist on embodying the myth. Beaten, bullied and tormented, not infrequently to the point of death, a woman will state in her dying words that her man is not guilty. Why?

The most obvious reason is that she is illiterate, untrained and unqualified to earn a living and support herself. To leave home is to court death on the streets. The other reason is that she is so indoctrinated with the ideals of honour and status and respectability that nothing will make her go against them. If she did, she would be questioning her own being – if she is not there to uphold the honour of her husband, her family, her society, then what is she *for*? What is her purpose, her meaning?

In India the gift of education is reserved for the sons and rarely given to daughters, just as the best food is given to the boy child and not wasted on the girl. So there is great illiteracy among girls just as there is malnutrition, and few Indian women have access to the printed word. What recourse has she to the law courts? What does she know of the constitution or of her lawful rights? And how can she publicise her condition? Most of the literature created by women in earlier times is poetry, which does not require literacy in either its creator or its audience. It can be memorised and recited. There is, in fact, a large body of work by Indian women poets. Very little of it was written down in their lifetime. What is curious is that the theme of most classical poetry is the pining of a woman for a man. Very often this is a camouflage for the pining of the soul for the godhead, a spiritual longing, but the women poets felt a need to express it in physical, sexual terms. The myth of Indian womanhood was too strong to allow for anything else.

Prose came to be written by women only in the twentieth century. The twentieth-century trend in literature of self-analysis and psychology, when attempted by Indian women writers, produces a curious sameness of tone – melancholy, complaining, tearful. There is no argument or criticism in it, because these are forbidden for women now as they were earlier – it is not their heritage, not their tradition. Criticism never having been encouraged – in fact having been firmly and actively discouraged – Indian women have not developed the critical faculty. They have a capacity for worship and a capacity for denunciation, but not for cool, reasoned criticism, and it is a sad shortcoming in their work. So is the evident absence of a wide experience of life. They have had to confine themselves to the domestic scene – few women have had any experience of the world outside their homes and families and so their area of study remains restricted, limited. So many limitations. So much censorship and self-censorship. Does this not amount to suppression, the suppression of a whole gender?

Very much the same conditions pertain to another prison-house – the prison-house of religion. We are brought up in India to think of religion as containing the highest truth, the greatest good, of the religious life as being the finest life, the one to which all Indians aspire, no matter what their beginnings. To question this would be to question our whole society – an intensely religious society, a country where religion is not reserved for one place or one day of the week but is everywhere, at all times, a way of life, dictating the way we eat, the way we dress, the way we bathe and marry and bring up our children, speak and live. To separate religion from such society would be to tear out its heart or remove its limbs. People would not know how to live with godlessness and unbelief. Who has the strength to face not God but – himself? Not the distant future – but the here and now? And so religion is not questioned. If it were, it would be the beginning of the end.

One writer who did question it was Salman Rushdie because he believed, as he stated in his Herbert Read lecture, that "To respect the sacred is to be paralysed by it. The idea tends to turn other ideas – Uncertainty, Progress, Change – into crime." Crime is what he was accused of when he wrote *The Satanic Verses* and as you know, he has been in hiding ever since, in fear of his life.

His case is an extreme and exceptional one, of course, but if there are not more such cases it is not because other iconoclasts have been luckier but because – in India and in the East generally – there are no iconoclasts, they would not be tolerated. If there are rationalists, those who like him believe in inquiry, dialogue and deconstruction, they have chosen not to speak, not to take such risks as he has taken. And that is a form of suppression, of imprisonment. Imprisoned inside a hidebound religious structure, whether Muslim or Hindu, too brainwashed or too browbeaten by religious leaders and the gullibility and naivete of those they lead, too weak and fearful to try and turn the tide – the writer is silenced, paralysed. So, on the two most absorbing themes we have on earth – the relationship of men and women, and the relationship of man and God – there is either silence or, if there are words, they are too often false and hypocritical.

The third area of suppression is economics. Who does not know the need to earn a living, to survive, and also survive better than the next? This universal need is as great an enemy of art and free expression as gender or religion. It dictates its terms to the artist – it tells him what is marketable, what will succeed. A situation any artist, and in fact any labourer, any producer in the world recognises. He learns the relation between demand and production – and naturally this affects the product.

But in India, poorer than most countries, in worse straits than most others, economics exerts another kind of pressure as well, a much more subtle and insidious one. If, whenever you leave your safe house – large and luxurious or small and cramped – you meet the face of hunger, the face of starvation and disease, can you then go back into your room and write a poem or paint a picture and believe that it matters, that it will do anything to fill that extended hand or heal that sick body?

If I go out, and meet people, there is this question, sometimes politely unspoken but often spoken very bluntly – what are you, an educated woman, doing writing novels, *fiction*? And I have no answer because a part of me agrees that yes, I should instead get together those beggar children and teach them to read and write so they could earn a better living than begging.

Should we be serving an urgent need or the eternal needs, the secret, instinctive needs too deep to name? Society demands one answer, the artist another. To listen to society is to have one's belief in art gradually eroded and destroyed. I need to remind myself, every so often, of the story told by Solzhenitsyn of a fellow prisoner in a camp who built for himself a small piano out of sticks – of necessity a dumb piano, a silent piano – and sat playing on it music only he could hear. The music saved his sanity; it spoke to him of values in which he could believe, which helped him survive. And perhaps it added to an insane world a note of sanity and was therefore worthwhile.

It is to that silent piano one must dedicate oneself when society becomes a gaoler, and forbids music.

The West has two fixed notions about India. One is that it is a romantic land, full of holy men, maharajas, palaces and elephants: the other is of India as a land of horrors – a place of intolerable poverty and squalor, hunger and disease. How can one country have two such contradictory images? The reason is that neither is true – or not wholly true. Each is only a half-truth. You may have been made familiar with the face of the maharaja and the face of the beggar child – but have you learnt anything of the human being within?

Indians have been as guilty as those in the West of the creation of these half-truths. You have heard of the dream worlds created by Indian film producers for the masses, masses that are hungry for celluloid dreams. The same reluctance to face the truth exists in our art and literature; it exists in our daily lives as well – consumed by a passion for gossip and scandal, we rarely bother about facts. And this reluctance to face the truth is shared by Western readers and viewers who also prefer either the romantic or the shocking version to dull actuality. Not out of malice or ignorance – although there is sometimes that – but because truth is so often ordinary, commonplace, colourless and dull. But I think that has a value greater than the other. I think that pinch of dust should be preferred to the paper flower and the tinsel, or to the rag and the begging bowl, because it has the value of truth. If literature, if art has any purpose then it is to show one, bravely and uncompromisingly, the plain face of truth, and here in the West, just as in the East, we must learn to distinguish and recognise, and to value. Once you have told the truth, you have broken free of society, of its prisons. You have entered the realm of freedom.

DOM MORAES

On God

THE CHURCH SMELT of incense and whitewash. Seven years old, I knelt by my mother in the family pew. Her dark eyes were on her missal: her lips moved soundlessly. All around us, strangers knelt, moving their lips in the same mysterious soundless way. Gold and marble shone by the red velvet of the altar, the swung censers breathed up smoke. The priest intoned, the choir sang in an unknown language, and the Indian sun set the coloured windows on fire.

All this filled with an intense physical sensation of awe. It was not a religious awe. It was the kind of awe I felt when I looked up into the afternoon sky, endlessly, burningly blue, and saw hanging at its centre a solitary hawk, quivering its spread wings, crucified on that emptiness. As the hawk was a symbol, so the gold, the marble, the incense, the choired voices, were symbols, not of a god but of a world. They were parts of an unbroken cycle which contained me and which I hoped one day to contain within myself.

My family was a Catholic one: our name, inherited from some remote proselytised ancestor, was Portuguese. Above my parents' bed a plaster Christ stood on a wooden shelf, his raw and revealed heart clutched in his hand. My mother lit candles at his feet, a process my father watched with a certain wry irritation. He was not religious. Because of my mother, however, our house was frequently visited by priests. At a certain time every year they sprinkled holy water over the floors, the sofas and the chairs to bless the home. The non-Catholic servants complained it warped the furniture.

Apart from pouring water about, the priest had another function. It was to instruct me in the faith. Flumped in their chairs in white cassocks, they told me about sin: venial sin, which I must try to avoid, and mortal sin, which I must shun absolutely. The consequences of mortal sin, they said, were awful. They described the consequences. These alarmed me beyond measure. God in my mind, like a furious schoolmaster, stood flourishing an eternal cane, and when they told me I should love him, I could see no reason why. An angel raped a blue wife in an orchard, and from that ethereal semen rose a son, to die horribly in the reek of blood and vinegar. God, who had made this happen, loomed violently over Golgotha, and a storm rose. There was no love in this: there was only terror.

But I grew older and ceased to be afraid. Adolescents rebel against their father. I rebelled against the deity. I started to disbelieve that such a thing as sin existed and, even assuming that it did, the fine distinction between one degree of sin and another struck me as irrelevant and silly. It was not to be ruled by these arbitrary edicts that from a bubble of lava, a sac of slime, a fish, and ape, a race had risen that could write poetry and compose symphonies.* I ceased to patronise the church and started to look around me and to write.

Now, for the first time, I saw what the people of Bombay really looked like. Somehow I had never noticed them before: as a child I thought always that the shrouded, bundled objects

*The start of this sentence seems a mistake. It should read: "Rebellion meant not being ruled by these arbitrary edicts and declaring instead that from a bubble of lava . . ." – Ed.

that lay along the pavements were some curious species of plant. But they were people, an army of the defeated, without food or money or the prospect of either, which was why they lay limply on the pavements, their ribs like birdcages, their eyes sunk black and silent into their skulls. Yet mothers put their hands out very gently to their infants, and drew them to dry nipples: and at night, as the last traffic moaned home, husband and wife, under one ragged sheet, made painful and difficult love.

There were also people who had employment, sepoys and clerks – people who had a little income and knew they would never have more, who knew that their lives would stop exactly where they had started. Whereas the pavement people had been defeated so completely that it did not show in their eyes, the eyes of these others were harsh with the knowledge or merely tired. In trains, in buses, on the burning pavements, I was surrounded by eyes.

One day on a train I shared a compartment with a young clerk and his wife. The clerk was dressed in a worn cheap suit, and his face was worn and somehow made cheap by his poverty. His eyes looked inward at it: he did not look at his wife or speak to her – her eyes also had this inward look. Something had died in them: their faces were as inanimate as the turnips in the fields we passed. It was impossible to believe that at some time they must have flirted, courted, been involved with each other instead of a mutual poverty, have loved, made love. Yet between them on the dusty seat was the proof of this love, a child like a flower, asleep. The child was beautiful: he should have been destined to touch music, write poetry, dance a bay horse through the sunlight. It would not happen. He would grow up in poverty, and if he was lucky become a clerk like his father. Love would touch him briefly and in some dingy room he would beget a child as beautiful as a flower. Then what had died in his father would die in him, as in time it would die in his son. God, like a violent robber, had taken life away from these people. It was not right that mankind should live like this.

I came eventually, by the time I was fifteen, to disbelieve in God. But at noon the solitary hawk still hung at the meridian: the gold and marble shone still in the church I did not visit. The parts were still there – what was the whole? Ever since childhood I had been subject to a curious experience of, I suppose, the spirit. There were certain times when I became numb and unconscious of what happened around me. It was as though I, whatever that was, reached from my name and my life, and looked at myself down a long alley of darkness. At these instants an intense sensation both of illumination and of terror swept over me. I no longer belonged to myself, but to something I did not recognise, something huge, silent and unfeeling. If there was a God, I thought, he was this immense loneliness.

I was fifteen then, and am now nearly thirty. In the years between I have written and travelled, made love and known friendship. Most of the things I wanted to do, I have done. But my dialogue with the humped invisible presence of which I am continually conscious has come to no conclusion. His name is often on my lips, but only as an exclamation of surprise or of dismay. Yet in the middle of famines or wars, in remote corners of the world, I have heard the starved, the wounded and the sorrowful call upon that name. You brought up this catastrophe, the wronged mothlike voices seemed to whisper, and if you will you can take it away. Christ also prayed that the cup might pass from his lips.

Karl Barth once wrote, "The tension in which the thoughts of Paul move is unprecedented . . . It is not tension of a successive order, but tension of an intertwining character . . . It is the tension of faith. If it seems unbearable to anyone, he should ask himself how the tensions of human life, of which we know more today than in other ages, are to be encountered except with the yet greater tension of faith."

But the faith of Paul, a planned and specific faith, does not apply in moments of extreme physical or spiritual stress. The starved Indian mother with a dead child in her arms, the Israeli soldier with his leg shot away, do not call upon the God of their priests, though they may use his name because it is the only one they know. They call upon some enormous presence beyond and outside themselves, as a child calls upon its parents, because if that presence did not exist there would be neither alleviation nor purpose for their suffering.

I recall a curious interview I once had with the Dalai Lama, immediately after his flight from Tibet. He lived then in Delhi, in a white palace full of gnarled black lamas. "Do not touch the Beloved One," they said to me. "Do not turn your back on him. It would not be respectful because he is God."

He was, in fact, a handsome, freckled boy, who looked very tired and depressed. Also, he was clearly very lonely. I made no move to touch him, but he touched me: he shook my hand when I was introduced, and while we talked he emphasised his points with taps on my knee. It was as though he was anxious for any kind of human contact. He spoke mainly of his desire to return to Tibet, and his sentences were punctuated with a phrase which the interpreter translated as "by the will of the Lord Buddha." Later I told a friend who knew Tibetan about my interview, and repeated the Dalai Lama's recurrent phrase. "It does not mean 'by the will of the Lord Buddha'," said my friend. "It means – how do you say it? – 'by the will of God'."

So faith rose like a staircase; the Tibetan people looked upward to the black lamas; they in turn looked upward to the

Dalai Lama, who looked upward at some invisible omnipotence. For myself this is impossible. Religion itself repels me: but even separated from religion, I cannot positively believe in the existence of a causatory and kingly power. I am prevented by logic, by anger and pity at purposeless human pain. Yet with Pascal, and no doubt everyone else, I am terrified by the eternal silence of the infinite spaces. The planet on whose rough pelt we are fleas spins through eternity and infinity. God does not manifest himself – therefore, to defy our terror, we must behave as though he did not exist. We must fabricate a human morality, and obey that, rather than any religious code.

Man must be man, born to work, procreate and die; not a prospective angel, not lost in a dream of wings and harps, of another life after death.

But not all truth can be demonstrated by a process of logic. All my life I have been haunted by a quality of landscape, by whispers, by the immense darkness into which, as when a child, I retreat and survey myself and my life from a long way away. Constantly, too, I am annoyed by the inexplicable. Telepathy between husband and wife, for instance, or between close friends, I know is possible – I have experienced it myself. Ghosts I don't know about, but I am prepared not to disbelieve in them.

The air we breathe is populated with mysteries. The God we have pinned down under the heavy cathedrals of Europe, the God we have praised and destroyed in words and music, paint and stone, has nothing to do with this. The God who destroys us, who permits suffering, who creates catastrophe, if he exists, manifests himself in these curious vibrations of the atmosphere. An unhappy monster, he lies down on us like a blanket, and we smother under him.

Tonight the black rain falls like confetti past my windows. God, is that you out there, perched like an owl in the dark?

The murmured rumours, the echoed wings that I hear, are they yours? I have heard them for nearly thirty years. I think perhaps it is you, that humped shape in the sycamore. Twenty years back you were gold and marble, incense and altar, and I was afraid of you. I am afraid of you still, if you exist. Is that you, God, out there? Perched like an owl in the dark, whose bones do you crack in your claws?

ADIL JUSSAWALLA

When Earth Rose Up to Get Me

When you faced the road and turned round to watch them dump fresh loads of earth, you couldn't see for the dust. When you turned towards the road again, you saw a line of lorries go by, their weighty cargoes of stone and rubble unable to stop their juddering and rattling.

One day, through the dust, I saw the shape of a cow galloping towards me. As it got nearer I saw that it was a cow galloping straight at me. I was walking a puppy, about eight months old. The cow snorted and lunged at the puppy. I picked the puppy up. The cow lunged at me holding the puppy. I put the puppy down. This time cow made contact.

Huge head tries to grind tiny puppy into ground. Puppy yelps. I scoop puppy up and run. Cow follows. If I zig, cow zigs. If I zag, cow zags.

"Don't panic!" a friend shouted from a distance, his legs spread like Wyatt Earp's hands by his holsters. Except that the chump had no guns, bullets or holsters on him. I panicked.

But a minute later came a skilful sidestep, the left horn of the cow grazing my sleeve; and I thought I was getting there. I saw a fruitful career in Spain ahead of me. I also heard heavy panting. A *bhaiya*, his eyes wild, sprang to restrain the cow, but it deflected off him on to the main road.

"What happened?" I asked, for the first time noticing that the owners of the cigarette stalls and the Bania shop around us, along with several pedestrians, were grinning instead of applauding. I gave them a sour look and heard the *bhaiya*'s answer. "*Uska baccha mar gaya*."

Its baby died. Just now. You see? I watched the cow running down Cuffe Parade. The *bhaiya* ran in pursuit.

I saw what the *bhaiya* meant and I didn't see. Maddened by grief, was the cow so deranged that it saw every little four-legged creature as its own lost baby? Or did rage make it want to kill every little four-legged creature because its own had just died?

I've often thought of the cow–puppy incident which took place during our first year in Cuffe Parade. Twenty-five years later I still don't know what drove the cow mad but given the evidence those years have provided, I'd say it was rage.

Grief, intense grief – and rage, wild rage – coexist, except perhaps in a few saintly people. They are a deadly mix, tending to ignore without reason, without a thought to time, place or occasion. Why should all of you be so happy and I so miserable? They shout together. Together they make a woman swear revenge on her in-laws for the death of her daughters, though the in-laws may have had nothing to do with their deaths. They voice our incapacity to endure the fact that just as we and the living things precious to us came into life, we and those same living things must leave it. They are our cry for life. They are our breaking, our shattering, our defeat, our *shikast*.

Cuffe Parade is supposed to be a posh and genteel neighbourhood and those of us who live in it usually turn away from its other side. We haven't been particularly moved by the deaths of construction workers or domestic servants, crushed under lorries or falling from heights. Nor have we responded much to fires which have razed large areas of *zopadpattis* on either side of the complex. But terrible things have happened within each building. Where do the children play?

Some never will. They have fallen to their deaths, been run over by their own school bus, died in road accidents. Grief and rage abound in the neighbourhood as in any other. They fill each window as bees fill a honeycomb. At night every single window seems lit as though for a carnival, each high-rise a cascade of silver and gold sequins. At times it's magic, at times, not. One bad night I wrote a line: "Every lit window a cry for help."

But it's at ground level that help is most sought and perhaps most given. A friend of mine once called Colaba, close to Cuffe Parade, "the anus of the world". Both he and I have seen worse anuses. Honolulu, despite the small houses crawling up its hillsides, is supposed to be a gigantic Cuffe Parade, filthy rich. But its one low-life area is as scary as it can get. People don't look at you there, they stare daggers. From every bar stool and table, that look of daggers. Anyway, I'm frequently at ground level and ground level to me often means Colaba, the streets and lanes of which I like to wander in. In search of? Well, nothing, really. We're just a night-pack of ghosts out there, some hunting, some being hunted, some begging, some mainlining, some hustling, clumps of street kids in the shadows, bent over cigarette foil, chasing.

Slumming, my cynical friends and enemies say. It's called slumming. Well, cynical friends and enemies, don't you remember the Robert Frost poem "To Earthward"? It begins: *Love at the lips was touch/ As sweet as I could bear . . .*

In the course of the poem, the poet regrets the inevitable dilution of early love's extremes of joy and pain, and ends: *When stiff and sore and scarred/ I take away my hand/ From leaning on it hard/ In grass and sand,/ The hurt is not enough:/ I long for weight and strength/ To feel the earth as rough/ To all my length.*

The hurt is not enough, domestic hurt is not enough, the pain in the windows – somebody else's pain – is never enough. That's why we go to the anuses of the world and into the entrails beyond them. We seek an underworld – Colaba is my pale bourgeois version of it – where we may, with luck, come across our alter egos: the murderer, the thief, the conman, the hooker, the sex offender, the person who almost committed the perfect suicide.

Suicide is a curious business – it's so easy to do and yet not do – and an editorial in *The Times of India*, on the Supreme Court's decision to overturn a previous ruling which decriminalised attempted suicide, adds a curious twist to it; it mentions something called "chronic suicide". I'd have thought all suicides are chronic – like the chronic cold, they won't go away – but what the term apparently defines is those who persist in drug abuse or alcohol abuse over a long period of time. Well, we've plenty of those in our neighbourhood.

Why try to hide the fact and where hide it?

You can't brush dirt under dirt no more than you can brush earth under earth. The earth, under your feet, under the pavement, has its claims and demands. It claims attention, it demands you be hurt and hurt again, if only to acknowledge how much you've been responsible for hurting other people. If you ignore these claims and demands for too long a time, if your life's just dreaming without responsibility, you may not stumble, may not fall, but be sure the earth will rise up to get you.

I'm a dreamer, always have been, and generally dream without responsibility. One night when I was happy, having gone from bar to bar through the entrails of Colaba, having decided that that was one way to escape the burden and boredom of responsibility, of numbing the pain of not handling it, I found I had difficulty walking. I'd got off a bus quite close to where I lived and discovered, to my stupefaction, that I couldn't walk.

I thought a meal would fix me up so I managed to sway, don't know how, into the nearest beer bar and had one. It was a spicy curry and rice. The spice, instead of damping the alcohol, worked on it like a drug. Soon I was out of the bar, shot out like a cork, I was dreaming, I was flying, I was moving faster and faster over heaps of small stones, I was going home . . . when I felt the taste of steel in my mouth. My head rang as though hit by a bell. The taste of steel was my blood. It filled my mouth. It began blotching my kurta.

CHITRITA BANERJI

Patoler Ma

CHILDHOOD IS FULL of mysteries, even the most mundane aspects of daily living piquant with the promise of revelation. The daily ritual in our house that intrigued me most was the processing of spices on the grinding stone. We did not have a refrigerator then. It was considered an unnecessary luxury – something only the very rich would waste money on. The buying, processing, and cooking of food, therefore, was a major part of the daily household activity. And the preparation of spices for cooking – the transformation of seeds, herbs, and roots into smooth pastes, each with its unique colour – was, to me, the most magical part of the daily rituals of food.

My parents and I lived on the third floor of my grandparents' large, rambling, three-storeyed house in south Calcutta. It was a typical Bengali extended family, the house humming with the comings and goings of parents, uncles, aunts, and frequent visitors. The kitchen and pantry happened to be on the second floor, directly below our rooms on the third. And every morning I listened for the sound of the upended *shil*, a large, flat block of stone with a deeply pitted surface, being lowered to the concrete floor from its rest against the wall. That was the signal that our daily maid, called, in the customary manner, Patoler Ma (or Mother of Patol, after her offspring), had arrived and was starting on her chores. Once she had ground the spices, the cook could start on his job of preparing daily meals for our large family.

I think it was the juxtaposition of Patoler Ma's skeletally thin body – especially her stick-like arms and legs – with the massiveness of the grinding stone, that gave me my very first sense of the unfairness of life, and particularly the unfairness that women contend with every day in many traditional societies. She seemed so pitifully inadequate to this Herculean task of grasping and moving the stone into the appropriate position for spice grinding, while our male cook looked on, never offering to help, despite his obvious advantage of size and strength. She hardly ever missed a day's work and the routine never varied – spice grinding was the first chore of the day. The stone and Patoler Ma pitted themselves against each other every morning, year after year, and she inevitably won, for otherwise I would not have seen the magical transmutation that was wrought on that subjugated stone.

An unspoken method seemed to guide her as she set about this daily ritual – as if she were an artist preparing her palette for the day. Whenever I could, I went downstairs to watch her getting ready for her task, squatting in the small passageway in front of the kitchen. First she sprinkled lots of water on the oblong stone surface of the *shil* and vigorously wiped it off with the side of her palm. The water fell in large drops along the edges of the stone, forming a translucent pattern on the floor. Then she took the heavy, pestle-shaped, rough-hewn bar of stone, the *nora*, and wiped it down the same way. Now she was ready for action.

The cook had already set out the spices on a large, white enamelled platter with a raised cobalt-blue rim. Patoler Ma liked to start with the rock-hard lumps of dried turmeric. That was the base ingredient around which you built the colour and texture of your food. And it was the hardest to process. Bang, bang, bang she went, pounding away at the recalcitrant lumps with the *nora* held vertically in her right hand, while the left hand balanced the pieces. I watched and trembled at the possible mischance of the stone landing on her thumb or finger. But miraculously, that never happened. Sometimes, a piece rolled off the stone and fell to the floor. But sooner or later, they were all beaten down into smaller granules, their tint deepening into sunflower yellow as they mixed with the water on the surface of the stones. Sprinkling more water on the turmeric, Patoler Ma then switched motions. Holding the *nora* horizontally in both hands, she proceeded to grind the spice into a sun-bright paste, while the signature odour of turmeric filled the air. As I watched her – body leaning forward between legs folded in the squatting position, a look of intense concentration on her lean face under a huge topknot of black hair, arms vigorously moving back and forth with the *nora* – I thought of her as a woman warrior, despite her frailty.

The transformation of dried red chillies was another fascinating process for me. There was always something threatening about them whether I saw them sitting in a bowl or being picked out from the large jar on the kitchen shelf. Unlike the fresh green chillies that were often used whole in cooking and were also served as an accompaniment during meals for those who wanted to add more zest to their food, these dried chillies seemed to be infused with a sinister potential. Perhaps it was because of the intensely pungent odour they produced when the cook fried them in oil as a flavouring for certain dishes. You could be up on the third floor, but they still inflamed your nasal membranes and plunged you into an epidemic of sneezing. I had also been burnt by their fire once when neither the cook nor Patoler Ma was watching. Picking up a chilli I broke it open with a little snap. Seeing the small, pale seeds spilling out, I took some and put them in my mouth. It brought tears to my eyes; and the trauma was intensified when I rubbed my eyes with fingers on which minute particles of chilli still adhered.

And yet, Patoler Ma seemed to have no fear of these lean and fearsomely pungent missiles. Breaking off the stems, she firmly placed them on the stone, sprinkled water over them, brought the nora down and started moving it back and forth. I watched as the skins split open and yielded up the seeds, which, in turn, became pulverised and blended with the now moistly red, rejuvenated flesh of the chillies. Soon, she was scooping out the smooth red paste from the stone and placing it on the waiting plate – next to the rounded ball of yellow turmeric. Often, I surreptitiously looked at her hand. The fingers were stained with the colours of the spices, the predominant tinge being yellow. And I marvelled at the nonchalance with which she went through the day, never afraid of touching her eyes or lips or nose with fingers on which the burning essence of chillies might linger. Perhaps such accidents did happen, but life was tough for Patoler Ma and she had to get on with it, despite a runny nose, teary eyes, or stinging lips.

By the time she finished, the rounded balls of paste on the white plate added up to a whole spectrum of hues. The dull, mousy browns of ground cumin and coriander were often enlivened by the creamy whiteness of Indian poppy seeds (so different from the black poppy seeds used in the West). But the most intriguing colour was that of ground mustard. This dark Indian variety has an exhilarating sharpness when it is freshly ground. To dispel its bitterness, mustard seeds are ground together with one or two fresh green chillies and a touch of salt. Sitting near Patoler Ma, I often leaned closer just to catch the mouth-watering whiff of this titillating combination. The final product, a yellowish brown tinged with green, looked, and often was, good enough to taste on its own. On hot summer afternoons, my mother sometimes took sour green mangoes and peeled, seeded, and sliced them. The slices were then mixed with salt, mustard oil, and the ground mustard left over from the morning's cooking. The result was an epicure's delight, to be savoured by itself, one delicate piece after another, the tongue shivering with both shock and joy, but always craving more.

On the infrequent occasions when we ate meat, usually for Sunday afternoon lunch, Patoler Ma had to contend with ingredients that had their own moisture – onions, garlic, and ginger – as well as the most aromatic elements in our kitchen – cinnamon, cardamom, and clove. The noise of stone on stone was very different when the element between them was a juicy allium or a fleshy root like ginger. Their fluid-filled substance cushioned the shock and was reduced to paste with relatively little effort. But of course such ease came at a price. By the time she finished with them, Patoler Ma had tears streaming down her face and had to sniff vigorously to control her runny nose. So it must have been a relief to switch to the harder, sharper, smaller and intensely fragrant spices that we called *garom mashla*. As she hammered away at the combined pile of cinnamon, cardamom, and clove, before making them into paste, I would draw deep breaths to hold in as much as possible of the scent that was released.

Once I asked Patoler Ma if these were not her favourite spices when she cooked for her own family, since they smelled so good. She turned towards me with the saddest smile I had ever seen. "People like me can't afford to buy *garom mashla*," she said, "we only handle and smell it in the homes of people like you." The starkness of the statement at first puzzled me, then brought home to me the iniquities of poverty and our day-to-day acceptance of it. What must it feel like, I wondered, to spend so much energy in processing ingredients that you may desire but could never obtain? My child's brain came nowhere near an answer, but the question lived with me and edged me towards the curiosity about other lives and other worlds that consumes all writers.

The days of the *shil* and the *nora* are long gone from my life – as far away, today, as my lost childhood. Now, as I pour out powdered spices from capped bottles or plastic bags, I mourn the absence of freshness and intensity that only fresh, stone-ground spices can produce, and miss the earthy magic of transformation wrought by stone and human hand. In my modern American kitchen I use different electrical gadgets to change whole seed or root into paste and powder, but it is a mechanical process. In this kitchen, there is no white enamel plate with an array of spices waiting to be transformed into the palette of life by someone like Patoler Ma. But despite the lack of immediate and visible alchemy in the preparation of my daily food, I do not yearn for that long-gone ritual of spice grinding. For whenever the image of that colourful plate of spices rises before my eyes, it is inevitably overlaid by a film of another colour – that of Patoler Ma's sadness.

IRWIN ALLAN SEALY

The Anglo-Indians

THE ANGLO-INDIANS are the first modern Indians. Before the Victorian Hindu renaissance, before the nawabi itch for things European, before the feringhee musings of the Great Mogul, there appears this community of committed westernisers who will speak the father's tongue and yet eat the mother's salt. The first mother must have felt this alien child move in her and wondered at the future she contained. It was the future of the world, but she may not have cared to look so far. Would the child look like her, she must have asked, or like the father, that pale ravisher unlike any she had known. Or might it be a mixture of the two, or something else again?

The first births across the land would have been fraught but novel events. As the novelty wore off, practicalities would have arisen: who would pay for the child's keep? What would he or she wear? Might the father be persuaded to acknowledge his child? If not to take it on at least to take an interest in its progress? But very likely the father had disappeared, moved on with his regiment, or his ship, or his convoy, and every so often in the streets of any city there might appear this startling cuckoo, a fair-haired frank in native clothes.

Let a generation pass by. During this time such children would have been raised by the mother if not taken on by an interested father. But lately, by an order of state, military orphanages have been instituted that take in such offspring regardless of their colour. Here the children are housed and taught by the East India Company. They eat with knives and forks, not always a diet the father or the mother would approve; they wear hats. They study and play and quarrel in the foreign tongue. There is no record of their dreams but we might fairly guess that whatever their imagery, they are already in English.

Now let seven years pass. The child who was brought in is educated and ready to step into the world. If it is a young man he will very likely become what is known as a writer, or as we would say today a clerk, keeping books for the Company. But he could instead learn a trade such as ship-building, or if he were a ready outdoorsman become a soldier or a surveyor in the same honourable service. A young woman of marriageable age will immediately find a husband from among the European community where there is no shortage of reluctant bachelors. A European complexion would be an asset, but a dark skin would not necessarily be a liability, for she would meet all the other expectations of language, religion, customs and habits of a prospective husband. Given the high mortality rate among the Company's officers, she might even find herself widowed and remarried within the short span of the dreaded "two monsoons", all a resident European in the field was rumoured to expect in a cholera-ridden land. It would of course be tempting for her to reach as high as she could among her suitors and this might see her absorbed into European society without a trace of her origins. It would be harder for the male, especially the dark-skinned male, to compete, in spite of his hat. But the school leaver might equally marry for love, one of his or her own kind, and set up a home in the European manner. In this way a new community, next to but apart from the Europeans, takes shape. In the early years they are called East Indians.

Within two generations, then, we find a distinct group of Indians, for all practical purposes a caste, existing in as yet easy proximity to the colonising race, and distinct from the remainder of the population. The East Indians, by virtue of their colour spectrum, merge with Europeans at the fair end of the scale and with their own darks at the other end. Even when the fair go to the fair and the dark to the dark, such is the nature of genes that neither can be at all certain of the colour of their progeny. This may cause anxious moments in the ninth month, similar to those experienced by our hypothetical first mother, but popular novelists have tended to overstate the neuroses involved. Already by the middle of the eighteenth century the great majority are marrying among themselves without the slightest thought for the colour of their offspring. This is in itself a trait so modern that most other Indians have still to acquire it in the twenty-first century.

It is not their only modern trait. Unlike the great mass of their countrymen, the newest Indians expect and offer no dowry; they do not favour sons or lament daughters or stigmatise widows; in time they will lead the way in female employment and emancipation. They are largely educated, to varying degrees and effect, and unless destitute are imbued with civic notions well beyond the mainstream. In religion they follow their fathers and are as pious as any other group in a pious land. But here the shoe is on the other foot: unlike the others they lack a book. A holy book of their very own, as opposed to the one they share with their fathers. For the sharing, sadly, will doom them to a life of imitation. Any book might have sufficed so long as it were theirs and theirs alone, but in faith as in language they are covenanted. Just as the language they share with the rulers will both guarantee them jobs and keep them dependent, the shared faith proves another article of indenture. They will be loyal subjects in this world because even in the next they are in effect one with the master, only less so. They are bound to him as a shadow to the man.

If in manners and morals the latest Indians modelled themselves scrupulously on the English, it was an imitation not craven or servile but occasioned willy-nilly by the vacuum into which a new thing falls. There was no, or no recent, precedent for this overlapping of Europe and Asia, and any group that sprang from it had to return to either the one or the other for its cultural ballast. Anglo-Indians chose the more modern of the two, a choice which other Indians are happy to repeat today. As British rule was consolidated the many European surnames – Portuguese, French, German, Spanish, Italian were simply tags of origin; one language and its ethos united the community, English. So when they spoke of *Home* they were not being ridiculous; the country they had never seen was the source of all that they valued deeply, while in the only language they spoke, the word *India* was itself still exotic. Their very persons, their lived experience, domesticated both words – and embodied the worlds they stood for. They were foreign and yet native, native and yet foreign, and in that vexed identity lay their double fate.

By the early nineteenth century, they are a separate group recognized as such by both the Indians they have left behind and the Europeans they aspire to become, and are already adapting as a new thing must. Their entire outlook may be governed by those aspirations, their customs borrowed from the land of their fathers, and yet in one regard they have dug their heels into the motherland. Their food, even when eaten at a table, with a cloth, off china, and with cutlery, leans heavily to the Indian. This is pragmatism at work; foreign foodstuffs, certainly dainties, are for the European upper classes. Even where the cook attempts a European dish the tropical kitchen imposes its regime. True, the England baker, with his risen bread, cakes, and biscuits, has a ready market in Grey Town, but at the same time the Anglo-Indian housewife's meat is highly spiced, her vegetables locally seasoned; the Anglo-Indians are veritable products of the pepper trade. And yet in desserts they take on board extravagances no Indian would recognise. They are becoming something unto themselves.

They are also bound by new grievances, having lately found certain jobs denied them by virtue of their birth. Besides, although by now endogamous, they still lack a law to govern their civil relations such as marriage. The East Indians lobby parliament without success, but continue loyal to their side. At length their demands are met: after the Crown takes control of the colony following the mutiny of 1857 they find reserved employment in government services such as the newly expanding railways. They are also engineers on the new network of canals, and officers in the post and telegraph services, customs, and police, middle-order functionaries as befits their intermediate position. Protection will lighten their burden but perversely it will also rob the community of its enterprise: from now on until reservations cease in a hundred years, these guarantees of employment will shape their character, fostering a sense of dependency during the British Raj and occasioning the flight of half the community at Independence. It is a mark of their confusion that they do not settle on a name – Anglo-Indian – until just short of the departure of the British, perhaps because they are choosing the very name their patrons are about to relinquish.

But patronage is not the whole story. From early on in their history they began to open little schools all across the country which offered to teach the populace the English language. It is a clouded fact that up to and beyond Independence English was diffused through this country not officially by the Raj, in spite of Macaulay's famous minute, but unofficially by the Anglo-Indians. In just the same way as today an entire cottage industry of "English-medium" schools parallels the formal sector in education, for some three hundred years Anglo-Indians have, with perhaps greater justification, been trading in their father-tongue. A whole century before Macaulay there are records of dame schools run by formidable women from their homes. Nor did such schools vanish with Independence: all through my early childhood in the 1950s my mother ran a dame school in the many little towns my father was posted in as an officer of the UP police. From her the sons and daughters of government servants and businessmen learnt Wordsworth under the mofussil sky. Nor was she alone: to speak just of our family, her sister taught elocution in a small railway town in Bihar, while an aunt on my father's side is remembered by generations of her students in Lucknow. Of course historically there were church schools as well, and these are the ones that survive, but here too the Anglo-Indian teaching staff invariably outnumbered the British. We forget that it is their demotic, not British English, that is spoken in this country today.

Pride of connection and security of employment blinded the Anglo-Indians to opportunities beyond their native language. By turns beleaguered and complacent, objects of protection and prejudice, they found relief in an insouciance whose pleasures were invariably conformist. There were always rebels in the ranks, but perhaps a more thoroughgoing tradition of dissent would have sharpened their critical and analytic tools and served them better as a group. Once too scattered to combine they are today too few to matter; critical mass was always beyond them. Those who stayed on are emblems of the deracination that modernity demands of nations.

MEENA ALEXANDER

In Whitman's Country

> I too had receiv'd identity by my body,
> That I was I knew was of my body, and what I should
> be I knew I should be of my body.
>
> – "Crossing Brooklyn Ferry"

I cannot imagine myself in America without Whitman. Sometimes, in times of difficulty, when reinvention of the self is a fierce necessity – a time such as now – I think of myself as having been wafted here by Walt, a creature with a tumbling grey beard, cap askew, bony wings sprouting out of his corduroy jacket.

There are bits of grass in his mouth, and when I am about to pass out, with all the air gushing through – we make a curious kind of airplane together – he pushes a few stalks into my mouth. The grass is filled with moisture, rather cold and glittery, and the bits of ice on the blades help moisten my tongue. I totter a little with the unsteadiness of it all. Am I on a "trottoir", as he called it? Am I really in Mannahatta?

I could not have come to America without Whitman. Now that would be an odd statement to make to an officer at the other end of the table when one is taking a citizenship test – How many stars, how many stripes, how many states? etc. What should I say? Whitman drew me here, and now I am a woman who must cast herself on the kindness of others:

I resist anything better than my own diversity,
Breathe the air but leave plenty after me,
And am not stuck up, and am in my place.

– "Song of Myself", sec. 16

*

How did I get to Whitman's country? November 2004. It's a moist fall day, and I put on a light coat and go to take my place in the line at the polling booth near Fort Tryon Park. I have come from India, the world's most populous democracy, and in India, returning after my studies in England, I read Whitman again. In me are the memories of voting lines in Hyderabad, where I used to live, old people who had trudged in from villages miles away, mothers with infants hoisted to their hips, labourers, teachers, and everywhere the dust rising in the dryness that grips the city before the rains fall.

Now in the dampness of a New York November I step into the sunlight, and my fingers close around the pages I have slipped into my pocket. The pages are dry and light, and they feel as if a current of air were still passing through them. When I first came to America, I bought a book. I see from the date on the front page, December 1979, that I purchased it a little over a month after I arrived in Manhattan. Books were a luxury then, but this was one book I did not want to be without. Even now, the pencil markings I made so long ago are vivid, new to me, just as the book is, though the glue is resolutely unstuck in that green-backed Norton edition of *Leaves of Grass*, and I can tear out hunks and carry pages with me without hurting the boundaries of poems. So it is that "Song of Myself" struck loose of the book has come to take up residence in my coat pocket. And I have recourse to the poem as I stand waiting for the old man in glasses to check out my signature, neatly xeroxed in the pad of voters' names in front of him. I am all ready for a hitch, but it seems to work, the tally of name and signature as I point out my address, the very last apartment building on Fort Washington Avenue, just before the park.

How far north can one go on this island and not fall into water? Just a few more miles towards Spuyten Duyvil and one can see the foam lapping at the grey rocks.

Every few years in my life I go through a blaze of reading Whitman, and there are always poems I return to, in some driven way: "Song of Myself", "Crossing Brooklyn Ferry", and from time to time "Out of the Cradle". So it was before I left India in late 1979, so it is now. Why?

I try to spell it out. It has to do with identity. *Identity*, that overused, much maligned word. In a very recent book of that title Zygmunt Bauman speaks of the "spectre of exclusion" that haunts us now, in this age of fluid, coursing borders. And it is precisely to that anxious reality that Whitman speaks. Reading the poet when I was a young woman in India, I was gripped by an excitement that is still in me when I open his pages.

Who else has conceived of the self as a cluster of jutting, jostling identities and dared to make an epic out of that chaos, cutting and clipping it into a *paysage-état d'âme* that is pronounced to be coextensive with a great continent? Who else has made such music out of self-division and then imagined a new, internally embattled nation as coequal to that self?

Sometime in that week when I purchased my now battered copy of *Leaves of Grass*, we went walking over Brooklyn Bridge. It was one of the first things I had wanted to do in Manhattan, see that bridge and if possible walk over it. It was a clear, cold day. I had not felt such cold since I left England six years earlier. The air was brilliant and clear. I felt a sense of elation at the sweet metallic grid that upheld the bridge and staring down at the waters below murmured the lines as if they were a blessing:

> Saw the reflection of the summer sky in the water,
> Had my eyes dazzled by the shimmering track of beams,
> Look'd at the fine centrifugal spokes of light round the shape of my head in the sunlit water . . .
>
> – "Crossing Brooklyn Ferry", sec. 3

As a child of six, in a mixture of awe and pleasure I had stared down at my own forbidden reflection in the well. The waters were dark, and sixty feet down I had seen a blurred image of a girl. Everything was misty as I stared down into the water I was told might swallow me if I looked. But I looked anyway. And what the darkness of well water gave back still haunts me. Here, though, in Whitman, was the possibility of brilliant sunshine, a benediction around a face, a blessing for a body that dared to cross a bridge.

That first time crossing the Brooklyn Bridge I remember looking up from bright water and seeing across the river the grim sign of Jehovah's Witnesses, a Watchtower sign, something I was familiar with from India. The end of the world was everywhere, in everything, and Whitman had dared to flow through into a eternal present that seemed vouchsafed in the idea of America.

Where else could I have come to from a country where the weight of centuries threatened to overwhelm? It seemed to me then that there was an odd fit between the burden of time that I was born to and the promise of space that I had chosen. But what sort of life could I make for myself here, what sort of poetry? Those are questions that only time will slowly answer.

Whitman did not abandon me. Last year, in March 2003, when I was working on a poem I eventually called "Triptych in a Time of War", I felt that pulse of anxiety that had sometimes hit me when writing, the sense that I was entering utterly uncharted territory. I was writing in a time of war. It was then I felt the presence of Whitman, the feeling that it was all right to go ahead and write in the strum and throb of a violent present, make a long line for the breath to weave through, try to make sense of multiple worlds, one layering over the other, make an American poem, whatever in God's name that might be.

And what of "The old knot of contrariety" evoked in "Crossing Brooklyn Ferry" and reappearing throughout Whitman's poetry, a tug of discordant elements, the dark, the hidden, the silenced, braided through the clear and sweet and light? There was a way in which Whitman spoke directly to the knotted, secretive life I had led. I was raised in a world of tradition and decorum where being born a girl meant that even if one were to receive an education and excel in that realm of thought and learning, the core sexual self was already mortgaged, bound into a shadowy zone of indebtedness. Hence the self-division that I learnt to live with, depending on the mind to free me, if only provisionally. For after all, who could lose her body? I will never forget the frisson that ran down my spine when I read the line: "Through me many long dumb voices" ("Song of Myself", sec. 24).

Mine was a world in which one could be ritually cast out. The world in which one could be born an outcaste was never far from me, in spite of the many miles I travelled as a child, from continent to continent, crossing waters far from Kerala. I think of Lalithambika Antherjanam, the great Malayalam writer born ninety years after Whitman and two continents away, on the south-west coast of India, in what is now Kerala. I think of the continental plates rubbing together as if the mists of time were upon us, as the poet from "fish-shape Paumanok" whispers to the poet born from a bolt of land said to have risen from an axe Parasurama tossed into the Arabian Sea. For Lalithambika started as a poet, though she went on to write in prose. Whitman draws his beard aside and whispers to her:

> This is the meal equally set, this the meat for natural hunger,
> It is for the wicked just the same as the righteous, I make
> appointments with all,
> I will not have a single person slighted or left away,
> The kept-woman, sponger, thief, are hereby invited,
> The heavy-lipp'd slave is invited, the venerealee is invited;
> There shall be no difference between them and the rest.
>
> "Song of Myself," sec. 19

The ritual displacement of women in traditional Namboodiri society forms the core of Lalithambika's work and stands at the heart of her novel *Agnisakshi* (Trial by Fire). The self doubles, splits into two: the self that endures, mute, voiceless, and the other self that bears witness, taking on the role of narrator. In the struggle with the prescriptions of an all-powerful culture, her own bodily self, passionate, desiring, violated, becomes the very source of speech. Elsewhere in my writing I have called this a "back against the wall aesthetic", a recourse to the most primitive ground: the body as the site of first and last resort. And it is precisely here I see her holding hands with Walt Whitman. In her sleep she speaks to him, and he, a gay man, shares with her the evidence of the senses, a vision of "the caresser of life wherever moving" ("Song of Myself", sec. 13).

I have no evidence that Lalithambika read Whitman. In fact, it is eminently possible that she didn't. But Whitman certainly has been translated into my mother tongue, Malayalam, an ancient coastal language of India, whose literature has been fed, as all great literatures have been, by streams of translation. Kerala has a long socialist tradition, and Pushkin, Tolstoy, Lorca, Neruda, and Whitman have all been translated into Malayalam. When I was a child in Kerala I used to hear cousins who went to school reciting bits of Whitman that they had "byhearted" in Malayalam, part of a long mnemonic tradition.

In a recent e-mail communication I asked the poet Ayyappa Paniker about Whitman. He sent me his poem "Yesterday I Saw Whitman" in an English translation he himself had made. The poem has a poignant opening:

> Yesterday, or was it the day before, I saw Whitman.
> Talking loudly about the multitudes,
> In loneliness I saw Whitman.
> Stretching his long shadow across the Long Island,
> the islander poet was counting the waves of the sea.

The e-mail he sent with the poem was eloquent. Ayyappa Paniker, one of the most important twentieth-century poets of Malayalam, told me that in his own imagination he connected Whitman with another great epic poet, Vyasa, the author of the *Mahabharata*. Each poet was born on an island. Turning to the other great Indian epic, news of which might well have reached Whitman, he reflects on Whitman's "Out of the Cradle": "the remaining or solitary bird perhaps echoes the survivor bird in the story of Valmiki, the author of the *Ramayana*" – alluding to how Valmiki was driven to write by the piteous cries of a bird calling out to his dead mate. Ayyappa Paniker closes by speaking of the "invisible threads" that surely bind us all our lives, reminiscing about an old man he knew who once lived in the city of Thiruvananthapuram. That man so loved Emerson, that everyone knew him quite simply by that name – Emerson. Dr Paniker concludes his e-mail by saying: "In the metreless metre of recent Malayalam poetry we may see the influence of Whitman, Neruda, Lorca, etc."

But the worlds that Whitman wanted to draw together sometimes threaten to split him apart, lay him waste, body and soul: "Is this then a touch? Quivering me to a new identity?" ("Song of Myself", sec. 28).

Was this the price to be paid for living in the American present, in a world that Emerson felt had no need of memory, where "history is an impertinence and an injury" (Emerson, "Self-Reliance"), where autobiography had to be inscribed "in colossal cipher"? Studying Whitman when I was a student in England, then writing about him in my dissertation, it was precisely the way in which he used his body to achieve, sometimes at painful cost, a flowing, liquid poetics, a life in letters, where the edge was courted, where breakdown was close, even necessary to free the quick of the desiring self – all this haunted me. I titled the chapter on Whitman that I drafted at the age of nineteen "Identity by My Body", little realising that this was to be the theme that would stitch itself through my work, even though Whitman's own name and presence might lie buried in the seams of my consciousness, the world he had drawn me to more than three-quarters of a century after his death, filling me up, tumbling me over.

Manhattan was hard to live in, and the question of race, of what it might mean to be an Indian poet here, was thrust at times into harsh relief. At times, Whitman turned into a good grey mother, a ghost who might suck me in without allowing me the soil, the ground I needed to survive. In those early days in America, I often spoke to my friend Joel Porte about Whitman, needing to understand how it was that both Whitman and Emerson struck such deep chords in me. Was it the promise of newness, of a self-invention that could cast itself loose in a massive, unnamed geography? And what of the urgent need, in those like myself, migrant poets, growing up with globalisation, to achieve a voice that sought passage between worlds?

As a small child in Kerala I used a stick to draw pictures in the dirt. Often I would draw rooms and even houses and then try to join them together in a figure of eight. Then I would use my bare feet to make the drawings disappear, and all that was left was the rippling figure of eight, that too disappearing in the garden dirt.

I turn to the figure of eight in order to try to draw my world together. This summer I was in Kerala to visit my mother, who lives in the house of her childhood and mine. It is built in the traditional *nalukettu* manner, red tiles and whitewashed walls, enclosing a gravel-covered courtyard where a mulberry bush still grows. She wanted to consult a lawyer about making a will, and we travelled to the ancient port city of Kochi to find a lawyer. The waters of the Arabian Sea were deep blue, a seamless silk drawn up and shaken out into tiny gleaming waves, and in Mattancherri Palace I stopped short, breathless, in front of a wall full of old maps of Kochi.

These maps seemed bland, colourless next to the room of intricate murals I had just passed through, the far wall filled to bursting with scenes of childbirth in the Ramayana, a unique set of images, the almond-eyed royal infants dropping clean out of their mothers' thighs, three boy babies in brilliant vegetable colours, seventeenth-century imaginings of grace and courtliness, a dream of natural continuity.

And the maps? The maps were Dutch, from the same period, representations of Kochi harbour. What made me stand still was their eerie semblance to maps of New Amsterdam made in the same period – the stylised mainland, the curved passageways for water, Vypeen Island, Governor's Island – they blurred and doubled in my mind's eye.

The Dutch had lost New Amsterdam to the British in 1664, precisely a year after they took Kochi from the British. This figure of eight stays with me – gaining Cochin and access to the spice trade in 1663; losing New Amsterdam. It takes a mythic turn in my mind, and I imagine the waters of the Indian Ocean and the Atlantic, which I have crisscrossed in my life. I need to stay with this loop in time and space and see how far it will take me. I need to pay attention to where the figure ruptures and how I might set down a small shelter made of words. And saying all this, it is clear to me, that without Walt Whitman I could never have ventured this far.

Tomorrow morning, if the weather is fine, I will put on my boots and walk north to the edge of the island, to Spuyten Duyvil. The northern side of the creek was called Shorakapok by the Lenape people who inhabited it. The word is translated as "space between the ridges" or "sitting down place". I will sit between the rocks and gaze at the waters of the river Hudson. My grandmother was born in Kozhikode, an ancient city where Vasco da Gama landed. I imagine Whitman, his beard speckled with salt spray, strolling where the Arabian Sea meets the land of Kerala. Lifetimes later, I am here at the Hudson's edge, haunted by what the poet in "Out of the Cradle" called "the unknown want".

I search for something that lies just beyond the reach of words.

In Whitman's country.

GAUTAM BHATIA

Art as Politics

SOME YEARS BACK, in the small *mandi* town of Bilaspur in western Uttar Pradesh, a nondescript statue of Ambedkar was attacked by an angry mob of students. They were protesting the fact that those among them who had failed their exams were being kept from proceeding to the next class – a reasonable demand in a system that only seeks to buy a diploma.

Political statues, such as the one attacked, belong to popular culture, not to high art. There are enough of them at provincial street corners, in parks and roundabouts; reminders of the sullied greatness of once-great men. Nehru in *achkan* and Gandhi *topi*, rose in buttonhole, gazing into the bright future of a Free India, with streaked hair and the fixed pitiless gaze of running an un-runnable country; Gandhi, with the enigmatic toothless smile, unsure why he has wasted a lifetime procuring freedom for a perpetually quibbling mass of humanity. Warm poses they are not, just the easily recognisable faces, their familiar stances in frozen body language. Collective images bred in stone. They stand there, by the roadside, at intersections, bereft and ignored, gathering dust, like files in government offices. Polychrome faces and marble bodies shrivelled in the summer light. If they have lost their ability to extract the intended awe, it is only because they have become standardised items of the streetscape: a little like a list of government-approved items in an office – "One desk D/2/Vig Bhav/Rm 7/Chair, Nos. 3, Paper Weight – two nos., Portrait of Gandhi – one".

Bilaspur's blue-suited statue of Ambedkar, pink-faced, with black-rimmed glasses, had withstood many such protests. But in the ensuing clash, someone knocked off Ambedkar's nose. Within hours, a Dalit rage engulfed the small town, leaving many injured and a few people dead. In an effort to quell the anger, the city administration quickly fixed the nose and, to keep the statue from further facial disfiguring, surrounded it with a high-strength steel cage, a structure so tightly welded, only barely could Ambedkar peer out at his devotees from his new jail cell.

It has taken the Indian politician and bureaucrat sixty years of tireless foreign study tours to look for urban solutions to Indian problems. A two-week tour of Sydney to study Olympic facilities, a week to study expressway interchanges in Los Angeles, a month of grave scrutiny of the Brazilian rainforest, a careful week-long assessment of Moscow's metro system, a thorough investigation of Singapore and Hong Kong airports, and when all else fails, there is the two-week executive course at Harvard. And at the end of all this, we have Ambedkar enclosed by iron.

His modern follower, Mayawati of Lucknow, is unfettered in this respect. She has absorbed the fact that memorials have only a political dimension – it may have been apparent to her from the kind of hectoring-from-a-high-pedestal statuary put up around the country. Of these, she has taken the prize for the most shrill and pushy form of public sculpture. Her memorials appeared during her chief ministership in virtually every public maidan, every respectable roundabout, and any place given to large-scale visibility. A larger-than-life Mayawati glared down the Bahujan Nayak Park. A bronze Mayawati stood at the Ambedkar Samajik Parivartan Sthal, Mayawati's own memorial to Ambedkar. At road intersections there may have been no policemen, but four Mayawatis stood tall in bronze or stone;

passersby view her front, back and sides, all at once. She stood larger than real life, higher than ordinary life, letting people know that one in flesh and blood and freshly poured bronze also walks upon this earth. Always there, always with them, at the low summer discount sale of rupees two to four crore per statue, not including VAT and entertainment tax. Gift-wrapped, and unveiled at critical state occasions: her birthday, Kanshi Ram's birthday, Ambedkar's.

The mismatch of India's real history with its street reality calls for clear action. It should hardly be incumbent upon a Dalit leader to continue proposing more statues of Ambedkar all over India, or a government to only propose memorials to a chauvinistic national greatness. No country's history is so shamelessly one-sided that it revels only in victory. From public representations, the Freedom Struggle would appear to be the single most crucial event that defines modern India. What then of social and economic struggles? Should a Patna gallery enact the Bihar famine? Should Bhoodaan and Narmada Bachao be preserved in some physical form? Rather than mindless statues of a united Ambedkar, should there be a museum at India Gate dedicated to caste and Dalit oppression? A more inclusive history would move from symbols to defining a picture closer to reality. The world over, governments are choosing to right the wrongs of history. Canada and Australia have apologised for the mistreatment of their indigenous people; German cities continue to build Holocaust memorials. If our government's public memorials are to have a semblance of fairness, for a while it will have to forget the grandiose and the monumental and concentrate on smaller corrections: return King George to the *chhatri* at India Gate, assemble the rubble from the Babri Masjid into a gracious setting of forgiveness in central Ayodhya; then act on local efforts: acknowledge the good education work of Christian priests in Bihar; rename streets and squares in Bangalore after Kannada artists, Kerala roads after local writers. To let future residents of these places know that their country's greatness was not just in freedom struggles, but in local, sustained, and ordinary battles.

The Indian politician holds a different view of the matter. "I always felt that memorials should be built during the lifetime of icons," Mayawati declared without a hint of irony. "This is why I got the statue of my mentor Kanshi Ram installed in Lucknow during his lifetime. But because he wished that I should also have my own statue next to his, I decided to go ahead." The absence of statues in Dalit history provided Mayawati the star-power in an idol. Here was a woman, a Dalit, who had taken centuries of oppression and turned it right-side up, into an asset. The oppressed still remained oppressed, but in symbolic terms they were riding the popular wave. Mayawati had pushed the Brahmins, the freedom fighters, the Nehrus and Annie Besants off their pedestals, and without so much as testing her own political strength, proclaimed her power.

Every seasoned politician knows the dividend gained by claiming the moral high ground, and the great potential in garnering goodwill through the noisy act of choreographed selflessness. So, the *padyatra*s come, long spells of endurance across India. So too come the fasts, always unto death, always in full view of TV cameras. The noise and clutter of physical action, and the need to express indignation at a national scale far outweigh the possibility of reconciliation through debate. No one understands this better than the older politicians, who know how easy it is to quickly feel the blaring pulse of India and move on. That statues of elephants can be built in place of schools, and vast memorials of self-portraits erected in the time of malaria only shows up politics as just another endurance sport. Like athletics and marathons, you cheat and lie and drug yourself to stay in the game.

It took only a short drive around the streets of Lucknow in those years to know that Mayawati was the new Gandhi. There she was, unlike a feeble Gandhi on the Dandi March, unlike an intellectual Ambedkar with his Constitution, handbag on her arm, gaze firmly fixed ahead, to a new future – her future. Her sculptor, Prajapati, had a set of standing instructions to always sculpt her features as if in an attitude of triumph. Image mattered. To counter any ill-fated attacks on her nose, he was instructed to make her in unbreakable bronze.

It was Mahatma Gandhi who said the poor imagine God in a loaf of bread. Before the election which brought Mayawati to power, the poor imagined God in her. They flocked to the parade ground to view her just like devotees at a temple; they prayed to her statues, as if to Goddess Laxmi; they sang her praises in a hypnotic religious trance. And they forgave her excesses even when they had to pay bribes for a street-cleaning job; even when they were denied a water connection in their colony, knowing full well that the water was being directed to the fountains at her memorials, it didn't matter. Mayawati was a sister, a Dalit, oppressed for a thousand years. And now, by becoming just another politician, she was correcting the course of history, for herself, for them.

A government clerk's daughter, for many, Mayawati was the Indian Obama. Similar portraits of the two appeared in magazines: Obama under the looming shadow of Abraham Lincoln at the monument in Washington: men of ideas, statesmen-like, whose lives had become entwined by political concerns and ideology. In her own portrait, Mayawati likewise stood under a statue of Ambedkar, seated ironically in the Lincoln pose. Clutching her handbag, she offered the same visual presence as the American president: confident, pensive, and caring. Reporters and journalists who questioned her on development and rural reform left her with no option but to answer by unveiling more statues of herself. A monumental memorial was unveiled on the outskirts of Delhi, others planned in towns all across her state. Her personal life of acquisitions, monuments built, houses bought, helicopters leased, diamond jewellery hoarded, extortion wealth amassed, came looming into the frame. It was Mayawati's way of scoring a point and letting everyone know that if there were enough visible signs of her presence, the poor would take care of themselves.

The urge to appropriate real estate among the political class in Delhi was only a minor aberration when compared to Mayawati's search for immortality in nearby Lucknow. In what was doubtlessly the most brazen act of self-promotion, large tracts of urban land combined with funds for public housing were used to erect bronze memorials to herself. As a Dalit and woman, Mayawati had not found a cause greater than erecting row upon row of stone elephants, fountains, and statuary all across the state to ensure that people were constantly reminded of her as a woman of the people. The same people who had lived through a summer of drought were all too often reminded of their water-free state when walking about the fountains of Mayawati's memorials. It was a paradox too delicious to bring to the attention of their leader.

Much before Mayawati's memorial building spree encountered rough weather, a Delhi architect, a Dalit himself, had proposed a thirty-storey statue of his leader to be built as a focus of a memorial in central Lucknow. The monument was to be 340 feet high, and if built would have dwarfed not just the tallest building in Lucknow but the Statue of Liberty as well. All thirty floors contained a variety of spaces: two museums to

Dalit history, another to Dr Ambedkar, and a fourth on Mayawati's own life story – all encased in an outer structural steel and concrete shell depicting Mayawati holding her favourite handbag. With an entrance near her toes, the building's two elevator banks would rise up Mayawati's legs to a series of mid-level restaurants in her stomach, past offices in the chest area and emerge into the museums located inside the head. The detailed plans, though secret, revealed a careful resolution of all the essential services: air-conditioning, garbage disposal, and plumbing – all concealed within the chief minister's body, a body which served a dual purpose, enthralling the public on the outside by the sheer size of her presence, and enclosing the weight of her intellectual message inside, in museums, research libraries, and restaurants. Fortunately, the plans of a Mayawati shaped as a building were safely secured in the drawers of an architect's office, the work, thankfully, never built. Yet the sheer audacity of its scope demonstrated not just the exaggerated possibilities of public expenditure, but the grotesque magnitude of political power gone to seed. The mere fact of its conceptualisation also raised larger questions of urban appropriateness and the public's view of politics as art.

Naming roads and renaming railway stations and airports has led every elected government down the path to urban sycophancy. Yet names by themselves were never as effective as physical representations of the hero. In a culture which reveres cardboard cut-outs of politicians, the search for an extravagant expression for a national icon invariably leads to a larger-than-life manipulation of statuary. Sitting on a committee to select a sculpture of Indira Gandhi, I once watched how works of art were commissioned by the government. Sculptors had submitted sketches; Rajiv Gandhi was to make the selection. From about twenty drawings that showed Indira Gandhi in rough loose chalk strokes, to a pensive Indira in formal view, to a comic Indira missing below the waistline, there was only one that could satisfy the criterion of sculpture for mass consumption: a larger-than-life Indira set on a high pedestal in direct frontal view, face grimacing downwards, presumably hectoring the masses at an election rally. What could be a more fitting portrait of an Indian leader? Rajiv set it aside from the rest.

A related case comes to mind: it took the Maharashtra government three centuries since Shivaji to finally come up with a Mayawati-like commemoration of the Maratha warrior, 309 feet high, set a mile into the Arabian Sea on a plinth containing a multi-utility complex, a public sculpture that would be India's Statue of Liberty. What in the present scheme of things stirs the state into decision is of little consequence. In times of religious polarisation and identity politics, the idea didn't hold water. If Mumbai's sizeable Muslim minority had no say in the selection of a Maratha icon it was only because their protests were drowned in a sea of Hindu voices which saw Shivaji's presence as a vindication of the ills plaguing the city.

In India the standard response to public deification is a form of exaggerated monumentalism. When L.K. Advani announced in all seriousness that the proposed Sardar Patel statue in Gujarat will be the tallest in the world, he sounded like a Dubai sheikh taking credit for the highest building, the biggest island, the largest aquarium. Something not for public good but for the *Guinness Book of Records*. Now that it is complete, the 600-foot statue, the brainchild of Narendra Modi, made of iron and concrete with a bronze outer layer, shines in the afternoon light as it faces the Narmada Dam. Leaving aside the sheer audacity of public expenditure and the gross misuse of political power to electoral ends, the statue's conception raises questions of ecological malpractice and the visual destruction of the landscape, not to mention issues of the public's view of politics as art.

The recurring notion seems to be to take an individual or an idea and build it tenfold; in so doing, convert a serious intent into a Disney cartoon. A 300-foot Shivaji on a horse out in the sea not only denigrates the serious philosophy of the man but casts it, Bollywood style, into the realm of the unreal and fantastic. That Shivaji worked with ordinary people, peasants, and had a human policy towards his administration and army is made entirely redundant. Moreover, the political purpose implicit in such public art denudes the piece of all artistic merit. In fact, the political party's endorsement of the idea in its manifesto and its willingness to shower funds for its construction only reduced Shivaji to puny irrelevance. The Maharaj, as just another party worker, needing sponsorship.

Thanks to a paternalistic attitude of reverence, politicians in India get the same treatment in death as in life. As the single-most lucrative professionals after prostitutes and drug smugglers, politicians occupy the largest real estate in the capital. Whether dead or alive, their entitlement to remain permanently in their constituents' memory has tarred acres of green, making Delhi one of the largest necropolises in the world. Its position as a world-class city of the dead is paramount: beginning with the Sayyid, Lodi, and Mughal tombs to colonial landmarks to dead kings and the collective cemetery of India Gate, the history of the city is itself preserved only in death. By adding the vast retinue of Indian politicians in Lutyens' row and at the various shanty *sthals* and shanty *vans* along the river, the modern dimension of remembrance is further enshrined. If Mahatma Gandhi and Sanjay Gandhi can be commemorated a stone's throw from each other, it says something about the persistence, rather than the content, of the recall. With its devotion to modern variants of the sarcophagus, Delhi turns even the unholiest of crooks into martyrs.

SHAMA FUTEHALLY

March

FOR ANYONE LIVING in Delhi, March is surely the season of the gods. The fresh wintry breeze, the trees in new leaf, the flowers making a "riot of colour" – all this evokes grateful surprise in a populace used to dust storms on the one hand and polluted winter evenings on the other. It is also a time for birds; since many trees are not in leaf, the flitting and darting and pirouetting of small shapes seems to be all around us. As I sit here I can see Rose-ringed Parakeets flying into the neem trees, their long tails gleaming blue in the sun. The peepul tree by the veranda, whose leaves are still tightly curled, harbours a family of Crimson-breasted Barbets. On the hibiscus bush outside my window a Tailor Bird is looking for nesting material, perhaps, along with an Ashy Wren Warbler. And on top of the hedge a Magpie Robin, glossily black and white and as self-assured as Clinton himself, is singing his heart out, because it is the courtship season too.

Further away, a tall pale tree is preparing to shed its leaves and cover itself with a washed lilac colour which could belong inside a Japanese painting. Because we have this blessing too – that when the freshness of March gives way to the sadder suns of summer, the flowering trees leap into colour, and they are colours so amazing that we should seriously consider banning them. The red silk cottons are already aflame, and alive with sunbirds, flower-peckers, bulbuls and mynahs. Then it will be the stunning yellow of the laburnums, and after that the frothy whites and pinks of bauhinias. Around our house some unnamed horticultural official, on whom be peace, has ensured that during the most despairing weeks of summer we are treated to a vision of purple jacaranda in full bloom. And, of course, for the rest of the summer life is worth living only because of the gulmohurs.

For the last two or three years, the advent of March has seemed to me peculiarly unexpected. The gentle message which it brings, i.e. that you never have a single season but a cycle, that every wheel comes full circle and today is not all, now appears both more reassuring and harder to believe. And that, I suspect, is because we live in a world where, increasingly, today is in fact all. The print media and the television, those two dictators of our lives, scream about Today in a way which drowns out both yesterday and tomorrow. Thus, in our personal lives, in our social life and in the national life, we grab for Today with a vehemence which is out of all proportion to its importance. And, as recent events have shown, we sometimes somersault right back into yesterday. Whoever planted the jacaranda was thinking about tomorrow, and contemplating it now may teach us more than we imagine.

AMITAV GHOSH

The Imam and the Indian

I MET THE IMAM OF the village and Khamees the Rat at about the same time. I don't exactly remember now – it happened more than six years ago – but I think I met the Imam first.

But this is not quite accurate. I didn't really "meet" the Imam: I inflicted myself upon him. Perhaps that explains what happened.

Still, there was nothing else I could have done. As the man who led the daily prayers in the mosque, he was a leading figure in the village, and since I, a foreigner, had come to live there, he may well for all I knew have been offended had I neglected to pay him a call. Besides, I wanted to meet him; I was intrigued by what I'd heard about him.

People didn't often talk about the Imam in the village, but when they did, they usually spoke of him somewhat dismissively, but also a little wistfully, as they might of some old, half-forgotten thing, like the annual flooding of the Nile. Listening to my friends speak of him, I had an inkling, long before I actually met him, that he already belonged, in a way, to the village's past. I thought I knew this for certain when I heard that apart from being an Imam he was also, by profession, a barber and a healer. People said he knew a great deal about herbs and poultices and the old kind of medicine. This interested me. This was Tradition: I knew that in rural Egypt

Imams and other religious figures are often by custom associated with those two professions.

The trouble was that these accomplishments bought the Imam very little credit in the village. The villagers didn't any longer want an Imam who was also a barber and a healer. The older people wanted someone who had studied at al-Azhar and could quote from Jamal ad-Din Afghani and Mohammad Abduh as fluently as he could from the Hadith, and the younger men wanted a fierce, black-bearded orator, someone whose voice would thunder from the mimbar and reveal to them their destiny. No one had time for old-fashioned Imams who made themselves ridiculous by boiling herbs and cutting hair.

Yet Ustad Ahmed, who taught in the village's secondary school and was as well-read a man as I have ever met, often said – and this was not something he said of many people – that the old Imam read a lot. A lot of what? Politics, theology, even popular science . . . that kind of thing.

This made me all the more determined to meet him, and one evening, a few months after I first came to the village, I found my way to his house. He lived in the centre of the village, on the edge of the dusty open square which had the mosque in its middle. This was the oldest part of the village: a maze of low mud huts huddled together like confectionery on a tray, each hut crowned with a billowing, tousled head of straw.

When I knocked on the door the Imam opened it himself. He was a big man, with very bright brown eyes, set deep in a wrinkled, weather-beaten face. Like the room behind him, he was distinctly untidy: his blue jallabeyya was mud-stained and unwashed and his turban had been knotted anyhow around his head. But his beard, short and white and neatly trimmed, was everything a barber's beard should be. Age had been harsh on his face, but there was a certain energy in the way he arched his shoulders, in the clarity of his eyes and in the way he fidgeted constantly, was never still: it was plain that he was a vigorous, restive kind of person.

"Welcome," he said, courteous but unsmiling, and stood aside and waved me in. It was a long dark room, with sloping walls and a very low ceiling. There was a bed in it and a couple of mats but little else, apart from a few scattered books: everything bore that dull patina of grime which speaks of years of neglect. Later, I learned that the Imam had divorced his first wife and his second had left him, so that now he lived quite alone and had his meals with his son's family who lived across the square.

"Welcome," he said again, formally.

"Welcome to you," I said, giving him the formal response, and then we began on the long, reassuring litany of Arabic phrases of greeting.

"How are you?"

"How are you?"

"You have brought blessings?"

"May God bless you."

"Welcome."

"Welcome to you."

"You have brought light."

"The light is yours."

"How are you?"

"How are you?"

He was very polite, very proper. In a moment he produced a kerosene stove and began to brew tea. But even in the performance of that little ritual there was something about him that was guarded, watchful.

"You're the *doctor al-Hindi*," he said to me at last, "aren't you? The Indian doctor?"

I nodded, for that was the name the village had given me. Then I told him that I wanted to talk to him about the methods of his system of medicine.

He looked very surprised and for a while he was silent. Then he put his right hand to his heart and began again on the ritual of greetings and responses, but in a markedly different way this time; one that I had learnt to recognise as a means of changing the subject.

"Welcome."

"Welcome to you."

"You have brought light."

"The light is yours."

And so on.

At the end of it I repeated what I had said.

"Why do you want to hear about *my* herbs?" he retorted. "Why don't you go back to your country and find out about your own?"

"I will," I said. 'Soon. But right now . . ."

"No, no," he said restlessly. "Forget about all that; I'm trying to forget about it myself."

And then I knew that he would never talk to me about his craft, not just because he had taken a dislike to me for some reason of his own, but because his medicines were as discredited in his own eyes as they were in his clients'; because he knew as well as anybody else that the people who came to him now did so only because of old habits; because he bitterly regretted his inherited association with these relics of the past.

"Instead," he said, "let me tell you about what I have been learning over the last few years. Then you can go back to your country and tell them all about it."

He jumped up, his eyes shining, reached under his bed and brought out a glistening new biscuit tin.

"Here!" he said, opening it. "Look!"

Inside the box was a hypodermic syringe and a couple of glass phials. This is what he had been learning, he told me: the art of mixing and giving injections. And there was a huge market for it too, in the village: everybody wanted injections, for coughs, colds, fevers, whatever. There was a good living in it. He wanted to demonstrate his skill to me right there, on my arm, and when I protested that I wasn't ill, that I didn't need an injection just then, he was offended. "All right," he said curtly, standing up. "I have to go to the mosque right now. Perhaps we can talk about this some other day."

That was the end of my interview, I walked with him to the mosque and there, with an air of calculated finality, he took my hand in his, gave it a perfunctory shake and vanished up the stairs.

Khamees the Rat I met one morning when I was walking through the rice fields that lay behind the village, watching people transplant their seedlings. Everybody I met was cheerful and busy and the flooded rice fields were sparkling in the clear sunlight. If I shut my ears to the languages, I thought, and stretch the date palms a bit and give them a few coconuts, I could easily be back somewhere in Bengal.

I was a long way from the village and not quite sure of my bearings, when I spotted a group of people who had finished their work and were sitting on the path, passing around a hookah.

"*Ahlan!*" a man in a brown jallabeyya called out to me. "Hullo! Aren't you the Indian *doctor*?"

"Yes," I called back. "And who're you?"

"He's a rat," someone answered, raising a gale of laughter.

"Don't go anywhere near him."

"Tell me *ya doktor,*" the Rat said, "if I get on to my donkey and ride steadily for thirty days will I make it to India?"

"No," I said. "You wouldn't make it in thirty months."

"Thirty months!" he said. "You must have come a long way."

"Yes."

"As for me," he declared, "I've never even been as far as Alexandria and if I can help it I never will."

I laughed: it did not occur to me to believe him.

When I first came to that quiet corner of the Nile Delta I had expected to find on that most ancient and most settled of soils a settled and restful people. I couldn't have been more wrong.

The men of the village had all the busy restlessness of airline passengers in a transit lounge. Many of them had worked and travelled in the sheikhdoms of the Persian Gulf, others had been in Libya and Jordan and Syria, some had been to Yemen as soldiers, others to Saudi Arabia as pilgrims, a few had visited Europe: some of them had passports so thick they opened out like ink-blackened concertinas. And none of this was new: their grandparents and ancestors and relatives had travelled and migrated too, in much the same way as mine had, in the Indian subcontinent – because of wars, or for money and jobs, or perhaps simply because they got tired of living always in one place. You could read the history of this restlessness in the villagers' surnames: they had names which derived from cities in the Levant, from Turkey, from faraway towns in Nubia; it was as though people had drifted here from every corner of the Middle East. The wanderlust of its founders had been ploughed into the soil of the village: it seemed to me sometimes that every man in it was a traveller. Everyone, that is, except Khamees the Rat, and even his surname, as I discovered later, meant "of Sudan".

"Well, never mind *ya doktor*," Khamees said to me now, "Since you're not going to make it back to your country by sundown anyway, why don't you come and sit with us for a while?"

He smiled and moved up to make room for me.

I liked him at once. He was about my age, in the early twenties, scrawny, with a thin, mobile face deeply scorched by the sun. He had that brightness of eye and the quick, slightly sardonic turn to his mouth that I associated with faces in the coffee houses of universities in Delhi and Calcutta; he seemed to belong to a world of late-night rehearsals and black coffee and lecture rooms, even though, in fact, unlike most people in the village, he was completely illiterate. Later I learned that he was called the Rat – Khamees the Rat – because he was said to gnaw away at things with his tongue, like a rat did with its teeth. He laughed at everything, people said – at his father, the village's patron saint, the village elders, the Imam, everything.

That day he decided to laugh at me.

"All right *ya doktor*," he said to me as soon as I had seated myself. "Tell me, is it true what they say, that in your country you burn your dead?"

No sooner had he said it than the women of the group clasped their hands to their hearts and muttered in breathless horror: "*Haram! Haram!*"

My heart sank. This was a conversation I usually went through at least once a day and I was desperately tired of it. "Yes," I said, "it's true; some people in my country burn their dead."

"You mean," said Khamees in mock horror, "that you put them on heaps of wood and just light them up?"

"Yes," I said, hoping that he would tire of this sport if I humoured him.

"Why?" he said. "Is there a shortage of kindling in your country?"

"No," I said helplessly, "you don't understand." Somewhere in the limitless riches of the Arabic language a word such as "cremate" must exist, but if it does, I never succeeded in finding it. Instead, for lack of any other, I had to use the word "burn". That was unfortunate, for "burn" was the word for what happened to wood and straw and the eternally damned.

Khamees the Rat turned to his spellbound listeners. "I'll tell you why they do it," he said. "They do it so that their bodies can't be punished after the Day of Judgement."

Everybody burst into wonderstruck laughter. "Why, how clever," cried one of the younger girls. "What a good idea! We ought to start doing it ourselves. That way we can do exactly what we like and when we die and the Day of Judgement comes, there'll be nothing there to judge."

Khamees had got his laugh. Now he gestured to them to be quiet again.

"All right then *ya doktor*," he said. "Tell me something else: is it true that you are a Magian? That in your country everybody worships cows? Is it true that the other day when you were walking through the fields you saw a man beating a cow and you were so upset that you burst into tears and ran back to your room?"

"No, it's not true," I said, but without much hope: I had heard this story before and knew that there was nothing I could say which would effectively give it the lie. "You're wrong. In my country people beat their cows all the time; I promise you."

I could see that no one believed me.

"Everything's upside down in their country," said a dark, aquiline young woman who, I was told later, was Khamees' wife. "Tell us *ya doktor*: in your country, do you have crops and fields and canals like we do?"

"Yes," I said, "we have crops and fields, but we don't always have canals. In some parts of my country they aren't needed because it rains all the year around."

"*Ya sakám*," she cried, striking her forehead with the heel of her palm. "Do you hear that, oh you people? Oh, the Protector, oh, the Lord! It rains all the year round in his country."

She had gone pale with amazement. "So tell us then," she demanded, "do you have night and day like we do?"

"Shut up woman," said Khamees. "Of course they don't. It's day all the time over there, didn't you know? They arranged it like that so that they wouldn't have to spend any money on lamps."

We all laughed, and then someone pointed to a baby lying in the shade of a tree swaddled in a sheet of cloth. "That's Khamees' baby," I was told. "He was born last month."

"That's wonderful," I said. "Khamees must be very happy." Khamees gave a cry of delight. "The Indian knows I'm happy because I've had a son," he said to the others. "He understands that people are happy when they have children: he's not as upside down as we thought."

He slapped me on the knee and lit up the hookah and from that moment we were friends.

~

One evening, perhaps a month or so after I first met Khamees, he and his brothers and I were walking back to the village from the fields when he spotted the old Imam sitting on the steps that led to the mosque.

"Listen," he said to me, "You know the old Imam, don't you? I saw you talking to him once."

"Yes," I said, "I talked to him once."

"My wife's ill," Khamees said, "I want the Imam to come to my house to give her an injection. He won't come if I ask him, he doesn't like me. You go and ask."

"He doesn't like me either," I said.

"Never mind," Khamees insisted. "He'll come if you ask him – he knows you're a foreigner. He'll listen to you."

While Khamees waited on the edge of the square with his brothers I went across to the Imam. I could tell that he had seen me – and Khamees – from a long way off, that he knew I was crossing the square to talk to him. But he would not look in my direction. Instead, he pretended to be deep in conversation with a man who was sitting beside him, an elderly and pious shopkeeper whom I knew slightly.

When I reached them I said "Good evening" very pointedly to the Imam. He could not ignore me any longer then, but his response was short and curt, and he turned back at once to resume his conversation.

The old shopkeeper was embarrassed now, for he was a courteous, gracious man in the way that seemed to come so naturally to the elders of the village. "Please sit down," he said to me. "Do sit. Shall we get you a chair?"

Then he turned to the Imam and said, slightly puzzled: "You know the Indian *doktor*, don't you? He's come all the way from India to be a student at the University of Alexandria."

"I know him," said the Imam. "He came around to ask me questions. But as for this student business, I don't know. What's he going to study? He doesn't even write in Arabic."

"Well," said the shopkeeper judiciously, "that's true; but after all he writes his own languages and he knows English."

"Oh those," said the Imam. "What's the use of *those* languages? They're the easiest languages in the world. Anyone can write those."

He turned to face me for the first time. His eyes were very bright and his mouth was twitching with anger. "Tell me," he said, "why do you worship cows?"

I was so taken aback that I began to stammer. The Imam ignored me. He turned to the old shopkeeper and said: "That's what they do in his country – did you know? – they worship cows."

He shot me a glance from the corner of his eye. "And shall I tell you what else they do?" he said to the shopkeeper.

He let the question hang for a moment. And then, very loudly, he hissed: "They burn their dead."

The shopkeeper recoiled as though he had been slapped. His hands flew to his mouth. "Oh God!" he muttered. "*Ya Allah*."

"That's what they do," said the Imam. "They burn their dead."

Then suddenly he turned to me and said, very rapidly: "Why do you allow it? Can't you see that it's a primitive and backward custom? Are you savages that you permit something like that? Look at you: you've had some kind of education; you should know better. How will your country ever progress if you carry on doing these things? You've even been to the West; you've seen how advanced they are. Now tell me: have you ever seen them burning their dead?"

The Imam was shouting now and a circle of young men and boys had gathered around us. Under the pressure of their interested eyes my tongue began to trip, even on syllables I thought I had mastered. I found myself growing angry – as much with my own incompetence as the Imam.

"Yes, they do burn their dead in the West," I managed to say somehow. I raised my voice too now. "They have special electric furnaces meant just for that."

The Imam could see that he had stung me. He turned away

and laughed. "He's lying," he said to the crowd. "They don't burn their dead in the West. They're not an ignorant people. They're advanced, they're educated, they have science, they have guns and tanks and bombs."

"We have them too!" I shouted back at him. I was as confused now as I was angry. "In my country we have all those things too," I said to the crowd. "We have guns and tanks and bombs. And they're better than anything you have – we're way ahead of you."

The Imam could no longer disguise his anger. "I tell you, he's lying," he said. "Our guns and bombs are much better than theirs. Ours are second only to the West's."

"It's you who's lying," I said. "You know nothing about this. Ours are much better. Why, in my country we've even had a nuclear explosion. You won't be able to match that in a hundred years."

So there we were, the Imam and I, delegates from two superseded civilisations vying with each other to lay claim to the violence of the West.

At that moment, despite the vast gap that lay between us, we understood each other perfectly. We were both travelling, he and I: we were travelling in the West. The only difference was that I had actually been there, in person: I could have told him about the ancient English university I had won a scholarship to, about punk dons with safety pins in their mortarboards, about superhighways and sex shops and Picasso. But none of it would have mattered. We would have known, both of us, that all that was mere fluff: at the bottom, for him as for me and millions and millions of people on the land masses around us, the West meant only this – science and tanks and guns and bombs.

And we recognised too the inescapability of these things, their strength, their power – evident in nothing so much as this: that even for him, a man of God, and for me, a student of the "humane" sciences, they had usurped the place of all other languages of argument. He knew, just as I did, that he could no longer say to me, as Ibn Battuta might have when he travelled to India in the fourteenth century: "You should do this or that because it is right or good, or because God wills it so." He could not have said it because that language is dead: those things are no longer sayable; they sound absurd. Instead he had had, of necessity, to use that other language, so universal that it extended equally to him, an old-fashioned village Imam, and great leaders at SALT conferences: he had had to say to me: "You ought not to do this because otherwise you will not have guns and tanks and bombs."

Since he was a man of God his was the greater defeat.

For a moment then I was desperately envious. The Imam would not have said any of those things to me had I been a Westerner. He would not have dared. Whether I wanted it or not, I would have had around me the protective aura of an inherited expertise in the technology of violence. That aura would have surrounded me, I thought, with a sheet of clear glass, like a bulletproof screen; or perhaps it would have worked as a talisman, like a press card, armed with which I could have gone off to what were said to be the most terrible places in the world that month, to gaze and wonder. And then perhaps I too would one day have had enough material for a book which would have had for its epigraph the line, *The horror! The horror!* – for the virtue of a sheet of glass is that it does not require one to look within.

But that still leaves Khamees the Rat waiting on the edge of the square.

In the end it was he and his brothers who led me away from the Imam. They took me home with them, and there, while

Khamees' wife cooked dinner for us – she was not so ill after all – Khamees said to me: "Do not be upset, *ya doktor*. Forget about all those guns and things. I'll tell you what: *I'll* come to visit you in your country, even though I've never been anywhere. I'll come all the way."

He slipped a finger under his skull-cap and scratched his head, thinking hard.

Then he added: "But if I die, you must bury me."

SARA RAI

On Not Writing

"KATHERINE MANSFIELD . . . You will be the Katherine Mansfield of Hindi." My father spoke slowly, placing an emphasis on each word. He seemed to be listening to a voice in his head. "Go on, write it down," he insisted, as though afraid he and I might both forget the ten words if they were not written immediately. His eyes were on my pen as it hesitated above a notebook. Did he really expect me to write that? It was an ordinary day and I still remember it. A crow-pheasant strutted about on the lawn, its tail feathers gleaming black. A dog barked and then there was quiet. I could hear the pressure cooker's whistle from the kitchen at the far back of the house.

He said this in March 1994, a few months before he died. He had recently moved back to our Allahabad home after having lived in Delhi for more than twenty-five years. When he arrived at the Allahabad railway station one winter morning, all he had with him were a few clothes in an old suitcase, an Onida television tied in a check tablecloth, and a sheaf of papers that he held close against his grey zipped-up cardigan, the only one he now possessed. I too had just about returned from Melbourne, where I'd lived the past five years. It was while there that I'd begun to write fiction in Hindi.

My father's hair was uncombed. Clean-shaven all his life, he now had a beard born of negligence. His nails were long and yellow, and a wilderness had taken over his eyes. He had grown senile. He would stand about in doorways, having forgotten what he had come to the room for. After my mother died he stood by her bed and looked at the bunched-up quilt as if he suspected she was underneath it. Never interested in food, he developed a sweet tooth. He ate the rasgullas that were bought for him from Hira Halwai with a focussed pleasure. Afterwards, he wiped his hands on his white dhoti. This was a father I did not know.

When I was in my late teens and still undecided about which language to write in, he told me that the language one is born into, one's mother tongue, can be the only possible medium for creative expression. The irony of his desire to see Katherine Mansfield in me, which would not have escaped him earlier, now escaped him entirely. I had begun writing in Hindi largely because he'd said fiction can only be created in one's mother tongue, and here he was now, setting up a New Zealand-born English writer as an ideal. But looking at the changed person he had become, I could not say this to him.

For most of his life my father, Sripat Rai, had been a Hindi editor and critic. Off and on, he translated writings into English from Hindi. He had also written a few Hindi stories under the pen name Akalank Mehta, but I did not know about these till after he died. I read a couple of them when they were posthumously published in a memorial issue of *Kahani*, the journal he'd edited. I realised how disappointed he must have felt after he wrote them. He was fond of saying that a failed writer becomes a critic. The weight of his literary expectation came, eventually, to rest on me. He seemed happy that I was showing an inclination for writing. "She will go far," he told my mother after reading the first story that I sent him from Melbourne.

My father's pronouncement on the mother tongue stayed with me when I later started writing fiction in Hindi. Another thing that I barely acknowledged even to myself was that I felt something like shame whenever I so much as thought of writing in English. It seemed wrong for a granddaughter of Premchand even to be thinking so. Our family had a certain linguistic pride. I knew that Premchand was famous, but I had not at the time realised the extent of his popularity. In the Hindi class at St Mary's Convent School, where I studied in Allahabad, the teacher would point me out to the other children when we came to the Premchand story, and everyone would turn to look at me. These were moments I dreaded from the beginning of term. And they were only the beginning.

The fact of Premchand, that I was his granddaughter, followed me everywhere. Everyone had a story to tell about their personal engagement with his fiction – the shopkeeper who said she went with a candle to dusty bookracks overhung with cobwebs in a dark and neglected village library in Bihar to find his books; the long-time cook in my father's Delhi house who wept over Premchand's story "Alagyojha" (Divided Hearths) which he read between cooking meals; the cyclist whom my family and I met at a wayside tea stall in Gopiganj, where we had stopped while driving to Varanasi, who recited whole passages from a favourite story. The list was long, for there was practically no-one who had not read something by him that had moved them. However, it was this very ubiquity, the reverence and love that he inspired in people, that made of him something too large for me to comprehend in the early years of my life. It led also to the strange feeling that, without having read him and just by being related to him, I had somehow inhaled his writing. The reading happened much later.

This connection with Premchand was only one of the things

that contributed to my confusion over which language to write in. And the question was never quite settled for me. I had been born into Hindustani, the mix of Hindi and Urdu that we spoke at home. We were forbidden to speak in Hindi at the English-medium school I went to, and transgressions were punished with a fine. We were embarrassed to speak in English at home. I did not know which my first language was. It felt more natural to be speaking in Hindustani, but the books I read were in English. The Hindi textbooks we came across in school, despite containing the rare interesting story, had seen to it that we stayed off Hindi literature for a long time. It was only later, when I was in my twenties and my father needed some help in sifting through the hundreds of stories that were sent for publication to *Kahani*, that I found myself reading Hindi literature. I could write more freely in English, being accustomed to it from school – so much so that in the '90s, when my early stories started appearing in Hindi, someone asked me if I'd drafted them in the Roman script. As a four-year-old I was on the lookout for simple ways to convert Hindi words into English, for I could not speak it yet – *khilao-d, baithao-d, sulao-d* (fed, seated, made to sleep) – as if merely adding a "d" to the Hindi word made it English.

The preoccupation with language went back a long way. The first story I ever wrote was in English, titled "Lucky Horace". I was eight years old and the story was modelled on the Enid Blyton books I'd read when I was very young. Later, in my teens, I had taken to translating into English stories from Hindi, as well as occasionally from Urdu, and some from English into Hindi. I now see that this was all a process of fumbling, of groping for a language that could be my own. I would wake up of a morning and start writing in English, or even come out of a dream in which I saw myself writing in English, much after two of my short-story collections had been published in Hindi. I was in a constant mental state of migration. It was only later, much later, that a startling realisation came to me: it was possible to write in both Hindi and English. One language did not cancel out the other. This had not occurred to me as I flitted from one language to its alternative, my restlessness not finding the necessary repose in either. The situation was further complicated by the Urdu factor. The Hindi taught at school, heavily influenced by Sanskrit, was a punishing, burdened language that we never spoke. What I wrote in, indeed could write in, was Hindustani.

My feeling of being a migrant was not confined to language. I had a sense of self that was transitive at a deeper level. Having become used to reading from an early age, my bookish life set me apart from the people around me, particularly school friends and those I came in contact with outside home. I seemed to be always travelling, from my world of books and the thoughts that they set in motion within me, to the provincial world that was Allahabad. The books I read formed the core of my deeply intimate self, and I wanted to keep it secret. I felt that if I talked about them I would be exposed, as if I'd undressed in public. I was very aware of being a literary and social itinerant, of being in search of a language into which I would some day fit perfectly. I belonged to a middle class that was still colonial and feudal in its attitudes, I had an English-medium education, I wrote fiction in Hindi which connected me to a circle of Hindi readers, but few of my English-educated friends read it. I was constantly moving between languages and from Hindi-reading friends to English-reading ones, or to those who read nothing at all in either language. Adding to the confusion was the Shia Muslim background of my mother and the secular Hindu worldview of my father and the polished Urdu of my grandmother – which on occasion she'd switch to a coarser idiom when speaking to a servant. "Should I wash my ass with this?" I once heard her ask a maid who had brought an insufficient quantity of water for her daily *vazu* before she started her namaaz. The linguistic hotchpotch did not end there. Awadhi was spoken by the servants at home, while at school the German nuns had a clipped English accent and were strict about enunciation, down to the syllable on which the stress should fall.

Even as I write this, I find myself wondering why I felt the need to write about writing at all; and why it is that I choose to do so in English when my fiction is primarily in Hindi. Could it be that I need the perspective of linguistic distance, or is it that some things are better expressed in one language rather than another? To an extent both are true, and yet neither is. Premchand did not write fiction in English. English, however, was the language he often used to draw up the extensive notes that he made before actually writing his stories. Can it be that English has an expressive economy which lends itself better to the conceptualisation and framing of a piece of writing? When I was writing stories based on my experiences of living in places like Allahabad or Delhi, the texture of things around me seemed to get woven more easily on the loom of Hindi. Yet when writing *about* the stories, about the complex process that goes into creating fiction, English was the language that came naturally to me. I had, after all, done most of my reading in it. Suddenly, it all fell into place, for how else is a literary sensibility formed except through reading books in which we experience worlds remote from our daily lives? I was writing about the local, but the lens through which I was looking had been ground by the English language. This was language migration. I was sure it could not be a migration particular to me, for there were many who wrote in Hindi or Marathi or Bangla whose reading was largely of books in English. But I had not read anyone else's account of writerly difficulties of this kind, and so I wondered what someone else would make of mine.

My mother, Zahra Rai, and her sister Moghal Mahmood, both wrote stories that were published in Hindi but which they first set down in Urdu. Both women were as talkative as my father was silent. They were linguistic conspirators who had, as many creative people do, invented a coded language of their own – the addition of an "f" after every consonant – and they used it to shut out the world beyond their own inventions. They would speak very quickly and the "f" sound, occurring so frequently in their speech, gave it a feathery quality, as though a breeze were rustling the leaves of a tamarind or gulmohar tree. The sisters talked all the time about the easy flow and refinement of Urdu and recited couplets to suit every occasion. They found fault with the Urdu used by the poet Faiz, whom they admired greatly, forgiving what they thought were idiomatic errors in his work by seeing him as a part of the unrefined Punjab. They had no doubt that the Urdu spoken in Uttar Pradesh was purer. The balance of a sentence, and the way a line could get "broken" by the use of an undesired word, was something they often spoke about. It strikes me only now, when they have been dead twenty-four years, that the parsing and unravelling, the stitching and unstitching of sentences which the loquacious sisters constantly engaged in, was my first lesson in the use of language.

My father wrote his critical pieces in a Hindi I found difficult to follow. He had spent some years in Calcutta and was a fluent Bangla speaker. If he happened to chance upon people who spoke Bangla, he relished conversing with them in that language, eagerly forsaking his mother tongue, Hindi. Bhojpuri was the dialect he was born into, the one he always spoke with his mother, Shivrani Devi. Whenever anyone from his village of Lamhi turned up, he would, like a fish released from an aquarium, slide into his natural element, into the waters of a river that flowed right back to his childhood. It is perhaps a necessary condition of living in India that one's awareness of language is permeated by a multiplicity of sounds. Anything written in one language must feel the presence of others: this too drew me to Hindi, in which it seemed possible to write by ear, to catch the sound of the spoken. What this meant was that one could use in a story, for instance, snatches of heard conversation that were sometimes in a different dialect or language. So, not only could one change the register in Hindi, but also layer the writing with resonances from other languages.

Writing could also be more easily adapted to the milieu one was dealing with. Speech changed across classes, but the class barrier was not easy for me to cross. English, with its middle-class orientation, seemed even less up to the task. So it seemed to me that writing in English would limit me from the outset. All that constrained the reach of writing in English also made the world beyond middle-class homes inaccessible, for catching a swear word or an exclamation as it flew across the linguistic sky, or a street vendor's cry enriched with layers of cultural memory, was hard enough in Hindi – in English it seemed impossible. Being a woman writer excluded me from other experiences that, had I been a man, I could have taken for granted. For instance, it would be difficult for me to walk around a provincial North Indian town at night, to see it while it slept. It is often the case in the hinterland that women are not visible and treated as if not there at all, especially if accompanied by a man, to whom all that is said is addressed. And yet, paradoxically, a woman in the same situation is also *too* visible, instantly noticed, stared at. It would be hard for someone not used to local norms in Allahabad to understand how the presence of a woman at a *paan* shop, for example, can make other customers as well as the shopkeeper uncomfortable. Women eat *paan* at home, but they are not expected to be seen at *paan* shops where men hang about discussing local politics and the little incidents that make up the life of a small town. So a chance for the ear to tune into the colloquial, the fine gradations of street-speak, the hum and buzz of the everyday, is lost.

But at the time I started writing I did not think clearly about all this. I only worked with an intuitive understanding of writing and what it involved. It seemed to be just something that one did, that one fell into. I had realised even as a child, though without verbalising it, that this was what I would be doing. There was just the problem of being able to begin. That was where the difficulty lay. Certain difficulties with vocabulary had to be kept in mind while writing – the cultural specificity attached to names, to caste, class, and regional backgrounds, for instance. Mr Srinivasan or Mrs Gupta or Mrs Kashyap or Mr Jhunjhunwala needed their particular background, their speech, moulded to a different geography of palate and tongue; their food, their style of dressing would have to be shown as authentically *theirs*. A talking parrot in a Shia Muslim or a Sunni Muslim or a Hindu Kayastha household would each speak in a distinguishable accent.

It was more than a question of choosing one language above another. I had led a rather privileged life in Allahabad, where the bungalows were far apart and there were few people to interact with. There was no class of society that I could honestly say I knew well. I was on an island and almost its sole inhabitant. Instinct told me that a writer lived within me, but it appeared that the writer had neither the material to write about nor the language to write it in. In all the years that I spent not writing, there was ample time to think – about words, their interactions with other words. And while I was fumbling to find my voice I realised that the Sanskrit-derived Hindi word *shabd* meant both "word" and "sound". This seemed serendipitous to me. The first time I learnt about its two meanings, the word drew for me a connection between written language and language that was only sound. The creaking of the wheels of a bullock-cart in Chhattisgarh, on which I once chanced to take a ride; the hollow sound of a hand-pump being worked; the whistle of a train engine – these were part of a language of sound that did not lead to further meaning. It was simply itself. Somehow this had implications for me as a writer. It occurred to me that the double meaning of *shabd* created for me a bridge between the heard and the written, that the craft of writing is auditory as much as it is visual, that a sentence or a paragraph, when it is written, must be heard as well as seen.

On the morning when he made his memorable Katherine Mansfield declaration, my father and I were sitting on the front verandah. The ground outside was sodden, the air saturated with moisture. It had been raining, though it was not the rainy season. The Mary Palmer growing right outside the verandah had pink and white blossoms. The rain had shaken loose the flowers and they had collected in the shallow water-race that ran round the house, looking profuse yet forlorn. Termites had been silently eating the books in the glass-fronted bookshelf in the drawing room that opened out onto the verandah. The spines were intact, but the pages had been hollowed out in the shape of ridges and terraces. I had spread the books out on the verandah floor, their leaves open, to let them breathe. There were a lot of books. Most of them were my father's, left behind in the Allahabad house when he'd moved to Delhi; he had given away the ones he had there. There was Oscar Wilde's *De Profundis*, a battered illustrated *Arabian Nights*, the Everyman's Library edition published in 1929 of Abbé Prévost's *Manon Lescaut* and Prosper Mérimée's *Carmen*, the *Collected Stories of Katherine Mansfield*, and two of the twelve volumes of *Remembrance of Things Past*, published by Chatto and Windus in 1941, with my father's name, the date and place where he'd bought the books written on the fly-leaf in his decorative hand – May 9, 1946, Lahore. The bright orange dust jacket of a collection of Proust's writings, chosen and translated by Gerard Hopkins, had been eaten away. What was left of the book crumbled first into paper flakes and then to dust when I tried to leaf through it. The fat volume of *Gitobitan*, containing the songs of Rabindranath Tagore, was intact, as was the English translation of Premchand's *Godaan* by Gordon Roadarmel, published as *The Gift of a Cow* by Allen and Unwin in 1968. My father stood in the midst of these books like a battle-weary king looking at his ruined palace. Some of the books that lay open on the verandah – *Treasure Island* and *Alice in Wonderland* among them – were the ones I had grown up reading. The books in the drawing room were housed in two shelves with sliding glass fronts and in two teakwood cupboards. The cupboards were built into the wall on either side of a blocked-up fireplace whose mantelpiece was of pale pink terrazzo. The doors of the cupboards tended to get stuck. When pulled open, there arose from inside a smell of fresh varnish, even though it was years since the painters had finished their job.

As a child I had developed a fascination for the written word, regardless of where I saw it. I read train timetables, dictionaries, cinema hoardings, and shop signs. Allahabad's roads had signposts with their names on them – Thornhill, Clive, Elgin, Hastings, Edmonstone – and each name seemed to have a distinctive colour and shape. I read the graffiti on the exposed brick walls that we passed on the slow train journeys that we took between Allahabad and Benares, or between Allahabad and Delhi. My eye caught the names of the stations, written in black on a sunflower-yellow background in three languages, Hindi, English, and Urdu: Handia, Jangiganj, Kachhwa Road, Madhosingh, Raja Talab, Manduadih. The names stayed in my visual memory long after the train reached its destination. It was while travelling through the bookish landscape which I first became acquainted with in my childhood that I made an extraordinary discovery. All the books were about me. They were set in locations thousands of miles away – St Petersburg, London, New York, Paris, or Rouen – and yet they spoke of things that I could have said. This was something that stirred me into restless excitement. Could I create a fictional world of my own? Many years later, while reading Proust's essay "Days of Reading", I came to understand how inextricably reading and writing are linked:

> The lazy mind can get nothing from pure solitude because it is incapable, unaided, of getting its creative activity to work . . . What, then, is needed is some sort of intervention, which, though it may come from elsewhere, does stir the requisite consciousness in ourselves, an impulse [that] has its origin outside ourselves but [is] received into the very centre of our personal loneliness. This . . . is the true definition of reading, and it fits no other activity.

The books that I read also led me to put on a certain weary pose, a kind of melancholic despairing stance that I associated with Kafka which, given my circumstances, was quite absurd. In my bookish life, the characters and landscapes in the novels that

I read were more real than the people we actually met. It was an imaginative world inhabited by fictive characters and their milieu, and it became a barrier between me and the world I lived in. No-one else seemed to care about books or writing, and I was not interested in the things that mattered to them. The questions that plagued me ("Will I ever be able to write? And if not, what then?") would have sounded laughable to them. At the age of twenty, I wrote in my diary:

> One needs to be alone to write. If you want to write, there is just one way – write. Acquire the habit of writing. Only when this initial stage is crossed does the eye become discerning and the brain perceptive. It is impossible that I can go on like this much longer. Dreaming, struggling to stop dreaming, and also to give expression to the many voices in my brain. Writing has become a question of life and death.

But as things stood, I spent years searching for the writer in me who was nowhere to be seen. It was like having a star-crossed lover. The writer and I could never meet. I would look at the shape of my hands to see if they looked like a writer's. I stared into my eyes in the mirror, wondering if they would reveal to me the writer that I was convinced I was, though there was little evidence to support the idea. When my father asked me to write down his words about Katherine Mansfield, one of my Hindi short-story collections had already been published. But that was where my writing aspirations seemed to have ended. I had not written a thing in months. And here was my father, asking me to do something more than just writing those words down. Something too large for me to grasp, something that I kept trying to escape from and that kept escaping from me, slipping through my fingers like glittering particles of mica. I wanted to hold on to it even as I wanted to flee from it.

My flight from the act of writing fiction went on for years. I could not face it; I thought that writing was all about not writing. After my father died, I wrote in my story "Biyabaan Mein" (In the Wilderness) about the struggle of writing fiction:

> I try to write. I want to focus my attention on writing. But my mind is empty like the sky that stretches in front of me. Sometimes groups of broken sentences, indistinct faces, the rags of days long past move across my mind in a procession. I am unable to grasp the forms and mould them into something that is whole. The images fly away into the sky like birds.

It took me a long time to realise that the process of writing begins much before one has put anything down, that one has, so to speak, always been writing. It was while chasing butterflies in the garden as a child or watching a tortoise-shell cat slink away into a dark alley that the writing was taking place. Like an invisible letter written with lime juice that only shows up when a hot iron is put to it, the impressions that have been written on to the memory all the while that life is being lived are revealed in the catalysing moment when pen meets paper. The city buried underground and long forgotten about is chanced upon, and not without a shock of surprise.

And so it was that, years after the house of my childhood had slipped into oblivion, I found myself writing: "Suddenly there was an army of mice in the house. Signs of their presence could be found in all the rooms, and especially in the storeroom. The scraps of nibbled paper, the pieces of roti, the mouse droppings inside the cupboards, under the chairs and behind the black iron trunk, were evidence of their being around."

When I wrote those words, the colour of the light from

that buried time, the clinking sound of the bunch of keys that my mother carried tucked into her sari, the whole breathing quality of the house as it was then, came back to me as though the past could never quite be past.

Recently, I found the ten words that had been uttered by my father almost twenty-five years ago, written in the orange notebook I had been using at the time, the long letters sloping to the left, the handwriting uncertain.

MUKUL KESAVAN

The Ugliness of the Indian Male

SOME YEARS AGO I was struck by the contrast between the beauty of Hindi film heroines and the ugliness of Hindi film heroes. After researching the matter I concluded that the explanation was straightforward: leading men in Hindi films were ugly because they were Indian men and Indian men were measurably uglier than Indian women. You don't have to take my word for it: cursory surveys of marriages, *morchas*, classrooms, offices, and homes will bear out this observation.

While my observation was accurate and the data I had gathered reliable, I made the mistake of attributing the ugliness of the Indian male to nature. I know now that Indian men aren't born ugly: they achieve ugliness through practice. It is their habits and routines that make them ugly. If I was to be schematic, I'd argue that Indian men are ugly on account of the three Hs: hygiene, hair, and horrible habits.

Let's start with their extremities. Examine the nails of any Indian man: the cuticles will be yellow with *haldi* and the underside of the bitten-off tip will be spotty with accumulated dirt. When you think of where they put those nails, this is not surprising. I've seen respectable men conducting conversations with their index fingers two-digits deep in their nostrils, digging with industrial enthusiasm. If you ever see a *desi* man delicately rubbing the tip of his index finger over the pad of his thumb, beware. Don't go near him: he's rolling the bogies he's mined into little balls. He uses those same fingers to adjust himself in public. All Indian men do this, without exception. The refined ones do it furtively, but the majority do it openly without shame or embarrassment. A famous Indian batsman does this regularly with the butt end of his bat handle under the gaze of thousands of spectators. You can't do this and be good-looking, you really can't. You could be John Abraham (an exception to our ugly rule) and your looks wouldn't survive this particular habit. And if it isn't the thumb and forefinger it's the pinkie inserted into the ear and vibrated with manic vigour. This generally comes with eye-rolling and little oinks of pleasure. You'll never see women doing this, only men. It's an important route to ugliness.

The sounds they make are crucial to the unattractiveness of Indian men. For example, an Indian man with a cold will, in company, try to snort up the congestion and swallow it. He'll do it over and over again, completely unaware of the revulsion it causes. When he eats, there's another repertoire of sounds born of the fact that subcontinental men don't keep their lips together while chewing. If you think this doesn't apply to you because you keep your mouth shut while processing food, you're wrong. A second before swallowing, you part your lips and swipe your tongue over your palate, to juice the last taste out of the morsel, and you make a sucking noise. If you want to test this out, use grapes: they generate the slurpiest sounds.

Hair habits do even more to intensify the ugliness of Indian men than the sounds they involuntarily make. Statistically, some ninety per cent of all South Asian men wear moustaches: their masculinity seems to be critically dependent on this growth. I don't mean the beard-cum-moustaches style, which is respectable, but the standalone moustache. Even here, a bushy, Zapata-style moustache has something going for it, but the styles Indian men favour are (a) the twirled moustache; and

(b) the little trimmed one. The first makes its host ridiculous, the second makes him look like a harried clerk or, if the hair has been trimmed into a thin line, like a sexual predator.

Middle-aged men improve on this by dyeing their hair a radiant black, then letting their roots show. Or, like General Musharraf, they will dye the hair on top of their heads but leave their sideburns grey because they've read somewhere that this makes them look distinguished. It doesn't: it makes them look like unreliable car dealers.

Indian men wear badly because they look into magic mirrors that hide the changes middle-age brings. For example, they don't notice the hair growing out of their nostrils in little tufts and consequently don't trim it. Even worse, the hair bristling out of their ears in great wiry jets is invisible to them because their narcissism is so complete, so proofed against reality, that what they see in the mirror is not their reflection but a favourite photograph taken twenty years and twenty kilos ago.

But speaking for myself, the oddest aspect of the Indian man is the things he's willing to wear, and I'm not talking about his dress sense because that would need a book. I'm talking, for example, about the thick bands of rotting pink threads that North Indian men wear around their wrists. I'm sure there's some respectable ritual reason that requires them to keep these threads on till they discolour and fall off, but why would you change your clothes every day if you're willing to wear something that you sweat into for weeks?

Then there's their keenness on necklaces. Not one, but as many as they can wear. Not content with doing this, they leave the top buttons of their shirts unbuttoned so you can see that tangled jumble of amulets and gold chains and lockets. Sreesanth and Ganguly wear so many that they look like shady trinket vendors.

Any inventory of the ways in which Indian men achieve ugliness has to include their relationship with rings. We're not talking about nice rings, say a discreet wedding band, but cheap rings with coloured stones in tarnished silver settings worn on every finger of both hands, not excluding thumbs. Since the average Indian man's fingers aren't long and slender, the net effect is one of sausages banded with metal.

Why are Indian men like this? How do they achieve the bullet-proof unselfconsciousness that allows them to be so abandonedly ugly? I think it comes from a sense of entitlement that's hard-wired into every male child that grows up in an Indian household. That, and the not unimportant fact that, despite the way they look, they're always paired off with good-looking women.

RAMACHANDRA GUHA

The Coconuts of Bengal: Brown Men, White Affinities

BACK IN THE 1970s, a group of political scientists advanced the theory that India was a "multinational" state rather than a simple "nation-state". It was said that like the Soviet Union the Republic of India was an artifice of history, the product of accident rather than of willed circumstance, an unhappy and unstable coalition of different nationalities forced to cohabit by a strong state. There, the Leninists had brought together Ukrainians, Latvians, Georgians and others under the control of a dominant nationality, the Russians. Here, the British and the Congress had forced the Bengalis, Andhras, Tamils and others to accept political union with, and political subjugation to, the Hindi-speaking nation.

I was reminded of this theory when, in July 1995, I visited Nirad Chaudhuri at his Oxford home. For two hours we spoke – rather, Chaudhuri spoke and I listened – about English literature, English crockery, English monarchs, English wars and French wines. Just before I left the telephone rang. The lady attending to the great little writer picked up the phone and told him it was his son calling, from "desh". Desh, not ghar; homeland, that is, not home. Other clues – for instance, his preference (a sensible one!) for *maccher jhol* over fish and chips – led me to conclude that Nirad Babu had two distinct nationalities, Bengali and English.

A friend of mine once described Nirad Chaudhuri as the President for Life of the Coconut Club of Bengal. The members of this (in Calcutta, at any rate) well-subscribed club were, like the coconut and Chaudhuri, brown on the surface and white within, Bengali by birth but English by habit and taste. In truth, the brown sometimes seeped into the skin, for the *bhadralok* intellectual would not wholly disavow his roots. Even when he studied at Oxford or declaimed Shakespeare, a part of his soul remained pledged to Bengal. This was true of Nirad Babu, and this was also true of roughly a million others. In this respect at least the writer who thought he stood alone was wholly representative of his time and class.

As a young man, Chaudhuri knew the Mother Country only from afar, but sons and daughters of better-heeled families were sent there to study. Once upon a time, it was not enough to take a PhD in history or chemistry from Dhaka or Calcutta; one had to obtain a second doctorate from Oxford or Cambridge. Meanwhile, the less scholarly minded *bhadralok* went to Oxbridge to get a BA, or qualified for the bar from the Inner Temple or Lincoln's Inn. These journeymen effortlessly fused English ways with Bengali ones, practising and promoting their dual nationality. On their return, they would appear suited and booted in the office but stay *dhoti-punjabied* at home. They would waltz when in the club but tunefully sing the works of Nazrul Islam in their *bari*.

A significant minority of these Coconuts converted to Communism while still in England. Thus they abandoned one foreign allegiance for another, Mother England for Father Russia. These turncoats included such well-known figures as Susobhan Sarkar, Hiren Mukherjee, Nikhil Chakravarty, and Jyoti Basu. However, one part of their self remained unchanged. That is, the *bhadralok* communist adopted a new foreign master without abandoning his language, literature, and cuisine. Just as one did not have to cross the *kaala paani* to be Bengali and English, one did not have to leave Calcutta to become Bengali and Russian. Some of the finest *bhadralok* film-makers, thinkers and writers of the post-Second World War era have displayed a pathetic loyalty to the Soviet Union. A Calcutta scholar of my acquaintance, an educationist of distinction now in his late sixties, once told me of his visit to the Party headquarters during the time of Stalin's last illness, in 1953. There he joined the ranks of his anxious comrades, all scanning the news communicated by telex and telegraph from the Kremlin, their Vatican. When the message came that Stalin had breathed his last, recalled this scholar, he felt more lonely than when his own father had died.

Three years later, Stalin's successor announced that the Father to generations of Bengalis was actually the greatest mass murderer in human history. The educationist, to his credit, left the Communist Party of India, and has retained a sturdily independent existence ever since. Numerous other *bhadralok* denounced Khruschev's "revelations" – revelations known to the non-communist world for decades – as bourgeois lies.

There was also a section that went in search of a substitute fatherland. The Soviet Union now stood exposed as a land of grisly Gulags, but there might yet be a Communist Utopia someplace else. A good proportion of the renegades settled on China, whose Chairman, it was suggested, was actually our Chairman too. Others, who could not ignore the casualty lists of the Great Leap Forward and the Great Proletarian Cultural Revolution, went looking for more exotic locations. And so there are activists and artists who have been Bengali and Russian, Bengali and Chinese, Bengali and Cuban, Bengali and Vietnamese, and Bengali and Albanian.

All told, the Bengali has shown a keener and more durable interest in other cultures than, for example, the Marathi or the Tamil. The foreign nationality might change, but not the native one. Thus, Satyajit Ray was at one point in his life both Bengali and British, but at another point, Bengali and French. (With the emergence of the EU, Ray, were he alive now, would perhaps be considered Bengali and European.) More recently, the collapse of the Berlin Wall and China's march down the capitalist road has caused some surprising shifts of allegiance. The United States of America, the Great Satan, the country so massively demonised in Bengali literature, art and cinema, has become an alternative homeland for numerous *bhadralok* thinkers. Emblematic here is the case of the Subaltern Studies project, the movement of new historical writing which was originally inspired, back in 1981–2, by the Collected Works of Chairman Mao. Within a decade, the project had been laid to rest in the universities of Chicago and Columbia. The very historians who were once Bengali and Chinese have now become Bengali and American.

From one point of view, this unique blending of nationalities could be called cosmopolitanism, illustrating a rare and untypical interest in ideas and movements originating outside India or, indeed, outside Asia. Moreover, the *bhadralok* dual national has embraced a foreign culture while holding steadfast to this own – he (and she) is a rooted cosmopolitan. From another point of view, however, this must be seen as a form of parochialism – as a characteristically Bengali lack of interest in other parts of this land. Thus, a well-regarded scholar who lives in Calcutta will not visit New Delhi, which he dismisses as "that imperial city". However, he is happy enough to spend half the year in New York.

Perhaps one man's internationalism is another man's chauvinism. And perhaps the last *bhadralok* thinker to be both Bengali and Indian was Rabindranath Tagore.

The first section of this essay was earlier published in that respectable *bhadralok* paper of Calcutta, the *Telegraph*. It was intended to provoke, and it did. The letters I received in response were a charming mix of approval and dismissal. I was accused of being a self-hating Bengali, or (if the writer in question knew that my surname actually conceals a Tamil identity) of being a professional "Bong-basher". "Have you ever seen anyone from Tamilnadu or Maharashtra derogating their own people in public," asked one correspondent. "Don't Tamils go in a herd to the US for IT jobs," asked another. These critics at least had the courage (and courtesy) to use their own names, unlike the two letter-writers who sought to hide themselves under those authentically Bengali titles, "Gabbar Singh" and "M.O. Gambo".

The most damaging criticism came from a lady who pointed out that "if you take a survey of the people who leave their homes on a regular basis either to travel around the country or to work elsewhere you will find Bengalis topping the list." She then quoted from a letter written by her son, in temporary exile in Scotland: "Late last night I was looking at the map and suddenly the tremendous romance of these places hit me once again: Peshawar, Aligarh, Allahabad, Meerut, Ambala. I will return I know for sure, and soon. I want to see Sasaram too." This was a salutary reminder, and indeed while writing my article I was not unmindful of the Bengali penchant for travel, as witness the bus companies and special railway compartments reserved exclusively for their journeys to temple towns and historic sites. I have an enduring memory of a cold bus ride up to Naini Tal with a Bengali tourist, dressed in shirt and chappals, his conversation periodically interspersed, as gusts of snow-laden air hit us, with a flick of the cigarette and an expressive "Ai, *shala!*" My *Telegraph* essay, however, did not really deal with these patrons of Kundu and other Travels; rather, it focused on the cultural aristocracy of Bengal, the writers and scholars and film-makers whose journeys, both mundane and imaginative, have generally been made overseas.

One correspondent, agreeing with me, succinctly suggested that for the Bengali dual national "the rest of India is a geographical obsolescence. Dum Dum connects straight to JFK or Heathrow." Juxtaposing this endorsement with the chastisements, I thought I should perhaps reformulate my thesis as follows: the ordinary folk of Bengal, the *sadharan lok*, are genuinely interested in other parts of India; the self-proclaimed intellectual, hardly ever. This amended thesis finds confirmation from the remarks and comments of other correspondents. One asked how I could forget the renaming of Calcutta, that Marxist-inspired act of linguistic chauvinism. He then recalled how the dismantling of a statue outside the KGB headquarters in Moscow had brought forth an instant rebuke from the Chairman of the Left Front: "We condemn this act of disrespect to Comrade Dzerzhinsky who is one of the greatest Marxists of all time."

Other writers amplified the theme of *bhadralok* hypocrisy. I was told of the romantics who wished to merge Bangladesh and West Bengal into a "Sonar Bangla", but who would not care to travel to the eastern side, while happy enough to exchange a comfortable life in Kolkata for a more comfortable life in London. Another correspondent passed on a delightful story of how the eminent historian Irfan Habib was once introduced at a public meeting by a *bhadralok* communist: not by his books, nor even by the length of his party membership, but by how he was linked by descent to the most sophisticated of Indian Muslim families, the Tyabjis.

Finally, there were those letter-writers who argued that my thesis, even if valid, really applied to the past. The question I should have addressed more directly was this: how would Bengalis fare in the homogenising and globalising world of the twenty-first century? One writer to the newspaper felt that they were indeed already "fast shedding or disguising their Bengaliness in an attempt to internationalise themselves." On the other hand, an economist friend believed that their history of rooted cosmopolitanism would stand them in good stead. The Bengalis, he perceptively remarked, were "actually survivors and the ones who can do so in new and hostile environments are those who can adapt." They had become coconuts – white inside, brown outside – to better cope with British rule. This ability to retain elements of your own culture while absorbing elements of another, suggested the economist, was a "special case of the general theory of adaptability that we are increasingly going to see in a borderless world."

Altogether the most curious letter came from a South Indian who claimed that the *bhadralok* "were merely self-deprecating slaves of some foreign master or the other, whether British, Russian or Chinese. All of them deserve to be held in the most profound contempt by all self-respecting people." For this correspondent, "a 'rooted cosmopolitan' can exist only in the imagination." Further correspondence revealed him to be an admirer of Bal Thackeray and Nathuram Godse, and the upholder of a chauvinism so extreme that even Gandhi was suspect for the sin of respecting the human rights of minorities.

I would recommend, to this gentleman in particular but also to all readers who might not have seen it, a book titled *The Mahatma and the Poet* published by the National Book Trust.

Edited by Sabyasachi Bhattacharya, this contains the complete correspondence between the two greatest modern Indians. Better than anything else I have seen, this exchange reveals both the perils and promise of what I have here termed "rooted cosmopolitanism". For, more urgently than ever before, the world we now live in forces us to declare our cultural affiliation – or affiliations. We really have only three choices: to reject everything "foreign" (as the Hindu and Muslim chauvinists prescribe); to unthinkingly absorb everything "foreign" (as American advertisers ask us to do); or to work out an honourable accommodation between cultures, thus to discard what is useless or reactionary in "ours" while absorbing what is genuinely useful or progressive in "theirs". In this vital and profoundly challenging exercise there can be no better – and still relevant – guides than the Gujarati-patriot-internationalist Gandhi, and the *bhadralok*-Indian-world citizen Tagore.

SUNIL KHILNANI

Gandhi's Styled Life

"MY WRITINGS SHOULD BE cremated with my body," Gandhi said in 1937, "What I have done will endure, not what I have said or written." It's an intriguing statement, especially coming from a devoted writer and speaker, someone whose collected words amount to a hundred printed volumes: and it underlines Gandhi's belief that his greatest political text is in fact his life.

Gandhi understood his life as an enactment of his thought. In the decades after his visit to London in 1909, when he delved into the world of clandestine Indian revolutionaries and plotters of terror and assassination, Gandhi made a point of living his own life without secrecy. No part of it was reserved from public view. In the communal life of his ashrams, during his times in prison, in his incessant correspondence and daily discourses, in his regular reports on his own doings in his newspapers and journals, and in the chapters of his autobiography, in his every gesture and action, he opened his life up to the scrutiny of others, invited them in – not just to his study, but to his kitchen, bedroom, and even his toilet. All could watch his doings, track his habits, eavesdrop: fellow Indians, both elite and poor; the British; and the world at large. Gandhi *wanted* his entire life to be observed, listened in on, like the Reality TV characters who nowadays populate our cultural landscape. But Gandhi's purpose was not to vault to minor celebritydom. It was to challenge himself, and others. He wanted to see if he could indeed achieve the self-mastery that he had urged in *Hind Swaraj*.

He wrote, "A portion of the whole theory of life described in *Hind Swaraj* is . . . being carried into practice," a practice which he insisted had nothing reserved or secret about it. Gandhi was, though, a careful stylist of his life, organising the haphazard trivia of his daily actions into formal order, to give them a shape and meaning. He was in pursuit of a unity of thought and action, theory and practice.

George Orwell, one of Gandhi's most insightful critics, and temperamentally distant from the Indian leader, was struck by the tensed, pageant-like character of Gandhi's life, his capacity to turn his deeds into parables of meaning. He observed, rightly, that Gandhi's "whole life was a sort of pilgrimage in which every act was significant."

Gandhi's artful choreography of daily living, intriguing in itself, is still more so because it was at the heart of his remarkable political achievement. The accessibility of his life, his candour about his flaws and his strivings to fix them made him not a minor celebrity but a major one in the eyes of the Indian masses. They were scattered across the vast subcontinent, unable to read the words or to follow the speechifying of high politics. Gandhi helped create for them a political world they could inhabit. He made powerless Indians believe that they had it in their ability to change themselves and, together, the world. It's a conception still alive in India's democratic politics today, where the poor and those in the countryside have among the highest levels of participation in elections, and are the ones who have deepest faith in politics as a means to improve their life-chances.

Gandhi's connection to the masses was not a born one but a made one. His background wasn't as privileged as that of some

Indian political leaders – for instance Nehru – yet it could hardly be said to be humble. Gandhi's father was a high functionary in a princely state, and Gandhi himself had studied at the Bar in London; he had lived in South Africa for two decades and had held down a successful legal career. But Gandhi understood, as no other Indian did, the need to transform politics from its existing image and routines – to chase politics out from the world of wood-panelled debating halls filled with men in stiff collars and too-tight shoes reciting purple bombast, and into the open, dusty air. He wanted to build, over the labyrinths of the powerful, the world of secret chambers and corridors sound-proofed against popular voice and hopes, a public space where the people could assemble, and come to see themselves as makers of their world.

In a society such as India, the ordinary masses were doubly excluded from the language of power. Literacy was the exclusive preserve of the Brahminic upper castes, and English was restricted to a still more elite circle within that. Gandhi saw the limitations of trying to convey political meaning through discursive means, or even through books like *Hind Swaraj*, with their lucid, unadorned style. And so he turned his own self, his small body, and all its attendant habits – into a language that could speak even before he himself had uttered a word.

His manner of dressing was one such silent signal to the masses. He spent months after his return to India in 1915 devising his headgear, trying turbans in all styles, before inventing the Gandhi cap. He practised his movements and gestures – the stoop, the arm over the shoulder, the cross-legged spinning. He thought out his way of speaking – in a low voice, sitting (in contrast to the populist demagogues at work in Europe). He gave ordinary Indians an idiom that was both intensely individual and one that they could make sense of.

Gandhi's dietary "crankisms" (as he called them), his sexual anxieties and habits, his bowel rhythms, fevers and black moods, his prayers, spinning, and walks, the drinking of a glass of orange juice to break a fast, gathering up a handful of dusty salt, even his silences themselves: these became sources of rumour, legend and inspiration among the masses. To his professed dismay, many Indians took him to be a messianic spiritual figure, a performer of miracles, possessor of superhuman qualities. Others, for instance those who plotted his death, read his idiosyncratic, crafted self as an insult to Brahminic strictures, and an unforgivable disruption to the hierarchies of the Hindu social order.

His disturbance of social order was wilful. In a fine subversion of the principle of Jeremy Bentham's panopticon, the original low-cost public prison, Gandhi saw that by exposing himself to constant public surveillance he might shake free of the stifling superstitions of Indian society. He desired, just as much, to escape the oppressive conformities of the modern world, in order to rule himself, to achieve Swaraj.

In opening his life to public view, Gandhi was not displaying a finished product. Rather, he showed the life of Swaraj to be one of constant testing of the individual's capacity for truth. He considered his life a series of "experiments". "The Story of my Experiments with Truth" was how he entitled his autobiography, and in it he revealed the extent of his compulsive self-tests. In dance and in householding, in education, washing and laundry, in healing and medicine, in hygiene, politics, in earth and water treatment, in friendship, in communal living, in sexual relations, and of course in truth. "I wore out my body experimenting," Gandhi tells his reader. But through such experiments, Gandhi came to confront and master his own shame and fears.

In the autobiography, he's frank about the breadth of his crippling anxiety and his fears. We feel his unease at nightfall and darkness; when he has to socialise with the Indian elite; when trying to make his career as lawyer; and perhaps most painfully, in the everyday routines of life. Buying a train ticket, travelling, puzzling over how to dress himself, even when walking down a street – all are liable to induce terror in Gandhi.

One of his greatest fears, he recounts, is the prospect of speaking – at school, on board ship, before the courts of law, even when, already a political personage, he was called to address the Congress. Even when he became a national leader and an international figure, he went to great lengths to manage and control his public appearances and events. He issued exact instructions about the pandals or platforms at which he was to speak, as well as specifications for crowd control. He would tell his audiences the behaviour he expected of them. They didn't always obey.

As he made his self public, Gandhi was a master self-publicist to match. Take for instance how he stage-managed his political campaigns. Perhaps the most famous of these was the Dandi March, the world-famous climax to the Salt Satyagraha that Gandhi led in the spring of 1930. He liked to describe as intuitive the decision to set off on the long walk to the sea, in order to make salt in defiance of what he saw as an unjust British salt tax. But he meticulously planned every aspect of the trek.

Gandhi took an ancient practice, the pilgrimage march, and reinvented it for the modern media age. Seventy-nine marchers accompanied him, each screened and personally selected – and a small enough number for him to personally manage. Gandhi wanted a representative of each part of the country. Moreover, he wanted marchers who were dedicated but relatively unknown – so that the focus of attention would remain on Gandhi himself. Their outfits were carefully designed (no political ensignia or markings were allowed), and Gandhi made sure that he was the only one to carry a *lathi*, or stick. He dispatched his lieutenants in advance, to gather the support of townspeople and villagers on his route. For the world media was coming along, and he wanted to minimise the unexpected.

Gandhi made very careful arrangements with the media. In the weeks before the march, he invited journalists, Indian and foreign, to his ashram on the banks of the Sabarmati river, allowing them to write up not only his public prayer meetings, but his private conversations with visitors and ashram members – which they published in reports across the world. The prayer meetings themselves became moments of high drama, with Gandhi telling his listeners that for the marchers this would be their last fight, while in the audience, mill owners mingled with the poor and lower castes. Most importantly, Gandhi – remember him as the critic of technology in *Hind Swaraj*? – invited several photographers and three film crews to accompany him on his march. They did so, in motorcars: and the jiggly footage they shot of Gandhi's fast-paced walk (he would speed up at certain strategic points) would be seen on cinema screens across the world. The image of the Mahatma, striding across the dusty plains leading his band of followers, was now burned into the imaginations of millions – the stick man showing up the imperial blimps.

Gandhi knew: when beliefs changed, in India and across the globe, empires would fall.

The political magic he was able to orchestrate around an event like the Dandi March – part charisma, part mental and physical rigour, part canny manipulation – was not a one-off, a kind of Obama lightning flash on the way to winning personal political power. Gandhi was able to sustain his ability to bring enchantment to politics for decades – not just the duration of an election campaign. And he used this gift to free his country.

This capacity to enchant had its enemies, of course – and not only among the British. Gandhi's assassin, Nathuram Godse, was a man profoundly influenced by the ideas of Savarkar, the young terrorist and ideologue of Hindu nationalism whom Gandhi had met and argued with in Highgate in the autumn of 1909. Godse was incensed by how, as if by magic, Gandhi's life and willpower could mobilise hundreds of millions of people. In his statement at the murder trial, Godse railed against Gandhi's "childish insanities and obstinacies", his "eccentricities, whimsicality, metaphysics and primitive vision." These qualities, along with "a most severe austerity of life, ceaseless work and lofty character," Godse went on, had made Gandhi "formidable and irresistible," the dominant force in the Congress Party and Indian politics.

Gandhi made himself the sole judge "of everyone and everything; he was the master brain guiding the civil disobedience movement," Godse raged on. "No other could know the technique of that movement. The movement might succeed or fail . . . but that could make no difference to the Mahatma's infallibility."

In the weeks before Godse did his deed, there had been several attempts on Gandhi's life – including, just ten days earlier, a bomb explosion at one of his Delhi prayer meetings. Gandhi knew there was a conspiracy, yet he refused extra precautions. He told those assembled at his prayer meetings that, even if a bomb were thrown into their midst, they must not budge. "I want to keep saying the name of Rama, even if there is shooting around me." And that is exactly what he did when, on the evening of 30 January 1948, Godse shot him dead.

Nehru marked with the right words Gandhi's exit from the world, after almost eight decades of painstaking, ingenious, world-changing life: "Even in his death there was a magnificence and a complete artistry," Nehru wrote. "It was from every point of view a fitting climax to the man and to the life he had lived."

SHOHINI GHOSH

Sky Above and Grass Below

In the year 2003 I was invited to a dinner at Delhi's India International Centre. I came face to face with a woman my age and began talking. We both agreed that we found each other very familiar and yet couldn't recall where we had met. Were we in the same school? No, we weren't. Were we in the same college? No, we weren't. Had we met when studying abroad? Certainly not. Then where had we met? "I know for a fact that we have met before," she said. There was something uncannily familiar about her, so I said, "I know that we have spent a lot of time together." Then, suddenly, it fell into place and we both asked, "Did you play cricket in Bibekananda Park?"

"Of course, I did!" we both exclaimed. "So that's where we met!"

In the 1970s and early 1980s I grew up in Hindustan Park, a neighbourhood in South Calcutta. My mother had spent many of her growing-up years in Hindustan Park, so my sister and I had heard of this place even before we moved into it from North Calcutta. Hindustan Park became much better known when Jyoti Basu, whose house was centrally located in the area, became chief minister of West Bengal. As he consolidated his position in successive elections, the house became bigger and the various hangers-on around the premises acquired an air of self-importance. The rapid transformation of the house led one wit to write graffiti on the walls that read:

Opore bhara, neechey bhara
Moddhye khane shorbohaara

Which, roughly translated, reads:

With a tenant upstairs and a tenant downstairs
Lives in between, the proletariat.

Hindustan Park was the target of both anger and envy for the rest of Calcutta because, as part of a VIP neighbourhood, we rarely suffered power cuts. So, during the city's worst experience of "load shedding", Hindustan Park was an idyllic pool of light in a city of literal darkness.

One day, I came home and told my mother that one of my girl friends had said I shouldn't be wearing boyish clothes all the time. My wardrobe was all wrong, she had said. My mother said, "They have not heard of tomboys? Don't you remember George from Enid Blyton's Famous Five? Tell them you are a tomboy." Then Pratima-di, my neighbour downstairs, told me, "Don't be silly and call yourself a boy. You can be a girl and still do all the things that boys do." I had never heard anything so sensible in my life. Pratima-di was my mother's contemporary and I should have addressed her as "mashi" (aunt), but we ended up calling her "didi" (elder sister). Her son, whom we called Ajit-da, was our childhood hero. He was "good in studies" and a badminton champion in his university. He played cricket well and seemed to excel in everything he did. It struck me that in our quiet and unambitious neighbourhood it was only Ajit-da who seemed to have a life.

My first lesson in cricket was from Ajit-da. He taught me the grip and stance with which to take the crease. I discovered that the correct grip was nothing like my father had taught me – clearly, he had known nothing about how to play the game. But could anybody hit the ball comfortably while holding the bat along Ajit-da's instruction? What was the purpose of such a contrived posture? Why couldn't you just hold it like a stick and swing it around any way you wished? His "correct grip" led to my being clean bowled several times. It was Ajit-da who told us that women's teams had been formed at Bibekananda Park, and that if I was really interested in cricket I should join the club and learn the game properly.

The following Sunday, I accompanied him to Bibekananda Park in South Calcutta. I was struck by what I saw when we reached. I had never seen so many women in white flannels playing cricket. There was a batswoman at the net and other women bowling to her. A man whose physique was scandalously unathletic was coaching them. He was genial and diminutive, with the hugest belly ever. Everyone called him Debu-da and Ajit-da introduced me to him. Debu-da asked me to bowl. Mercifully, if there was anything I did consistently well, it was bowl. It turned out to be one of those good days when I was able to maintain a good line and length. Debu-da was thrilled and Ajit-da looked very proud. As we walked back home he patted me on the back and kept saying I had bowled very well. I felt vaguely conscious of being happy in a new sort of way.

Meanwhile, the street matches continued right in front of our houses. We were so possessed by the game, it hardly mattered that the ball was regularly crashing into the neighbour's house. Then, one day, my mother joined the neighbour in scolding us. The cricket ball had upset the goddess Saraswati and she had taken a tumble. I may have felt bad for a few minutes. I can't remember.

I was now visiting the nets regularly. One day, during a mock match, I bowled out the captain of our team, who was horribly taken aback. She was an excellent cricketer and couldn't believe that this slip of a girl from nowhere had uprooted her middle stump. She remained at the crease and continued to stare uncomprehendingly at the umpire, whose raised finger looked like an insult. Then it was my turn to bat and the captain insisted she bowl to me. The balls were hurtling towards me and I felt terrified. "Keep your eyes on the ball," Debu-da kept shouting. "If you keep your eyes on the ball, you'll see a football." Now what the hell did that mean? I played too many on the back foot even when they weren't short pitched. Then I nicked one to the wicketkeeper. The captain and I became very good friends later and not only did we play together, we hung out, visited each other's homes, and watched movies.

The grip and stance that Ajit-da had taught me was fast making sense. Now I couldn't understand how people had at any time in human history held the bat like a stick. Debu-da had asked me to focus on forward defensive. I played backward defensive well but seemed to misjudge the length when it came to playing forward. One day, I was deeply embarrassed when I was playing on the streets of Hindustan Park and a man started hollering from a rickshaw. It was Debu-da returning from Gariahat after buying vegetables with his wife. "Put your foot forward and keep your eyes on the ball. Understand?" he shouted as he trundled by. Everyone, including my father who was taking a walk, had stopped to watch. It became less and less embarrassing as this peculiar spectacle became more and more frequent.

I was opening batsperson and a medium-pace off-spinner in the team. Now, here's a secret I never got to share. I hated matches. They were more about winning or losing than simply enjoying the game. The pressure to score runs after every shot took away the pleasure of stroke-making. I would often forget to take runs and this was certainly inconvenient for a team playing to win. It was worse if we had to field in the second half.

Then we were not even allowed to eat a good lunch. I much preferred net practice, which allowed me to play and correct my mistakes. Under Debu-da's good-natured tutelage, I began to understand what it meant to keep my eyes on the ball. When I did consistently manage to keep my eyes on the ball – there were many days when I didn't – it did turn into a football. It seemed bigger, slower, and much easier to hit. What an amazing thing that was!

I owned no cricket gear of my own except an old bat that I polished with turpentine every week. But that wasn't good enough for the nets. I could only shadow practice with it in front of the mirror. Debu-da had asked me to practice my back lift endlessly – I had knocked down the wicket with my own bat a couple of times. The gloves and pads that had made my early batting days a nightmare were now beginning to become indispensable. Playing without method seemed madness. As a result, playing on the streets was beginning to lose its charm, it seemed now random and arbitrary.

The news that I played regularly for a club was beginning to spread through our neighbourhood. One day, I was buying something from Nabin's shop when an elderly lady, who was also buying provisions, exclaimed she hadn't realised that I was a girl. "And do you know how well she plays cricket?" said Nabin proudly, "She plays at the club in Bibekananda Park." The lady patted my back.

But all was not equally well for women's cricket. The *Ananda Bazaar Patrika* group had launched a new sports magazine called *Sportsworld*. I had decided to unsubscribe *Sportsweek* and replace it with *Sportsworld* because Mansur Ali Khan Pataudi, my favourite cricketer, was its editor. One day, a letter from Shillong appeared in the magazine saying women shouldn't be playing cricket at all – because the very idea was ridiculous. The letter was a description of how absurd women looked when they played cricket, and then argued that the travesty should be stopped. Encouraged by my mother, I wrote back a passionate defence of women's cricket, adding that I suspected the hostile letter writer had never seen women play. The fellow wrote back to say that, indeed, he hadn't seen any woman play, nor had he any intention of doing so because didn't the whole world know women playing cricket was a ridiculous sight! On this rather persuasive note the editor, without a single line of refutation, decided to close the debate. How I wished Nabin from the grocery store had been the editor of *Sportsworld*.

Sunday mornings were reserved for cricket practice at Bibekananda Park. Boys and girls played in adjoining nets. There were several young men like Ajit-da who took interest in women's cricket. They bowled so that we could practice batting or batted so that we could bowl. They would hit the ball hard and high so that we could take turns catching. For some strange reason, everybody was required to shout "Lebbit" before catching the ball. Someone later explained that it was to prevent all of us from rushing to take the same catch and knocking each other down. So, whoever was best positioned to take the catch was supposed to tell the others, "leave it". That made sense. But when too many coaches began teaching us, Debu-da firmly put an end to it. Thank god for that, as some of us were getting really confused.

Then there were young men whose interests were not limited to the game. And one member of our group was a budding actress. Her lack of skill at the game was amply compensated by the aura of glamour that surrounded her. An over-protective father notwithstanding, she had managed to acquire a band of willing tutors. These incidental developments did not make Debu-da very happy but he battled on with the rest of us.

Then there were days when I played badly. I had no idea why I couldn't keep my eyes on the ball. I would see it coming and suddenly it was gone. Instead of turning into a football, the cricket ball was beginning to vanish as it came up to my bat. One day, I got hit and lost my nerve. It had become a habit for me to look at Debu-da for approval every time I played a shot. If I managed to play my strokes well, he would ask, "Do you feel good about it? If you do, you know you've got it right."

I loved to collapse on the grass at the end of the practice and stare up at the sky. I grew up imagining that I would always be enveloped by so much sky above and so much grass below. Very often, the other team members would join me in lounging around. Sometimes we would cross the street to eat the *aloo dum* that the Lake area was famous for. Then we would go home, to return the next weekend. The person I met many years later in Delhi was often a companion on these restful jaunts.

Having finished my school, I was ready to move for college to Delhi. I had never thought that the hardest thing about leaving Calcutta would be the parting from my cricketing days in Bibekananda Park. In fact, my separation from the game was so painful that I decided never to talk about it. Of course, I never missed the matches. But I missed everything else. When I lost cricket, I lost an entire world.

Sometimes, the world comes to me as phantoms in restless dreams. Sometimes, I see the ball coming towards me and turning slowly into a giant red football. At other times I seem to miss it. Sometimes I play a stroke perfectly and I can hear Debu-da ask, "Are you feeling good about it?" I never know what I will see in my dreams. But I do know that when I wake up I will see no sky above or grass below.

SANJAY SUBRAHMANYAM

Another Booker Flop

ANYONE WHO HAS read the inside pages of Indian newspapers over the past few decades will be familiar with the recurring stories of violent urban crime. Some concern "crimes of passion" and use a peculiar Indian-English journalistic vocabulary, involving such terms as "eve-teasing", "absconding", and "paramour". Some of the stories have to do with incest or close family relationships – say, between father-in-law and daughter-in-law – while others are tales of paedophilia and "child molestation". Another popular subject of which Delhi residents will be well aware are the crimes committed by the "criminal castes", often linked in the neocolonial imagination of the city's bourgeoisie to the villages and smallholdings that are gradually being asphyxiated by Delhi's expansion. It's been an urban legend since the 1990s that people are being bludgeoned to death in their houses with blunt instruments even though they haven't resisted; and that the intruders show their contempt for their victims by defecating in their living rooms. Class elements are present in the reporting of crimes of passion, which the elite naturally associate with slum dwellers and squatters: the second type of crime involves something approaching class warfare.

But the dominant topic of the past decades has been domestic servants, an indispensable part of life but also a source of endless paranoia in metropolitan households. These domestic servants come in various guises. Some commute to work by public transport, perform tasks in several households, and return home at the end of the day. Many others are children, or barely adolescent, and sleep in the house where they work (though they aren't usually allowed to use the same bathrooms and toilets as their employers). They may be poor relatives; or they may be adults from outside the family. They have no fixed hours, though in some cases they are given a day off every week or every fortnight. The government recognises their existence by providing every state employee who attains "officer" status with a flat or house that has "servants' quarters" attached to it. Here, in the alleys at the back of government residential areas, a world exists in parallel to that of the houses and flats that look out onto the streets and gardens. It is a curious form of what the Brazilian sociologist Gilberto Freyre, in his discussion of the relationship between plantation owners and their slaves, called *casa grande e senzala*; sometimes the children of the masters and those of the servants can be found spinning tops or flying kites together.

Servants are naturally a favourite topic of conversation. "They are so difficult to get and so hard to keep." "They don't know their station any more." "It's not like it was in the good old days when they were so loyal that they were really members of the family." And so on. The paranoia resurfaces every time there is a story in the papers about an elderly couple found murdered and robbed by their resident servant; and the paranoia increases when the police, as they usually do, place advertisements in the papers advising employers to run "background checks" on potential employees. Attempts are made from time to time to introduce identity cards for servants, and urban Indians wistfully say how much better arrangements are in Singapore, where servants are strictly regulated by the state, have just one day off a month, and women are kicked out if they get pregnant.

A bourgeois household may have washing machines, vacuum cleaners, microwaves and other domestic aids, but who can live without one servant, or several? Every American, European, or Japanese who lives in an Indian city succumbs soon enough to the Servant Raj.

Some time in the 1980s, a friend of mine had a lavish wedding in one of the cities. Though he lived and worked in India, his family was spread across the West and they turned up in large numbers, accompanied by Western friends who were not above a bit of freeloading. The wedding was an extended affair and what began cordially enough soon deteriorated into squabbling. Some of it was the usual friction resulting from familial proximity, but there was another, more peculiar cause. Some of the relatives from abroad announced that they were appalled by class relations in India. They didn't just mean the rickshaw-pullers on the streets: what troubled them was the position and treatment of domestic servants, who had been mobilised in large numbers for the wedding. They were there to clean up after parties that ended in the early hours of the morning, and yet had to be up to make masala omelettes for the honoured guests when they rolled out of bed. All this smacked of a dreadful feudalism to those whose parents had lived in India a bare generation before, surrounded in all probability by even larger numbers of servants. It seemed archaic and primitive, unworthy of a democracy, an affront to liberal principles. Eventually, many of those who had come from abroad stormed off with their moral superiority intact, leaving their Indian relatives bemused.

Social scientists reflecting on India tend to discuss class in its rural version (relations between landlords, peasants, and wage labourers), or in its classic urban incarnation of the factory and shop floor, or in terms of what has been termed "footloose labour" – which is to say the labour used on construction sites or for contract work on piece rates or for a wage. Even the broad intellectual grouping known as Subaltern Studies hasn't taken domestic work into account, save for the occasional moment when a conversation with a servant provides the researcher with an anecdote or factoid to motivate an essay on some profound question or other. It is very hard to define or measure class in a country where data on personal income and assets are extremely hard to come by. It is even harder to know for certain what has happened in the past two decades since economic liberalisation was proclaimed. But there are clearly very rich people in the cities now with fancy imported cars, expensive watches and clothes, and showy lifestyles, and they live side by side with slum dwellers and those who sleep on pavements. There are urban and suburban developments that boast such names as Malibu Towers, Beverly Hills Residence, and Bel-Air Estate. This is growth all right, but of a sort that can induce vertigo. It is what Aravind Adiga's Man Booker Prize-winning *The White Tiger* is ostensibly about.

The book purports to tell the story of a murder committed by its narrator, Balram Halwai (also known as "White Tiger"), from the eastern Indian state of Bihar, who moves first to the prosperous suburb of Gurgaon near Delhi to work for Mr Ashok and his wife, Pinky Madam, and then to the booming city of Bangalore in South India, which together with Hyderabad is associated in clichés with the country's recent economic transformation. We learn the fact of this murder some thirty pages into the book, at the end of the first chapter: "Eight months later, I slit Mr Ashok's throat." The plot has no twists and turns, no real surprises; there is no sleight of hand. The novel just rolls on like an Indian Railways train, from one stop to another, over seven chapters that are notionally recounted over seven nights.

Why Bihar? It is a state that has some of the lowest economic and developmental indicators in modern India, and is also part of a large swathe of territory where Naxalite (or Maoist) groups operate with impunity. Urban Indians, especially from the great metropolitan centres, love to sneer at Bihar as the worst part of the so-called Cow Belt, a place where banditry, caste warfare, and feudalism are rampant and where one of the leading politicians is Laloo Prasad Yadav, who provides much hilarity in the salons of Delhi, Mumbai, and Bangalore (and who has a role even in this novel). Balram refers to Bihar as the world of "Darkness", a term that appears repeatedly in the book in opposition to "Light" – i.e. the sophisticated urban destinations to which the narrator is headed. People like him don't speak the increasingly standard Hindi of northern India, but rather its eastern Indian versions, such as Maithili and Bhojpuri, the dialects spoken by nineteenth-century working-class migrants to Calcutta, Fiji, Mauritius, and Guyana. Even now, they are mocked as rustics because of it.

Balram hates Bihar and hates his ancestral village of Laxmangarh, which is apparently only a few miles from Bodh Gaya, the pilgrimage site where the Buddha is said to have attained enlightenment: "I wonder if the Buddha walked through Laxmangarh – some people say he did. My own feeling is that he ran through it – as fast as he could – and got to the other side – and never looked back!" Balram is cynical about the Hindu religion, which he views in an entirely instrumental manner. He despises the holy river Ganges, which for him is no more than a large open drain. His village is a place "split into two" by "a bright strip of sewage", and where there are "three more or less identical shops selling more or less identically adulterated and stale items of rice, cooking oil, kerosene, biscuits, cigarettes and jaggery." It is this background, the anything but bucolic world of Laxmangarh, that propels him to seek employment in the provincial city and mining centre of Dhanbad.

Here, after a bit of instruction from a local taxi driver, he finds work as a driver with a powerful family that controls large parts of his native region. The next sections of the book trace Balram's rise through the household of this master, where, after first being obliged to drive the humble Indo-Japanese Maruti Suzuki, he reaches a triumphant position behind the wheel of the family's chief car, the luxurious Honda City. Balram has had to exercise his ruthlessness to get there, developing the skills he honed while working in a teashop, doing his job "with near total dishonesty, lack of dedication, and insincerity." His rise involves betraying and blackmailing another driver, a secret Muslim, pretending to be a Hindu called Ram Persad. By stages, Balram is elevated to serve the family at a far higher salary, in Delhi and Gurgaon, where it has sent its sons so that they can live out of harm's way (further away from the Naxalites) and closer to the centres of political power. A hundred pages into the novel, we have migrated from Darkness into Light, from the feudal world of Bihar into the suburban and metropolitan one of Gurgaon and Delhi.

Adiga's may be the first novel in English to attempt to come to terms with the phenomenon that is Gurgaon. It is, to put it mildly, a curious place. A quarter of a century ago, it was an agrarian region in the state of Haryana on the fringes of Delhi, inhabited by Jat agriculturists and Gujjar pastoralists and farmers. As Delhi expanded southwards, it became a place of opportunity, with the state of Haryana offering incentives for entrepreneurs to invest. In the late 1980s, I remember the first condominiums going on sale there, and Non-Resident Indians (NRIs) buying into them. The car firm Maruti Suzuki, one of whose products Balram drives in Dhanbad, opened a factory.

Money began to flow in, often in obscene quantities. I recall visiting a bank in Gurgaon in the mid-1990s; the manager proudly pointed to a large and freshly cemented patch in the roof where armed robbers had broken in one night a couple of weeks before and fought a pitched gun battle with local police.

There are now enormous malls and glass towers housing firms such as Alcatel and Siemens. But it is an insecure world, where employees walk to collect their cars with what I gather is an understandable nervousness. Muggings are frequent, as are kidnapping and carjacking. Last year IBM apparently issued a memo to its staff advising them to take a long list of precautions. The following story from the *Hindustan Times* of 2 September gives a flavour of the situation (and of Indian journalese):

> Yet another incident of carjacking was reported from Gurgaon on Monday. Two armed youths reportedly snatched the keys of a Scorpio (HR 26 AH 8100) that was parked in DLF Cyber City from its driver and drove away with the driver still inside. The incident occurred at 11.15 p.m. when hundreds of other vehicles were parked in the area.
>
> The SUV belongs to a businessman who lives in Sushant Lok, Phase I. Ashok Kumar, station head officer of DLF City police station said driver Rajeshwar Mandal was sitting in the vehicle and the owner, Vikram Veer, had gone to a restaurant at Infinity Towers.
>
> "Two youths armed with pistols entered into an altercation with the driver saying he had hit their car. The youths then pushed the driver inside and drove the car away," Kumar said. The robbers snatched Mandal's mobile phone and other belongings and stripped him before dumping him near Palam Vihar.
>
> In June this year, the Gurgaon police had issued a word of caution to people driving their cars at odd hours. It had cautioned a motorcycle-borne gang of carjackers was on the prowl in Gurgaon

and was snatching cars at gunpoint. In August also, Gurgaon police commissioner Mohinder Lal had said a gang of professional auto-lifters from neighbouring towns as well as from Bihar and West Bengal were active in Gurgaon. As many as 1100 auto theft cases have been reported till date in Gurgaon as against 950 cases in the corresponding period last year.

In this Wild West atmosphere, which Gurgaon shares to an extent with other prosperous Delhi suburbs such as NOIDA and Faridabad, nothing is quite what it seems. There are shoot-outs in courtrooms. There are swanky clinics with five-star decor and marble floors where medical attention borders on the criminally negligent. Gurgaon is fragile, but many NRIs are happy to buy into it because they want to believe in the illusions it seems to support: the illusion of security, of the safety of gated communities, the illusion that one is not living in India because one is surrounded by Benetton, Nike, Pizza Hut, TGI Friday. But these are illusions that can be sustained only because the drivers and domestics, the cleaners and sweepers, not to speak of the armed security guards, are all in place. I imagine that large numbers of executives fly into New Delhi's Indira Gandhi Airport in business class, and return to Paris or Düsseldorf three days later without having set foot in any part of India other than Gurgaon.

It is this world that Adiga sets out to dissect in the most ambitious part of the book. Balram lives in the servants' apartments in Buckingham Towers B Block. It is, as he describes it, part of a "warren of interconnected rooms where all the drivers, cooks, sweepers, maids and chefs of the apartment block can rest, sleep and wait." Balram's master and mistress, Mr Ashok and Pinky Madam, the son and daughter-in-law of his feudal Dhanbad employer, live on the thirteenth floor of the apartment block in a flat that their driver finds cramped after the Dhanbad house. Mr Ashok, it turns out, is a wishy-washy liberal who was educated in the US, unlike his brother Mukesh, a more rooted and vicious representative of the Bihari landlord class. He has, however, had the courage to oppose his family in marrying Pinky, presented less as an NRI than an ABCD (American-Born Confused *Deshi*), an Indian-American who is also a Christian. Balram lusts after Pinky, her fancy perfumes, skirts, and low-cut tops, through the rear-view mirror. Pinky, for her part, sneers at Balram and his crude English and his habit of scratching his crotch while working in the kitchen.

In an improbable moment, a drunken Pinky insists on taking the wheel and accidentally runs over the child of a pavement dweller. There is an attempt to persuade Balram to take the rap and he signs a statement falsely admitting his guilt. But this is unnecessary: the poor have no rights and no one has registered the hit-and-run accident. Still, a disgusted and somewhat remorseful Pinky departs for America and asks for a divorce. Mr Ashok falls into despair, drinking and puking his way through the next few pages. He begins to frequent former girlfriends and the odd blonde Ukrainian prostitute in seedy hotels. Balram is torn between a certain sympathy for his misery and a contempt for his lack of gumption. Contempt triumphs and he begins to contemplate his employer's murder. One rainy night when Mr Ashok is in possession of a large sum in cash, he draws him out of the car, claiming that a tyre needs repair, and kills him with an empty bottle of Johnnie Walker Black Label, smashing his head in and then cutting his throat. Accompanied by a young nephew, he decamps for Bangalore. Of course, Balram knows that his employer's family will visit vengeance on his. But he doesn't care. His brothers and their children may be slaughtered, the women of the family may be raped, but he is indifferent. Adiga wants us to see all this as emblematic of the new Indian tough guy, the murderous entrepreneur who will step over any number of dead bodies to get his way.

The idea of a resentful, oppressed protagonist murdering his employer and getting away with it in pursuit of his ideal of social mobility is not much of a novelty. Any innovation must therefore be sought in the novel's narrative voice. But there is also a framing device that should be mentioned: each chapter consists of a message sent by Balram to Wen Jiabao, the prime minister of the People's Republic of China, who is about to visit Bangalore. This adds nothing to the novel beyond permitting Balram to present himself as a Third World rather than a merely Indian racist. Consciously or not, it also imitates far funnier and more successful examples, such as John Barth's "Petition" from *Lost in the Funhouse*, addressed to the King of Siam.

The novel is not, contrary to confused assertions in the Indian press, another attempt at a form of Indian magical realism in the wake of Salman Rushdie and Arundhati Roy. No one has telepathic or supernatural powers here; time is broadly Newtonian in its flow. This is a novel that wants to be realistic, even if the realism is meant to be understood as tinged with black comedy. There may even be some moralising intention, with Adiga denouncing the greed and corruption of the New Indian Society. But the merit of the book must eventually rest on the credibility and verisimilitude of the voice of Balram Halwai.

As it turns out, the Halwais are an upper-middling caste of sweetmeat-makers, resident across large swathes of northern India and often using the caste name of Gupta. Balram is presented in the novel as impoverished but with some education, even if it doesn't give him access to English. "Neither you nor I speak English," he writes to Wen Jiabao at the outset of the novel, and yet the novel is written in English. We are meant to believe – even within the conventions of the realist novel – that a person who must really function in Maithili or Bhojpuri can express his thoughts seamlessly in a language that he doesn't speak.

This is a problem that takes us back to the roots of the Indian novel in English and its two broad categories. One type deals with Indian characters who speak English because they have had a Western education (as in the work of Vikram Seth), and often involves middle-class angst, urban lust and loss, or satirical views on post-colonial pretension. Some of these novels describe more or less ironically the tragic fate of anglicised members of India's elite colleges, rotting away in the 1980s in the wilds of places like Dhanbad while dreaming of Fleetwood Mac or Supertramp. At its most genteel, this attitude may be found in an Indian-American writer such as Jhumpa Lahiri, whose work would never embrace the subjectivity of a crass chauffeur from Bihar who smashes his employer's head in with a whisky bottle in Dhaula Kuan while chewing betel-leaf.

The other – more common – type of novel tries to represent in English dialogue spoken in another language. Some writers, like Raja Rao, adopt an elaborate sing-song tone supposedly intended to correspond to the rhythms not merely of the various Indian vernaculars but of Indian life itself. Others, including Rushdie, have tried the macaronic solution, sprinkling their English with Hindi or Urdu words or even inventing words. Still others, such as Lee Siegel (who navigates between Indology and fiction writing), have attempted for comic effect to have Indians speak in a drolly exaggerated way, through the use of odd vowels and diphthongs. None of these solutions really works; what they bring to mind are the SS officers in World War Two films speaking English among themselves with a strong Mitteleuropean accent. Rushdie's characters sound like no known Indian, but this is not meant to matter because his novels are not realistic. None of these writers has the ethnographic ambitions of a Zola, attempting to capture, notebook in hand, the vocal nuances of the Other.

What of Balram Halwai? What does he sound like? Despite the odd *namaste*, *daal*, *paan*, and *ghat*, his vocabulary is not sprinkled with North Indian vernacular terms. His sentences are mostly short and crudely constructed, apparently a reflection of the fact that we're dealing with a member of the "subaltern" classes. He doesn't engage in Rushdian word-play. But he does use a series of expressions that simply don't add up. He describes his office as a "hole in the wall". He refers to "kissing some god's arse", an idiomatic expression that doesn't exist in any North Indian language. "Half-formed ideas bugger one another, and make more half-formed ideas" and the Chinese prime minister is advised never to "let that blasphemous idea into your yellow skull." On another matter, he sneers: "They're so yesterday." A clever little phrase appears: "A statutory warning – as they say on cigarette packs – before we begin." Dogs are referred to as "mutts". Yet whose vocabulary and whose expressions are these? On page after page, one is brought up short by the jangling dissonance of the language and the falsity of the expressions. This is a posh English-educated voice trying to talk dirty without being able to pull it off. This is not Salinger speaking as Holden Caulfield, or Joyce speaking as Molly Bloom. It is certainly not Ralph Ellison or James Baldwin, whom Adiga has claimed as his models in speaking for the underdog. What we are dealing with is someone with no sense of the texture of Indian vernaculars, yet claiming to have produced a realistic text.

Imagine recording the speech of your interlocutor – a driver encountered in a car park in Gurgaon, say – in an Indian language and trying to render it not literally, but credibly, and with some effort at verisimilitude, into English. This is no easy task. The translator always faces dilemmas, of course, and can never get it quite right. But we also know what it is to get it disastrously wrong. It is when the "autobiography" of an Indian untouchable woman appears in French using expressions from Victor Hugo. The falsity in *The White Tiger* goes much further. It means having a character who cannot read Urdu, and certainly has no notion of Persian, tell us that his favourite poets include Jalaluddin Rumi and Mirza Ghalib. It means having someone who can't read English being able to recall a conversation in which his interlocutor speaks of books by James Hadley Chase, Kahlil Gibran, Adolf Hitler, and Desmond Bagley. Try that lot out on a Hindi speaker who knows no English next time you are in India.

Adiga gets the tone right only when he writes of the world of the bourgeois. Some of this is quite funny and rings partly true.

> "Ashok," she said. "Now hear this. Balram, what is it we're eating?"
> I knew it was a trap, but what could I do? – I answered. The two of them burst into giggles.
> "Say it again, Balram."
> They laughed again.
> "It's not piJJA. It's piZZa. Say it properly."
> "Wait – you're mispronouncing it too. There's a *T* in the middle. *Peet. Zah.*"
> "Don't correct *my* English, Ashok. There's no *T* in pizza. Look at the box."

Some two decades ago, Gayatri Chakravorty Spivak wrote a celebrated essay, "Can the Subaltern Speak?" At the time, a folklorist is said to have responded: "More importantly, can the bourgeois listen?" We can't hear Balram Halwai's voice here, because the author seems to have no access to it. The novel has its share of anger at the injustices of the new, globalised India, and it's good to hear this among the growing chorus of celebratory voices. But its central character comes across as a cardboard cut-out. The paradox is that for many of this novel's readers, this lack of verisimilitude will not matter because for them India is and will remain an exotic place. This book adds another brick to the patronising edifice it wants to tear down.

AMIT CHAUDHURI

Money Matters

ONE OF THE THINGS that's long intrigued me about this country is its curious, grudging relationship to money – by which I mean not markets, capital, financial gain or material success, but, specifically, the individual banknote and small change. I was reminded of this when, a few days ago, taking out a new 500-rupee note to pay a bill at a nursing home, I was made to notice the razor-thin tear in the crisp paper, and given it back. "I just got this from an ATM," I said, shaking my head; the receptionist, noticing my look of exasperation, and mistaking it for pique at the cash machine, commiserated by sharing his own experiences with me: "These days even banks aren't reliable. They . . ." and continued with words I couldn't hear properly.

I gave a comparably crisp note, a flawless one this time, and suppressed the urgent question I often feel like asking and sometimes have: Why will a note with blemishes not do? People's responses are varied: some grin, as if, like a child, I've gone straight to the heart of the matter without any understanding of what it is that makes our lives what they are – complex and sometimes opaque. Others, with downcast eyes, pretend not to hear; they are helpless – silent adherents to a law that only a fool or a saint or a foreigner would have no inkling of.

What was the next sensible step, though? Would I have to go to a bank, in the near-forty-degree Celsius brunt of the morning and return this note for another one? Instead, I had a cappuccino at one of those coffee-shop chains where the note changed hands without comment or scrutiny or judgement. Maybe the thin, placatory young man (little more than a teenager) hadn't seen the tear, which was almost invisible unless you shook the note. Or maybe he'd noticed it, but both he and the chain he worked for, and for that matter the coffee he served, represented a new order, to which the physical state of the banknote had suddenly become irrelevant. This development had occurred belatedly, unevenly, but it's possible to hazard a guess and say it has occurred, at least in some enclaves of the rapidly changing metropolis we now inhabit. The only other party in this city that will accept a damaged-looking note occupies an axis opposite to the one the coffee chain represents: I mean the much-resented parking attendant. This ghost of the licence raj, darkened and attenuated by exposure to the elements, but impelled by a sudden breathless energy that can make him cover half the length of a street in seconds, knows the money he collects from the car isn't seen as a legitimate fee at all, but as gratuitous commission. Though he's seldom tested – because the imprimatur of the state clings to him like a faint film – he's aware he has little authority. He will accept any kind of note at all, new or aged or tattered. He represents the rarely but oddly accommodating nature of the old order; of how it's based on a mixture of complicity, mistrust and mutual understanding – a DNA of co-operation that's changing, but hasn't gone away.

The realisation that the physical condition of a banknote is unimportant came to me in my years in England – not in a flash of light, but over time, semi-conscious, semi-attentive, as ragged five- or ten-pound notes, a few even rescued by a simple and firm band of Sellotape, changed hands without a word. At some point, nations made the transition from coins – which, in their weight, their detailed, minted appearance, the longevity for which they'd been designed, seemed to contain the value they represented – to notes, which no one could confuse for having any value at all. There lay the paradox of money as we've understood it – why the world abounds in it, and why so little of it's available. To ascribe value to a piece of paper is, of course, to be part of a contract, as well as to be involved in a willing suspension of disbelief. The sheer literal worthlessness of the frayed note makes its symbolic value transcendental and near indestructible. In India, though, this isn't the case. The symbolic worth of the note is almost overwhelmed by its physical, worldly incarnation, and by the loose but inescapable aesthetic guidelines that inform our scrutiny. As the torn, perishable note threatens to fall apart, so does the value it represents; in this, it almost becomes indistinguishable from the commodities in the market it was assigned to purchase. Only yesterday, I heard my mother, taking out a fatigued-looking twenty-rupee note from her purse, complain, "Where does he get them from?", referring to the driver of her car. She was speaking of the note as if it were a vegetable or a fruit the driver had brought back home; it had begun to wither; it lacked freshness.

This leads me to the other mystery in our daily lives related to the monetary: the curiously perennial shortage of change. Give a 500-rupee note to a shopkeeper (it used to be a 100-rupee one) and he will close ranks, his expression giving away nothing and everything. Then there's the inscrutable, sly, adamant refusal to part with coins, leading to the swift, across-the-counter yogic calculations peculiar to Indians; for instance, if, on being presented with a bill for sixty-two rupees, you were to give the shopkeeper a hundred rupees, he will say, "Do you have two rupees?" This is the default query; if you don't have two rupees, it results in a mixture of accusatory silence and introspection.

And who can forget those pregnant moments in taxis our lives expand to make room for, when the driver, having been handed a large note, first rummages tiredly in one pocket, then another, then takes out a carefully folded wad and looks at it in the half-light? Then the coins appear in one palm; money is broken into smaller and smaller units because you had no change; almost a minute passes in the heat, and nothing happens. This is when you might wonder where all the change goes; what causes this constant paucity; why we all hoard coins and notes of smaller denominations, and lie about not possessing change even when we have it in our wallets; that the paucity doesn't even necessarily have anything to do with the general or literal or metaphorical lack of wealth in circulation.

The poet C.P. Surendran once gave me an insight, in Delhi, into why the situation as we know it exists. We'd arrived in Khan Market late in the morning; we had to pay the fare; not a single auto driver, though, among the line of autos parked in the front, could give us change for a hundred rupees. My old puzzlement came back: "How can not one of them have the money?" C.P. said, "These people don't bring the last day's earnings when they return to work. They begin each day afresh." And this was the first time someone had said something illuminating to me on the subject, and opened my eyes to the most common sort of employee around us: the daily-wage earner. This person goes back home at night, possibly having spent part of his money on *beedis*, *gutka* or drink, possibly giving some of it to the family, or part to an employer to whom he owes a species of mortgage. The next day he's back, like a migrant, to whom the business of livelihood is old and inevitable, but to whom money is always new. He could be anywhere. Having money doesn't mean owning it; it means to relentlessly make or break the makeshift rules of exchange. Change isn't hoarded for the purposes of saving or spending, but because it constantly needs to be earned. Others, in the salaried middle classes, or in trade or business, have to deal with this person in their own manner: by outwitting or outwaiting him, or – what's more common – by mimicking him.

PANKAJ MISHRA

Mashobra

I SPENT MUCH OF my twenties in a little Himachali village north of Shimla called Mashobra. It was a serene and fulfilling time; and like most good things in life it came about with a minimum of fuss, with no anticipation or planning.

I had gone to Shimla in the spring of 1992 in order to find a cottage I could rent cheaply for a few summers. For the first couple of days, a lethargic estate agent showed me around a few sunless houses with damp cement walls, and it became clear that the silence and seclusion I associated with living in the mountains weren't to be found in the city's aggressive favela-like squalor. I had given up on Shimla; and that morning, when I took the bus to what had been described as a "nice picnic spot" in my guidebook, I was hoping only to kill some time before taking the train back to Delhi.

The half-empty Himachal Roadways bus never stopped groaning as it travelled through the broad open valley that slumbered peacefully in the pale sunshine. After about half an hour, we were surrounded by damp pine trees, and didn't regain our freedom for some time. Miniature mountain ranges of snow sat muddied beside the rutted road; at tea-shacks in dark little clearings, men in woollen rags hunched over pine-cone fires.

The bus left the highway, stuttered down a steep road cramped by tottering houses of wood and tin, and then abruptly stopped. The driver killed the ailing engine, and everyone got out.

I was the last to leave. After the warm pungent smells of the bus, the cold came as a little shock. I saw that I was on a long ridge, facing a vast abyss filled with the purest blue air. The overall view, extending far to the East, was clear and quite spectacular: a craggy row of white mountain peaks, watching over, along with its minor underlings, the layers and layers of hills and ridges, a deep wooded valley.

The cliché fantasy broke with renewed force into my mind: wouldn't it be wonderful, I thought, to live here? I wondered if I should ask someone about places to rent. But the bus had emptied fast – I had been the only tourist on it – and there was no one around. It was then that I noticed the red tin roof of a largish house, and the steep spiralling dirt path that seemed to lead towards it.

The house was indeed big and handsome, if in an old-fashioned unostentatious way – it had been built, I later learnt, in the early seventies, when wood was plentiful and cheap. Flower pots with peonies hung from the eaves; on the wide sunny porch, some red chillies lay quietly drying on a bright yellow sheet.

A window on the second floor was open; so was the main door that opened, I could see, on to a wooden staircase. I knocked and then heard the thump of bare feet on the floor. Someone appeared in the second-floor window: a boy. I tried to explain what I was looking for. He disappeared and then a little later Mr Sharma came down the stairs.

He was a tall man, and seemed even taller in his Fez cap, which I didn't see much as the years passed, and the air of sombre dignity it gave Mr Sharma deepened by itself, became an air of mourning.

I told Mr Sharma, a bit awkwardly, that I was a student from Delhi, had spent two summers in Mussoorie and was now looking for a place in the mountains where I could read and write for a few years.

Mr Sharma gazed uncertainly at me for a moment, and then said that he would show me a cottage he had just built.

We walked through an orchard – I didn't know then that these were apple and cherry and peach trees – and came to a narrow spur at the corner of the hill. It was here that a small cottage stood, directly above a cowshed and what looked like storage rooms for fodder.

It was just about functional: there were altogether three rooms, built in no particular order or design, but plonked next to each other; a bathroom and kitchen had been tacked on to them almost as an afterthought. The rooms were still full of the aroma of wood shavings – it stayed for many months until pushed out in October that year by the fragrance of freshly plucked apples stored underneath.

It was the balcony, however, that held me. It had the same view I had seen as I came out of the bus – the valley and the sky locked in a trance so private that you could only watch and be still yourself. In my mind's eye, I could already see myself sitting there on long evenings and gazing at the darkening world.

To my surprise, Mr Sharma asked for only Rs 1000 per month. He said that he too had come to Mashobra many years ago, wanting to read and write. His father had set up the first Sanskrit college in Shimla; he himself published a magazine in Sanskrit. He said he hadn't built the cottage to make money; it was meant to host needy scholars like myself.

I felt uncomfortable with being called a scholar: I had two mediocre degrees in Commerce and English; I hadn't written anything more than a few ill-considered reviews; I had barely any idea of what I could write about. But I didn't correct Mr Sharma; I did not wish to disappoint him. I had lived far more precariously in Mussoorie, at boarding houses run by Christian missionaries who saw me as a potential convert, who accosted me on my evening walks and wished to know the state of my soul. As I saw it, I was closer to being a scholar than a Christian.

And then it didn't really matter after I moved to Mashobra – just a few days after my first visit – and began to look like, with all my books and my steady absorption in them, a scholar of sorts.

I was awakened very early in the morning, the sun bullying its way even through the thick coarse-textured blue curtains of my window. The day stretched long and somewhat emptily, even though I went to bed babyishly early, at around nine p.m., by which time the whole village was already asleep. I read all morning and then walked up the hill for lunch at a dhaba called Montu. It was run by a hospitable Punjabi couple from the Kangra valley who lived in two low-roofed rooms at the back, curtained off from the dhaba with a torn cotton sari. I seemed to be their only customer at lunch: I sat alone on the wooden bench, under the outdated calendar with pictures of Shiva's exploits, and read the censorious articles in *Punjab Kesari* about masturbation (bad for eyesight) and blue jeans (bad for blood circulation), while Neeraj, the couple's young son, kept bringing in warm chapatis on a small aluminium plate.

The food was unremarkable; the menu unchanging. There was frequently a lot of something called "mixed *daal*", which was all people could afford by way of *daal* in those days of post-liberalisation inflation. But Neeraj asked hopefully each time if I had found the food satisfactory, and I had to lie.

On the way back I stopped at the post office, a large dusty room with a disused telephone booth and an old damaged clock. There usually wasn't much mail for me; but the ageing postman was always grateful to give some for my landlord and save himself the steep walk to and from the house. I, in turn, would hand it to Mr Sharma's mother who sat knitting at the open second-floor window. She would sit there from late morning, all through the long drowsy afternoons until the sun disappeared behind the hills to the West, when the shadows glided swiftly across the orchard and the valley, and the soft golden peaks in the distance seemed to hold, briefly, all the light in the world.

The days acquired a rhythm; began to pass. The Sharmas sensed my mood and left me undisturbed, except on early mornings when Mr Sharma's mother would send around a plate of aloo parathas and a steel tumbler with steaming chai.

The Sharmas themselves lived quiet if disciplined lives, except when a special occasion – a festival, a *shradh*, or a *yagna* – brought the scattered family together in a happy whirl of silk *chunnis*, crying babies, and sizzling *puris* (some of which came my way). Much of their time went into tending the fruit trees and the cows. Mr Sharma's father, Panditji, a sprightly octogenarian, was also known as an astrologer; people from places as far off as Chandigarh came to consult him. And each month, Mr Sharma brought out a Sanskrit magazine, *Divyajyoti*, from an antique printing press kept in one of the dark rooms just below my cottage.

Mr Sharma told me that it had a circulation of 500 copies, and it went out to Sanskrit colleges and institutions. He wrote most of the magazine himself during the first half of the month – articles on social and political issues – and brought the loose pages to the press, smiling awkwardly when I passed him on the narrow path through the orchard. For the second half of the month, Daulatram, the big round-faced jovial printer and handyman, would laboriously hand-typeset the longhand version, a lonely figure in a corner of the dark room messy with wooden galley trays and metal sticks: the tips of his finger were stained black when he came up to my cottage to replace a fuse, or to offer some peaches. A week before the 15th of each month, the issue would be printed. The press would begin to loudly hum as Daulatram turned on the power, and then, after an uncertain staccato start, ease into a regular beat, its rhythms as peculiarly soothing as those of a train at night. Then, on the morning of the 15th, Daulatram would jauntily walk up the hill to the post office, holding the finished copies in a small bundle under his giant arm.

My association with the Sharmas gave me a certain status in the village. Strangers said namasté as they passed me on the road; the *dukaandaar*s, idle behind open sackfuls of *rajma* and *chana* and rice, were attentive, eager to talk, and offer me gossip about panchayat politics. But I was shy with them. I did not want to get too involved in the life of the village, or with anything that took me away for too long from reading and writing and the silence of the valley.

I was grateful for the lack of middle-class people in the village; it would have been more difficult to avoid them. The owner of the small fruit juice factory, a certain Mrs Jain, rarely left Delhi, and left most of the management to an old Gurkha. I did see once or twice the retired colonel who lived in a strange-looking house which I subsequently realised had been modelled on the semi-detached houses of England. He made mushroom pickles, and sold them in jars of Kissan jam that were placed in neat rows on a rickety table underneath a fading beach umbrella in his front lawn.

There were other old houses, built during British times, and never properly possessed by their later owners. One of these, I heard, belonged to Waheeda Rahman, although I never saw her in Mashobra, never saw the chains taken off the iron gates to her house. One summer, the gates were painted over with black. I thought then that she might be on her way. But weeks went past; the monsoons came; the paint began to peel off and reveal the rust underneath; and the tufts of wild grass covered the cobbled driveway to the house.

The bells on the old church that loomed over the village were silent on Sunday mornings, until the time the local diocese set up a drug-rehabilitation programme there, when trendy-looking young men from Assam and Meghalaya appeared in the *kiraana dukaan* with unusual demands for Maggi soup; and you heard, passing below the church, the soft guitar chords of songs by John Denver and Simon & Garfunkel.

The summer months saw a few bored-looking tourists in the village. They didn't stay for more than an hour or two; there was little to hold them: most people, I had heard, came to Shimla for the promenades on the Mall, *idlis* and softies at Baljis, and the video-games parlours.

When I came to live in Mashobra, its first big hotel called The Gables had just come up. I went there occasionally, when wearied by Montu's unchanging fare. The vast panelled lobby and giant-size paintings of durbars and banquets could be unsettling after the dusty shabbiness of the village. The menial staff consisted of villagers who were always embarrassed to be found out in their Raj-style cummerbunds and tunics. Conversation with them was always strained in that setting, the stylish young manager from Sector 17, Chandigarh, watching us warily from behind the reception counter. I was always relieved when the time came to pay the bill.

Another tourism venture began to come up towards the east of the village, in a hamlet called Daojidhar, where fluorescent-bright tents appeared one day on a grassy spur. I often went walking there; the views of the snows and the valleys were more extensive from that side of the hill, beyond which lay Kufri and Wildflower Hall, the house Kitchener, the C-in-C of the British Indian army, had lived in. One evening, I met the entrepreneur. His name was Bakshi. He was from Shimla, and restless with plans. Shimla was dead, he declared; it had been killed by tourism. Mashobra could be a wonderful alternative to those who loved quiet places in the hills.

He had some partial success, I think, with backpacking students. On cool summer nights, I saw bonfires on his property, and heard sounds of singing: once again, college-festival favourites. But the summer remained serene for the rest of the village. The afternoons were particularly still, for the inhabitants found the 30 degree C. heat excessive. Maruti vans loaded with tourists and blaring Hindi songs would arrive at the spot where I had my first glimpse of the valley and then hurtle off to Craignano, two miles north, where an Italian adventurer had built a house in the mid-nineteenth century. Meanwhile, the *kiraana dukaan*s remained closed, the men retired for siestas behind wooden multi-hinged shutters covered over with faded photos of Hema Malini endorsing Lux beauty soap, and Dara Singh weighing in for Milkfood ghee.

The village looked even more withdrawn during the monsoons, when some shops didn't open at all for days on end, the empty road offered a hundred small and big muddy mirrors, and the damp drew the map of the former Soviet Union on the white walls of The Gables. It rained heavily and almost constantly, but you got used to it quite fast – so much so that on nights when the drumming on the tin roof finally ceased and the thousand nameless creatures in the forest took up an eerie chant, I would wake up, feeling a bit desolate, and only renewed rain could then send me back to sleep.

The day was a grey blur; stray clouds kept sneaking into the house; you couldn't see more than a foot or two ahead. The sun would timidly break through occasionally, and then the rain-battered roof hurriedly tried to dry itself and cracked its joints in short sharp impatient bursts.

The rain abruptly ceased in mid-September. It was rarely overcast again before the first snow of the winter; and it was the best time of the year, the present, as well as the future, brimful of bright clear days. The apples were lazily picked; the corn cobs laid out on the roofs; and the long grass cut and patiently stacked into little igloos which were sunburnt blonde in a few weeks.

On autumn afternoons, it was chilly inside the house, and I lay on the grassy platform above my cottage. I smelt the dew-damp earth, gazed into the deep blue endless sky, which faded just above the snow-capped peaks, and felt the blankness that I was beginning to recognise as part of being happy and content.

Such luck! I felt blessed, but also anxious. I hadn't signed a lease with the Sharmas. I depended on their goodwill, but it could run out any moment. Even after many years in Mashobra I couldn't quite believe my good fortune; never ceased feeling the fragility of my claim upon the place; and I returned to Mashobra at the end of each winter burdened with a grim sense of foreboding, my imagination hectic with scenarios of rejection and disappointment.

There were other, related insecurities. Mr Sharma had seen in me a needy scholar; he wasn't entirely wrong. I wasn't really a scholar but I was certainly needy not so much for money, whose lack didn't preoccupy me as much as my desire to write, a desire that I felt I had no choice but to fulfil, but which seemed impossible to realise until I knew what writing was all about.

I thought I would find out by reading more books in Mashobra; but it didn't work that way. I felt dwarfed by many of the books I read; whatever skill and intelligence I managed to see in them seemed beyond my capabilities; and it didn't help that I was trying to assess them in print. Reviewing is and should feel like a fraudulent activity until you have done at least some good writing of your own; and I was troubled by the ease with which my callow glib judgements travelled into the world. I felt I could go on churning out these 800-word reviews and remain as clueless as before. I tried my hand at a couple of novels; but I quickly lost momentum after the energetic starts.

Then, one afternoon, when I hadn't gone out for lunch, the postman brought a letter from a publisher in Delhi. He had seen my reviews and he now wanted to know if I was interested in writing a travel book. I wrote back, proposing a book on small towns – somewhat rashly, since I disliked even the trip I had to make to Shimla once a month.

But the book was an opportunity to redeem at least partially all the promises I had made to myself; and for five months I travelled across small-town India. During that long absence, I never really stopped missing my life in Mashobra, never stopped wishing that I was in my cottage instead of the grim dhaba-hotel full of echoing TV noises where I usually found myself at the end of a day's journey.

It accounted for the impatient, frequently intolerant tone of the book I wrote, working flat out in Mashobra for three months. I barely looked at it again after I sent it off to the publishers. I went out of my way to avoid reading the reviews.

As it turned out, the book was noticed. The postman suddenly had more mail for me. One of the letters asked me if I was interested in a job in publishing. I should have said no. I had spent too much time by myself; I could no longer work in an office. But I was seduced by publishing's glamorous image.

And the decision exposed me to many more worlds and people than I had known in Mashobra. I travelled to England and America. My desires began to change, became more complicated, until the point where I couldn't quite recognise them as mine. They involved me with more and more people; kept me out of Mashobra for long stretches, and took me back there only for very brief periods.

On one of these short trips I learnt that Mr Sharma's mother had died the previous week. Mr Sharma and his father had just returned from immersing her ashes in the Ganges at Haridwar. The next issue of *Divyajyoti* was dedicated to her memory. The cover had a photograph of her, taken one bright summer afternoon from my camera. Inside, there were tributes from her son, daughters, sons-in-law and other people whose lives she had touched, even altered, in small but significant ways. It made you see how much solid endeavour and achievement even a restricted life as hers could contain.

There were other losses. The entrepreneur at Daojidhar abruptly died. The brightly hued tents disappeared; tall wild grass grew in their place; no excited singing voices drifted in from the east any more. Wildflower Hall was burned down in one of the mysterious fires that had claimed many old buildings in Shimla. I went to see the charred ruins. The flower beds still bloomed in the blackened lawns and tourists in Himchali folk-dress posed for pictures amidst them.

The Sharmas' big house now felt oddly empty. The second-floor window, where Mr Sharma's mother had sat on sunny afternoons, lay open as before, but the new void there came as a pang each time I walked past it. I noticed grief beginning to work upon Mr Sharma's face; deepening the melancholy in his eyes; lining his mouth.

It was a difficult time for me. The publishing job had ended badly; and I hadn't known what to do for some time. I saw myself drifting, and felt powerless before the fact. It was really out of boredom and confusion that one day a stray memory of an earlier time in Benares came to me.

I started to write about it. The piece went through a couple of drafts before being published. It found appreciative readers; and then grew, in my mind, into a novel. I went back one summer to Mashobra to write it, and had new reasons to feel grateful for the silence and the solitude that I had come almost to take for granted.

It has been two and a half years since then. My life has changed even more. I feel much less insecure as a writer. I travel a lot, mostly for work. It has become harder to spend time in Mashobra. I once thought of it as home; I am no longer so sure what or where home is. The cottage is still there, with my books and music. But I really can't go back for too long, and I can't be too sentimental about it. The longings and aspirations that gave point and urgency to my time in Mashobra have been partly realised; they now take me further away from it, and into the larger world.

In any case, time hasn't quite stood still for Mashobra. Places as much as people can be unfaithful. My slow betrayal of Mashobra has been accompanied by its own keen embrace of the modern world. You can buy Maggi soup as well as Tropicana orange juice in the jazzed-up *kiraana dukaan*s. The Gables has a new wing. New buildings, some of them hotels, have come up in the vicinity of my cottage; the seclusion I so cherished, that made possible all my reading and writing, is gone.

This at least is what I tell myself – if not always convincingly. On days when I am far away from Mashobra, in very different landscapes, I only have to see a patch of mellow light on a lawn, only have to feel a fresh bracing quality in the air, or hear the rain being fierce with a roof, to know that I want to be back, and never leave; and it's no use reminding myself then that the senses – those semi-magical faculties of sight, smell, hearing – hold not only your most truthful memories but also your most hopeless desires.

HEDGEHOG AND FOX

HISTORY AND POLITICS SERIES

"The fox knows many things, but the hedgehog knows one big thing"

General Editor **RUDRANGSHU MUKHERJEE**

MONOGRAPHS

Steven I. Wilkinson ARMY AND NATION

Thomas R. Trautmann ELEPHANTS AND KINGS

Partha Chatterjee, Sudipta Kaviraj, Nivedita Menon THE INDIAN IDEOLOGY

Nayanjot Lahiri ASHOKA IN ANCIENT INDIA

Nicholas B. Dirks AUTOBIOGRAPHY OF AN ARCHIVE

Vasudha Dalmia HINDU PASTS

Dipesh Chakrabarty THE CALLING OF HISTORY

Sunil Agnani HATING EMPIRE PROPERLY

Mahesh Rangarajan NATURE AND NATION

Bhavani Raman DOCUMENT RAJ

Sumit Guha BEYOND CASTE

Iqtidar Alam Khan INDIA'S POLITY IN THE AGE OF AKBAR

Linda Hess BODIES OF SONG

Charu Gupta THE GENDER OF CASTE

Ajay Skaria UNCONDITIONAL EQUALITY

Velcheru Narayana Rao TEXT AND TRADITION IN SOUTH INDIA

Udaya Kumar WRITING THE FIRST PERSON

Chinya V. Ravishankar SONS OF SARASVATI

Christian Lee Novetzke THE QUOTIDIAN REVOLUTION

B.D. Chattopadhyaya THE CONCEPT OF BHARATVARSHA

Sumit Sarkar ESSAYS OF A LIFETIME

Sudhir Mahadevan A VERY OLD MACHINE

Sanjay Subrahmanyam EMPIRES BETWEEN ISLAM AND CHRISTIANITY

Neeladri Bhattacharya THE GREAT AGRARIAN CONQUEST

Chetan Singh HIMALAYAN HISTORIES

Yogendra Yadav POLITICS, ELECTIONS, AND INDIAN DEMOCRACY

Arvind Krishna Mehrotra TRANSLATING THE INDIAN PAST

Francis Robinson THE MUSLIM WORLD IN MODERN SOUTH ASIA

Joya Chatterji PARTITION'S LEGACIES

Jennifer Dubrow COSMOPOLITAN DREAMS

Sumit Guha HISTORY AND COLLECTIVE MEMORY IN SOUH ASIA 1200–2000

Partha Chatterjee I AM THE PEOPLE

Tanika Sarkar HINDU NATIONALISM IN INDIA

Mohammed Ayoob and Danielle N. Lussier THE MANY FACES OF POLITICAL ISLAM

Sherali Tareen DEFENDING MUHAMMAD IN MODERNITY

INDIAN HISTORY and POLITICS CLASSICS

Ranajit Guha A RULE OF PROPERTY FOR BENGAL

Ranajit Guha THE SMALL VOICE OF HISTORY

Romila Thapar THE PAST BEFORE US

Muzaffar Alam THE LANGUAGES OF POLITICAL ISLAM IN INDIA

Asok Sen ISWAR CHANDRA VIDYASAGAR AND HIS ELUSIVE MILESTONES

Rosalind O'Hanlon CASTE CONFLICT AND IDEOLOGY

Arvind K. Mehrotra, ed. A CONCISE HISTORY OF INDIAN LITERATURE IN ENGLISH

Ramachandra Guha AN ANTHROPOLOGIST AMONG THE MARXISTS

Partha Chatterjee DEAD MAN WANDERING

Partha Chatterjee EMPIRE AND NATION

Partha Chatterjee THE BLACK HOLE OF EMPIRE

M.S.S. Pandian BRAHMIN AND NON-BRAHMIN

Nayanjot Lahiri FINDING FORGOTTEN CITIES

Iqtidar Alam Khan THE MUGHAL NOBILITY

Srinath Raghavan WAR AND PEACE IN MODERN INDIA

Sudipta Kaviraj THE ENCHANTMENT OF DEMOCRACY AND INDIA

Sudipta Kaviraj THE IMAGINARY INSTITUTION OF INDIA

Sudipta Kaviraj TRAJECTORIES OF THE INDIAN STATE

Sudipta Kaviraj THE INVENTION OF PRIVATE LIFE

David Hardiman GANDHI IN HIS TIME AND OURS

Christophe Jaffrelot INDIA'S SILENT REVOLUTION

Sunil Kumar THE EMERGENCE OF THE DELHI SULTANATE

Christian Lee Novetzke HISTORY, BHAKTI, AND PUBLIC MEMORY

Ramchandra Gandhi THE AVAILABILITY OF RELIGIOUS IDEAS

Brijen Kumar Gupta SIRAJ-UD-DAULAH AND THE EAST INDIA COMPANY

Francis Robinson THE ULAMA OF FARANGI MAHALL AND ISLAM IN SOUTH ASIA

Niraja Gopal Jayal CITIZENSHIP AND ITS DISCONTENTS

Michael J. Fisher COUNTERFLOWS TO COLONIALISM

Jahnavi Phalkey ATOMIC STATE

Ramachandra Guha THE UNQUIET WOODS

Rudrangshu Mukherjee AWADH IN REVOLT

Sarvepalli Gopal IMPERIALISTS, NATIONALISTS, DEMOCRATS

HISTORICAL SOURCEBOOKS IN CLASSICAL INDIAN THOUGHT

Patrick Olivelle, ed. A DHARMA READER

Sheldon Pollock, ed. A RASA READER

Johannes Bronkhorst, ed. A SABDA READER

INTERNATIONAL FICTION CLASSICS

Joan Sales UNCERTAIN GLORY

Jaan Kross THE CZAR'S MADMAN (forthcoming)